The Music of The Statler Brothers

AMAZING! *The Music of The Statler Brothers: An Anthology* is an amazing piece of work covering in detail the amazing songs and recordings of an equally amazing group. I was there the night Johnny Cash first saw and heard The Statler Brothers and changed history by hiring them for his show. And I've followed them every step of the way since. Congratulations to Don Reid, his work ethic, and his amazing memory for recalling the minutia and putting this collection together in such immaculate fashion. Actually, I'm jealous, because he and I are about the same age, and I can't remember what I ate for breakfast.

—Bill Anderson, member of the Grand Ole Opry
and the Country Music Hall of Fame

I was night-riding through Los Angeles recently, in a black car with stylish wheels, sporting lots of chrome, enjoying the sights on Sunset Boulevard. Palm trees were swaying, busy people were moving fast up and down the sidewalks. I had pop music playing on the radio. "Flowers on the Wall" came bursting out of the speakers. I couldn't get it loud enough. I was in the presence of one of the best records ever made. Two minutes and eighteen seconds later, the song was over. It quietly disappeared into the California darkness. As it faded away, I thought to myself, there goes one for the ages. And just like The Statler Brothers themselves, in one way or another, they'll be around forever—true classics. With love to the Brothers.

—Marty Stuart, Grammy Award-winning singer-songwriter
and member of the Grand Ole Opry

I grew up listening to and loving The Statler Brothers, the Gospel/Country vocal group that dominated the charts for a career that spanned 40 years, 45 albums, over 250 published songs, and a list of awards longer than the funnel cake line at the county fair in my hometown. Don Reid was more than lead vocalist for The Statler Brothers—he remains one of the most creative and nostalgic storytellers in show business. The songs of The Statler Brothers evoke memories, smiles, and even tears, but in this true treasure of stories behind the songs, Don reveals where the songs came from, what they mean, and how they were recorded. You'll better understand why you have always loved The Statler Brothers. There is an authenticity and clarity about the music that was often copied, but never duplicated. Your soul will be stirred, your heart warmed, and your face will form in an uncontrollable smile when you read this priceless book, *The Music of The Statler Brothers: An Anthology*. If you don't love the book and their music, you're probably a snob and I bet you don't even like dogs, cornbread, or fried catfish.

—Mike Huckabee, 44th Governor of Arkansas

MERCER UNIVERSITY PRESS

Endowed by

TOM WATSON BROWN
and
THE WATSON-BROWN FOUNDATION, INC.

The Music of The Statler Brothers

An Anthology

Don Reid

Lead singer of The Statler Brothers

MERCER UNIVERSITY PRESS
Macon, Georgia
MMXX

MUP/ H990

© 2020 REID PARTNERSHIP, LLC
Published by Mercer University Press
1501 Mercer University Drive
Macon, Georgia 31207
All rights reserved.

25 24 23 22 21   9 8 7 6 5 4

Books published by Mercer University Press are printed on acid-free
paper that meets the requirements of the American National Standard
for Information Sciences—Permanence of Paper for Printed Library Materials.

Printed and bound in the USA.

This book is set in Adobe Caslon Pro (text) and Georgia (display).

Cover/jacket design by Burt&Burt

ISBN 978-0-88146-751-2
Cataloging-in-Publication Data is available from the Library of Congress

For allowing us artistic freedom,
for giving us the benefit of his amazing talent,
and for his undying friendship,
this chronicle of our music is dedicated to
Jerry Kennedy

Love you, my friend

Other Books by Don Reid

Heroes and Outlaws of the Bible

Sunday Morning Memories

You Know It's Christmas When...
(with Debo Reid and Langdon Reid)

Random Memories
(with Harold Reid)

O Little Town

One Lane Bridge

The Mulligans of Mt. Jefferson

Half and Half

donreid.net

Contents

Foreword   ix

Introduction   1

1: Flowers on the Wall: 1966   3

2: The Statler Brothers Sing the Big Hits: 1967   20

3: Oh Happy Day: 1969   29

4: Bed of Rose's: 1970   38

5: Pictures of Moments to Remember: 1971   48

6: Innerview: 1972   58

7: Country Music—Then and Now: 1972   68

8: The Statler Brothers Sing Country Symphonies in
    E Major: 1972   78

9: Carry Me Back: 1973   89

10: Thank You, World: 1974   101

11: Sons of the Motherland: 1974   110

12: Alive at the Johnny Mack Brown High School: 1974   122

13: The Best of The Statler Brothers: 1975   127

14: Holy Bible: 1975   130

15: Harold, Lew, Phil, and Don: 1976   143

16: The Country America Loves: 1977   152

17: Short Stories: 1977   160

18: Entertainers...On and Off the Record: 1978   168

19: Christmas Card: 1978   178

20: The Originals: 1979   186

21: The Best of The Statler Brothers Rides Again
    Volume II: 1979   199

22: 10th Anniversary: 1980   203

23: Years Ago: 1981   214

24: The Legend Goes On: 1982   225

25: Today: 1983   235
26: Atlanta Blue: 1984   244
27: Pardners in Rhyme: 1985   254
28: Christmas Present: 1985   265
29: Four for the Show: 1986   275
30: Radio Gospel Favorites: 1986   285
31: Maple Street Memories: 1987   292
32: The Statlers—Greatest Hits Volume III: 1988   302
33: Live and Sold Out: 1989   308
34: Music, Memories and You: 1990   316
35: All American Country: 1991   325
36: Words and Music: 1992   334
37: Gospel Favorites: 1992   344
38: Home: 1993   353
39: The Statler Brothers Sing the Classics: 1995   363
40: Showtime: 2001   379
41: Amen: 2002   390
42: Farewell Concert: 2003   402
Acknowledgments   415
Index   417

Foreword

When we were high school English teachers we used to study a play called *Our Town* by Thornton Wilder. It was about a town much like the one we still live in and not so different from Staunton, Virginia, where the Statlers grew up. In the play, a girl named Emily lives out her short life in such a small town, goes to school, marries her high school sweetheart, then dies giving birth to their first baby. She is allowed by an omniscient Stage Manager to go back to the living "just for a day." Overwhelmed by the beauty of an ordinary day, Emily can't bear the revelation of what she'd always taken for granted. Finally, she asks the Stage Manager, "Does anyone ever realize life while they live it...every, every minute?"

"No," the Stage Manager answers. "Saints and poets maybe...they do some."

He's right; most people don't. Most of us stumble right past the wonder of life and love and beauty and even pain. That is exactly why we so need the songwriters and the people who make us laugh at ourselves and hold up for us mirrors of words and music and poetry and story so we can recognize our core selves and put our successes and failures into perspective.

Maybe even more than most preachers and psychologists and politicians, in their forty-three years of traveling, the Statlers saw and captured the true identities of human beings. They held up mirrors so we could see both our flaws and our perfections, our loves and our propensity for betrayal. They gave us hope and sometimes called our hand when we tried to fool ourselves. They saw—and made us see—life and the multifaceted wonder of it.

Great writers are most often molded by learning to appreciate good writing, or, as Don Reid once said, "If you aren't a real writer, find good songs. If you *are* a writer, find only songs you wished you'd written." Early on, these guys could recognize a good song, and that served them well until their own incredible ability to write was discovered. From their beginning, even as a teenaged gospel quartet, and later as an emerging performing group, it was great songs—country songs, gospel songs, pop songs, folk songs—that got their attention and became their instruments of communication.

From their first fifteen-minute stand on the Johnny Cash programs to becoming the creators of some of America's greatest country songs and comedy routines, it was their astute observation of what we all have in common and the ability to be honest about it that drew audiences to their songs and performances. Their "realizing life while they lived it" spilled into hundreds of hits, scores of recorded projects, years of television shows, and more concerts than they can probably count.

Even though they sang mainly in the secular country music field, they seem to have never been able or willing to separate their country music from their gospel roots. And how does one separate the sacred from the secular if all of life is a prayer of sorts—a prayer of gratitude, a sacrament of celebrating the holy in everyone we meet, a telling of what is true?

What can we say about a group that made us double over laughing at the antics of Lester "Roadhog" Moran and His Cadillac Cowboys at the Johnny Mack Brown High School, and then brought us to our knees singing us through the Bible—both the Old Testament and the New. They drew us into their discovery that there is "more to the Bible than we learned in Sunday School," insisting that we not "look at the scriptural characters with our mouth open but with our minds open" and "take them off the pedestal and put them on the street," because "Jesus knew the worst of this world and the best of another."

How do you dissect or catalog the recordings, live performances, and television shows of a group of guys who genuinely liked each other and worked night and day and in between, capturing the human nature of us with whom they rubbed shoulders every day in the regular simplicity and complexity of life?

As all faithful songwriters know, some songs are the result of knowing the craft and exercising hard work and discipline, but the best songs are the ones that come after the writer. We don't capture these songs; they capture us. As Don says in this fascinating book: "A song can crawl up your back and demand to be written any time of the year or any time of the day or night.... The best ones just come down on you like noonday sun, and you couldn't escape giving into the urge until you find a little shade and a pencil and paper."

This book is about songs, the way they are written and chosen for recording projects, and how they make their way to the intended audience. It's full of secrets about the people artists travel with and those they meet when they get there. It is a big letter of gratitude to the amazing studio musicians who created the sound that makes each song unique and shoot it straight to the heart. It is a love note to all the beautiful people who gave the Statlers their start, encouraged them along the way, and welcomed them to cities all over the world.

It's about the magic of regular daily life, the human emotions and the treasured memories that make songs worth writing; it's about the simple beauty of the small town that sent these boys out in the first place and remembered who they really were when they quit the road and came back home.

—Bill and Gloria Gaither

IN MEMORIAM
HAROLD REID
8/21/39-4/24/20

I delivered this finished manuscript to Mercer Press
in December of 2019. My brother read and
approved every page and every word as I sent him
each chapter as I wrote it.
We both wanted this story told and I only wish
his energy those last few years would have
allowed us to co-write it
but that was not God's will.
We were brothers, best friends, business
partners, and confidants.
This is a chronicle of our musical life together,
and it was important to me that he agreed
with every memory I recorded here.
He did.

Introduction

The Music of The Statler Brothers

As a part of The Statler Brothers, I enjoyed around forty years in the music business, depending on where you start counting. Personally, if you start in 1959 when I was fourteen years old, I can mark the date I started singing with the Kingsmen. (That's what we called ourselves in those early days.) We—Harold Reid, Phil Balsley, Lew DeWitt, and I—were just a weekend quartet singing wherever they would give us ten dollars, and if they didn't have the money, we'd give them ten dollars to let us sing. I was still in high school, and Harold, Phil, and Lew had day jobs. So until that final concert on October 26, 2002, that would put me at the forty-three-year mark. But if you start counting the day we turned professional and began to actually earn our living by performing, the starting point would be March 8, 1964, when we went to work for Johnny Cash. That would then put me at the thirty-eight-year mark. I'm going to measure it the first way because those five years between '59 and '64 were great learning years for us. We learned to sing and write songs and developed a stage presence, and we learned how to put a show together, stage comedy, how to dress, how to talk in front of people, and how to get on and off the stage gracefully.

I always tried to learn from everyone, especially the old-timers. There was an interesting old country comedian named the Duke of Paducah on our first professional tour. He dressed in funny country clothes, as most "hillbilly" comics did in those days, and had a standard line he closed every comedy routine with as he walked off the stage: "I'm headin' for the wagon. These shoes are killin' me." And he was also the emcee for the whole show on that tour. He brought every act on and off stage. And every night I stood by the curtain and watched what and how he did it. He saw my hunger for wanting to learn every aspect of performing and came to the side of the stage one night and said to me, "Son, always remember when you bring an act on stage, find out in advance which side they're entering from so you won't bump into them and spoil their entrance." I wondered at the time why he was telling me this, but it was only a few short weeks later that I was given the job of introducing all the acts on the Cash tours, a job I did for many years to come. Don't know how the ole Duke knew that, but he had a sense of it some way or another. I never saw him again after that first tour.

So, either way you measure it, it's a long time, a lot of songs, a lot of miles, a lot of hours in the recording studio, and a lot of time writing music. And that is what I wanted to make this book about: the music. Why we sang what we sang and how we got there by singing it.

My sons, Debo and Langdon, and I eat lunch together every Wednesday since I retired and sometimes more than just once a week. They've asked me about a lot of things over the years about the Statlers' career and have pushed me toward chronicling this epistle to document some history and some understanding of just who we were musically. Remember, the main object here in these pages is the music. Because when it comes down to the skinny of it all, it's simply about the music. That's what motivated us and made us. That's what maintained us and kept us. It starts with a song, then an appealing arrangement, capped with a personable performance. Lyric + melody + performance. It's all about the music.

—Don Reid

1

Flowers on the Wall

1966

After meeting Johnny Cash back in Virginia (that story was told in detail in a previous book, *The Statler Brothers: Random Memories*), he told us to come do a show with him in Canton, Ohio, on Sunday March 8, 1964. My brother, Harold, Phil Balsley, Lew DeWitt, and I packed our car, a 1952 Cadillac limousine that had seen better times, and headed northwest with enough clothes to last us for weeks. We planned on doing the one-nighter with John, with the promise of more dates that week, and then head to New York or Nashville to see if we could find a place for ourselves in the world of music. We arrived at 8:30 A.M., showered and shaved at the George Washington Hotel, went to church at First Baptist, and were at the Canton Memorial Auditorium at 2:30 for the matinee. In hearing this story, some people have marveled that, in facing maybe the most important and challenging day of our lives, we took time to go to church that morning. My only answer is that this was just who we were and are. It was Sunday morning and we never considered not going. And what better place to start off maybe the most important and challenging day of our lives? It prepared us spiritually and bolstered us for whatever we may be facing.

We were the first ones there at the auditorium, and as the rest of the cast started to arrive—George Hamilton IV, Bill Anderson, Sonny James, the Duke of Paducah, and John's band, the Tennessee Three—we learned that none of them knew we were to be on the show. John and June did not arrive until after intermission, but by the grace of God everyone believed our story when we assured them John was expecting us, and we were put on the show to do our fifteen minutes. We opened with a couple of songs—an old folk tune "I Am a Rovin' Gambler" and the perennial standby spiritual "Swing Down Chariot." Then we introduced a skit of imitations that included Ferlin Husky, Minnie Pearl, George Jones and Melba Montgomery, Tex Ritter, Roy Rogers and Dale Evans, the Sons of the Pioneers, and, yes, Johnny Cash.

In case you might find this interesting, this was one of three different shows we kept in our rotation. We had a set of impersonations for country audiences and for pop audiences. This being a country show, we pulled out the country artists. Harold did a great straight-out version of Ferlin singing "Gone." It was so on the money it needed no comedy punch. He's always been good at voices and accents. Lew donned the straw Minnie Pearl hat with the price tag hanging from the side and did a crystal clear and strident "Howdeeee! I'm just so proud to be here!" That was all that was needed to take the crowd from laughter to applause. Then Lew and I did a hit song from that era in the voices of George and Melba, "We Must Have Been Out of Our Minds." It was good and very country but nothing compared with what followed. That would be Harold's over-the-top send-up of one of our childhood heroes, Tex Ritter, singing the theme from *High Noon*. Best I recall, he also put on an ugly cowboy hat and did a drunken Tex for no particular reason—just because it was very funny. (Only a few weeks later, when Tex himself would join the tour and be with us nightly and stand in the wings and watch, Harold never let up. And Tex loved it! And we loved him. What memories we made with him and his family through those years.) Phil and Lew would then put on cowboy hats and give their version of Roy

4

and Dale singing "Happy Trails" just before we all four-stepped center stage as the Sons of the Pioneers. Now I realize there are those who may read this and be too young to know any of the above, but trust me, they were all giants in their fields at the time, or a few years prior. But without a doubt, the bravest act of them all was Harold twitching and singing and offering up a parody of Johnny Cash, who just happened to be the star of the show. Phil, Lew, and I did the trumpets with our mouths in three-part harmony while HR did John singing "Ring of Fire." It was a showstopper, and John was told all about it and got us to do it just for him between shows that same day. He loved it so much that by the second night he insisted we come out on his portion of the show and do those trumpets on his performance of "Ring of Fire." We did because he was the boss, but this left us with having to make a major change in our comedy routine. Harold did it gracefully by simply switching songs and singing an even funnier version of "I Walk the Line" with these lyrics:

> *I keep my pants up with a ball of twine*
> *I keep my eyes wide open all the time*
> *I keep the ends out for the tie that binds*
> *Just say you're mine, then pull the twine.*

The comedy and the singing were hits, and to be unabashedly honest, we killed 'em. The audience was howling for us, and we were the only folks on the show who had no hit records and the only ones they had never heard of. We walked on that stage but we floated off it.

When John arrived for the headliner portion, he heard all about what we had done and how well we had been received. He always called all the cast out during a final curtain call after his show to take a final bow. And right along with George, Bill, Sonny, and the Duke, he called out The Statler Brothers, and we took a bow like we knew what we were doing. We were giddy.

The evening performance was at 7:00 P.M., and the time between the two shows was spent in John's dressing room singing whatever songs he and June and the Tennessee Three could think to throw at us. We sang gospel and country and pop, and they laughed and applauded each song like the friends they all came to be. On the spot, he hired us and asked us to finish

5

the tour of one-nighters with him, which ran through the next Sunday night in Davenport, Iowa.

One of the songs we were asked to sing that night in the dressing room was "How Great Thou Art." Luther Perkins of the Tennessee Three and the boom-chicka-boom sound of the electric guitar asked if we knew it. With our Southern gospel background, we had a full vocal arrangement on it and gladly sang it for him and all those present. Sometime on every tour thereafter, Luther would catch us backstage before a show and get us to sing it for him. One night, as we were getting more and more stage time and needed to add a couple of songs to our show, Luther insisted we add HGTA. We wondered how it might fit in with all the country songs and if it would be accepted, but because Luther loved it so, we sang it that night on stage for him. It got a standing ovation and every night for the rest of our career until our final concert we sang that song with the same reaction from every audience. It became more associated with The Statler Brothers than some of our major hit records. And all because our buddy Luther kept wanting to hear it. We never sang it in all those years that we didn't think of him. But the most memorable performance of that song came a few years later, in August of 1968 in a Baptist church in Hendersonville, Tennessee, when we sang "How Great Thou Art" at Luther's funeral. There were four men there who almost didn't make it through the song.

From here, there are a thousand road stories, but focusing on the music, as I promised to do, the important fact is that exactly twenty-seven days after first singing with Johnny Cash, he took us to Columbia Studios in Nashville and got us a record deal. Looking back on that, in today's world, it sounds as if I'm lying. Less than a month in the business and we were recording for a major label. John went with us to that first session on April 3 and performed on both sides of our record. This was our first chance at presenting ourselves musically to the world, and although well intentioned, it was not very well received.

We recorded a new folk song that had been written by a lady, Lucille Groah, from our hometown of Staunton, Virginia. She was the mother of Danny Groah, who would become Alan Jackson's longtime lead-guitar player decades later. The song was called "Hammers and Nails," and it had a recitation piece in the middle of it that John wanted to do. And he even showed up on the flip side, "Wreck of the Old '97," blowing a train whistle in the background. Both of these songs represented the times and the musical climate of the country at the time. It was the era of hootenannies, and folk music groups like Peter, Paul, and Mary and the Kingston Trio. We were doing it all at this point—Southern gospel, country, folk, pop—and folk music is just the one that popped up on our radar at the time. John and the whole troupe was sure this was what we should do, but Columbia and America were not of the same mind.

By the end of July this same year, the 28th, to be exact, we were back in Nashville and back in the studio for another pass at making a record. The label had agreed to give us three chances before throwing us out on our ear, or whatever part of our body we might land on. They were not real happy with us as we were being force-fed to them by their biggest record seller and there was literally nothing they could do about it. It was decided that John would not be a part of the session this time, even though he was there in attendance. We recorded one of his past hits that he had written with his nephew Roy Cash Jr., "I Still Miss Someone." Then, for the flip side, we set a precedent of considering our own material. Harold, Lew, and I had been attempting the art of songwriting and thought we might as well give one of them a try. We decided on "Your Foolish Game," one I had written and that we felt had some promise. It didn't, but it was fun hearing my own creation on an actual record.

Two things come to mind when I think of this song. In order to join Broadcast Music, Inc., the agency that pays songwriters for all airplay on radio, TV, and electronics, you had to have a song recorded. And in order to get a song recorded, you had to belong to BMI. To save going through all that red tape again, I gave half of this song to brother Harold so that we would both be ready and set for our songwriting career. Both our names are on it even though I wrote it. Also, at the time, I was still a teenager and not legally able to enter into a contract by 1964 law, so my mother had to sign for me to join BMI.

These sides were where we first found some country roots in our singing. No more folk music influence would be heard from us for the next thirty-one years when we would record "Tom Dooley" on the album *The Statler Brothers Sing the Classics*.

John was working on an album called *Ballads of the True West* at Columbia in Nashville. We were there with him in the famous Quonset Hut studio off the back parking lot of the Columbia building, singing backup as we did on most all of his records at the time. It was March 13, 1965, just a year and five days from when we signed on with him. We recorded two songs with him that day—"Rodeo Hand" and "Stampede." Between cutting those two album songs, John left the studio to get something to eat and left us and all the musicians standing around waiting for his return. Never wanting to leave the clock running in vain, Don Law, the producer, came out of the control room, looked at us, and said, "You know we told John we'd give you guys three chances at a hit record. You've already had two. You've got till he gets back from lunch to try for number three." Then he turned and went back in the control room, and we knew our destiny and future depended on what we did in the next hour or hour and a half. It depended on just how hungry John was as to how long we had to seal our fate. We silently said our prayers while we grabbed instruments and began teaching the pickers a couple of songs we had in mind. Lucky for us they were all pros and fast learners. We had a song written by a disc jockey we had met back in Roanoke that we had been carrying around for a couple of years. The song was called "Billy Christian" and the writer was Tom T. Hall. He was yet to come to Nashville, but we had told him that when we got the chance, we were going to record his song because we loved it and thought it had great potential.

Check it out on YouTube sometime. You can see us performing it on *The Johnny Cash TV Show* with John, with Barbara Mandrell on her TV show in Hollywood, and by ourselves on our TV show in Nashville. We got a lot of juice out of this very early Tom T. song even though it was never really a hit for us. And that's because it was eclipsed by the other song we recorded that same day.

The second song we cut that day was "Flowers on the Wall." Lew wrote it and had been working on it but still didn't even have a title for it. He was calling it "The Big Kick," and he had written it to the tune of "Jingle Bells." Some fast transitioning took place as the four of us huddled in a corner and came up quickly with the arrangement you hear on the record. By the time John got back, we had two songs down and were ready to continue his session. "Flowers," of course, was a monster hit on both the country and pop charts. A million-seller. And we put our name on the map with it, but to say we found our style and sound with it would be misleading. We tried hard to follow it but didn't really know how because we weren't sure of the elements that made it a hit. We spent countless hours analyzing what made it so appealing to the public. The banjo fills? The Captain Kangaroo line?

Harold's little gimmick "Kang- Kangaroo"? The sudden stops after each chorus? What did we do and how could we do it again?

Music is a mystery and style is something you can't manufacture. It's all a perfect marriage of a good song and a good performance, and if you think about it too long and too hard, it clouds the senses and leaves you with vacant and useless answers. But the hit took us back in the studio for a big-selling album by the same title. Some of the songs were good and some were just passable. I look back at them now and find it easy to be honest about each one of the other eleven tunes and remember why we chose them to be part of our musical history and our first album.

As FOTW began to hit and climb the charts toward its million-seller status, I remember John saying to us one day in an airport, "You never hear your own songs on the radio as much as other people do." We laughed then but it took on more meaning with each future hit because it was so true. It's kind of the Lord's way of keeping you humble by not letting you see or hear all the accolades, and that's a good thing.

"My Darling Hildegarde"

I wrote this and I'm not real proud of it. It was what we call a ditty. Very little substance and it never set a particular mood of any kind. It was 1965 and too much of that era and too little of a country influence could be found in it. It was our second single off that album, and even though it charted both country and pop, it didn't do the job that needed to be done. And, most importantly, it had hardly any hint of Statler Brothers on it.

"King of the Road"

Roger Miller was a good friend and one of the most prolific and cleverest songwriters ever. He could write deep, he could write silly, and then, as time proved, he could write a Broadway play. We had great times with him on the road and on our television show. He guested on one of our Christmas specials in '85, and we literally laughed so much while we were trying to get it all on tape that we all five lost our voices. In 1965, just about everyone was singing KOTR and putting it on their albums. During this period, we were told by a reliable source that Roger said in an interview, "King of the Road has been recorded 110 times, but it's only been sung twice. Once when I did it and once when the Statlers did it." I never confirmed this with him, but it's good company he put us in.

"Memphis"

Yeah, the old Chuck Berry rock 'n' roller. We sang this song for years on the stage as our opener. It was lively and always fun to sing. We were on a show with Chuck Berry in Carnegie Hall in June of '65. What an original, with his little duck walk across the stage and the way he could turn a lyric. He wrote a lot of standards in the field, and this one fit us perfectly for the times. A little rock influence that seeped into our makings.

"I'm Not Quite Through Crying"

Looking back, for years I've thought that this would probably have been a better choice as a follow up single to "Flowers." It had the guitar licks, the harmony, the little tricks that sometimes catch the ear of the public. Lew wrote it, and it was fun to sing and certainly had more potential than it was given.

"My Reward"

I mentioned in passing earlier that we had three different shows in those preparation years that we were ready to perform at any time. The Southern gospel set that was closest to our hearts, the country set with all country songs plus the impersonations I outlined, and the pop set. We used this for any banquet and dinner work. When we were booked for a date in those very early days, we would actually ask the buyer/promoter, "What do you want?" And we'd offer these three shows. Got us a lot of work.

On the pop set we would sing old standards such as "Autumn Leaves" and "Moments to Remember" and then we'd throw in impersonations to fit the show. Harold would do Tennessee Ernie Ford—"Sixteen Tons." He did a killer Dean Martin where he would walk out to a table and pick up someone's water glass and spill it all over the floor before he finished singing "Memories Are Made of This." Phil, Lew, and I did the McGuire Sisters, and it lit a fire every time we hit the first line of "Just for Old Time's Sake." (Thirty years later they guested on our TV show and racked their brains for a song all seven of us could do together. I wish I had thought of suggesting "Just for Old Time's Sake." It would have been a hoot.) Then somewhere in there, Lew would do his Eddie Fisher and we all closed out the skit with the Ink Spots singing "If I Didn't Care." I hope you don't mind me saying we nailed them and also made it funny. Of course, I know so many of you have never heard of these stars and these songs. Look them up, because their era, a bit before us, was one filled with great personalities and fantastic talent.

Soooo...I tell you all this to tell you about this song. John without a doubt, knew more songs than any one human I have ever known. He knew all the words to any hymn you could name, any old obscure folk song, old classic country songs from the thirties and forties, and any pop song he ever heard once on the radio. He was a walkin', talkin', singin' musical encyclopedia. Every song from Jimmie Rodgers to Fanny Crosby to Bing Crosby—he knew. Therefore, we weren't surprised when he walked into our dressing room one night before a concert while we were running through our Inkspots number and said, "My favorite Ink Spots song is 'My Reward.' Do you guys sing that one?" We looked at one another and confessed to him we had never heard of it. He proceeded then to take the guitar and sing it to us. Wow! What a beautiful old song. We got him to write down the lyrics immediately on one of those brown hand towels from the bathroom (we used those a lot for writing down lyrics and also writing songs), and we carried it with us for days until we memorized all the words and came up with an arrangement. To this day, I still haven't heard the Inkspots version, but I sure love our version, all thanks to John's ironclad memory.

"This Ole House"

We have been singing this song since day one. And we could sing it on any show because it was originally written as a gospel song. Rosemary Clooney had a pop hit with it, and it had the perfect bass hook line. We were singing it then, and we were still singing it four decades later on our final concert. Some nights we would stop in the middle of it, and Harold and I would do a comedy routine that never failed to stop the show. Great fun! Great song. Written by Stuart Hamblen, whom we were honored to do a TV special with later in the sixties. He was a character actor who also wrote such classics as "It Is No Secret," "These Things Shall Pass," "Until Then," and so many, many more.

"Billy Christian"

Originally called "The Ballad of Billy Christian," we fully believed this would be the A-side of the record. Again, many reading this may not be familiar with A- and B-sides of 45-rpm records. It is an anachronism in today's world but a very important element all artists and record labels had to consider at one time. It was only after many months of promoting this song to radio and record stores that a major station would turn it over and play the B-side. Once they did, everybody did, and we had our first major hit.

"The Doodlin' Song"

A clever, clever song. You can tell it came from the comedy-writing mind of brother Harold. It was a novelty song, which I called a ditty earlier. This song was a good flavor for the album and showed we could do many different types of music and attitudes. Harold and I had not really started to write together at this point. That teaming would start a few years later.

"Quite a Long, Long Time"

Lew had been writing and had a nice little storehouse of songs saved up. Then, shortly after this, he slowed down and his input wasn't as heavy on later albums. But this song, out of all he ever wrote, was always a favorite of mine. I liked the content and our performance.

"The Whiffenpoof Song"

I'm not sure I can explain, even to myself, how this one got in there. A little history: it was an old college song from Yale University. The lyrics came from a poem by Rudyard Kipling back around 1900. An a cappella group from the school called themselves the Whiffenpoofs after the poem, and, as far as I know, the Whiffenpoofs, whose members change with each graduation, are still in existence. Lots of folks have recorded it, such as Bing Crosby, Rudy Vallee, and even Elvis. But no one ever gave it the tempo and energy we did. That tempo came about from the pop show on stage I told you about earlier. We needed a closer and that was it. And a darn good one. So when we needed another song for the album, we just did something we already knew. It's fun to listen to and to sing, but it has very little commer-

12

cial value and doesn't fit into any sort of developmental aspects of our musical career.

"I Still Miss Someone"

If you recall, I said the label gave us three chances to try for a hit. Of those first four songs we recorded that made up our first and second attempts, this is the only one that made it to our first album. "Hammers and Nails," "Wreck of the Old '97," and "Your Foolish Game" died out there somewhere in limbo. They may have shown up later on compilation collections.

Columbia released these songs as singles, but they, like some others I'm going to tell you about, never found a place on an official album. Wish I could tell you why, but I can't. Just some of those decisions that are now lost to time.

Looking back, "I Still Miss Someone" would have been a great choice for a second single from this album. It already had a history with country music as John released it back in 1958. That familiarity alone is often a good ear-catcher for disc jockeys.

Songs in Limbo

For the five years we were at Columbia, 1964 to 1969, we released only three albums. We recorded a lot more songs than that, but it was a restless and unfulfilling period in our musical history. We were bounced around from one producer to another. We often were given songs by the label we had no interest in singing. Even though Harold, Lew, and I were writing feverishly all the time, we weren't allowed to cut very much of our original material. In all, we recorded twenty songs at that label that never appeared on an album at that time. Later, they were in included in compilation albums the company would put together to create a new product to sell without having to pay us for recording new material. Many of these songs were released years later, after we had left the company and became popular artists at another label, Mercury. This is pretty standard practice with any record firm, as they own the recordings in perpetuity, and there is no way an artist can challenge an old release.

Years after we had left Columbia and were enjoying great success at Mercury, our old label decided to release some of our old songs and called to ask for a new and updated picture for the album cover. It was an obvious maneuver to cash in on our current success so we ignored them. We told them if they were going to release old songs, use an old picture and not try to fool the public. After numerous subsequent requests, we finally just gave them a flat no. Months later, the album came out with a brand-new picture of us performing on stage. They simply hired a photographer and sent him to one of our concerts. When all the fans came to the front of the stage to snap pictures, he joined in the crowd and got his shot. We had to laugh at that one. They outsmarted us and got what they wanted.

In addition to the three aforementioned cuts, "'97," "Foolish Game," and "Hammers and Nails," these seventeen titles never appeared on any album until one of those compiled in later years.

"Green Grass"

We've had to tell this story many times. But for those who haven't heard, the label gave this song to us and we were told to record it. So, on April 1, 1966, fittingly April Fool's Day, we did our duty as we were instructed. Oddly enough, it turned out pretty darn good. It even grew on us and we got to where we were in agreement it should be our next single. With great expectancy, it was released and the first word we got from it was it was selling like crazy. The next word we got was the company was pulling it off the market. We were baffled and pretty angry. Apparently, the publisher, who usually has nothing whatsoever to do with what songs an artist or record company releases, was the culprit. Al Gallico was a very powerful publisher, and he wielded a lot of clout with a number of major labels. Unbeknownst to our producer at Columbia, Gallico had promised Liberty Records that Gary Lewis and the Playboys could have that song. Without further ado, our version was pulled and Gary's version was released, becoming a top-ten record for them. We never really knew Gary. We ran into one another in a restaurant one day in Los Angeles but it was never mentioned. As it shouldn't have been. Water under the bridge.

I think it was a blessing it happened. If that song had hit for us, it would have thrown us back into the pop field as "Flowers on the Wall" did, and we were very uncomfortable in that environment. We hadn't yet made our all-out country commitment, but we already knew in our hearts where we wanted to be.

"The Right One"

We were sure we had found the next best thing since chocolate. Cowboy Jack Clement wrote this song and brought it over to the studio to us. He was a powerhouse writer and had a lot of history with John, as he started out as an engineer at Sun Records in Memphis. He wrote "I Guess Things Happen That Way" and "Ballad of a Teenage Queen." He had written for George Jones and Jerry Lee Lewis and Jim Reeves. Therefore, when he handed us this song, we grabbed it and ran with it. It got on the charts and kept our name out there until the right one really did come along, but it wasn't a career builder for us. And that intro and ending—obviously a rip off of "Flowers" that the producer thought was a fabulous idea. We did it, but we cringed every time we did.

A side note here that has more to do with our lives than with our music, but the day we recorded this song, April 29, 1966, was the first day we met rock 'n' roll legend Carl Perkins. He was good friends with a lot of the Johnny Cash troupe, and we had heard great stories about him for some time. Marshall Grant, who was playing bass on all our sessions at this time, brought Carl with him that day. We were overjoyed to meet him and never considered letting that kind of talent sit on the sideline while we recorded. So, we invited him to sit in with us and pick, and that was the beginning of a long, wonderful, and close friendship. He joined the Cash troupe shortly after, and we traveled the world together for the next six and half years.

"Is That What You'd Have Me Do?"

This was the flip side of "The Right One." Good song, written by Lew. He loved the augmented chords and used them often and nicely. This is a very pretty ballad and the perfect kind of song you would want on any album to add flavor.

And that is Grady Martin featured on the guitar. You may know his work from Marty Robbins's "El Paso" and "Don't Worry 'Bout Me," and he later traveled as part of Willie Nelson's road show for many years. Grady was a stalwart fixture in Nashville history.

"That'll Be the Day"

I was not a big rock 'n' roll fan in my teen years, and I honestly was not familiar with Buddy Holly's song with this same title. My head and heart were in Southern gospel and country, and when I wrote this song I didn't know about the other one. They're nothing alike, and you can't copyright a title, so all was well. It was a single for us but, again, we were just chasing the dream with it.

The Carter Family also recorded this on their *The Carter Family Sings the Country Album*. They did a great job on it, and it was a sweet feeling having Mother Maybelle, one of the inventors of country music, singing my words and my music. And, of course, the sisters, June, Helen, and Anita. They were a part of our extended family for so many years.

"Makin' Rounds"

As a writer, I had my first double side because this was the B-side of "That'll Be the Day." What a strange little song. Listening to it today, the verses sound spooky. The guitar breaks are original and good, but I don't think I'll find myself whistling this tune while skipping down the street any time soon.

"Half a Man"

On this song, pitched to us by an outside writer, and even on some of the songs we ourselves wrote during this period, there was always a chorus in minor chords. All of this was from the influence of "Flowers," and until we finally shook ourselves of this habit, or even stigma, we would never find The Statler Brothers sound. It wasn't completely our fault, as the label and the producers pushed that thought process into every recording. It was like short pants—we just had to outgrow them and it took time.

But the more interesting thing about this song is the banjo. You wouldn't guess in a hundred years who was playing it: Jerry Reed. It was the first time I remember ever meeting him. Here we had one of the greatest guitar players sitting in on one of our sessions, and somebody put a banjo in his hands. We laughed about that with him years later, and no one laughed about it louder than Jerry himself.

I would love to stop here and tell about ten Jerry Reed stories, but I was the one who said this was going to be about the music, didn't I? One of life's most unique characters! I laugh just thinking about him.

"Do You Love Me Tonight?"

Another very sweet love song from Lew's pen. I listen and marvel at how high we sang in those Columbia days. We had not yet discovered the intimacy that would later evidence itself when we sang a personal love song. Later, at Mercury, we would sing with more heart and a step or two lower. It would set a warmer mood.

"'Scuse Me, Miss Rose"

Oh my golly! What happened here? Well, I'll tell you the best I can. The Nashville office heads changed a lot during this era. In early 1967, they brought in Bob Johnston to run the show. He had produced Bob Dylan and made a name for himself in the rock field, and he decided he was going to put his mark on The Statler Brothers. Bob wrote this rock song and pitched it to us and finally had to put the pressure on us to get us to commit it to tape. We hated it from the first note and saw that it became the first unissued song we ever had. That simply means it was *never* released. It is decaying somewhere in the dank dungeons of Columbia records, covered in dust and mold where it belongs. We worked with Bob a lot afterward, so there were no hard feelings on his or our part. Matter of fact, he produced our next album, and we were with him at Folsom Prison and San Quentin on those albums he produced for John. The music business is a fickle and capricious business. You often have to make merry music with people you don't agree with and with whom you have nothing in common. And you have to make it appear as if there is harmony and accord at every turn.

This brought us up to March of 1967, when we began our second album. The Statler Brothers sound had not been found or established by this time, but it was evident we were working hard on it. With so many outside influences, such as record producers and songwriters and musicians that we were constantly handling, I think we came out pretty good but not close to what it would be in three years. But until then, we had a lot of recording time ahead of us, and we realized every time we stepped in front of a microphone we were in an experimental era. We were not completely sure of what we were looking for, but we knew we would know when we found it.

Here's a little folk history on the Statlers during this period that you may find interesting. We have performed on stage sans each member a few times in our early years. It was never easy for us and sometimes awkward for the audience, I'm sure, but circumstances take precedence sometimes, and you do what you have to do.

Circa 1967, when I was twenty-two years old, Uncle Sam called me to come take a physical and board a plane to Vietnam if I passed it. When the Uncle called, we were in the middle a Canadian tour with the Johnny Cash show, so I had to fly home to Staunton to board a bus to carry me, along with fifty other contemporaries, to Roanoke to be stuck, poked, and inspected by a series of army doctors. (It was a policy with John that anyone who flew to, from, or during a tour, flew at his expense; he never let anyone pay for a flight for any reason. Just another endearing tidbit most people don't know about the man.) When I flew out of Toronto, there were three days of shows left, and Harold took over my lead singing, with Phil and Lew keeping their parts intact. (Footnote to this: I did not pass the physical. Uncle found a heart arrhythmia I had been aware of since my teens and decided he didn't want me getting in the way of America's best able-bodied men. I never missed another performance in the next forty years.)

In February of 1966, we were on tour somewhere in the great Northwest when Harold got a call that his number-three daughter, Kodi, was about to be born. He left the tour and flew out in a snowstorm and arrived in Virginia to another snowstorm but made it to the hospital just in time. Phil, Lew, and I sang as a trio and finished up the remaining dates.

Brother Lew suffered from stomach ailments most of his life. It was finally diagnosed as Crohn's disease, but in the meantime, we had to check him into numerous hospitals across the country as we traveled. So, there were a number of times Phil switched to the tenor part and Harold and I alternately filled in the baritone part to fulfill the dates.

And then the most comical calamity of all somewhere in this time period found two Statlers missing and two on stage. I wish I could remember the exact town, but it slips my memory and that may be no accident.

John and June and two of the Tennessee Three, Marshall Grant and W. S. Holland, along with Carl Perkins, often traveled in a mobile home/camper kind of contraption. Luther Perkins traveled separately with his wife in his personal camper. The Carter family, Mother Maybelle, Helen, and Anita, were in their Cadillac, and we, the Statlers, were in our Cadillac. This particular day, John and June were flying, so when we all stopped to gas up and eat, Harold and Phil got on the mobile home to visit with Carl, Marshall, and W.S. Somewhere along the line, miles got between each of the vehicles, and the mobile home broke down. Lew and I and the Carters were way ahead, never knowing any of the problems going on behind us. Luther comes along and finds the camper sitting on the side of the highway and stops to help, and after they get embroiled in trying to fix it and find a mechanic, they aren't just late, they all end up missing the show that night. Remember this was the mid-sixties and long before cell phones. What a different world it was!

For the evening performance, the Carters go out and open the show. Come time for "Ladies and gentlemen, here's The Statler Brothers," and out walk Lew and me. Two Brothers on stage and two somewhere sitting on the side of a Midwestern highway. Lew played guitar, as usual, I played bass, and the singing was pretty good. But it was the comedy routine we tried to do in Harold's absence that kept us laughing for years to come. Harold was doing an opening joke at the time that went like this:

> Don was standing out there before the show, and a lady came up to him and said, "Are you okay?" He said, "I'm fine." She said, "Are you nervous?" He said, "No, I'm not nervous." She said, "Then what are you doing in the ladies' bathroom?" (I know it sounds silly today but it was a rip-roaring opener the way Harold told it back then.)

Lew and I decided, after singing a couple of songs, we would try the routine and he would do Harold's part and tell the joke on me. He started right off with, "Don was standing back in the lobby before the show...."

I knew immediately the joke was dead. Not standing in the LOBBY! That kills the punch line of standing in the LADIES' BATHROOM! But it was too late to stop him and too late to correct it. The whole thing fell as flat as a year-old Pepsi.

Then when John and June hit the stage, we had to be their band. John banging on a rhythm guitar, Lew playing an electric guitar, and me thumping a borrowed electric bass. Sometimes the memories just overtake the heart.

2

The Statler Brothers Sing the Big Hits

1967

Our new producer was now Bob Johnston. It was his idea to do an album with this title that would feature ten current hits and standards with one slot open for an original song that would be the single. We listened to stacks and stacks of songs sent from publishers from all over town. With Bob ignoring our input as writers and us trying to keep him at bay as a writer, we were giving every songwriter in Nashville an opening for that single that would lead the album.

"Ruthless"

This is the one we all decided on. Bobby Braddock was a fairly new writer in town, and we were one of the first artists to record one of his songs. Bobby, of course, would go on to be a major force in the business, writing "D-I-V-O-R-C-E" for Tammy, cowriting "The Bird" for Jerry Reed, and cowriting "He Stopped Loving Her Today" for George, plus so many more. He was a clever composer in the vein of Roger Miller. He.could take a common phrase and find a new twist to it you would never expect. And that is just what charmed us about this song. A guy with a wife named Ruth who walked out on him and left him "Ruthless." Pretty cute. And it served its purpose well. It was a top-ten song on the country charts for us. But the fact that it fell into the category of a novelty song, which is what many folks saw "Flowers" as, we felt a little typecast with it. Lighthearted. Frivolous. Fun. And, yes, that is all four of us whistling on the intro. But after all was sung and done, we weren't real sure we were comfortable with this style and this category.

Here is the best part of this session and this day, March 14, 1967. On this song you can hear the musical future of The Statler Brothers in the Dobro guitar intro and fills. This was the day we first met and worked with Jerry Kennedy, who in three and a half years would become our longtime producer and best friend. We worked together as producer and artists for more than thirty years. He gave us the freedom from day one to be ourselves. But much more about that later.

"Green, Green Grass of Home"

Now we start the list of "Big Hits," as referenced in the name of this collection. Porter Wagoner had a hit with this song a year before Tom Jones got a hold of it. This is a perfect example of what the label was playing off of to sell this project. They didn't care how we sang them, only that we sang them. The song titles were to be the drawing card, not to mention how a record company could stack up favors from a publishing company by using their recent hit songs on as many releases as possible. This reciprocates favors so that they might get first shot at the best the publishers have to offer for another artist on their roster. This country classic was written by Curly

Putman, who wrote the other half of "He Stopped Loving Her Today" with Bobby Braddock.

Harold's performance here shows the grasp we were getting on using different sounds and combinations. He did a great job with it and with the recitation (which isn't easy to do), which points to other arrangements we would use in featuring him when we earned that freedom in the future. And more great Dobro guitar work from Jerry Kennedy.

"Release Me"

This one fell in the grouping of both a recent hit and a standard. Ray Price hit with it thirteen years before (in 1954) and Engelbert Humperdinck had a giant pop hit with it just two years before (in 1965). It's a song we might have chosen to do later in our career, and I think we would have done it much better in another decade. I was just shy of twenty-two years old, and my voice was too young and inexperienced to do what the solo demanded. That element sticks out terribly to me today, and the track had none of the meat and potatoes we could have given it a few years later.

"Walking in the Sunshine"

A fun and enjoyable Roger Miller song. But then he never wrote a bad one. Sounds like we were in a whistling frenzy, and this time it was Lew doing the honors. I am stunned, in listening to it today, that Columbia sprang money on trumpets for us. They must have been left over from a Johnny Cash session!

"Funny, Familiar, Forgotten Feelings"

Mickey Newbury wrote some fabulous hits that have been recorded by countless singers. Although this is a very good song, it's just not one we would have ever thought we should record. There was so much of Don Gibson on it (who had the hit) and just not a lot of us, but then we were doing what was being strongly suggested to us by the powers that be. It's sad that so many decisions in the music business are made by people in power who know nothing whatsoever about music.

Mickey was in the restaurant at the old Ramada Inn Motel in Nashville with us one night back in the summer of '69. We were practically living there while taping the Johnny Cash ABC television show. He would often come over and hang out with us, and we all had mail delivered there. It was not long after Kenny Rogers and the First Edition had had a monster hit with Mickey's "Just Dropped In to See What Condition My Condition Was In." That night the mailman brought him his first big BMI check after that song had hit. I won't reveal how large it was, but Mickey was stunned and ecstatic, we were impressed, and he was moved to buy all of us dinner.

"Ruby, Don't Take Your Love to Town"

The experimenting was finally paying off. This arrangement was what The Statler Brothers would come to sound like. This is as close to a bridge between the two eras as there would be. We found something we liked here. We jelled, which was a word we used a lot when we felt something come together and ring true with our harmonies. But then it's hard not to hear something good when you're singing a Mel Tillis song. We've sung his songs, worked dates together, he's guested on our TV specials, and we've written comedy for him and performed comedy with him. What an all-around talent this man was. We loved Mel and loved his songwriting.

"You Can't Have Your Kate and Edith, Too"

Bobby Braddock strikes again, this time with Curly Putman by his side. The next song off this album for the second single was just like the first. A clever, twisted composition in the novelty class we weren't sure we were comfortable with. But Bobby and Curly were such good writers and we gave a certain energy to both of these songs, so we weren't surprised when this one put us back in the top ten. Jerry Kennedy was back on his signature Dobro guitar. (You'll remember Jeannie C. Riley's "Harper Valley PTA." That was Jerry on the same guitar. He's a master.)

Shortly after this song hit for us in the fall of '67, Jim Nabors and fellow actor Glen Ash sang it on the *Gomer Pyle* TV show. And still to this day you can buy birthday cards with the song title and girls' pictures on it, playing off the old saw of not having your cake and eating it, too. You can find them on just about any greeting-card rack you look through. I can't begin to tell you how many of those cards we have received on our birthdays over the years.

"There Goes My Everything"

Dallas Frazier (yes, the same guy who wrote "Elvira") wrote this classic. A perfect solid country song that anyone should be glad to sing. Jack Greene had the hit just a year before we cut it for this collection. It was the Country Music Association "Song of the Year" and "Single of the Year." This was the kind of song we would look for in years to come to flavor our albums. This vocal arrangement was typical of the way we would present them, although maybe a step lower for the sake of intimacy. Hats off to the powers that be—they didn't have to twist our arms on this one.

"Almost Persuaded"

Not the old hymn, but the David Houston hit. Good song. No one will argue that. But just not Statler material. We never did drinking songs as none of us drank. So, had the decision been left to us, this would not have made the list of songs we wanted to sing and be associated with. Plus, the piano drives me crazy. I remember who it was, and he was probably getting double union pay and wanted to be sure we got our money's worth. We did, with change.

"I Can't Help It If I'm Still in Love with You"

You can't do a country hits album without a Hank Williams song. The singing here is fine, but I'm a little ashamed of the recitation lines I did. I just wasn't "ready for prime time" when it came to the talking parts. Harold was always good at that, and I don't know why he didn't do it on this song. We did other Hank tunes in the years to come and did a better job for him on those.

"Shenandoah"

An old public domain classic that has been around forever. We sang it on stage, on television, on record. It never failed to kill in front of a live audience. Some say the song is about an old Indian chief. Some say a river. When we sang it, it was about the Shenandoah Valley of Virginia. It served us well. It was all our arrangement and all our decision to include it on this album. And it still kind of makes me weak with memories whenever I listen to it. Memories of Harold, Phil, and Lew. I can't listen to it often.

Songs in Limbo

After the second album, there came another stretch of songs with no particular home. We would release singles, but none of them wound up on albums, thus, after they served their purpose on the charts, they would just die on the vine. It was like buying a new shirt, wearing it once, and then throwing it away. None of them had a great effect on our development musically or on our career progress. They were there for a moment and then vanished in quick time. They may be found on YouTube today. I can't say. I haven't looked.

"Jump for Joy"

Hey look! It's Bobby Braddock again. Three singles in a row. This one is as clever as the other two, but we were getting close to being pegged as a novelty song act. Have you ever looked at a picture of yourself from early in your adult life and you just couldn't relate with that even being you? That's how I feel when I listen to some of our music from this era. It's as if I'm listening to someone else. Some other group I don't know all that well. Truly an out-of-body experience.

"Take a Bow, Rufus Humfry"

This was the B-side of "Jump for Joy." If somebody had written a song with a funny name in it or a funny twist of phrase, the word was out. Send it over to Columbia and they'll get The Statler Brothers to record it. You got a nice love ballad? No, don't send them that. Don't you have anything comical or at least tongue-in-cheek? These guys are becoming the court jesters of Music Row, so just send it to their producers and they'll get them to cut it.

"Stella Malone"

I can tell you so very little about this one. I can't even hum you the tune. All I know is what I learn from looking up the files. It was recorded in Studio A on January 11, 1968, and the producer was Bob Johnston. And here's the real kicker: it was never released. Not on an album or a single or as a prisoner on probation. "Unissued" is its official status. Recorded that day and buried that day in the vaults of doom somewhere on 16th Avenue South. So be it.

"Don't Think Twice, It's Alright"

This is another one that is lost to the ages. To my knowledge, it was never released to the public in any form. To be honest, I'd love to hear it but I don't have it either. None of the Statlers have it. I always liked the song and would love to hear what we did with it.

One night back in the sixties, we were hamming around backstage between shows. John was singing "Understand Your Man," which, of course, he had written. I said, "John, you know you stole that melody from Bob Dylan's 'Don't Think Twice, It's Alright,' don't you? You ever worry he might sue you?" He said, "Naw. He ain't gonna sue me. He stole it from Paul Clayton." Turns out he did.

"Sissy"

Not sure why I even wrote this one. But when a young songwriter is in the throes of passion about his craft, he writes about everything. At this phase in my creativity, if you said hello to me I would write two verses and a chorus on it. Everything was fodder for a song. And when there was a coal-mine accident in the news, I just couldn't look away. It is all about a boy telling his little sister that their daddy has been lost in the pit of a mining accident and they don't know whether he's dead or alive. It's pretty raw in places, and one of the lines I always liked was, "Lord, if you don't save his life, then God, please save his soul."

It was on the charts but not really a mainstream country song. It was the type of song that was great for an album but probably better left out of the singles competition.

"I'm the Boy"

I like this song. This was getting us closer to where we were going. It had the signature Statler harmony that was getting better with each trip to the studio. It had the lyric, catchy without being cutesy. It had the stops and even the "Third Man Theme" fills on the guitar. Lew penned this one and I think did a fine job. It didn't do much for us on the charts, as it would be the last charting record we had while still at Columbia. And that wasn't a bad thing. We were itching to go.

"Staunton, Va."

Carl Perkins, bless his rockabilly heart, wrote this strictly, especially, and personally for us. We had spent so much time together on the road, and he had heard us talk so lovingly about our cherished little city in the valley, that he wrote us this tribute to our hometown. A clarinet intro with an almost Dixieland-band break midway through joined by a trombone. Not the country sound we were looking for, but this sweet little song served its purpose, if not on vinyl, then on stage. For twenty-five years we did a big charity show in our hometown on the Fourth of July. Many of those years we opened the show with this song to great acclaim. We had special guest stars most years such as Reba McEntire, Conway Twitty, Johnny Cash, Tammy Wynette, and so many more. Carl came and did the show with us on two different occasions, and to my recollection, he was the only person we ever had twice. I always thought it odd that our friend, who had never been to Staunton when he wrote it, would be the one to write this tribute to the town we grew up in instead of one of us. I loved that guy and still miss his humor and talent. He could write a song faster than anyone I have ever known. The Beatles loved him and recorded his songs as did Elvis, so we felt in good company when he wrote for us.

Carl and I used to sit in dressing rooms in theaters all over the world and pick guitars. I mostly play rhythm, but we had these funky little syncopations we would do, and we'd write lyrics and melodies that we never committed to paper. Every night we'd jam, just to the two of us, in some secluded cement room in the basement of a concert hall. The cast would pop in all the time and listen and sometimes join in. Harold dubbed us "Pork n Beans," and that became our renowned name throughout the troupe whenever we pulled out acoustic guitars. Funny thing, lots of times I was playing rhythm on Mother Maybelle's F-Hole "Wildwood Flower" guitar. By the way, Mother Maybelle taught me that famous bluegrass lick from "You Are My Flower" on that same old famous guitar. I recently saw it in the Country Music Hall of Fame Museum. I stood for a long time just staring at it, sitting there in its glass case, and It and I had a few nice memories together before the crowd moved me along.

"That Certain One"

I wrote this song, we recorded it, and then it fell off the face of the earth. I don't think it was ever even used on later compilation albums the label put out on us after we left. It may have been, but if so, I'm not aware of it. But the song itself got new life when Tommy Cash, John's brother, had a hit with it in 1972. Tommy recorded two more of my songs that were hits for him: "One Song Away" and "So This Is Love," cowritten with Lew.

"Confused"

I know nothing of this. I have no memory of a song by this title, but the official files say it was recorded and never released. I only have their word for it.

You can see how haphazardly our label handled the recordings we made. Too many unissued songs. Too many songs recorded and then just discarded. This is not how we would run our musical or business career once we were out from under this contract that the label never wanted anyway. First, they didn't want us recording for them; then, when we had hits in spite of their non-efforts, they wanted to dictate to us what to record. It was a stressful and trying time for us, and they weren't through messing with us yet. There were more songs and recording sessions that would be wasted that I will address in a third chapter of "Songs in Limbo" later, but the next project was one they thought would capture our hearts. It would be our third and final studio album for Columbia.

3

Oh Happy Day

1969

The recording and piecing together of this album was the most confusing and convoluted planning you could ever imagine. With what I have remembered and what the official files that were kept can prove, this collection of gospel music was two years in the making. And it just should not have been that complicated.

It started with a new producer at Columbia, George Richey, who had his musical roots in Southern gospel as a piano player. When the label decided we should investigate our roots and record a gospel album, Richey seemed the ideal man to head up the project. We felt relatively comfortable with this arrangement and began the venture with as much enthusiasm as possible. That passion was doused in cold water when we went in to the actual sessions because we recorded the entire album, eleven songs, all in one day. This was and is unheard of, but I get ahead of myself. Let me tell you a little bit of who we were in a musical sense before we ever came to Nashville.

We grew up fans of Southern gospel. This is a dying genre that has been overtaken by contemporary gospel, black gospel, country gospel, bluegrass gospel, and any other field of music that wants to add their name in front of, well, the gospel. To describe it properly would be to simply give you a couple of perfect examples of it. In the 1950s that we grew up in, it was James Blackwood and the Blackwood Brothers and Hovie Lister and the Statesmen. They were each a four-man quartet with a single piano player as accompaniment. They could sing and entertain in a manner that no other category of singers and entertainers could touch. They were our musical idols. There were many others in their field—the Speer Family, the Harvesters, the Florida Boys, the Chuck Wagon Gang—we were fans of them all. When they would travel through the Shenandoah Valley, we were there in the front row soaking in every note and nuance. That is what we wanted to be. That is how we wanted to sound. That was our musical education, goal, and ambition.

Though he grew up three states away from us, Bill Gaither had the identical musical upbringing as we did. Bill has become a great friend over the years, and we admire so much what he has done to preserve the Southern gospel field of music. A few years ago he invited us out to his hometown of Alexandria, Indiana, to spend a few days and just talk about and revisit the glory days of the quartet era that we all had grown up in. We had a terrific time and cemented a friendship that will last forever.

We never got away from our love of gospel songs and gospel arrangements, and as I have said elsewhere in these writings, we expanded into country and a little into pop and folk to sustain ourselves in those early years. But throughout our career as country artists, we never abandoned our gospel music roots. We always included a gospel segment during our stage shows, we included a gospel song on most of our albums, we wrote and recorded our double album *Holy Bible—The Old and New Testaments*, and on our television show on the TNN network for seven years in the nineties we closed every show with an old hymn or gospel song. So, when our record label wanted us to do an album of those wonderful old songs, we were ready and prepared. Maybe not prepared to cut eleven songs in one day (and to be honest, some of them were recut and some were replaced), but this is the album as it was released as our third and last for Columbia Records.

"Oh Happy Day"

This was a hit on the pop charts for the Edwin Hawkins Singers in the spring of '69. Hawkins's arrangement was based on the old English hymn "Oh Happy Day, That Fixed My Choice," written in 1755 by Rev. Philip Doddridge. You might find it in any old church hymnal. The label thought if we could mimic the Edwin Hawkins arrangement, we could build an album on it and ride on its popularity. This wasn't our style, musically or businesswise, but we didn't have the freedom to impose our values during this time in our recording history. So, we sang it and it is what it is. Listening to it now, so many years later, I have to admit it's better than I thought it was at the time. So many other issues and feelings were involved, maybe we couldn't make an honest assessment back then. I don't remember ever singing this song on stage.

"King of Love"

Brother Harold wrote this beautifully constructed song years before we got into the business professionally. We had sung it in church programs and gospel concerts and knew it would be a perfect new song for this project. It consists of three verses: one—Jesus's birth; two—His life; three—His death. (I loved singing this song and John loved it, also. We recorded it with him three years later in 1972 when he put it on his *The Johnny Cash Family Christmas Album*.) It has a fantastic key change just before the last chorus. And isn't that just the simplest and most powerful title you have ever heard for a song about Christ?

"Are You Washed in the Blood?"

Harold, Phil, Lew, and I were and are Presbyterians. We laughed many times (and in later years with Bill Gaither) that we were the only Presbyterians involved in any way in Southern gospel music. Everybody in the industry was Baptist or Pentecostal, but here was a wonderful old hymn written by a

31

minister in our denomination. Elisha Hoffman wrote others, such as "I Must Tell Jesus," but this one is a classic all to itself.

I'm not sure if Elisha would have approved of the flatted seventh chord we sang in the verses, but we thought it gave it some nice flavor. This one we dusted off and sang some twenty-five years later as a closing hymn on our weekly television show, *The Statler Brothers Show*. We used the fading ending on the record, which was not of our choosing, but we certainly corrected that years later on TV when we sang the endings we liked.

"Daddy Sang Bass"

We were in the dressing room with Carl Perkins the night he wrote this song. As he put it together, we all sang it together, and we knew it was a killer hit from the minute we heard it. We even asked Carl if we could have it to record, and he said yes. But a few weeks later, John called us to come to Nashville to record his next single with him, and guess what? It was "Daddy Sang Bass." Just one of those things that happens in the ole music game. It was as perfect a marriage of a country song and a gospel song that I have ever heard. It's fun to sing and always a crowd-pleaser.

In 1994, right in the heat of our number-one television show, we celebrated our thirtieth anniversary in the music business. TNN wanted to televise it, and we had a great cast of some wonderful folks who dropped by to help us celebrate. Foremost, was our old boss and mentor, Johnny Cash. We had not seen one another in years simply because of our individual schedules and career paths. Since we had last seen John and June, Jimmy had replaced Lew, and he had never met either one of them. Being the original thinker he always was, John said he wanted to do the show, but he didn't want to get together or see us until we walked on camera live. He wanted that true-to-the-bone honesty and energy of old friends reuniting after all those years. Fine with us. He was introduced, and we all five walk on stage, and if you get a chance to see this anniversary show floating around out there somewhere, you'll see what I'm talking about. We had a very emotional moment of old kinship before we broke into song. And it was this song. Jimmy has laughed for years that he sang with Johnny Cash before he ever met him!

"Just in Time"

A beautiful song. Lew writing at his best. The duet that Phil and Lew perform on the chorus is sweet to the ear. This is a peaceful song to listen to and get lost in. Without even trying to remember, I can listen to it and tell that we arranged it totally. Our hearts were in it.

"Less of Me"

During this period, we were singing this Glen Campbell-written song in concert every night. Glen didn't write a lot, but when he did he made it count. The lyric is very philosophical as if it is a page of proverbs set to music.

"Pass Me Not, O Gentle Savior"

No matter what denomination you may be, at some time or another you probably have sung this song in church. Fanny J. Crosby wrote some of the best and most long-living hymns that we have. We arranged this rather simply but with a lot of power that I love to listen to as well as sing. This is one of those songs that when you announce to a studio full of musicians waiting to hear what's next, you can see their faces light up with joy and anticipation. They all know it without taking any kind of notes, and they dive into it with a fervor and a passion that is just not evidenced in other songs. In the beginning days, we would sing this in churches on Sunday nights and also in country music parks on Sunday afternoons. The reaction was the same no matter where it was heard.

"Led Out of Bondage"

This was a wonderful hit, written by Bob Prather, for the Statesmen Quartet in the gospel field. It was from one of their early albums on RCA Victor in 1957 titled *The Statesmen with Hovie Lister*. They had an energy and a glow on stage that I have never seen matched in any field of entertainment. This was their arrangement, hands down. We admired them so much and learned so much by listening to their songs, as well as those by the Blackwood Brothers, for hours and hours on end as we were growing up. We four could sing anything either group ever recorded at the drop of a hat.

Harold's performance was a tribute to the Statesmen's bass singer, Jim "Big Chief" Wetherington.

Harold and I were eating lunch one day in the fall of 2017, talking about this book, and he said something that I had never thought of before. He said he believed our name, The Statler Brothers, was a subconscious, unknowing choice derived from our hero worship of these two groups. He said we surely got the S-T-A-T from Statesmen and the Brothers from Blackwood Brothers. I sat amazed at the revelation. It had never crossed my mind, but I had no argument for it. That is why that box of Statler Tissues sitting on that bureau so many years ago caught our collective eye and why we added the fraternal "Brothers" to it, even though none of us were Statlers and only two of us were brothers. I think he was on to something. Well, we couldn't have paid homage to any better or more inspiring artists.

"Things God Gave Me"

I wrote this song and we all agreed it would be good for the album. I don't recall that we ever sang it anywhere or anytime except when we recorded it here. This is true of so many songs throughout our career. Once they were committed to tape, unless they were to become a single, chances are we'd never even memorize the lyrics. We used lyric sheets and notes on the music stands in front of us during a recording session. I've saved all of those and have quite an archive of transcripts. They are a history to themselves.

"The Fourth Man"

What a song! Written by Arthur "Guitar Boogie" Smith, this composition had it all. It was up-tempo. It told a complete and accurate Bible story from the book of Daniel. It had rap verses before rap was even invented. It had bass solo lines in the chorus, which is always, always a hit. We began singing it way before the Cash days, so we pulled it out of our old bag of tricks to fill this slot on the album.

Arthur Smith had a syndicated TV show in the sixties and early seventies originating from Charlotte, North Carolina. He had hit records such as "Guitar Boogie" from as far back as 1949. He was the writer of "Dueling

Banjos" from Deliverance. He wrote other religious songs such as "I Saw a Man."

The song is fast and there are a lot of words in the rap verses I mentioned. They were my responsibility and it was fun singing them on stage for so many years. They are still imbedded firmly and forever in my mind.

Since we have retired, I often dream about the old days on tour. Sometimes those sweet dreams turn into nightmares. I can't tell you how often I have awakened in a cold sweat because I was dreaming about all of us going back on stage and once I grabbed the mic to start singing, I realized I couldn't remember all those words to "The Fourth Man."

"How Great Thou Art"

I am sure we have sung this song more than any other song in our repertoire. It was recently pointed out to me that we recorded this song multiple times, more than any other song in our recording history. I can't begin to count the number of times we performed it on television. It is without question our own very original arrangement. The ending is the tour de force of the performance. On stage, Lew or Jimmy and I would kick off the first half of the verse. Phil and Harold would duet on the last half. This was visually effective with two moving back and two moving up. Then all four of us would step center stage for the chorus. Then the fade back for the repeat procedure for the second verse. Then the chorus again and the power key change and the big ending. You can hear on this first recording that I sang the duets with both Phil and Lew. Without the need for the visuals on record, Harold felt it more in my range to do both duets, so I sang his part on both verses.

We started singing this hymn in churches in the very early sixties, and the response it would draw was amazing. The melody and the words are so powerful and on point, and we felt all of that come together with each performance. Once we put it on the concert stage, it became even more magical. There wasn't a night we sang this song that it didn't produce a standing ovation. Always. Therefore, we had to be careful where we placed it in the song list. It quickly found its way toward the end of the show as we built toward a musical climax. Of all the hit songs God so graciously placed on our path, this song could overpower any of them if put in the wrong place. It was hard to follow. We are so thankful for our relationship with such a classic spiritual composition. As I told you earlier in these pages, we sang it that first night we joined the Cash troupe. We sang it for our buddy Luther at his funeral. We sang it every night on stage. And we were still singing it the night of our final concert. This song is so powerful that when this album was reissued years later, it was no longer called *Oh Happy Day*. It was retitled *How Great Thou Art*.

Songs in Limbo

Songs you have recorded for a particular record company but have never released are referred to as "what you have in the can." There are pros and cons associated with having songs in the can. A pro for the company is that if they let an artist under contract leave, and that artist gets hot at another label, the company has music they can legally still release to cash in on his/her/their new popularity. A con for the company is that they have money tied up in every unreleased song left in the can, and if they never have an opportunity to release those cuts, that is money left on the shelf and lost forever.

That same system of pro and cons works for the artist. You want to leave as little material behind, should you leave a company and go to another one, because you don't want two labels releasing your music to the public at the same time. Some of the old material may not be what you want to sell at the time, and it confuses the music-buying public as to what is your latest and what is three or four years old. A pro for the artist is, with any luck at all, maybe some of the earlier product you really didn't care for gets buried deep in that can and is forgotten and never again heard from. Like life, without knowing the future, you have no idea which way is best for you at the time.

When we left Columba in early 1970, we had, to the best of my recollection and file-surfing, nine songs in the can. Oddly, they were all gospel songs. We would record eight of them on later albums, so I'll talk about them in subsequent pages. The lone track that no one ever heard was a beautiful song called "He." I have no copy of it, but I can still hear it playing in my head. In 1955, when I was just a child, it was a big hit for both Al Hibbler and the McGuire Sisters. This was a gospel song right at the beginning of all the rock that was floating about, and this fabulous melody cut through all the drum licks and electric guitar breaks and made a statement for the times. Don't know why we didn't record it again in later years. But that is a conundrum with music. Once you arrange and put all your heart into a song, you often just never have the energy or the sparkle to do it again with any success.

As this page turns, it takes us to a new and glorious chapter in our music. I look back on these years I have just chronicled with some regrets, a few joys, lots of learning, and a considerable amount of pain at us not being able to reach the level of creativity we wanted. But that would come, and very soon. Onward to the Mercury years.

4

Bed of Rose's

1970

The Statler Brothers' five-year contract with Columbia Records ended around midyear to late summer of 1970. Months before, we had already discussed and planned how we were going to handle our departure. What we were not planning on was their insistence and pressure that we re-sign. How could a company who had been so disdainful of us and our creativity want us back on the label? We were a little confused and greatly amused by their sentiments. It became our unanimous decision that Columbia would be better than no record deal at all, but only a little. If we failed at all other attempts down Music Row, then we'd talk to them, but we weren't even interested in opening negotiations.

What we *were* interested in was that fantastic guitar player who had worked so many of our sessions in the last five years who was now head man in charge of the Nashville office of Mercury. We had become friendly with Jerry Kennedy, liked him a lot, and he was our first choice and first phone call. When we asked him if there was any place for us on his roster, his reply almost caused us to jump out of our seats, if not our skins. He said, "Guys, I would love to have you, but I am so busy over here I just wouldn't have time to find and gather material for your sessions." What's that, Br'er Rabbit? Please don't throw us in that briar patch. We said, "Jerry, we have three writers in the group and songs coming out of our ears. You'll never have to look for material. We'll take care of that end of the business." His answer was simple and quick. "Let's do it."

We crossed the side avenue, Hawkins Street, about twenty steps from Columbia's Quonset Hut backdoor, where we had recorded "Flowers on the Wall," to the front door of Mercury, where we would find a new home and cut our next album and single, "Bed of Rose's." And many, many more.

The album cover was shot on the set of *The Johnny Cash Show*. This was a variety television show on ABC that we were currently regulars on each week. We were still a part of John's concert tours and his albums, along with all the dates we were doing on our own. It was a very busy and demanding period for us.

"Bed of Rose's"

Brother Harold Reid wrote this classic country song a couple of years before we recorded it. We couldn't drum up any interest for it at our previous label, so we began pitching it around Nashville to other artists. Everyone we sang it for loved it. You can tell when you hawk a song to a singer if they are sincere in what they're telling you. You have to watch the eyes and the body language, and we have been on the other side of that coin so many times we knew all the stock things to say to get a songwriter out of your office if you didn't like their material. But everybody loved the song. It was hard-core country. It was four chords. It was well written. Simple story and easy melody. But it scared everybody we sang it to. The content was just too risky and risqué. A woman of the evening and a young boy just barely the age of consent. Too many hurdles for most. Some took the song, kept it for a few months, and then called and said no. Kenny Rogers was the last I remember who had it. He liked everything about it and wanted to do it, but in the end just wasn't sure how it would fit his image.

And in all honesty, it didn't fit our image either. Not at all. But we believed in it so much we threw fate to the four winds, and on September 11, 1970, at 2 P.M., we walked into the Mercury Custom Recording Studios and sang our debut song. It felt good. The musicians Jerry had put together for us were top of the line, and that core group would perform on all our records for decades to come. "Pig" Robbins on piano. Harold Bradley, bass guitar. Ray Edenton and Chip Young, twin rhythm guitars. Bob Moore on the upright bass. Buddy Harman at drums. And Jerry Kennedy, guitar and Dobro guitar. The most talented and easiest group of pickers you could ever dream about working with. They immediately invented a unique and recognizable intro. Bom—bom/bom. Bom—bom/bom.

That intricate little intro that is so recognizable was invented on this particular session. Bob Moore and Harold Bradley are responsible for its creation. I am told it still floats around record sessions to this day, and when anybody wants that certain beat, it's called either "speed bumps" or "Bed of Rose's lick."

We were off and running. Me singing the first four lines, Lew joining me on the next four, then all of us on that full, hearty chorus. This was it! At last we had truly found our sound. And that last chorus, where Phil and Lew take the harmony parts up, rode it out to a perfect ending.

Some songs are made for the studio, some for the stage. This one worked for both. Harold wrote a masterpiece and we found ourselves. A new phase of our career had been born. We would never have to fear being one of those one-hit wonders—"Those 'Flowers on the Wall' guys." With this song, and our feet set firmly in the country field, we were The Statler Brothers.

"New York City"

Never ask a writer where he gets his ideas. Chances are he'll give you an answer, but it won't necessarily be the truth. Because, trust me, he doesn't always know the truth. Writing is a passion, and you write because you can't not write. Every phrase you hear, every sight you see, every piece of gossip someone shares, and every wild thought that just blows through your mind are all fodder for a song or a story. You may start to write a particular piece and end up with something on the paper so foreign to you even you will wonder where it came from. Such was the case with NYC. My original plan was to write about a girl's adventure in the Big Apple who was there for the first time—what she saw and did and how it affected her. I had the title "New York Cindy." So, go figure. From that linear idea came this storyline I never intended or dreamed of.

You can hear the intimacy in our singing and in Jerry Kennedy's Dobro guitar. This is a true Statler song, arrangement, and presentation. I was surprised many years later in an interview when we were asked what was each Statler's favorite song we had recorded. We each had a different answer, of course, but Phil's answer was "New York City." He'd never told me that.

"All I Have to Offer You Is Me"

It was an early practice of ours to mix in a couple of recent and familiar hits on each album. It gave the collection a nice flavor, and as a fan stood in a record store and perused the back of the album jacket, they would see a title they recognized which might help sell them on it. It was a good marketing tool, plus we loved getting a chance to sing some of those songs we liked. This one was written by Dallas Frazier and Doodle Owens with Pete Drake on the steel. Such a rock-solid country composition that fit perfectly with our harmonies. And it was a Charley Pride hit, and we liked old Charley.

Minot, North Dakota, October 16, 1999: we were playing the Hostfest, a four-day event. They have shows going on nonstop and fantastic acts every year. We were in one building and Charley was in another at the same time. We both had overflowing crowds. I look to the side of the stage after a few songs, and sitting in the shadow of the curtains is Charley's wife. I say, "Folks, looks like we have a special guest tonight," and I introduce Rozene. Then I take the mic over and say, "Your husband is next door doing a show. How come you're over here?" And she says, "Oh, I can see him anytime. I told him tonight I'm going to see The Statler Brothers." She got a great hand for that and we had lots of laughs with Charley later. Two wonderful people.

"Neighborhood Girl"

I love the story songs. If I had had my way, I would have written nothing but story songs my whole career. Most times I wrote them alone, but this was one of a few Harold and I penned together. We wrote as easily and as comfortably as a twosome as any blood brothers ever have. Never a falling out over the direction a song was taking. Never a harsh word when one of us would reject the other one's suggestion for a word or a rhyme. We just flowed together and were always of the same mind on the finished product.

Listening back to this song after we recorded it, I was surprised that it had no chorus, just verses. I don't think I even realized that as we were writing it. But in the final cut, it didn't hurt it at all. And with the up-tempo and the Bobby Thompson banjo, you have to listen closely to catch that it is really a sad song. Yet I can hear the joy in our voices as we performed it. I can listen to it today and tell how happy we were musically in doing our own material and arrangements.

"Fifteen Years Ago"

Phil solos on this and does a fantastic job. I can't begin to tell you what a musical influence he was on each of us. He had all our parts in his head and showed each of us, sometime or another, where we should be in a chord. Phil is the most modest human I have ever known. Usually you have to ask him before he offers any of his knowledge simply because he never wants to appear to come on too strong even with the people closest to him.

On songs where Phil solos, I would then grab the lead on the choruses to maintain the full Statler sound because it would change when any of the other three sang the melody. Of course, when we changed keys in the middle of songs and Lew or Jimmy took the lead, Phil and Harold and I would harmonize around them. But then we were going for the change in sound to create the excitement. This song had the built-in Statler-style lyric, and it was on this album because we loved it. Conway Twitty had just come off of a number-one hit with it, and we loved Conway, so all of this was reason enough to include it.

We were sitting on Conway's or our bus, I don't remember which, one night behind an auditorium just after he had had such bad luck with his Twitty City adventure, and we had dropped a bundle on a chain of restaurants we were involved in. We were lamenting to each other about it all, and Conway looked at me and said, "You know if we would just keep all the money we make from singing instead of trying all these investments, we'd never have to worry about anything." We laughed for twenty minutes over the wisdom and irony of that statement. What a good guy he was.

"The Junkie's Prayer"

This is the most un-Statler song we ever sang—anywhere, anytime. We always stayed away from drinking songs and drug songs because we didn't drink or drug and didn't want to glorify it. Lew wrote this song and it is well put together. It's just the subject matter that is at issue. Different artists showed interest in it at the time. While doing Porter Wagoner's TV show one night, Lew sang it backstage and Porter flipped out over it and said he wanted to record it. He finally backed out on that decision but still wanted to publish it, and I think he did have half of the publishing when we recorded it.

For my money, I wish it wasn't in our history and discography, but I have to say vocally we did a good job on it. We never sang it again after that one time of singing it in the studio.

"We"

This is so very much a song of the era in which it was written, and I had a ball writing it. Most of the events each line mentions never happened, but there were a few near-true ones you might find interesting:

We spent a winter in Winnipeg and a summer in Mississippi's sun

We learned early on in our career to never go to Canada in the winter or the Deep South in the summer. You only have to come out once at 6 A.M. in Winnipeg, Manitoba, in 25 degrees below zero and find your car tires frozen to the pavement. Or perform an afternoon, outdoor show in Hattiesburg, Mississippi, in the dog days of August with the sun beating down and glaring directly in your eyes.

We hit Keno in Reno and lost it all in Vegas the very next night

Show me anybody who has hit both towns on back-to-back nights and hasn't done this.

We checked in all the big hotels then used the fire escape to get away

Early on, in the very young days of our travel, when we had more dreams than dollars, two of us would go to the front desk and check in. Then the other two (we rotated) would sneak up the back stairs and four of us stayed for the price of two. Not that I'm proud of that deception, but it's a part of our history and an inspiration for that line.

And finally, there's the line in the last verse that says:

We got stranded in a snowstorm with some girls from Salt Lake City on a train

So, here's the truth that started the whole writing idea and process of this song. The four of us were on a train from Baltimore to New York in the dead of winter. We were going up to record a television commercial for Beechnut chewing gum and we thought it would be fun to take a train for a change. I remember being asleep in a window seat and sleeping through all the little stops along the way but was suddenly aware of someone standing in the front of the car making an announcement. I shook myself awake and realized it was the train conductor, and he was saying there was engine trouble and we would have to sit on the track while the engine was towed and a new one arrived and it could be hours.

So, there we were, sitting in the middle of a snowstorm somewhere in the northeast United States, waiting for a train in a train with no heat. When I stood up to move my very cold feet back into circulation, I looked back through the passenger car and saw that it was full of Catholic nuns. It was just us and a carload of Sisters. Trying to capture the irony of this and kill some time, I pulled out my trusty pen and paper and began to write a song. But in the end, the Sisters never made the final cut. It became "girls from Salt Lake City," and don't even ask me why. It's just the way a song often takes on a life of its own and writes itself.

Bill Anderson and Jan Howard covered this song on one of their albums and did a terrific job with it. Bill is one of our best friends in the whole music industry. I love him dearly. He said to me a few years ago, "Do you realize The Statler Brothers only cut one of my songs their whole career?" I said, "Well, you only cut one of mine your whole career so we're even."

Yes, that's Charlie McCoy wailing away on the harmonica. He became a staple to our every session because he could play literally any instrument in the room.

Johnny Cash used to hold what he and June called "Guitar Pullins'" at his house out on Old Hickory Lake. It was just a bunch of invited songwriters who would gather and pass the guitar around the room and everybody would sing whatever song they had just written. I remember one night in the early seventies singing this song at one of those parties. There were always interesting people, old and new in the business, who would show up. One night we were leaving through the kitchen and ran into Merle Travis sitting in the window pickin' his guitar. We had never met him, but he was an icon we had admired all our young lives. Needless to say, we didn't leave as soon as we had planned and he played every song for just the four of us we could think to request.

"This Part of the World"

This is a prime example of Lew experimenting with his writing. The song has two tempos it keeps switching back and forth between. Each of them is good, but to my ear it is very annoying. I wish we had settled on just one and left it at that. But that was the hook in the song; it's particular personality. Good lyrics and good singing. Just a little bothersome with the rhythms.

"Tomorrow Never Comes"

A very simple bread-and-butter country song written by Ernest Tubb and Johnny Bond. Ernest had a major hit with it in 1945, so it had been around awhile. But we heard something in this old tune that had never been tapped. We made a production number out of it. Harold and Lew each sang a verse, and they were both crooning at their very best. Then we all hit the chorus and added that powerhouse ending. When we sang this song on stage, it was always a showstopper. It was never a single but it should have been. It became one of our most requested songs in concerts.

"Me and Bobby McGee"

I don't like repeating myself, as Harold and I told the stories behind these next two songs in a previous book we wrote together, *Random Memories*. Maybe you have that book and maybe you've heard the stories, and maybe I'm going to tell you again anyway.

Kris Kristofferson is perhaps the best country songwriter of all time, and this is maybe the best country song of all time. And that's my opinion. In 1969, 1970, and 1971, we were practically living in Nashville, as we were part of the Johnny Cash ABC TV show. We hung out with a lot of songwriters, and Kris was one of them. He used to come over to our hotel and sing us new songs he had just written. We heard all the great ones before they ever got recorded, but when he sang this one, we jumped at it. He assured us we could have it to record, but when we got back to Nashville after a few days of being at home, things had changed. He came with his head down and confessed he had gotten a little drunk over the weekend and had given the song to Roger Miller, who had already recorded it. We were disappointed but happy for Roger, and to show Kris we weren't upset with him, we still recorded it as an album song.

Our version differed from Roger's and the subsequent cut by Janis Joplin in the la-la-la ending. We didn't do that. Instead we added a line of our own, *I still hurt for Bobby McGee*. I think our ending was more in line with the mood of the song. And speaking of mood, the Jerry Kennedy Dobro guitar added the perfect touch of soul it needed.

"The Last Goodbye"

Harold, Lew, and I were the songwriters in the group. Phil seldom showed any interest in creating lyric and melody. But one night at the old Ramada Inn Motel in Nashville on Capitol Hill, fighting boredom, we created a little game. Let's each write an opening line to a song. Then we'll go around the room and each will sing his and we'll vote on the best line and then write a song. Kind of a silly little game for a bunch of grown men? Not really, because we got a pretty good song out of it. Phil's opening line won:

Afraid her tears might move my mind...

And we were off to the races. I distinctly recall I played the guitar while Harold jotted down all the ideas we came up with and the final lyrics. Listening to it today, I can't remember who wrote what lines. I just remember it as a collaborative effort. But I do know the punch line still gives me chills whenever I hear it: *All the goodbyes came out sounding I love you.* Way to go, guys! I love this song.

It's the only one Harold, Lew, Phil, and I ever wrote together, and it was the flip side of "Bed of Rose's," our first single on the Mercury label.

The first day we started this album with the recording of "Bed of Rose's," I wore an old green hat to the studio. I'm really not a superstitious guy, but I also avoid walking under a ladder if at all possible. From that day on, I began either wearing or carrying that old hat to every record session henceforth. I kept it hanging in my office until we retired. My son Langdon has it now. But there was a time when Jerry Kennedy would walk into the studio, look around and say, "Where's the hat?" before he would ever let the music begin.

5

Pictures of Moments to Remember

1971

This is as good a time as any to explain how we chose the songs we record-ed. With a single artist, it's no problem. He or she decides, for whatever rea-son, that they would like to sing a song, and they simply do it. When you have four opinions to consider, it gets a little more complicated. Thus, we invented what we called for the rest of our career "the 4-Star System."

We would sit down at our offices in Staunton, weeks before we were due in Nashville to begin a new album, with a stack of tapes and lyric sheets in front of us. Each of us would bring songs we had written, songs we had been pitched, and old songs we thought we could give a new spark to, and we would sing them or play a tape of them for the other three. As we lis-tened, each of us would make a list of the titles, and after hearing them all, we would vote on them. We may have twenty songs or more, we had to choose eleven from for the album, and this is how we did it. We gave each song anywhere from one to four stars on our individual lists. Maybe you'd give one and a half stars to a song, maybe three or three and a half stars, and on and on. If you really loved a particular song, you'd give it the highest rating of four stars. After voting, we'd all give Phil our lists to add up. (Not sure why, but from day one, it was always Phil.) After the addition, each entry would have anywhere from four to sixteen stars. The eleven highest rated songs would be our album, and any that earned sixteen stars became the singles.

So there. Can you think of a fairer or more diplomatic way of each partner getting an equal vote? We couldn't, so that was our star system, and it always worked for us.

We wanted this second album for Mercury to be a theme album, and we wanted the theme to be memories. I think we were heavily influenced by Johnny Cash all those years we were with him. He had done lots of theme albums: gospel, Old West, American Indian, comedy. And we were on all those with him, so maybe it seeped into our thought process along the way. We loved talking about our childhood memories as we traveled, and it was an easy decision to decide on an album title of *Moments to Remember*. This was an old song we all remembered and loved from the fifties sung by the Four Lads. We were just kids, but we were fans of all those groups of that era: the Four Aces, the Ames Brothers, the McGuire Sisters. But then something magical happened that steered the course of our music and changed the title of our album.

We got together in a hotel one afternoon and Lew said, "I wrote a song last night." This got to be a common statement through the years as we always sang our new material to each other before anyone else heard it. But then he didn't sing us anything. He read us the lyric and we flipped over it. "Where's the melody?" we asked, but he threw the paper down on the coffee table and said, "I don't have one. Can't come up with one." And he threw his late-night scribblings at me.

I went to my room with a guitar and in minutes we had a song. It just fell in place. I went back and sang it to my partners and we all agreed this was the lead song for the album and should be the title song. But what about the title we had already decided on? That's when four heads are better than one. Just combine these two perfect titles, and we'll have the all-time perfect title for a collection of songs about memories. Thus, *Pictures of Moments to Remember*.

That even gave us our album cover. We all went to our old family picture albums when we got home, and we used actual snapshots pasted all over the front of the cover. In the center was a present-day picture of the four of us singing, again on the Cash TV set, and we were ready to set all those pictures and memories to music. New songs we had written, old songs that told a great nostalgic story. We didn't care. Just as long as they were good and pulled heavily on the heartstrings.

"Pictures"

I've already told you a lot about the writing of the song. The performance was just as if we were sitting around a living room leafing through one of those old family albums. *Here's a picture that we took in Cincinnati...*, and *Here's the best one that I've ever seen of Daddy....* It was very conversational and laid-back. And with this attitude, we created another arrangement style we would use many times thereafter—the style of dividing up verses into four solos. We did it first here and then subsequently with "Monday Morning Secretary," "Thank You, World," "Class of '57," and others. We knew we had found one sound and style with "Bed of Rose's," in which Lew and I were duetting, with all four of us on the chorus. And now this new technique would sustain us further. And if you note, we used both of those styles on this particular song.

We were credited with a major part of the nostalgia craze that swept the seventies decade. And this was the song that started it all. *Grease* was on Broadway. *Happy Days* was on TV. *American Graffiti* was on the big screen. And *The Statler Brothers* were all over the radio, television, and record stores. And that double-lick-speed-bump rhythm was back in the chorus. It was a musical trademark, and it served us well.

"Moments to Remember"

This song was a smash hit for the Canadian group the Four Lads when I was ten years old. We were all charmed by the words and the performance, and, as kids, we sang along with it every time it was on the radio. And it was on a lot! Listening to our arrangement today, I notice something interesting

I'm not sure I can explain. On the original Lads' version, there is a recitation midway through that is spoken by an uncredited female voice. On our version, we omitted that recitation altogether, and I can't really say why, because we recorded this beautiful song again in 1995 on an album called *The Statler Brothers Sing the Classics*, and on this version, twenty-four years later, we included the recitation. We, too, used a female voice, and she did a fabulous reading of it. You'll know her, but I won't tell you who it was. You'll have to wait till we get to that album, and no fair looking ahead! And then, seven years later, it was on our very last and final album, *Farewell Concert*. We sang "Moments to Remember" in concert quite often, and as you'll see on this concluding live performance, I did the recitation. It was one of my favorite songs to sing on stage. Not my very favorite, but I'll tell you what that one was when we get to it, also.

This may have been the first time we used that lush bed of strings on a record. And the man to thank for that was arranger Cam Mullins. When we finished a session, before it was ever mixed or overdubbed with any other instruments, Jerry would sit down with Cam, and for hours they would listen and discuss possibilities. Jerry would show him where he wanted the strings and how much or how little. Cam would then write violin and cello arrangements to fit the holes we left for him, and what he filled them with was music on a cloud.

"Second Thoughts"

It was a year or two before we got our first bus, and we were still flying a lot on tour and sometimes still driving between dates. We were coming through a desert somewhere in the great Southwest about 5 A.M. one morning. Phil and Lew were asleep in the back, I was asleep in the front, and Harold was driving straight into the rising red sun. When I opened my eyes, I looked over at him, and he was driving with one hand and writing on a piece of paper with the other. The paper was lying on the seat between us and he never took his eyes off the road but just kept scribbling. "What are we doing?" was my first question.

"Writing a song," he said. "Reach back there and get a guitar and take this paper and pencil." He then recited me the lyric he had already written, and it was the most sarcastic song I'd ever heard and yet it made me smile.

"Okay, who are we mad at?" I asked as we began putting the music to it with another verse and chorus of more stinging words. I was loving it, and in minutes we had a darn good cynical, nostalgic song. We had hit a mood we had never hit before and maybe never would again.

Harold's son Wil and my son Langdon make up the country duo Wilson Fairchild. Forty-six years after we wrote this song in the early morning desert, they recorded an album called *Songs Our Dads Wrote*. Harold and I were honored to be in the audience when they introduced this collection of songs in a special concert not long ago. They told a story neither one of us knew. Wanting to be totally true to our original lyrics, they sang the opening line, *It was in the high school yearbook dated May of '55* as we had written it. When each son played the unreleased version to their dads, Harold and I, unbeknownst to one another, said the same thing. "You ought to change that first line to 'May of '95.'" They went back in the studio and updated it all because they didn't want to offend our senses by changing it on their own. Good sons.

"Just Someone I Used to Know"

As I indicated elsewhere, the song was always the thing with us. We didn't care if we wrote it or some other writer had written it or someone years ago had penned it. We wanted the right song for the right mood, and this song fit like a Grand Prix driving glove. Written by Cowboy Jack Clement, this song was recorded by George Jones in 1962 under the title of "A Girl I Used to Know." Why the change? I have no idea. Too late to ask Jack or George. Jack had written "The Right One" for us a few years prior, and as a staff engineer for Sam Phillips at Sun Records during the glory years in Memphis, he had written quite a few for John. I'm just reminded of the absolute first Jack Clement song we ever sang.

It was that first night in Canton, Ohio, when we joined the Johnny Cash show back in '64. John was so excited to have us on board he immediately wanted us to do songs with him on stage where we would be featured. Two Clement songs that had been hits for him, "I Guess Things Happen That Way" and "Ballad of a Teenage Queen," came up instantly. We knew the first one easily but weren't sure of all the lyrics on the second. June went in the bathroom, pulled down about three of those rough brown paper hand towels, and wrote out the words to "Teenage Queen" for us, and we carried those towels on stage with us for the first night or two until we learned every word. Show Business!

"I Wonder How the Old Folks Are at Home"

This is *the* classic old-time folk song. True folk music is handed down from one singer and picker to another with each making their own little changes and additions until it becomes something just a little bit different to anyone who touches it. This is so true of this American jewel that it is diffi-cult to ascertain exactly who originally wrote it. You will find a long list of names listed as its progenitor, such as Harry Lincoln, Herb Lambert, M. Christian, F. W. Vandersloot, and A. P. Carter. So, being as I remember sitting backstage as a teenager and Mother Maybelle picking it for me on her famous 1928 Gibson L-5 F Hole Guitar, I'm going with A. P. Carter. (The Carter Family recorded it in 1930.)

We didn't need to look up any lyrics on this one. We all had known them since childhood. And you have to note how much Lew sounded like Mac Wiseman on the last half. Not an accident. This was our salute to Mac, who was born and reared just fifteen miles down the Virginia highway from us. This song is probably more associated with him than with any other singer in the industry. Hats off to Mac!

If you are going to record such a bluegrass standard as this, why not get the best performers to give it the right flavor. Why call in a banjo picker and tell him to play it like Earl Scruggs? Why not just call Earl Scruggs? So, we did. And what a thrill to have the five-string master in the studio with us. Heck, hats off to Earl, too!

"Things"

This represents Lew writing at the top of his game. If I had to pick a fave from his pen, this is it. The song is virtually a look at things that have changed throughout life, and the mantra of the piece is that "things just ain't the way they used to be." And I have to imagine that this is the sentiment of every generation. Our grandparents must have said it, I know our parents said it, and now we're saying it and feeling like we're the first to ever notice such horrible things.

A little writing touch I really like here is Butch Carter. He's first mentioned in the song as a childhood bully, but then at the end he's described as having "gone to working for the Lord."

"You Can't Go Home"

Thomas Wolfe wrote the novel *You Can't Go Home Again*, and it was just sitting there waiting for a country songwriter to come along, drop the "Again," and write a song with wistful leanings and longings to go back to the good old days. And that sentimental busker was me.

Ninety-eight percent of this story is fiction. To give a little insight as to how little of a seed it takes to inspire a song, I'll share the process with you. First, I was not raised by an aunt and uncle, and I had no cousin named Freddy. My mother lived to see Harold and me retire, and we loved and enjoyed her every day of her ninety-two years. I did have an uncle who used to come to our house in his suit and tie and dress hat and sit on the floor of the living room and play the harmonica until our aunt looked over the top of her glasses at him and warned him it was time to go home. From that I created Roy, *teaching me the Fox Chase on the harp*. The aunt with the glasses was truly named Kathleen (Aunt Kat) and thus the tale was born.

The line *she washed my socks and damned the pox that kept me out of school from fall to fall* was a little risky for 1971. I'm really not one to test the boundaries, but it felt right and no one ever complained about it. I think it's safe to say it was the first song we ever sang with even a mild profanity in it. Probably one of the first that anyone used in the country music industry. I'm not praising that certainly, but just stating a fact.

There's an old family story that is told repeatedly about Harold getting in trouble for breaking the butter dish when we were kids. His version of it was that he was getting the butter dish out of the refrigerator to make me a sandwich and it slipped out of his hand and I told on him. What a little brat I was if this is true, and I'm sure it is. That incident inspired the line *Freddy used to lie for me whenever something valuable got broke*. With fiction you can turn meanings around and still use the emotion in the moment. Everything that is mentioned in that verse is true of what my big brother taught me and did for me.

The chorus says, *Freddy's off somewhere to fight a war*. We were in the heat of Vietnam. It was on everyone's mind. It needed no more of an explanation at the time. My favorite line of the whole song is the last one. *I'm only proud that you're the ones who're proud of me.* My sincere feelings for my mom and dad.

Cam Mullins steals the show again when the violins come in with such a swell on the second verse. Still gives me chills even though I know they're coming. We had more choruses and more punches, such as *Freddy died in someone else's war,* but we faded the ending and lost these lines because we knew we wanted to use the song as a single, and it was going to be too long without the fade. Love the story. Love the memories.

"Tender Years"

This is the song that made me a country music fan. We grew up with Southern gospel—the Blackwood Brothers and the Statesmen—and with pop music—Dean Martin and Eddie Fisher. We knew country music, but it was third down the line for us, me in particular. But I can remember hearing this song when it was a hit for George Jones in 1961. He and Darrell Edwards wrote it, and it grabbed me in the heart from the very beginning. *If I can't be your first love, I'll wait and be your last. I'll be somewhere in your future to help you forget the past.*

I think I'm safe to say this is the first song where you can hear our salute and the paying of respects to the Louvin Brothers. Ira had a unique way of switching parts and moving away from Charlie on the melodies instead of following along with him. We really liked the way they did that and had worked with them and watched them maneuver their notes on stage. We borrowed often from their style to honor them. That harmony will show up more times through the years.

Wilson Fairchild opened the tour show for George Jones the last three years of his life. They were with him on his last date. During their tenure with him, Harold and I traveled to see them one night in Charlottesville, Virginia. We hadn't seen George in a while and we sat backstage that night, just the three of us, and talked for a long time. It was a pleasant and good talk, and I had the opportunity to tell him what I'd never told him before. That it was he and this song that got me interested in country music. He was touched by hearing that. I was touched by being able to tell him.

"Makin' Memories"

Harold and I loved tackling different genres of songs together. We wrote love songs, comedy songs, novelty songs, story songs, even a quiz song. And this one that I'll call a retro song. Musically, it has a 1930s sound to it. And the ukulele that kicks it off and runs all through it just adds to that flavor. (The uke was played by Harold Bradley, who usually played electric bass guitar on all our sessions, not to be confused with the electric bass. It's an entirely different instrument.) The song is full of sweet memories of a couple who have been together for years, married and now raising some boys of their own.

Phil solos, and, again, the melody goes back to me on the choruses to where we are all in our own parts, maintaining the familiar Statler sound. Something very inside that we have never revealed before might help other group singers in their phrasing: *S*'s can be very troublesome when they come at the end of a line. If all four don't hit it exactly together, you can get a "s...s...s...s" sound. So, the trick we used in all these cases was I, as the lead singer, was the only one that put an "s" on the end of the word. That way, there was no chance of getting that staggering, sloppy "s" sound. And now you know everything I know. We might as well close up shop right now and go home.

"Faded Love"

The Bob Wills family wrote this old Texas standard. I think his daddy and his brother were all in on it. The melody was another of those old folk melodies handed down through generations from the mid-1800s. It was originally called "Darlin' Nelly Gray," and then the Wills family tinkered around with a few new words of their own, and they had a song that has been recorded by scores of artists since. Everyone from Elvis to Harry James to Patsy Cline has tried their hand at it.

The charm for us was in that flowing melody and in the looking back on a lost-love theme. It was exactly what we were going for in this album concept. The strings send me to another atmosphere. As does the harmony. I like this a lot.

"When You and I Were Young, Maggie"

What! Another old song from the nineteenth century? "Why?" you may ask. Because we knew from whence came our music heritage, and we were proud and respecting of it. Again, there are countless writers claiming ownership and no way to determine who is right and who is wrong. Harold sings a fantastic solo toward the end, and I remember rewriting parts of that verse to make it a little more modern. I threw out words like "sprightly" and a whole line that read "as spray by the white breakers flung" and added a touch of 1971 to it. But we never touched one note of that magical melody. It's a masterpiece of mood and sweetness. And then it gets personal.

I sang the song and listened to it as many times as was necessary for us to determine it was like we wanted, and then I put it out of my sight for the next forty-some years. I have not listened to it again until I reviewed it for this book. It is much too sad for me to endure. My mother's name was Mary Frances, but for some unknown reason to all our family, my dad's nickname for her was Maggie. It conjures up in me more than I'm willing to deal with.

This has long been one of my favorite albums. So many pictures of so many memories.

6

Innerview

1972

Innerview became our third album at Mercury where we had complete creative control, and we were proving that we were on the right track. Three of us were writing, Harold, Lew, and myself, and even though we were able to record any songs we wanted to, we only used five of our original songs on this collection. We used six songs by other writers, proving that the finished product was more important to us than sticking our own personal song on the record at any cost. So many artists do this. They find a strong single then fill the album up with tunes they have either written or they have publishing on. That fills their pockets until the public catches on that the quality of songs suffer in the listening.

This album is probably best described as a bread-and-butter production. It's solid and it's country, and we were true to our style, our sound, and our fans. The title says it all: it's an inner look at us and our music. An inner-view of what we were becoming musically. The front center photo was of us sitting in the studio listening to playbacks after a day of sessions. We always did this together. We did everything possible together, especially when we were on the road or recording. It helped cement our harmony both on and off the stage. Some groups, you may be surprised to know, don't even record together. The lead singer will go into the studio by himself and put down the melody. Later, sometimes days later, another member comes in and puts down his part and then another and so on. They're never actually all there at the same time. We were always there at the same time for the cohesiveness and continuity and fellowship of it all. In the long run, you could hear that closeness on the record. Those little things matter.

Around the edges of the front cover, there are individual pictures of each of us, but in the center, where it matters, we were grouped together. Every performing group should learn early that even the small things that seem unimportant at the time can be so very important in the end.

"Do You Remember These?"

At the time, we were writing for the House of Cash Publishing Company. This was John's publishing house, of course, and everything we wrote went through it. Larry Lee Favorite was the manager in charge of songs and writers. He used to hang out with us on the set of the Johnny Cash TV show in the Ryman Auditorium all day, and we'd kill time singing songs and exchanging new ideas. One day he said to Harold and me, "I have a great idea for a song that only you two could write." He knew we were deep into nostalgia and had dipped our pens in it musically on the previous album. He said, "How about a list of things you remember from childhood and call it 'Do You Remember These?'"

We agreed to think on it, and when we got back to Virginia and had a few days' rest, we got together on Harold's front porch, me with a guitar and him with a legal pad and pencil, and we wrote verse after verse of things we grew up with and even things we didn't remember at all. We had so many verses when we finished we had to throw sheets away. The only problem we had was finding a stopping place. The memories just kept coming and wouldn't stop, but we knew we had to end it gracefully someway. And I think the best part of the writing experience that day was when we came up with the perfect way out. We ended it with a musical knock-knock joke.

Knock–Knock
Who's there?
Dewey
Dewey who?
Dewey, remember these, yes, we do
Ah, do we, do we remember these?

Larry had given us a great idea, and in return we gave him 25 percent of the song, because without that seed there would never have been a song. It was the fastest rising single record we ever had. Six weeks from the day of its release, it was number one. I think *Billboard* archives will tell you it was number two on their charts, but in those days there were three major charting magazines; *Cashbox* and *Record World* were the other two.

The record itself sounded like a party, with clarinet fills and a slide whistle on the ending. It was fun and loose and it solidified our influence on the nostalgia trend of the seventies that looked back on the fifties with so much love.

Note, too, we utilized the arrangement of featuring all four Statlers on the verses. I don't think any group had ever done this before, but it was a wonderful way for us all to be heard and a great fan-pleaser.

"I'd Rather Be Sorry"

Kris Kristofferson was the hottest writer in town and was making the argument of being the best by the hordes of artists standing in line for his material. Ray Price had just come off of this chart-topper, and it was an easy decision for us to include it here. It had a special hidden meaning to me that always brought a smile to my face because of something my dad had said to Harold and me in his later years. The song says, *I'd rather be sorry for something I've done than for something I didn't do.* It's in reference to the old saw of "the sin of omission can be just as damaging as the sin of commission." Our dad, in a philosophical moment, said to his sons, "Always remember, a woman will get madder at you for something you didn't do than for something you did." There is not a married man reading these words right now who has to have it explained any further. Harold and I used that in one of our later songs to salute our dad, but we'll talk about that when we get to it.

I solo on the front verse, which sets a very warm and intimate mood. Lew joins me on the first two lines of the chorus before we all come in. Key change, and Lew sings the second verse with Phil joining him on the first two lines of the second chorus. Now, on most all duets, the one harmony part being sung is the tenor line over top of the melody. But when Phil joins Lew, he sings the baritone (alto) part *under* him. And what a beautiful sound that was. I could listen to this smoothness all day long.

"Every Day Will Be Sunday Bye and Bye"

From the time I was nine years old, I wanted to sing in a group like the Blackwood Brothers. We went to their concerts and bought all their records and knew all their songs. And when we decided to include this song as a perfect inner view into each of us, we didn't even have to write the lyrics down for the session. I keep good records and files, and I have every lyric sheet filed by each record session for more than thirty years. But there is none for this song anywhere in the files because there was never one made. We knew it by heart and sang it by heart.

In the seventies and eighties, there was an abundance of country music parks all over the United States. We, and everyone else in the industry, would play these parks on Sunday afternoons. They all basically looked the same and held the same schedule. They were outdoor parks, and the first show was at 2 P.M. with a long break for signing autographs followed by a second show at 5 P.M.

What made these park dates so different was that the first audience generally did not leave, and a new audience came in at 5. So, you were singing to the same folks both shows. We always gave them an entirely different performance for the second show, comedy and songs included. And we learned how to use that one-on-one time while signing autographs. We listened to their requests. This would usually determine what songs we would do for the later show. Invariably, this song was always requested, and we jumped on it because we loved singing it. Then that would remind of us other old gospel songs we knew, and we would have a feast of memories and melodies, us enjoying it just as much or more than the folks out front.

You know, these are the types of things I miss. Remembering how happy we were coming off those stages, wringing wet, exhausted, and smiling real deep down inside.

"She Thinks I Still Care"

Hey, another George Jones song. You can't go far awry of country music by covering GJ. I remember distinctly that Harold was the driving force in our singing this song. He always thought it was one of the best ever written, and who could argue.

Dickey Lee was a singer at the time with a few hit records but none that brought him more honor than having written this song. We developed a tradition of going to dinner every night after a record session. Always the four of us and Jerry Kennedy. Often, other folks would join us, and Dickey was one of those who would come along sometimes. We liked him and his songs, so it was only natural that this jewel of a classic would find its way into our inner circle.

And listen for more of that "borrowed" Louvin Brothers harmony on the second and third verses. It just flows, as did so much of our music from this new era. As I relisten to many of these songs after decades of not hearing some of them, I realize just how easy our producer, Jerry Kennedy, made the recording process. Compared to the first five years across the street at the other label, JK allowed us to do what we wanted to do and how we wanted to do it. To his credit, the tempos were right. Laid-back when needed, full of energy when called for, and always in just that right groove for the right mood. I never felt we were screaming into the microphone the way I felt we were with other producers. This performance is the perfect example of giving a song just the right touch.

Ten years earlier, Connie Francis had a pop hit with this song, but the title, of course, was *He* Thinks I Still Care." Hers was just as good as George's in its own right. But this fact got me to thinking about Connie. In the nineties, during *The Statler Brothers Show* on TNN, our agent got in touch with Connie, who was living in Florida, and invited her to guest on our show. She said she would but only if Harold and I would call her personally. We did, talked a while about some music we would do with her, and all was well. A few weeks later, she was on stage with us in rehearsal singing, I think, "The Wabash Cannonball." Because of the key it was in,

Jimmy was singing the lead and I was singing harmony. After one run-through, expecting me to be singing the melody, she turned to me and said, "I see you don't know this melody any better than I do." A little confused, I said, "I wasn't singing the melody. I was singing a harmony part." "Oh," she said. "Then maybe I better stand beside Jimmy."

"Got Leavin' on Her Mind"

I have already mentioned a number of Jack Clement-written songs and exclaimed how much we thought of Mac Wiseman, so put the two of them together, and why wouldn't we drop this gem in the old musical bag. It was fun to sing. It was up-tempo, something that so many artists overlook when putting an album together. It was an all-around good song. It really had it all except length. This cut of ours was only one minute and 34 seconds long (1:34). We could have easily stretched it out a little with a hot guitar or piano break, but that just wasn't what we were about at the time. We were all about harmony and lyrics. That's what we looked for in a song, and once we had it, that's what we used. This one was harmony all the way. Like a fleeting fling, fun and quick!

"I'll Take Care of You"

If I had to judge my own songwriting, and I'm glad I don't and certainly won't put myself on the spot to do it here, but if by chance I did, I would put this one close to the top for me. The first thing any good song has to do is set a mood. That happens immediately with the music and the words. We had a soft, intimate, warm feeling from the first note. My heart was in every word and every phrase. Then Pete Drake makes the sweetest and most haunting key change on the steel guitar that brings in the Cam Mullins strings. If I may, I'll swelter for a moment in my own words that I am humbly aware that all comes from above and not from me, and tell you my most inward thoughts. Of all the verses I have written in a lifetime, given to me by God to claim as my own, this is one of my favorite verses:

When you grow tired of spending evenings
Lacing twilight to the dew

When you grow tired of velvet people
Honey, I'll take care of you

Add this to the glorious performance of the other three Statlers, and I could never get tired of spending twilight to the dew listening to it.

"Country Roads"

What a song! The Blue Ridge Mountains and the Shenandoah River run right through our home state, just like they do in West Virginia. This is a must to put in this inward look at The Statler Brothers. But how about this, we said to ourselves, how about we make it even more ours by using these opening lines:

Almost heaven, Old Virginia
Blue Ridge Mountains, Shenandoah Valley

Yes, this will work. No one could possibly have a problem with this exclusion of West Virginia. No one except the entire state of West Virginia. In all of the years and all of the millions of wonderful fan letters we ever received, we never got a negative fan letter except for:

1. Changing West Virginia to Old Virginia
2. When I grew a beard

We realized immediately we should not have messed with West Virginia. It was written as a nice salute to their state, and I don't blame them one bit for feeling slighted in our alteration of lyric at their expense. It's a great song and one that should be sung with the earnestness with which it was written. To be honest, we played the state of West Virginia hundreds of times after this, and not one person ever mentioned it. But I still get a bang out of how passionate those few were who felt the need to write.

Love you, West Virginia. You've been like a neighbor to us.

"Daddy"

A sentimental salute to our dad, Sidney Boxley Reid. He passed away August 16, 1967. Harold and I wrote this song for him one night in a Nashville hotel room about four years later. His passing was still fresh on our minds and in our hearts, and it gets fresher with each passing year. Dad had nicknames for each of us. He called Harold "Buck" and called me "Pete."

Harold sang our words beautifully with just the perfect inflection and feeling. I am touched beyond words every time I listen to him. Daddy, of course, never got to hear his song, but I know what he would have said if he had. "That's pretty good, Buck."

"Never Ending Song of Love"

I'll start right off by saying this one should have been a single. It has one of the best instrumental tracks I have ever heard on a country record. Again, we got this from Dickey Lee. He didn't write it, but he had a top-ten record with it. He was of the same opinion as we were on the matter of songs. He didn't automatically cut one he had written. He looked for the best ones out there, as we did, and it worked for him, too.

The acoustic guitar break, I think, was Jerry Shook. That sawing fiddle was Buddy Spicher, who on our next album would be the instrumental sound of the Ol' Roadhog. Good musicians can make a singer's life a breeze. When you have to worry if they will have something new to bring to the table each time, it takes away from the confidence of your performance. But when you know, without a musical doubt, that they are on top of each attack and cutoff and filling in with original licks every time the red light goes on over the studio door, then you can lay back and give it all you've got. We never got less than 100 percent from anyone on any of our sessions, thanks to Jerry Kennedy and to the fact that we liked all these guys and they liked us.

And JK was not above setting up an extra microphone in the middle of a session and getting himself a chair and sitting in with the band on any given day. It was always fun to have everybody there knocking on the ceiling of their talents and enjoying themselves. You could hear it in the finished product. You could hear it in the music. And you can hear it in this song.

"A Different Song"

With our gospel roots in tow, and now being entrenched in country, I found myself at this point in my life trying to incorporate the two. It became a mission of mine as a songwriter. I experimented constantly to find that right marriage of the two fields in one song. I wanted the country melody but wanted words that lent themselves to both. I wanted to say something spiritual and meaningful but with guitars instead of a Southern gospel piano. I could hear it my head. Getting it to the paper was my struggle. But I didn't stop trying. Even after this song came out of me and I was completely satisfied with it, I wanted to go a step further, and I did on the next album. But let's not get ahead of ourselves.

I can't help but share just a few lines as an example of what I was shooting for:

I've sung everything from hard times to heaven
To the cold wind that chills my very soul
I've sung everything from lonely nights and taverns
To dime store women on the troll

I don't think there was another single act or group at the time who would have given this combination song a second thought. I have to thank my Brothers for understanding my passion, dipping their toes in the pond, and giving it a hearing. We liked the finished creation so much we even recorded it a second time years later with Jimmy.

I've read it in the pages of Matthew, Mark and Proverbs
Daniel, Revelation, Timothy
And the wisdom I discovered from cover to cover
Was enough to scare the devil out of me

And what a presentation from both the pickers and the singers! They all outdid themselves, and I thank them again all these many years later.

"Since Then"

An excellent melody. Just beautiful. This really was Lew's strong suit in his songwriting. All of those nice augmented and diminished chords I think I have mentioned before. And that is one of the things that has been a mystery to me looking back over all these songs we have written together. Lew and I, just the two of us, wrote three songs together. Two of them were for the Statlers and one we wrote for Tommy Cash. He had a single with it, "So This Is Love." However, on all of those three, Lew wrote the words independent of me, gave me his paper, and I went off and put the melody to them. We never sat down together to actually write in the same room. But the point is Lew was a fantastic guitar player, and I play just enough to write with one on my lap. But he would hand off his lyrics to me for the musical half of the composition. I find that very odd looking back over all these songs today. At the time, I never questioned it or really thought too much about it. When he did write the music, as you can hear in this song, it was something to cherish.

I have files of all our scribblings, and I sometimes laugh to myself when I run across an old yellowed piece of paper with Lew's lyrics and notes on it. He had his own version of shorthand, so easily recognized even after all these years. If he was going to write the word "heart," he would just draw a heart. If he wanted to write the word "star," he would draw a star. He used the quotes (") underneath words anytime possible to keep from writing out the words again. Looking back, I remember so many of these little things I never thought would be important to me. It takes a toll on the heart when you laugh and cry at the same time.

7

Country Music—Then and Now

1972

Most acts, certainly most rock acts, easily take a year to cut an album. In 1972 we released two albums. We recorded *Innerview* in November of 1971 in three days and had it ready—overdubbing, mixing, artwork—for a February 1972 release. We left for a European tour in February just as that album was coming out of the chute, toured every month that year, doing all of the Cash dates, new dates on our own, and dates with Tennessee Ernie Ford, recorded two albums with John (*Gospel Road* and *Johnny Cash Family Christmas*), and were in the studio putting down two Statler albums, *Country Music—Then And Now* and *Country Symphonies In E Major*, the latter ready for a 1973 release. From January to December, it was a blur.

It was also the last year we would be a part of the Johnny Cash touring show. The five of us had a heart-to-heart and knew it was time for us to sprout new wings and go. We left with his blessings and maintained our friendship till the end. We even did some dates with him the very next year, and he and June came to Staunton for our Happy Birthday USA Fourth of July celebration. Twenty years later, they were our primary guests on our thirtieth anniversary television special. Our bond lasted until the very end, at John's funeral. But my heart just got ahead of my hands, so give me a moment to reign in the sentiments of the time and get back to the nuts and bolts of album making.

It's 1972 and we have a killer idea for our fourth and next album with Mercury. We would record six new songs on one side, five old songs on the other side, and call the collection *Country Music—Then And Now*. We loved it. Jerry loved it. Mercury loved it and all was well in Music City USA. But that original idea would never come to fruition. Somewhere along the way, at about 36,000 feet in the air, it all got changed and a new route was taken. But that will come with the telling of these stories and the singing of these songs.

Sometimes my head hurts from all the remembering and the struggle to chronicle the facts so that they make sense in a chronological sort of way. And yet it amazes me how, as I do strain my brain to get it right, I so clearly remember who said what and how they said it, where they said it and how it was received. It's as if there is a CD playing in the back of my mind, and it just needs to have the dust blown off it so it won't wobble in the player. Once it smooths out, then I'm ready for the next memory.

"When My Blue Moon Turns to Gold Again"

This was an old song from the 1940s that would go on the "Then" side of the album. It had been recorded by a long list of folks in country music. Cindy Walker, the classic songwriter, had a hit with it early on. Cliffie Stone charted with it a few years later. (You likely don't even know these names today, but they were strong influences even before my time.) And even Elvis himself sang it on one of his appearances on the *Ed Sullivan Show* in '57. Merle recorded it. It was just a staple and a good song that kept banging its way around from album to album and artist to artist.

I think the melody was more magical than the lyric. It has a lot of highs in it and flows rather nicely off the tongue. We used Harold and Lew as solos here, as we often did in the same song. It tended to show a scope that most acts couldn't achieve. A bass, then a tenor lead is fun to the ear. And don't miss Jerry Kennedy's guitar intro and ending.

I've told this story before at different places, but the mention of Cliffie Stone always brings this life-changing tale to mind. It was 1965, before "Flowers," and Cliffie, head of Capitol Records in Hollywood, took the four of us to brunch at the Brown Derby one day. He had seen us on the Cash tour and offered us a sweet and tempting job in Los Angeles. He said if we would move out there, he could see that we would become the "Jordanaires of Hollywood." We could ditch our luggage forever, buy beach houses in Malibu for our families, and do backup work on sessions for the rest of our lives. I have no doubt that he could have made it all happen if we had just dropped our forks and made the commitment. But we didn't. We didn't even blink. We graciously said thank you and assured him that we were Virginians at heart and had no desire to leave Staunton for any reason. We never even left it for Nashville. We commuted our entire career by car/bus/plane to record and do TV in Music City, but we have never lived anyplace except the Shenandoah Valley. No regrets here. Retired, I still go to the movies in the same theater where I used to lay my quarter up as a kid to see Roy and Gene. Still go to the same church where I was baptized and Sunday schooled. Stand on the same corner year after year to watch the Christmas Parade that I used to march in when I was in high school. Memories are so important to us because we're still living them.

"No One Will Ever Know"

Mel Foree and Fred Rose wrote this song. You can't get more old school than that. If you want country music "Then," you have to have Fred Rose represented. He wrote classics for classic singers such as Gene Autry, Roy Acuff, and Hank Williams. The list is as impressive as it gets: "Be Honest with Me," "Take These Chains from My Heart," "Kaw-Liga," "Blue Eyes Crying in the Rain."

I have always been a believer in the theory that you should know the history of what you're doing, whether it's cooking, architecture, raising a child, or writing a song. So many are blinded by youth and think they are the first to think, feel, and express an emotion. They never bother to listen to those who have come before them, study their style, and really pay attention to what they were saying. I was at a place where I wanted this so very much, and these old songs spoke to me and led me in my thinking and in my techniques.

I'll even make believe I never loved you
Then no one will ever know the truth but me

Here is a lyric choice that makes me smile each time I hear it:

No one will ever know how much I'm pining

"Pining" is a very old-fashioned word, and I don't think anyone would use it in a song today or even in 1972. We didn't change it out of respect and the need to show the "Then" side to a country song. Today, I think a writer might say:

No one will ever know how much I want you

The line doesn't have to rhyme, so it could easily be changed, and writers are used to singers putting their own touch to a line and sometimes even a meaning.

Now to the singing. We gave it a very soft yet strong reading. The simple melody just gave more strength to the lyrics. We did a dominant key change in the last verse that was most unusual. For those who are musical, you will understand that going from the key of C to the key of F is simple if you're going from your base chord of C. But in this case, it is going from the five chord of G7 to a C7, then to the new base chord of F. Simply put, this is rather hard to hear. So hard that in the session, when the string players, who are accustomed to playing by the notes and not by the ear, heard us do it, they stopped, stood, and applauded us for the unusual and difficult change of keys. These are the kind of real-people musicians you were working with every day in Nashville. You seldom get applause in a recording session.

"The Class of '57"

December 17, 1971, is the birthday of this song. We were home on Christmas vacation. I called Harold after dinner and said, "Do you want to write tonight?"

He was hesitant, as I knew he would be. I usually had to twist his arm to get him to sit down and write. He put me off by saying he would first look at the *TV Guide* to see if he wanted to watch television instead. And to be honest, I was a little surprised when he called back a few minutes later and said, "I was looking through the *TV Guide* and the name of the *Ironside* episode tonight is "Class of '57."

A little puzzled, I said, "Then you're going to watch *Ironside?*"

He said, "No. I want to write a song using that title."

"I'll be there in 30 minutes!"

At his house, in his office, we wrote three songs that night. All three got recorded, and I'll clue you in on them later as they come up. But it was a very successful night of songwriting. "The Class of '57" was a career-building hit for us. There are hits, and then there are important hits. Hits keep you sustained on the charts and in concert between the important hits. A hit can be a number-one song but not necessarily important to the career development of the artist. Everyone has these. You can go through the discography of any of your favorite singers and pick out the titles that should be printed in bold letters. Ours, so far, were: "Flowers on the Wall," "Bed of Rose's," and "Do You Remember These?"

"The Class of '57" would not only be a career-building hit, it would become an image-maker. The nostalgia and memory songs before it would pale in popularity with this class reunion remembrance. There would, thank God above, be more to come, but this one was a giant in so many ways. It also earned us our third Grammy Award.

A little piece of trivia. Here are the nominees for "Best Country and Western Performance by a Duo or Group, 1973":

–The Statler Brothers—"The Class of '57"
–Johnny Cash, June Carter—"If I Had a Hammer"
–Conway Twitty, Loretta Lynn—"Lead Me On"
–George Jones, Tammy Wynette—"Take Me"

–Mother Maybelle Carter, Earl Scruggs, Doc Watson, Roy Acuff, Merle Travis, Jimmy Martin, Nitty Gritty Dirt Band—"Will the Circle Be Unbroken"

We won and it was a heavy category. I think the oddest feeling was beating out John and June after being a part of his company for so long. We were happy but not thrilled because we didn't want to look as if we were taking any joy in beating out our mentor, because we didn't. The first two Grammys in 1965 were pretty sweet though. One was in the country category of "Best New Country Artist, 1965," where our fellow nominees were Wilma Burgess, Norma Jean, Jody Miller, and Del Reeves.

We won here, green as we were. We were working a tour in Canada at the time, and John let us off one night to fly to Nashville to attend the awards ceremony. What a sweet time we had.

But this next one topped it all.

Nominees for "Best Contemporary Performance by a Group, 1965":

–"Help!"—The Beatles
–"Mrs. Brown, You've Got a Lovely Daughter"—Herman's Hermits
–"Wooly Bully"—Sam the Sham and the Pharaohs
–"Stop! In the Name of Love"—The Supremes
–"Flowers on the Wall"—The Statler Brothers

This was the pop field, and we were the dark horse. This one really felt good!

For "The Class of '57," we used the four-solo arrangement again, and it made each line more personal with an individual singing it. After it was a hit, we heard from Perry Como's people. He wanted permission to record it but tailor it more to his age group and call it "Class of '37." Harold and I said, "Sure." But it never happened for some reason or another.

You must note some Jerry Kennedy thoughtfulness and ingenuity during Harold's solo on the final verse. When Harold sang, *Linda married Sonny and Brenda married me,* Jerry had the cellos and violins play "Moments to Remember" underneath. Harold's class was '57 and Brenda is his wife's name. It was just a nice and personal touch he did without Harold ever knowing about it till it was done.

One of the best philosophical lines we ever put in a song was the third line in the last chorus. I can't tell you how many times I've applied it to situations that arrive in everyday life.

And the Class of '57 had its dreams
But livin' life day-to-day is never like it seems
Things get complicated when you get past eighteen
But the Class of '57 had its dreams

"Stranger in My Place"

This one fell on the "Now" side of the album. New songs. Current songs. Anne Murray had just come off a hit with it. Kenny Rogers and Kin Vassy cowrote it. They were both members of the First Edition. We'd worked TV together, and we liked them both. Of course, Kenny came from that group, as did Mary Arnold, who would marry Roger Miller. All of this really had little to do with our choosing to record the song. In the end, it was because it was one heck of a good song. It had nice setup verses and a fantastic chorus. I mean, what else do you need?

Arrangement-wise, we actually did it backward from the usual mode. We sang harmony on the verses and then I soloed the chorus. It worked and I still like to listen to it. Kin died way too young and would surely have written more good songs if given the chance.

"Jesus Take Another Look at Me"

On the last album, I explained how I was working on marrying the country and gospel genres in order to create a different, sensitive, and meaningful song. I was close to finding what I was looking for in "A Different Song," but when I wrote this one, I knew I had been given what I was hearing in my head. I wanted a love song with a spiritual sense. Maybe a melody and story version of something akin to the "Song of Solomon" in the Old Testament.

I was able to combine eros love (man and woman love) with agape love (the unconditional love God has for us.) Not to exclude sin and second chances and prayer. Then, given the powerful performance of my Brothers, I

74

felt we hit a homer here. Note the swell on the name Jesus in the chorus. We were together all the way in presenting something a little diverse with maybe an offbeat flavor. Thank you for the indulgence and tolerance.

"1953–Dear John-Honky-Tonk Blues"

Alright, this is one of those three Harold and I wrote the night we wrote "Class of '57." It's a ditty. Just a little nonsense melody with not a lot of substance. We wrote it with Dave Dudley in mind. Everybody remembers "Six Days on the Road." And Dave cut it and put it on one of his albums.

We referenced a lot of songs from this early era of country music. Can you believe they actually had songs back then called "The Huckle Buck" and "Roly-Poly"? And so often we would throw people's names in as a shout-out. There's a line here that says, "A golden oldie for Carl and his brand-new wife." That was Carl Perkins. He was a great friend who was traveling with us at the time, and we thought it would be funny to use his name in a secret sort of way.

Trumpets?

I have no idea why there are trumpets on this record. They are playing Dobro licks and really getting on my nerves. But this little ol' song is whatever it is and doesn't need to be taken very seriously at all.

"Under It All"

From Lew's pen and guitar. I remember when he first sang it to us, we looked at him and said, "To the tune of 'Amazing Grace'? Really?" But he very much wanted to do it, and the lyric is pretty darn good. So, we went with it, but I really do wish he had spent another few hours on it and given it a less familiar melody. We sang it well, and it served as another tune on the "Now" side of the album.

"Every Time I Trust a Gal"

From Lew again. And this one had guts and substance. Tempo is good and the story is strong. I liked the way we changed person in mid-verse. On the first line of each verse, it is Lew/Phil/Don telling the story in second person. Then it switches to Harold in first person. Back to the three of us in second person and then to Harold in first person again. I think that's clever and

75

very unique. Never heard another song do this. Also, in the first line, Lew used his own birthday:

He was born on the 12th of March and the winds did blow

I love what Harold does with the solos and what Charlie McCoy does all through it with the bass harmonica. This is a perfect song to spice an album. It was fun to sing and to listen to. And if you're counting and can still remember the name of the album, that gives us eight songs total, with the "Then" side coming up a little short. And the reason for that was that 36,000-foot flight I mentioned.

"The Saturday Morning Radio Show"

On the late evening of Tuesday, February 22, 1972, we, along with John, June, Carl Perkins, and the Tennessee Three, left New York for a nine-day European tour of Holland and Germany. While everyone else ate and then settled in for a little nighttime sleep, the four of us pulled out our legal pads and pens and started listing songs we wanted to do on our new upcoming album. We found ourselves to be three songs short on the "Then" side. Somewhere over the mid-Atlantic, the songs we were discussing turned into a comedy routine, and we began creating what would come to be known as Lester "Roadhog" Moran and His Cadillac Cowboys. This was a parody of all the local country musicians who had radio shows on local stations all over the USA. We created characters for each of us: Phil was "Red Vines." Don was "Wesley Rexrode." Lew was "Wichita Ramsey." And Harold became "Lester 'Roadhog' Moran."

We wrote and laughed all the way to Amsterdam, Holland. When we would calm down a little, Harold would just give out another "Mighty fine!" and we were back to rolling in the aisles. No one seemed annoyed with us. As a matter of fact, those strangers around us seemed taken by what we were doing and joined in the laughter.

Afraid it might be more jet lag than humor, we decided to wait till we had a few hours sleep on the ground the next day before we deemed it a part of the album. But the next night we were still laughing about it and gave up permanently on coming up with three more songs. This comedy sketch we had just written was 9 minutes and 37 seconds long, and that would easily take the place of three songs.

When we got home ten days later, we called Jerry Kennedy and told him what we had, and he was as ready as we were. By April 13, about five weeks later, we were in the studio in Nashville recording as our alter egos. The musicians caught the gist of what we were doing immediately and put their own twists on what we asked of them. We only asked that they play off key and out of rhythm. The only problem was getting through a take without one of them, and to be honest, one of us, breaking up laughing. There are hilarious outtakes no one but a handful of us have ever heard. I wish they were released so that all the Roadhog fans out there could enjoy them as much as we have.

We scripted and timed exactly what you hear on the record, and it was a worldwide hit. It was such a hit that Mercury asked us to do an entire album of Roadhog and His Cadillac Cowboys. We did and it, too, was a hit. Today there is a Roadhog album on just about every bus that rolls out of Nashville, because even the new guys love the satiric take we did on the industry when it was young and more innocent and on a local level.

We have enjoyed everything we have ever done, but Lester and the boys hold a special place in our hearts to this day. We still have the original costumes we wore on the front of the album. The picture of the Statlers in normal dress was taken at the Woodrow Wilson Birthplace in our hometown.

Funny thing we learned recording this album; after years of practice trying to do it the right way, it is harder to sing off key than it is on.

8

The Statler Brothers Sing Country Symphonies in E Major

1972

First things first. This album had an official scheduled release date of December 15, 1972. If that happened, and after all these years I have to trust that it did, then this would be our third album in that year. We were big album sellers, and Mercury liked to "make hay while the sun shined." But knowing the record business and marketing as I do, I'm sure it was well into 1973 before it was firmly in the stores. (Such an anachronism in today's vernacular, "in the stores." This was a time when the only place you could buy a record was in a physical brick-and-mortar store. There was no Internet. No downloading. No iTunes. This really dates us but it's our history and simply the way it was.)

Second thing—that title. We so often had our tongues in our cheeks throughout our career. This was one of those times we looked at country music through a classical eye and had a ball doing it. For the cover, we dressed in tuxedoes and sat in the ballroom at one of Nashville's classiest country clubs, surrounded by chandeliers and gold décor. Of course, we also wore black cowboy hats. Why E major? Ask any country music enthusiast. E is the fullest open chord on the guitar and gives the best full-throttled ring for any rhythm guitar that sets the opening scene for a country song. We sat in a semicircle in the style of a string quartet with a single gold music stand in front of us. That music stand has a history all its own.

We were at John and June's house one day, and in their music room sat this beautiful little brass music stand. June was a great collector of antiques and had a house full of them. I stopped and admired the stand, as it was really an attractive piece. As we were leaving, she came to the door with it in her hand and gave it to me. What a sweet gesture and precious gift. I have it to this day. I cherish the gift and the memory. Sweet June.

We even followed through with the liner notes in the same mode. We listed all the session musicians on the back and used their real and full names. We exposed steel guitar virtuoso Pete Drake's real name as Roddis Franklin Drake. No kidding. Famous piano player "Pig" Robbins was revealed to really be Hargus M. Robbins. And our fiddle buddy, Buddy Spicher, was really Norman K. Spicher. It is probably the only time their real names were ever publicly printed. But we wanted everything comically formal. We even listed ourselves thusly:

1st Bass...Harold Wilson Reid, Esq.
2nd Bass...Donald Sidney Reid, Esq.
3rd Bass...Philip Elwood Balsley, Esq.
Shortstop...Lewis Calvin DeWitt, Esq.

The stage was set. Bring on the music, which was as country and Statler as all our albums. We didn't change the product, only the package.

"Monday Morning Secretary"

I wrote this in the summer of 1972. It was July, the month we usually took off for vacation from touring. But that didn't mean your mind quit working. A song can crawl up your back and demand to be written any time of the year or any time of the day or night. Those are the ones I like best. There are times you have to sit yourself down and make yourself write. You have to schedule it like you would any kind of workload. But I always found the best ones just came down on you like the noonday sun, and you couldn't escape giving in to the urge until you found a little shade and a pencil and paper. My only thoughts going into it was to salute the working ladies—the secretaries who ran the offices and, in kind, ran the companies that all the bosses got credit for. She was overworked and underpaid and underappreciated. I wanted to tell her story and give her a little shine she never got enough of. This song was special to me in a lot of ways that I'll tell you about now.

Although profanity has never been a major or frequent part of my vocabulary, this was the second song I had written with a mild curse word in it. (The first was "You Can't Go Home.")

She laughs off his pass, like she's done in the past
She knows all those lines so well
At five she goes home, to her cat and two rooms
And cries cause she's lonely as hell

This was nothing earth-shattering but worth mentioning because of how it went against the grain of our image and general nature. No one seemed bothered by it, and it probably drew some extra attention to the song, even though that was definitely not why it was in there. It was there because it fit.

I liked the way we each performed our verses and that quickly recognized Jerry Kennedy intro. And here's something I can't explain to any satisfaction, but I originally wrote the opening line as:

She comes in at eight, a little bit late

80

But on the session, just before the red light came on and we started the first take, I changed it on my lead sheet to:

She leaves home at eight, a little bit late

That may seem terribly minor to just about everyone, but it's a textbook example of how a writer is never through writing and rewriting himself. (I hear songs of mine to this day on the radio that were recorded thirty years ago and think, *I wish I had changed that line.*)

"Monday Morning Secretary" represents a major milestone in our business development. 1972 was our last year with the Johnny Cash organization, and for all those years, we had been writers with his publishing company, House of Cash. Now that we were setting out on our own, we formed our own company, American Cowboy Music, and published our own writings. This was the first song we recorded for our new adventure. The first single to take our music to a business level that would allow us to own all our own words and melodies. We were ecstatic and ready to take on the industry wearing another hat.

On the liner notes, you will see toward the bottom:

Water and crackers will be served in the Great Room at Intermission
Waiter: William G. Hall

This was another time when we included a personal shout-out by using a friend's name in a clandestine sort of way. Bill Hall was one of the most respected publishers in Nashville, and he was instrumental in setting up and managing our company. We still get benefits from things he did and taught us how to do businesswise. I miss that little gray-bearded man every day.

"Burning Bridges"

Jack Scott had a pop hit on this little jewel in 1960. It was the perfect country song, written with that simple two-verse, strong, solid four-line chorus. Anybody could sing it and put their own brand on it without much effort. When you have an opening line of *Found some letters you wrote me this morning*, there is no limitation on where you can go with it. In any direction, it's going to be good. In this case, it was fantastic. This could have been a single for us if we had been in the habit of staying with an album longer. I feel we sang it so well and with such a winning formula that I think this is a good place to share a little shorthand from inside the group.

I told you earlier how we had borrowed on the Louvin Brothers' (Ira and Charlie) style of harmony. We liked them and their style so much that we used it frequently. And like all friends who work closely together over time, we developed shortcut words for things. So often, while just the four of us were alone in our conference room at the office or on the bus arranging songs for the next album, we would just take off singing a song until someone heard something and made a suggestion. Harold had a great ear for a lot of our arrangements. For instance, Lew and I sing the second verse here with straight lead/tenor parts, but when we got to the third line in that second verse, Harold yelled out, "Lugan," and we knew without questioning him what he was hearing in his head and what he wanted us to do. Forever after, "Lugan" scribbled on an arrangement sheet simply meant to emulate the Louvin Brothers harmony. This was our inside shortcut word for it, and there is no better explanation of what it sounded like than listening to the lines before and after this one and comparing the two sounds.

The last time we saw Charlie was at our Hall of Fame induction in 2008. We had a chance that night to tell him how much the duo had meant to us musically and how bad we had felt when they broke up back in the sixties. He thanked us sincerely and then sadly said, "Boys I just couldn't take it any longer. I got tired of being in a trio with me, Ira, and Jack Daniels."

"I Want to Carry Your Sweet Memories"

It's surprising to me, looking back, just how often a bluegrass song shows up in our repertoire. We liked listening to it and we liked singing it. And you just can't cut one of these without calling a banjo picker. This time it was Bobby Thompson, who showed up on our first album for the label two years before. He did his usual terrific job, as did all of our regular pickers. And they did something really special for us on this tune.

The bridge goes:

I don't want to be your servant anymore
I don't want to be your slave

I just want to remember all the good times that we shared
And carry those sweet memories to my grave

We wanted to do lines one and three real soft and then come down hard and loud on two and four. We could have done this electronically in the post-mix, but instead, we told the musicians to do the dynamics with us live. They did, and it gave a real feel and excitement that would never have been there with the twisting of the knobs.

"I Believe in Music"

Mac Davis wrote it and sang it and had a nice hit with it. We added a lot of little tricks in our rendition. It started with the first note taking pitches on the word "I." We did this throughout. The band played the rhythm in double-time, and we sang in half-time. And Phil, bless his gentle heart, crooned this in his laid-back gentle style that just charms you to the core.

We ran into Mac from time to time. He guested on our TV show. But out on the road, we saw him at a state fair one night. We were playing a show a little earlier than his, and as we were about to pull out after ours, he jumped on our bus and we sat and talked for a little while. He said, "I really envy you guys and your audience. You have adults out there who sit and actually listen to your songs and your comedy. I've got teenyboppers out there just screaming no matter what I do. I'd love to play to your crowd."

Mac was right about our crowd. Our fans. They were the best and most loyal folks you could ever ask for. They sustained us for forty years in a fickle and changeable business. God bless them, every one.

"A Special Song for Wanda"

Remember the night I told you about when Harold and I wrote three songs in one sitting? This was the third one. "Class of '57." Then "1953–Dear John-Honky-Tonk Blues." And "Wanda."

Who is Wanda? And don't think songwriters don't get asked that question. So do novelists. Fans (and even family) get to believing everything they hear is true. This is the perfect opportunity to clear up all those questions. We never knew a Wanda who was a Navy wife who lived in Newport News, Virginia. She was as fictional as the story she inspired.

Together, Harold and I had a knack for coming up with interesting storylines. I think we could have written a novel together, and I often wish we had. That's really what a good story song is. It's a short story. A short novel. A short fiction with a beginning, a middle, and an end.

What I said earlier about "Burning Bridges" holds true with this song, also. When you luck out with an opening line such as *Wanda was alone at nights while he was somewhere sailing,* you can go anywhere you want. She can 1) be at home crying herself to sleep every night with a broken heart; she can 2) become a sad widow in the final verse; she can 3) discover she's pregnant shortly after he shipped out and face motherhood alone. Or she can be

A navy wife with too much spare time on her hands

I never had more fun writing than when Harold and I wrote together.

"I'll Be Your Baby Tonight"

If they asked, "Who is Wanda," then trust me, they asked, "Why Dylan?" because Bob Dylan wrote this baby 100 percent, lock, stock and barrel. And most people don't couple Dylan and the Statlers in the same musical vision. Being painfully honest, I think he was a good songwriter when I could understand his lyrics. I understood "Don't Think Twice, It's Alright" and "Blowing in the Wind," but past that, I have to look them up online to see what all the noise was about. We ran into Bob a few times. We did TV with him, but he was the most inward, quietest person you can imagine, so much so that I would be hard-pressed to give you even an interesting memory about him. But, boy, I liked this song.

The whole form of it was country from the front to the end. We told the pickers to play it funky, and they did. Jerry, Pete Drake, and Charlie McCoy outdid themselves. And a top-of-the-line performance from The Statler Brothers.

"Woman Without a Home"

I always wrote with a guitar or a piano except for one song. (I'll tell you about that one in a minute.) This one, I used a piano intentionally because I knew what I wanted to write before I sat down with no idea in my head. I told Harold beforehand that I wanted to write a pop song. Nothing country. Something maybe, oh, I don't know, something Steve Lawrence might sing. I was always experimenting and challenging myself just to see if I could do it. I had an old upright in my office at home and used to go in there after everyone went to bed and write all night. So, I started noodling on the white keys, (I'm not really a piano player) until I hit on a little melody I liked. I knew I had someplace to go when I wrote the first two lines in my head because the rhyme pattern hit me hard, as if someone else had written it.

She was young and I was older
She believed everything I told her

That's when I rushed over to the desk for pen and paper. From there, it kept coming, and I was touched and a little baffled by what was flashing into my head.

Sometimes I lied to make her happy
Sometimes she lied to see if I would lie some more

I wrote three verses and a chorus and realized I almost had the story and emotion I wanted, but I had not repeated any lines at all that would give me a title. I had an almost-finished song I was falling in love with but no title in sight. And that didn't come till the very last line.

I hope life there is better
But I hope he won't let her
Have too much time to spend alone
'Cause she's a woman without a home

I never meant this song for the Statlers. Never meant it for anyone. Just for me; to see if I could do it. When I sang it to Harold, he insisted we sing it. We did it very simply. Pretty much sounded like it did when I sang it to my partners. Except for those fabulous strings and how big Harold, Phil, and Lew made that chorus. I get chills.

Of all God has given me through my pen, this is one of my all-time favorites. I was emotionally drained after writing it, and now I get that same feeling just listening to it.

Oh, yes. That one song I wrote with no instrument at all. It was April 29, 1971 (I keep good records). We were in the Carlton House Hotel in Pittsburgh on one of the top floors. I got an idea for a song, and, as is so often the case, if you don't put it down immediately, you lose it. I have tried waiting till morning because I was too tired to write when the idea hit me, and almost every time it's gone when you try to recall it. It was late, our transportation was parked a block down the street, which meant that was where my guitar was. I would have to get dressed, go down in the elevator, through the lobby, well, you see the situation. So, I just grabbed a pad by the phone and a pen by the bed and wrote down the words with a melody in my head and prayed I wouldn't forget it.

I didn't. This one was not for the Statlers, either. The title was "He Taught Me All the Right Ways to Go Wrong." But it was worth the trouble. Anita Carter recorded it and did a beautiful job with it.

"Delta Dawn"

Tanya Tucker had the country hit. Then Helen Reddy had the pop hit. And we liked the way the melody flowed, so we chose to include it here with a new innovation. For this song, we invented a new harmony format that I don't think had ever been done before or since except when we used it a couple of times later. Note the opening and closing choruses. Harold is singing lead. Phil is singing the baritone (alto) up an octave. I am singing the tenor part down an octave. And Lew is singing the bass part on the very top. We came up with this by simply fooling around. We hit on it and knew it was different and good. Until now, I don't think we have ever told anyone exactly what we did to get that unusual sound.

Harold's performance was easy and relaxed, which gave even more punch to those choruses at the front and end.

The mention of Helen Reddy reminds me of a long-ago fair date in upstate New York. It was August of 1974, and Helen Reddy and the Statlers were playing to a huge outdoor crowd. Or, at least, it was supposed to be. The problem was it had rained mercilessly hard all day and did not let up at all come showtime. We looked out from backstage, and there were maybe a dozen people in the whole stadium, and they were bunched under umbrellas and raincoats and drenched to the skin. The promoter called Helen and her husband and the four of us over to a corner and said, "I'm getting word from up front the show has to go on."

"You have to be kidding," was our response in unison.

He said, "I'm sorry. They won't postpone. If you'll go on in the rain, everybody will get paid. If not, we go home empty-handed."

We and Helen got our heads together, noticed there was a little over-hang above the stage, and decided, "What the heck! Let's do it." So, we each went out and sang in the rain to those dozen, soaked, loyal fans. Show business at its best!

"Wedding Bells"

Hard-core country. A Hank Williams classic but not written by HW. The legend behind this little gem is that back in the forties, a Knoxville guitar picker by the name of Claude Boone got his name on this composition but not by writing it. He paid an unknown Jimmy Pritchett $25 for it and slapped his name on the copyright and made all the big bucks. This is not a unique, one-of-a-kind story in our industry. Many of you may be aware of the most famous "sellout" concerning "Family Bible." Willie Nelson wrote this one in his lean and hungry days, and a Texas musician, Paul Buskirk, paid him $50 for it. Buskirk pitched it to Claude Gray, and they had a hit with it, with Buskirk and Gray both listed as writers. There are so many more of these sad stories in the music jungle, all interesting, but each one a trail of tears on someone's unenviable journey.

Our cut was intimate and an easy sell with those sadly sweet or sweetly sad lyrics. Listen for more "Lugan" harmonies.

"Too Many Rivers"

I can't tell you how much I love this Harlan Howard masterpiece. The power of that chorus when H/L/P join me makes me rise up out of my seat even after all these years. JK laid down the Dobro guitar for this one and picked up the electric, and it sounds like a fifth voice. It just makes me smile all over myself. You know Harlan Howard was the one who summed up country music in the best, purest definition ever offered. He said, "Country music is three chords and the truth," and this song is a flawless example of what he was describing.

And when you try to put love back together
There's always a few little pieces you can't find

One of the nicest compliments we ever received as writers was from this man. We had created quite a nice style with our nostalgia and memory hits, and one day Harlan and Jerry Kennedy were talking about songs. Jerry asked him if he had any new ones to pitch him, and Harlan asked who was recording next. Jerry said, "The Statlers are coming in next week." And Harlan said, "I have tried to write what those guys write but I can't touch 'em."

Thanks, Harlan. I just smiled all over myself again.

"They Can't Take You Out of Me"

A basic bread-and-butter country song Harold and I joined together in writing. A lament over a lost young love. It says all it needs to say on its own. "They" is identified as the virtual enemy here, and "they" can be anyone you want it to be. Could be society, the times, family. It's amazing who all we can blame when we don't want to shoulder any responsibility on our own.

They took you out of my Saturdays and Sundays
But they can't take you out of me

I am struck, listening to this, how complementary the tempo is to the lyric. There is a certain groove that fits every song, and it can't be measured. It has to be felt. Buddy Harman was our drummer on all these records, and he helped us set and hold those perfect rhythms. It's easy to determine who "they" are when we hear something on a finished record we like. It's all those talented people in that studio who do what they do best. They are the folks who make each album good, really good, or great. They come each day with their extraordinary gift and offer new innovations that catch our ear and make us smile. They give energy and beauty and excitement and then go home and come back the next day and do it all again. And most people never know their names. But they, the session musicians, are the ones who make an album a joy to listen to and make you want to hear it again. No singer can do that without their backing and support. *E Major* is a really good album, and those loyal pickers deserve as much credit as ol' Harold, Phil, Lew, and Don.

9

Carry Me Back

1973

We were waist-high and knee-deep in nostalgia. We were the vanguard for the rage that was sweeping the nation in every possible way. Music, fashion, décor, hairstyles, plays, TV shows. Everybody was looking back at the fifties, and we were reveling in every phase of it. This album was intentionally a retrospective of all the memories of an era that was already considered the best decade ever. This album was more about the songs than it was the singing. It was more about the words than the music. Each song was just another chapter of remembrances and tender recallings, such as young love, sock hops, and drive-in movies. We even captured it in the album cover.

In our hometown of Staunton, Virginia, there is a restaurant called Wright's Dairy Rite Drive-In. It was the place all teenagers circled a hundred times every Friday night after the football and basketball games and every Saturday night with dates. It still stands today on the very same site and has the best hamburgers and foot-long hot dogs the law will allow. To put a picture on our music, we and our wives dressed up in fifties attire and sat on the back of cars, just like in the old days. We shot it at midnight in a warm, summer A.M., and it gave an authenticity to each word inside the jacket cover.

As in all our music collections, each song had its story and, I think, told it well. We were in a soft, caring mode when we wrote and sang these tunes, and they all still leave me a little sentimental with each listening.

"Carry Me Back"

This was the lead single that set the tone for all the songs that followed. It began in a dressing room in Regina, Saskatchewan, at the Center of the Arts Theater. We were on a co-tour with Marty Robbins that began in Spokane and took us east across Canada and landed us in Regina for two shows on Friday March 16, 1973. (I told you I keep good records.) The most boring downtime at concerts was the dead zone between shows, so Harold and I often took advantage of that stretch and would write. This night—and I can see the dressing room as if I had been there just yester-day—we wrote "Carry Me Back."

The opening line *Is Jimmy through serving his hitch with Uncle Sam* would hold an interesting footnote ten years later when Jimmy Fortune came into our lives. Then we changed the first line, to sidestep confusion, to:

> Is Johnny *through serving his hitch with Uncle Sam?*
> *Do the kids still spend Saturday nights driving 'round Hamburger Dan's?*
> *Did Jackie ever make it to the streets of Hollywood?*
> *And Bobby, I'd love to see him again and I would if I could*

Another line that created a lot of questions and speculation was the last line of that first verse. When folks asked at the time, I didn't always give an answer because I wasn't moved to. It was very personal to me, but now that I'm analyzing these words and musings, I think I should. I grew up with a best friend, Bobby, living next door. We played ball together, went to church together, went to the movies every Saturday morning together, and

90

discovered girls together, from birth to our teens. When I was fifteen and he was sixteen, he was killed by a drunk driver on Christmas Eve. It made a difference in my makeup as to who I would become. It showed up in my lifestyle, in my zero tolerance for alcohol, and in my writing and the things I hold dear and the degree to which I hold them. He was young and it was unfair, and now I'm old and sometimes I think that is unfair, but it was God's will, and I have lived my life in search of a profound understanding of what happened and why. I have placed a Christmas wreath on his grave for sixty years. This line was a personal testament to the fact that we have a lot to talk about and laugh about and catch up on and that I'd love to see him again. And I will.

Carry me back and make me feel at home
Let me cling to those memories that won't let me alone
Where it was always summer and she was always mine
Carry me back, Lord, while I've still got the time

"Woman I Still Love"

If I were a painter, they might call this my Blue Period. My songs were intimate and introspective and all about emotions and man and woman things. You may say that's what most all songs are about, and you'd be right, but I was writing a different brand than I had ever written before. Memories plus lost love plus caring plus an openness of unbridled feelings. It was a very tender time for me as a writer, and I can hear it in the words and in the singing from us all. For example, this is the best solo I've ever heard Lew sing. Listen to it with your eyes closed.

The personal style of this song reveals itself in the first word of each verse. I started each verse with the word "And," showing that this guy has been haunted and worried way before the music ever begins. He eats and sleeps the misery this woman has left him in.

And what will happen to you
Are you sure you'll be alright?
When you walk away from me today
Into a brand-new life

91

I wrote it in July of 1972. There is no better time to write a love song that jumps out of the heart than on a hot summer night. Something is imbedded there that leaps out of the pen and comes storming through the microphone.

And if you think you've found
The man you've been dreaming of
Ask him, please, to treat with ease
The woman I still love

The Cam Mullins Orchestra doesn't hurt any, either.

"What Do I Care"

Johnny Cash has never received enough credit as a songwriter. He has penned some absolute pearls. Some of my faves from his earlier days: "Give My Love to Rose," "Come In Stranger," "Understand Your Man." And this one. It's carefree and touching at the same time. If you're talking about a strong memory song, this one is it. Just consider what these lines are saying about the power of a sweet memory:

Anything that I may miss
Is made up for each time we kissed
You were mine for a little while so what do I care

He was a straightforward, no-frills writer. What I call a no-fat-meat style. He used raw words and not many flowery adjectives. He wrote like he sang and like he lived.

John was our mentor and guru in so many ways. He gave me the best and most lasting advice I ever received as a writer. The whole troupe was in an airport waiting on a flight one afternoon, and I had my notebook out working on a song. I got stumped on how best to express a line, so I walked over to him, read what I had, and asked him how he'd fix it. He didn't tell me how to fix it, but he gave me guidance that would help me solve problems that would come up in all future years. He said, "Remember, Donnie, [he always called me Donnie] the best way to say anything is to just say it."

Wow! No flowers or fat meat. No dancing around what you want to say with clever turns of a phrase. Just say it. I have carried that with me to every page I have ever written since. He knew what he was talking about, and he practiced what he preached.

What do I care if I never have much money
And sometimes my table looks a little bare?
You were mine for a little while
So what do I care?

"If We Never Had"

It is common knowledge that songs are some of our best references to the past. We remember eras of our lives by the songs that were popular. Hearing one on the radio transports us to a time and place we haven't been for decades. And it is amazing the memories that pop in my head when I hear one of our songs forty-some years later. This one, written in the spring of 1970, takes me to a thousand hotel rooms. I would sit and pick the guitar in the long afternoons, and sometimes a good melody and some decent words would come out of it, and sometimes the trash can would be full of scribblings before an hour was up. You never knew. But this must have been a good day because this little tune has stuck with me and means a lot to me. Without a doubt, it may be the most philosophical poetry I ever wrote:

If we sorta made a mess out of what we had together
Still it's better than if we never had

Every experience we have in life, good, bad, or indifferent, makes us who we are in the long run. Everyone you meet, either briefly or for longer, has an effect on who you become.

If we both die tomorrow and never see each other
Still it's better than if we never had

The musical arrangement was very simplistic. We often did this consciously so the music would not get in the way of the lyric. More often than not, we were selling words just a little more than we were music. Too much

93

instrumentation can cover up good lyrics, and if the voices are not on top of the music, then all is lost, in our way of thinking. (That is what bothers me most about today's country music; the instruments are more prominent than the singers.) But with that said, Chip Young's underlying acoustic guitar roll throughout sells this song like a fifth voice. And that is called good mixing and producing by Jerry Kennedy.

If we loved a little hard and died a little trying
Still it's better than if we never had

"Take Good Care of Her"

This song had been recorded by lots of folks. Elvis, Johnny Mathis, Adam Wade. But the one we remembered best was Sonny James back in 1966. Sonny was on that first tour we joined in '64, and we had a great friendship with him through the years and lots more tours. Here was a guy with something like twenty-six number-one songs under his belt, so he knew a good song when he heard it and, boy, could he ever sell it. This one, written by two guys we never knew, Kent and Warren, will just tug at your heartstrings. We gave it the Statler treatment as if we had written it our-selves because it fit this album like a waiter's glove.

Sonny was the most caring, Christian man you would ever want to meet. He was also a stickler for perfection. He rehearsed his band every day before a performance, and he checked everyone's tuning personally before walking on stage each night. A familiar sight you could count on seeing each evening behind the curtain, just before his introduction, was his bass player, Milo Liggett, holding the end of his electric bass in Sonny's ear with Sonny turning the keys and fine-tuning it. I never knew until then that you could even do that, but the vibrations are very clear and it works!

Sonny retired early. In the mid-1980s he became almost reclusive and just walked away from everything show-business related. We were in contact but never really saw him until the night of our Hall of Fame induction in 2008. He came. And when I turned and saw him, still tall and straight and now bearded, I couldn't hold back the tears. It was an emotional night for sure, but knowing Sonny had come out for it just brought a lot of old cher-ished memories from the early days crashing down on us. He was such a good man.

"Streets of San Francisco"

I don't really know why I wrote this song. *The Streets of San Francisco* was a hit TV show at the time starring Karl Malden and Michael Douglas. (Yes, that's how the billing was. Michael Douglas was just coming into his own at the time.) The title had a nice little beat to the way it rolled off the tongue, so I thought I'd put a story to it. Not a pretty story, but one you couldn't ignore if you had ever walked down Times Square in those days or driven down Sunset Blvd. I see in my notes that I actually wrote this song in Hollywood in February of 1973, so I'm sure I was reflecting the sights I was currently seeing on the streets. There are a lot of sad lines that make up this song, and I think it tells its own story best.

Musically, you can hear the signature speed-bump rhythm with the bass drum on the choruses we talked about earlier. Then there is the fabulous guitar work of Ray Edenton and Chip Young setting the walking mood from the very introduction.

"Whatever Happened to Randolph Scott?"

I'll be happy to answer that question because it is a beautiful story. But first, to the song. It was simultaneously a salute to the western movies of old and a slap in the face to the westerns of the day. That Randolph Scott had retired completely from the business (see Sonny James) and disappeared from the face of anything resembling the movie industry gave great meaning to the line:

Whatever happened to Randolph Scott has happened to the industry

He was gone and so was the movie-making business as we knew and loved it. We referenced all our old cowboy heroes, saving RS for the title and punch line:

Whatever happened to Randolph Scott riding the trail alone?
Whatever happened to Gene and Tex and Roy and Rex, the Durango Kid?
Whatever happened to Randolph Scott, his horse plain as could be?
Whatever happened to Randolph Scott has happened to the best of me

Once in an interview, a lady reporter asked us what RS's horse's name was. Without missing a beat, Harold said, "Plain-as-could-be." She said, "Oh, that's nice," and wrote it down.

Harold does a fantastic and energetic job with the verses, and we had a ball with both choruses, naming all those old heroes of ours. And that's Jerry Kennedy on the guitar intro, break, and ending. What a great, original lick.

Years later, in the nineties on our Saturday night TV show, we had Jerry as a guest and got him to play some of the famous licks and intros he had invented on sessions of the past. Those were his fingers creating the electric guitar lick on Tammy's "Stand By Your Man," Orbison's "Pretty Woman," the Dobro guitar work all through Jeannie C. Riley's "Harper Valley PTA," and so many of ours, including "Randolph Scott."

In the mood to write, I asked Harold one day if he had any good ideas for a song, and he came out with this title. I stood and looked at him trying to decide if I was crazy enough to take him seriously or if I should just continue on with what I was doing and ignore him. The fact that I'm writing about this song after all this time tells you what happened.

It was the second hit single from this album, and after its run, we were in Hollywood in our hotel rooms one evening when a call came through from Pat Scott, wife of Randolph. She invited us over to his offices in Beverley Hills to visit the next day. Such a kind and gracious lady, she met the four of us in the lobby and took us up to see the man. He was standing behind his desk in a pinstriped suit and tie. The most perfect Southern, Virginia gentleman you could ever meet. We shared a home state but that day he shared memories of the old days in Tinsel Town that we just ate up and cherished. Our relationship did not stop there. They stayed in touch with us and we with them for many years until his death in '87.

Pat told us a story that describes the man's character so perfectly. She said when he retired from the movies and went strictly into the business of buying gas and oil stocks and bonds (that made him extremely wealthy), he maintained an office on the second floor of their home for a few years before setting up an office in town. She said every morning he would get up, shower, shave, and dress in a suit and tie and walk twenty feet down the hallway from their bedroom to his office and work all day behind his desk. (I, too, am retired and in my office just twenty feet from my bedroom as I write these very words. But I have on a sweatshirt and a ball cap.)

Whatever happened to Randolph Scott has happened to the best of me.

"I Wish I Could Be"

I wrote the arrangement of this song before I ever wrote the song. I had in my head to write four short, four-line love stories. One for each of us to sing. And we each did, in our own chosen way. This would become the only song The Statler Brothers ever recorded where we never sang a note together. Not one phrase of harmony in the whole piece. Just four solos. One inside joke was in Harold's verse. I wrote:

I'd sleep tonight in Little Rock if I could fly a plane

Just the mention of a plane is enough to make him cringe. He hates flying. We owned buses for thirty years so he wouldn't have to get on another airplane. I loved the way each Statler handled his verse. My favorite lines fall at the end of the song:

I'd give everything I have if things had just begun
And you were lying there in North Carolina's sun
And everything we had was still yet to be
Carolina, you sure got the best of me

"We Owe It All to Yesterday"

We were playing Mobile, Alabama on April 20, 1973. Brother Harold and I were lounging in the Holiday Inn knowing that we needed material for this upcoming album. We wrote this song on that day and were recording it in Nashville a month and two days later. This one was tailor-made for the memory theme of this particular album. The first verse instigated a funny moment that happens sometimes to writers:

Do you remember my old Ford, how cold it used to get?
And the blanket that we used to wrap up in?
Well, you that Ford and blanket all got away from me
God, I'd love to get you all together again

When a friend of ours heard this, he laughed and said, "Wow, you guys know what you're talking about. Those old Fords had the worst heaters in them ever invented. It took twenty minutes to get a car warm." I know nothing about cars and just lucked out on this fact that he deemed so important. But it's a lesson to all writers to know your subject thoroughly, because you never know what fact a listener or reader will latch onto and consider important.

Without question the favorite that Harold and I ever wrote together was the last line of the second verse. We have discussed it many times. It says so much:

> *Do you know I think about you too much for my own good?*
> *Everything I said then I still mean*
> *If we could do it over I wouldn't change a thing*
> *Your bobby socks keep dancing in my dreams*

Just a few years after we wrote this song, we started getting offers to talk about doing a TV series. We heard from networks and individual television producers who thought our brand of music and humor was a natural for that medium. We turned all comers down because we were loving making records and touring and doing exactly what we were doing. But Harold and I did talk between ourselves that the chorus to this song would make a really good theme song for a segment of looking back on memories. We called it our "Yesteryear" segment. It was nearly twenty years later that we decided the time had come, and we agreed to do a Saturday night, one-hour variety show on the TNN network that would run for seven years. We did indeed use this chorus for a segment of that name, and it fit perfectly with the change of only the last word in lines 2 and 4:

> *Yesterday will never be forgotten*
> *Tomorrow's ten thousand years from here*
> *Everything we ever had together*
> *We owe it all to Yesteryear*

We never throw anything away!

"When I Stop Dreaming"

We finally got around to saluting Ira and Charlie, the Louvin Brothers, in a proper way.

They wrote this song and had a major hit with it. It was their signature song and we all got to join in the "Lugan" harmony on this cut while Phil shines in the solos.

While we were still a weekend quartet, about 1961, we got a job at a nearby country music park one summer opening the show every Sunday afternoon for the star act. We were really just kids, but we got to rub shoulders with some of the great old-time stars: Cowboy Copas, Hawkshaw Hawkins, Buck Owens, Kitty Wells. This was where we first saw the Louvin Brothers. We learned so much by just watching and absorbing everyone we were privileged to work with. We took a little something from them all and carried it with us while we were developing and becoming The Statler Brothers.

"The Strand"

Lew wrote a nice history of what happened to the theater we all four used to go to every Saturday morning to see our western heroes. The addition of this one actually made two songs saluting those stalwart men of the screen from our childhood on this album. But the underlying story here was one of urban development that has taken the heart and soul out of our downtowns and sent everyone fleeing to the outskirt malls like teenagers on a Friday night. In doing so, our town razed our temple of hero worship and left us with only the memories of those times forever past.

But they say it's over and I guess it's true
They'll park their cars where horses used to stand

And they did. We have a large municipal parking garage on the site of that hallowed small-town theater. Cars and trucks stand where Trigger and Champion roamed. Tex Ritter became our good friend as adults, but it was in the Strand where we first saw him in person with his horse, White Flash, as front-row kids.

Just two days ago I parked in there, but I still feel a little guilty every time I do it. Like I'm not being loyal to Tex and Roy and Gene and Harold and Phil and Lew.

10

Thank You, World

1974

This was the tenth studio album of our career and the seventh for Mercury. The title was obviously taken from the single that would lead the album, and being a statement to our fans, to the world, we thought it would be best to have the album-cover picture taken of us on stage. The label sent a photographer out on tour, and he took dozens, maybe hundreds, of shots and poses of us in action while we sang. Why we chose one taken from the back and out of focus is beyond my conscious memory. But apparently we did because there it is.

"Thank You, World"

We were riding in a car on our way to National Airport in Washington DC (later to be known as Reagan International Airport) to catch a plane for points west. Somewhere along the way, Lew said he had written a new song. We said, "Let's hear it," as we always enjoyed singing our newest creations to one another. Someone said, "But we don't have a guitar in here." Lew said, "That doesn't matter because I don't have a melody for it anyway. But I'll read you the words."

He read us the words and we liked it immediately. We started dividing up solo verses and discussing arrangements even though there wasn't even a tune to the lyrics we liked. When we got to the airport, he flipped the handwritten sheets of paper to me and said, "Here, put a tune to it," just like he had on two previous occasions I told you about ("Pictures" and Tommy Cash's "So This Is Love"). This was March 13th of '73, and we already had sessions booked in Nashville to start a new album in May.

I want to thank you world for letting me belong
I'm just one-fourth of one small group that sings your songs
I know that there are others who have served in bigger ways
All I can do is sing your music all my days

After putting the music to it and making it an up-tempo foot-tapper, I had an idea for an intro and an original lick to run through the song at every turn. As the musicians were warming up and tuning on the 10:00 A.M. session on May 24, I took Jerry Kennedy aside in the control room and sang him the little rhythm intro I had and he loved it. He said, "Go out in the studio and just sing it to the pickers." I did, and without missing a beat or a note, together they played it back at me immediately. It was magical and set the tone for the whole song. We used this song as an encore in concerts from then on until our final concert, twenty-nine years later. It rocked on stage and the audience never failed to clap with us on beat every night.

I may not ever stand like Stonewall Jackson stood
But standing on that stage to me is just as good

Country singer Stonewall Jackson was working a show with us one weekend, and as he was packing up his gear and leaving, he came by, shook hands with each of us, and said, "I thank you boys for putting me in that song." I don't know to this day if he was kidding or if he thought we were singing about him.

Without a place here in this world I know that I'd be lost
Thank you, world, for letting me contribute to the cause

"City Lights"

You can take the perfectly pretty melody away and you still have some of the most magnificent poetry ever offered a country song. Bill Anderson writing at his best. Of all the great songs he wrote, this was his first hit as a composer and the one that brought him to Nashville; and the one we chose to give the Statler treatment. I really like what we always called the "zip-zip" fiddle intro. It is so Grand Ole Opry. And then the flood of lush violins that just pour all over the last verse and chorus.

Bill was our first friend in the business from that initial Johnny Cash tour in '64. We have maintained that friendship all through the years. For twenty-five years, 1970 to 1994, we gave a free concert for charity in our hometown on the Fourth of July. Most times we had guests, friends from the music business, come and perform with us. Bill came in 1974, the year we recorded this album. He did something with us no other guest ever did. Having a softball team consisting of himself and his touring band, he often would play games for charity events. So, on the afternoon before the concert in Staunton, we put a ball team together and we played one another. He has accused us for years of stacking our team with ex-major leaguers and owes that to the fact that we won. (In all honesty and friendship, I have no argument for that.)

We would pay back each guest performer, who came free of charge, with whatever they asked us to do in return for them. Some would have a charity event of their own that we would travel to and perform at for free. Some asked us to record a song of theirs. With Bill, we gladly did both. He didn't ask for the song, we just did that because we loved both the song and the man.

You don't get much better than:

103

A bright array of city lights as far as I can see
The great white way shines through the night for lonely guys like me

From these lines you would think he was looking out of a New York City hotel window when actually he was sitting on the flat roof of a radio station in Commerce, Georgia, using his imagination. Take that to heart, all you young writers!

"Sweet Charlotte Ann"

I wrote this little number about the prettiest girl in school that all the boys dreamed of and how she handled each one of them through her life. It had a nice punch line and it was fun to sing. I knew it wasn't single material, but a perfect flavor for any album. I mentioned before I/we would sometimes hide little personal references and names in our songs. In this one, during Harold's solo, I wrote:

Then the flowers started and she got woman-hearted
and Snappy Simmons kissed her in his car

Being the ultimate and best comedian in the world, Harold did a number of characters, on and off the stage. Snappy Simmons was one of his best off stage and definitely Carl Perkins's favorite. I have seen Carl laugh at Snappy until his stomach ached, and he would literally beg Harold to stop. I threw in old Snappy for Harold and Carl.

The song leads the listener into a false expectation of what the sweetest part of Charlotte Ann was, which is the charm and the punch of the whole thing:

Everybody had a part of Sweet Charlotte Ann
She's that certain someone in the past of many a man
They'd kissed her lips and held her hand and maybe touched her knee
But the sweetest part of Charlotte Ann was always saved for me
Yeah, the sweetest part was Charlotte's heart and she saved it all for me

"Left-Handed Woman"

When Harold and I wrote together, instead of complimenting or praising a stereotypical character, we often created a complex antithetical one.
(Boy, that was a mouthful! Sorry, didn't mean to get so analytical there!) We
came up with this not-very-admirable, untrustworthy woman:

She can cry when you're leaving
Then laugh when you're gone
That left-handed woman is right when she's wrong

There aren't many redeeming values in the girl we invented here, and,
of course, we were presenting it in an almost funny, sexy, and ironic way:

She loves being warm and hates being cold
She's proud of being pretty and scared of gettin' old

Many years later, our sons, Wil and Langdon, known as Wilson
Fairchild, included this song on an album of theirs called *Songs Our Dads
Wrote*. I would sit in the audience and listen to them perform it and have to
laugh privately to myself. I am so glad they have given new to life to this
creation musically, but I have to ask myself if this wicked, conniving, evil
left-handed woman deserves all the attention.

If you've ever seen her living
Then you know that when she dies
You can't bet she ain't breathin'
'Cause of the way she lies
She's good when she's lonely
And great when she ain't
That left-handed woman I love and I hate

"The Blackwood Brothers by The Statler Brothers"

This song took me a lifetime to write. It started when I was nine years
old, just discovering Southern gospel music and seeing the Blackwood
Brothers in person. They were the best, and James Blackwood and J. D.

Sumner became good friends of ours as adults. What a storybook blessing, as I look back on all of it.

The first two verses set up our hero worship of the group, and then the rest of the piece is simply song titles of theirs, songs they had hits with in the gospel field. They would perform these songs in concert, and we and all the others in the audience would clap till our hands were swollen to get them to sing them all again. I can't begin to tell you how much fun and how nostalgic it was in that studio the day we cut this song. There was a sincere and extreme excitement and even reverence about it all. Jerry even called in Larry Butler, a gospel piano virtuoso who had traveled with us back in the Cash days, to capture that authentic Blackwood style.

The ending brings me to my knees emotionally even after all these years. It begins where the music slows and we sing:

> And God if there's an old schoolhouse in heaven let me be
> Somewhere close where I can hear R. W. sing for me
> The Robe, the Robe, the Robe of Calvary

After the session that evening, the 27th day of November 1973, we took the rough tape of this song across the street to play it for our publisher, Bill Hall. We wanted him to hear it because we were so proud of it. As fate would have it, on the way, we ran into Ron Blackwood and a friend on the sidewalk. We grabbed him by the arm and told him to come with us as we had something he was going to want to hear. I remember standing in Bill's office with the song filling the room, everyone listening intently. When it reached the line *Somewhere close where I can hear R. W. sing for me*, Ron turned to his friend, and, with tears streaming down his face, said, "That's my daddy they're singing about."

The last note, when I hit the falsetto, was for James.

"Cowboy Buckaroo"

We really found our niche with those B-western cowboy star salute songs. Mason Williams had written this one a few years earlier. He was a West Coast guitarist/performer/writer. We just couldn't let it pass without giving it a dose of our nostalgically wistful style. Harold does a caring and authentic delivery but saves the best for the last chorus when he does a Tex

Ritter impersonation. And I think the ending is worth an honorable mention. We did the Eddy Arnold "Cattle Call" falsetto riff in four-part harmony.

Good job, guys!

"She's Too Good"

December 2nd, 1972. This was next to the last date the Statlers played as part of the Johnny Cash road show. We finished our eight-year-and-nine-month stretch the next day in Lakeland, Florida. In January of '73 we were on our own, building the next step of our career. But back to December 2nd—Harold and I wrote this song in a hotel room in New Orleans. Looking at them together, this song is the positive to "Left-Handed Woman." This woman we created was not evil and malevolent. She was basically good but life had turned her into something and someone else.

I cringe just a little today at the chorus where we wrote:

Maybe she ain't good enough to go to heaven
But heaven knows she's too good to go to hell

We took some theological liberties there. No maybe about it, she is *not* good enough to go to heaven. None of us are. Grace is needed for that. But past that little wrinkle, I like this song and what we did with it. Artists and producers in what is considered country music today would sneer at the slight production put into a cut such as this. It's stark with no frills or overpowering, driving instruments. The sound is pure to the ear and the senses. You can clearly hear each word, and the music complements, instead of competes with, the lyric.

Yeah, I like it. Wilson Fairchild recorded this one, too. And they stayed true to all the appealing elements that make a song something to enjoy. I love what they did with it.

Listen closely and you'll notice a constant snap or click on the rhythm track just under the voices. That is not a drum of any kind. That is Buddy Harman, the percussionist on practically all of our Mercury sessions, with his shirt rolled up, slapping his belly in time. It's hard to sing with a straight face when you're watching that across the room.

"Baptism of Jesse Taylor"

Johnny Russell had a hit with this just the year before we recorded it as one of the cover songs on this album. When we were in Jerry's office before going down to the studio that day, we noticed he was digging around on his desk for something and finally came up with a tape. He said, "This Jesse Taylor song was brought over here for you guys over a year ago, before Russell ever recorded it." We asked why he hadn't given it to us, and he paid us the nicest compliment one could offer. He said, "You guys bring such good material in here, I didn't figure you needed to hear all the outside stuff I get pitched to play for you. So I don't even bother." We could have had this hit before Johnny, but I don't begrudge him that. He did a fantastic job with it, and we had fun doing the cover version to round out this collection.

It is no secret that Johnny Russell was an all-around entertainer. He was one funny son of a gun on stage. He did a lot of concerts with us; he even came to Staunton for one of our Fourth of July shows in 1975. Anyway, out on tour, he would often get on our bus and travel with us to the next town, and we'd sit up all day or all night and laugh the whole way. It is also no secret that Johnny was a large man, and he frequently made jokes about that. We often had to tell him that he couldn't ride with us on a particular trip because we had a long way to go and had to make good time. We told him we didn't have time to stop every two hours to get something to eat because that is what he wanted to do way too often. He was never offended by that honesty. He'd just say, "No problem. I'll ride with you tomorrow night." Johnny met a hard end to life and we miss him. A good friend.

"The Streets of Baltimore"

Harlan Howard, joined by Tompall Glaser, wrote this one and told a catchy little story about the lovesick working man. Not a lot to add about the arrangement. It is what it is—a good solid country ballad and we did it well.

Of course, this was a hit for Bobby Bare. Nobody sold a song like Bare did. I could listen to him sing "Mary Had a Little Lamb" and never tire of it. He was another one who rode our bus with us when we worked the road together. He chewed all the time and carried a Styrofoam spit cup with him everywhere. I told him one day when we were sitting on the sofa on our bus riding down the highway, "If that thing spills, we're going to have a mess." He said, "That's okay. Harold will clean it up."

"Margie's at the Lincoln Park Inn"

Tom T. Hall wrote it and Bobby Bare sang it. That is a surefire hit. Both of these guys were label mates of ours at Mercury. Our arrangement was so different from Bobby's. The tempo is the first thing you notice. Ours is up and his is down, and there is no real comparison at all to the two over-all performances. For my personal taste, and I think for the other Statlers, also, this is the best of all the great things Tom ever wrote. What a story. What a punch.

Next Sunday it's my turn to speak to the young people's class
And they expect answers to all of the questions they ask
What would they say if I spoke on a modern-day sin?
And all of the Margies at all of the Lincoln Park Inns?

The Statlers and Tom went into the Hall of Fame the same night, June 29, 2008, during the same ceremony.

"The Boy Inside of Me"

This was Lew's "coming of age" song. He wrote from his heart on this one, and it shows in every line. I'm going out on a limb here, but I think men are more likely to retain and cherish the boy inside of them than women are to recognize and allow the girl inside of them to offer any influence on who they are. Maybe that's why they say girls mature faster than boys. They're smarter and more willing to grow up than we are. Whatever the answer, there isn't a male out there anywhere who can't relate to something in these lines. I leave you with these words:

Things slowly fell together, I grew into a man
I learned to live with politics and tie a four-in-hand
I've taken on a family and paying for a home
And live life so my son can have a hero of his own

11

Sons of the Motherland

1974

For years on our office stationery we had simulated Mount Rushmore with the likeness of our four heads. We decided to use that replication as a cover for this aptly named album. We wrote our own liner notes on the back, and, ironically, we did in short-form with each song what I am doing with this very writing. We penned a little summation of the song under each title, and I think it only appropriate that I include them here. I will do that under each song title in bold before I add my "today" memories.

"All American Girl"

She's sugar and spice and everything nice. She's yours, she's mine, she's one-of-a-kind. And you're in love with her.

We have told this story a number of times because it is so very unusual. Any songwriter will tell you it may take fifteen minutes to write a song or it may take months. This one took five years. Once upon a time, Harold and I were strolling down a beach in Hawaii and wandered into a little tourist-trap gift shop. There was, of course, a ukulele hanging on the wall, and I took it down, pulled it in tune, and played it. (I learned to play the uke as a kid before I ever even owned a guitar.) Standing there, we got to writing a song. He went over to the clerk and got paper and pencil, and, on the spot, we wrote a pretty cute little first verse:

She's got a Texas smile you can see for a mile and a Georgia tan
A dimple in her chin and soft brown skin like Florida sand
She's got an L.A. walk, a Mississippi talk, and a Boston grace
An Indiana, apple pie, hope I die, mother-lovin' face

It lay in our file of scribblings for something like five years before we rediscovered that forgotten piece of paper and finished the song.

She watches her stories on TV everyday
And eats at McDonald's once a week to get away

At the time, there was a McDonald's jingle that said, *You deserve a break today, so get up and get away at McDonald's.*

And that is where that line came from. This is a fun song that did its job for us on the charts as the second single from this album. And it was a nice, sweet salute to the mid-1970s All-American Girl. Today, most of the young ladies wouldn't find it complimentary, but trust me, it was meant to be.

She likes changin' her hair, something new to wear and playin' coy
But she likes it most lying close to her All American Boy

"A Letter from Shirley Miller"

No matter who you are, where you are, or what you're doing, everybody has a memory that won't go away. If you knew Shirley, you'd think she had it all together. And then again, you just might know Shirley, so listen to her story and you decide.

When Harold and I wrote together, I can honestly tell you it is impossible for me to go back through the song and pick out which lines he wrote and which lines I came up with. Once it was committed to paper, we just didn't choose to remember that sort of petty picking. We both saw it as a "we" project and never cared who contributed what. The same can be said for this little story song that Phil was a part of. What I do remember and have files for is that we were sitting on our tour bus in Portland, Maine, on January 27, 1974, and bro Harold and I were attempting to write this piece about the fictional Shirley Miller. (I stress fictional because it's a common name and someone is always claiming we wrote something about them when, in fact, we certainly didn't.) Phil was sitting nearby in the bus lounge drinking coffee and reading the paper, *The Press Herald*, I'm sure. Getting stuck somewhere in the process, one of us said, "Hey, Phil give us a line." At which point he did, and wide-eyed and grateful, we wrote it down. Note, I never said Phil *couldn't* write, only that he *didn't* write. And you'd have to know Philip Elwood Balsley to understand that. And right here, that "we" project kicks in, and I, for the life of me, cannot remember which line it was that Phil contributed. But Harold and I cut him in on the song and his name is on it right along with ours because when it mattered, he saved our bacon.

> *I got a letter today from Shirley Miller*
> *She's living in Ohio in a Presbyterian home*
> *She's married a preacher and raisin' a family*
> *She said she wrote the letter 'cause she was scared to phone*

Here is one of those little things you have to tinker with and tweak in writing a verse. Originally the next two lines were:

> *She says she still remembers things she said she wouldn't*
> *She asked about my travels and if Akron's on my route*

Before we recorded it, we scratched Akron and used Cleveland. Cleveland is just a little more musical and rolls off the tongue a little clearer than does Akron.

"A Few Old Memories"

If you've ever dug around in the closets of your house or your mind, you've probably found a few old memories. An old song you used to dance to, an old movie you didn't see the end of or that special thing you just thought of while reading this.

The near-perfect memory song that we were always striving for. Burning old memories is the common and accepted way of ridding oneself of past loves and past lives, both in song and in life. Not meaning to crow or boast, but looking back and reviewing these entries, I think Harold and I wrote seamless songs together. And by that, I mean they flow as if one writer had written them, and there is no evidence that two men discussed and decided what the next word or phrase was going to be. That's because we thought alike and knew one another so very well that we could anticipate what was coming from the other one before it was ever spoken. (We used to do this on stage practically every night when we would ad-lib comedy and lead one another in unforeseen directions right in front of thousands of spectators with no fear whatsoever. That's called brotherly love.)

> *I burned all those pictures at least ten years ago*
> *That one of you beside the car was hardest to let go*
> *That shoebox full of memories, promises, and lies*
> *The smoke from those old letters still gets in my eyes*

Usually the more personal and intimate a song is, the harder it is for multiple people to write it together. One person can let their thoughts flow more easily from heart to paper without having to explain why or express how they think this way is better than another and etc. With us, we could let it flow without any explanation at all. Such as this second verse:

> *There's still a silver bracelet around the house somewhere*
> *It's probably in that old trunk we keep beneath the stairs*

The words you had put on it have tarnished and turned
It and a few old memories were all that wouldn't burn

"You Can't Judge a Book by Its Cover"

If you don't like our cover, don't judge it till you've listened to our book.

We were writing like crazy. To date, this album had more original Statler-written songs than any yet. Out of eleven, Harold and I had written eight between us and one of our band members had contributed one. Only two covers on the whole collection, and this was one of them. Looking back and trying to determine why it is one of them presents somewhat of a quandary to me today. Not sure why we threw in a bluegrass song right here, but with that decision made I'm sure we chose this one because we remembered it as an old Mac Wiseman song. We had great love and respect for Mac. Bobby Thompson (banjo) and Buddy Spicher (fiddle) give us the proper bluegrass credentials, so we were off and runnin'.

"Together"

Together is the way we've seen America. *We've traveled every road I know, from Canada to Mexico.* **And enjoyed every mile, every mountain, and every minute.**

Carroll "Bull" Durham joined us in 1974 as a bass player. A year later, when we enlarged our band and got them a bus of their own to travel in, Bull switched to piano. He was very good at both. Then he showed us another side of himself when he came to us one day and sang this biographical story song to us that was about us. We sat up and took notice and liked it very much. The song was so well done and beautifully put together we anticipated a new writer in our midst who would keep us steeped in new material. But even though he was with us for many years thereafter, this was the only song he ever wrote for us. I'm really sorry because the finesse of this one tells me there were more songs inside him that should have come out.

"Susan When She Tried"

Everybody's got a memory, whether her name is Susan, Charlotte, Goldie, or Peggy. The little darling you thought in your heart was the best but in your mind you knew was only a fling. She were some little lady, yes, she were.

Oh, boy! I could write half a book on this one. There is so much to tell and it rings up so many memories. We'll start before it was even written. Our attorney at the time was a gentleman named Cal Thomas. He said to me one evening, "Sometime when you're writing a song and need a name, would you use my wife's? That would really mean a lot." I said that I'd be glad to. Now if her name had been Esmeralda or Helga, I wouldn't have been so quick to comply, but she was a very sweet woman with an equally sweet name. Cut to an entirely different world. I was reading a favorite novelist of mine at the time, Ed McBain (aka Evan Hunter), and he had written a book with a fantastic title: *Sadie When She Died*. Well, I don't have to tell you any more for you to know where this goes. I got a song title, Cal's wife, Susan, got her name in a song, and we had a hit that we owed a lot a people for.

I wrote it in a state of relaxation over the Christmas holidays in 1972. Our next recording date was on May 23 of '73, and I remember so well the evening we cut it. As was our usual pattern, we listened to the playbacks in the studio and then headed to one of our two favorite restaurants in Nashville for dinner and to discuss the day's work. That night we all agreed we were so taken with this song that we would put it in the can and hold it until a time when we were up the creek for a single. We felt so strongly about it that we just knew it would be good for us whenever we decided to release it down the road. We held it for two albums, nearly a year and a half, before we finally, out of being antsy and anxious and wanting it out there, decided to lead this album with it. It was a hit, served us well, and proved to be a great concert song also. I never got tired of singing this one as it kept its spark all through the years.

It also attracted some attention we weren't expecting. Elvis heard it and put it on his *Today* album. I was invited to his session the night he recorded it but wasn't able to go. His arrangement is very similar to ours, and I'm honored he liked it as much as he did.

115

I was asked a few years ago to write about "Susan When She Tried" for a book about Elvis. I did and even found the original scratch sheet of paper I wrote the words on that night in '72 that I sent along with the article.

One final note about how you can still be writing while the tape is rolling in the recording studio. My original opening line was:

I got over Shirley Thompson, Goldie Johnson, Lord, they done me wrong

On my paper, I scratched through *Shirley* and wrote in *Charlotte*. The reason for that last-minute change is lost on me today and forever. Also, I call your attention to the line:

And it's bad in December when they play those Christmas songs

Knowing now when it was written may explain how Christmas popped into the lyrics.

And then, lastly, Harold's bass line on the chorus, I think, had as much to do with selling this song as anything else. And that's about all I have to say about Susan except she sure was good to us in so many, many ways.

"You've Been Like a Mother to Me"

Each year in our hometown we sponsor an annual Fourth of July celebration called "Happy Birthday USA" to raise money for charities. Last year we introduced this song on stage, and 40,000 people stood up because they were proud of America. 40,000 people can't be wrong.

It opens with something you have never heard before—Harold and I singing a duet in unison. The assumption is we're singing a mother song. Then Phil and Lew singing a duet in unison. Still a mother song. Now it's all four of us but just the melody and one harmony part. Still mother. Full, strong four-part harmony and the reveal that it's not mother we're singing about but America. It keeps building with violins and changing keys until it explodes into a powerful marching song with a tuba accenting every beat. It's a true flag-waving John Philip Sousa-meets-the-Statler Brothers experience. We sang it at many of our Fourth of July celebrations in our hometown and it was always chilling. We did a video on it years later but nothing as effective as one memorable night when we sang it for the president.

I've told this story before, but I'm going to tell it again because it might mean more to me than anything I've ever written. Certainly, the reception it got, and from whom it came, meant more than I can properly express.

We have been invited to sing at the White House for Presidents Nixon, Carter, Reagan, and Bush 41. Multiple times for Carter and Reagan. The occasion pertinent to this song was September 23, 1981. There was a "casual" barbeque on the lawn of the White House, and everybody who was anybody in Washington was there. We were the sole entertainment and we did our full concert closing with this patriotic song. There is a line near the end of the song that says:

America, stand up and show it, that you're proud of the red, white and blue
You love her and you know it 'cause she's been like a mother to you

The first person to hit his feet with his hand over his heart was President Ronald Reagan. We finished the song with tears in our eyes, chills down our backs, and our hearts pumping like a new backyard cistern. After three encores, he came to the stage, shook our hands, and said these words verbatim: "We have not only been extremely entertained here tonight, but we have been inspired. The lady they sang about is very important to us all. Sometimes we cross state lines and party lines, but we all must try to talk to each other and not about each other."

He then turned just to us and said, "Any time you're in the area, I'll be at the show." And true to his word, we were with him a number of times thereafter. I miss that kind of unbridled patriotism, dignity, and heart in the seat of power.

"Eight More Miles to Louisville"

We've been hearing Grandpa Jones singing this song most of our lives. When we decided to record it, we asked him to play the banjo as only he can. He graciously consented, and that is him you hear on the song. "Thank you, Grand-Father Jones."

You might call this "old country" or maybe bluegrass. If you go with the latter, that makes two for this album, and I'm not sure why. Just don't remember the discussion or thought process, but I really like the arrangement. The contrast of Harold and Lew soloing and then Phil on the last verse and those rousing choruses. We did the dynamics again with the musicians getting soft and then loud with us on the next line for the ultimate effect.

And that is Grandpa Jones on the banjo. Old-time country-strumming banjo that was his trademark. He would throw his foot in the air and strike a chord so loud it would make your ears ring. We toured together often in the sixties and got to know him and Ramona. What a beautiful and sweet woman she was. By the time we knew G-pa (Harold first called him that and then we all started), he had grown into his character. He was in his sixties and didn't use makeup anymore to draw the lines on his face to make him look like an old man. But as he told us, he created the character in 1935 when he was about twenty-five years old, so to the public, he had been an old man all his life. He wrote this song, Louis Marshall Jones, and when we called and asked him to come play the banjo, he was there in a Nashville minute. Later, his son Mark worked on the road with us as a lighting technician.

"One More Summer in Virginia"

After all is said and all is done, wouldn't you like to spend one more summer at home? Virginia is our home, but all you have to do is put the name of yours in the song. (Even New Jersey will work here.)

Well, if I'm here to be honest, and I guess I am or I would have no other reason for doing this, then I have to make a candid and true confession. This one leaves me kind of weak in the stomach. Even after all these years, no, *especially* after all these years, it comes home to me from the first line to the last. I wrote it in a sentimental state of mind and it has its effects on me to this day. We sang our hearts out on this one and put everything I heard as a writer on the record for all to hear. We didn't wait for Cam Mullins to bring the strings in half way through; we let him kick it off with them, and he got right to the heart of the matter immediately. This one is truly a love affair with the state of Virginia. The Old Dominion. And I said everything I wanted to say and exactly like I wanted to say it. We started in Virginia, have always lived in Virginia, and retired to Virginia. Thank you, Lord.

One more summer in Virginia
One more August in her arms
Let me sit and rock on her front porch and watch the nights go by
Let me spend just one more summer in Virginia before I die

Virginia has been looking for a new state song for years. Some feel the one we have is outdated and not suitable for all our citizens. When Chuck Robb was governor from '82 to '86 and our US senator from '89 to '01, he had us to Richmond during his term for different occasions, and he and Lynda Bird have been guests of Debbie's and mine in our home in Staunton. He told us even back then to give him a song and he'd see that it got all the attention it could get to be the next Virginia state song. People encouraged me to submit this one as a front-runner, but as time went on, we had friends that got in that contest of submitting their songs for that honor, and I decided I didn't want to get in that horse race and turn friendships into competition.

I've got friends to thank, a wife to hold, and kids to kiss goodbye.
Let me spend just one more summer in Virginia before I die.

"I'll Be Here"

This is a testimonial song for all of us who have found the right one and know that we are going to grow old together. You'll be here and so will she.

May 9, 1974, I wrote this very positive yet melancholy look back at a lifelong love affair. A promise to be there no matter how many years pass. That is what I loved about writing for The Statler Brothers. We wrung every emotion out of each word that I felt while I was writing it. I never worried if it was going to be interpreted correctly or deeply enough. I knew it would be. From Jerry Kennedy to the Nashville pickers to my Brothers standing on each side of me, they always had my musical back. I put a lot into the writing of this song and they got every drop out of it that was ever meant to be.

I'll be here when things don't seem to fall in place
I'll be here when they have drained the roses from your face
And when time has left you nothing but memories and tears
Don't you worry, honey, I'll be here

"So Mary Could Make It Home"

This is the story about a childhood sweetheart you grew up with, went through school with, and then lost track of for a few years.

Until one day...but, then, you listen to the song.

A song idea is a lot like the flu. It hits you with no warning and you cannot ignore its impact. You have to give into it or suffer great consequences. The consequences of not paying attention to a song idea is the threat of it leaving you and you'll never remember it with the fervor it once had. I have done this and I've fretted over every lost inspiration. And a good idea will hit you anywhere and at the most inconvenient time.

I spent a lot of time in the backyard playing ball with my sons, Debo and Langdon, as they were growing up. This was the summer of '74, and Debo was six years old. The yard was full of neighborhood kids. Mary from across the street had just hit and was on third. It was Debo's bat, and as I was about to pitch him the ball, he yelled out to me, "I'm gonna knock this way out in right field so Mary can make it home!" My arm was in mid-flight so I finished the pitch but my heart froze and didn't beat for what felt like a full minute. You know when you hear a good line and this was a beautiful one delivered in all innocence and good nature. I got to the end of the inning and told all the kids to take a rest and get a drink, and I ran for the piano in my home office. In minutes, this song was finished and I was back out on the mound, pitching my heart out. Some of the lines still bring a smile to my face after all these many years and innings later:

From the first day school let out each summer, all the kids would come
To our backyard and we'd play ball and keep count of our homeruns
All the boys would do just fine but one thing was never known
I sacrificed my backlot average so Mary could make it home
I always hit to the right fielder's mitt so Mary could make it home

Debo is married and has two kids. Mary is married and has two, also. We still see her around town, and she knows the story behind this song. We all hug and laugh about it and remember that day so vividly. One of the many charms of life in a small Virginia town. You never lose touch with the things that matter. And you never lose all of yesterday because you still see evidence of it every time you walk out the door and open your heart.

12

Alive at the Johnny Mack Brown High School

1974

From that nine-minute comedy sketch on *Country Music Then And Now*, this full-fledged comedy album of Lester "Roadhog" Moran and His Cadillac Cowboys was born. The sketch was so popular and successful on that album from two years before that Mercury flew a VP in from Chicago to take us out to dinner one night in Nashville. The whole purpose of his trip was to talk us into doing this comedy album. We had never considered such a thing, but we were very aware of how the popularity of these characters we had invented was growing. On college campuses all over the country, Roadhog clubs were being formed, and when they saw one another, they had to speak in their Roadhog voice. Our fans were hollering for the characters during our concerts. Television shows were wanting the Hog and the

Boys to come on as guests in full costume. And now our record label was wanting to promote these country oddballs by giving them their very own album.

We thought about it. The workload was on us. We first had to write the comedy, probably expand and create some new characters, then perform it. One of the problems we had already run into was that growling Roadhog voice. It tore up Harold's throat so badly doing it that he was unable to sing properly if he did it for too long at a time. So, we ate their steak, scratched our heads, discussed the ups and downs, and decided there weren't enough downs for us to say no. The Hog and the Boys were off and running.

Comedy is best heard and experienced and not explained, so I won't spend a lot of time telling you too much about it. I'll just tell you to listen to it, but when you do, here are a few things to listen a little closer for.

"Saturday Morning Radio Show #1"

Radio announcer David Deepvoice is Harold. Having not heard this album in decades, I just now listened to it again and laughed out loud at his weather report of a low of 4 degrees and a high of 95, at the time being "9:35 A.M. and FM," and at his pronunciation of Lester Moran as Lester *Moron*.

On this cut, Phil and I, as Red and Wesley, sing "Why, Baby, Why." To appreciate this story, you have to know that George Jones wrote and sang this song, and it was his very first hit record twenty years previous. George and Tammy were riding in their car one day and this came on the radio. George angrily reached over and turned it off and said, "They shouldn't let people that bad even sing on the radio." Tammy turned it back on and said, "Wait a minute, I think there might be something more to it than we first thought." At that point they discovered it was the Statlers and a comedy album and all was forgiven. They both told us this story, and they were two of the biggest Roadhog fans ever from that day forward.

If you have access to the album and to the pictures, Burford was played by our bus driver, Dale Harman, and Ruby Lee, the Roadhog's wife, was Harold's wife, Brenda. The little saws and sayings that the Hog quoted as the music played at the end were so much fun to gather. The one original adage was my favorite. We were quoting an old friend of ours from the

Shenandoah Valley who once said, "A man that don't lie ain't got nothing to say." It still brings a smile to my face.

"Johnny Mack Brown High School Dance"

In the middle of this mess, a fight breaks out at the dance. In order to simulate the noise, we had all the ladies from the Mercury office upstairs to come down and be a part of the session. We also had asked them to save all the glass soft drink bottles for a week, and we literally threw them against the wall for the authentic glass-breaking sounds you hear. (When the janitorial staff came in that evening for the daily cleaning, they just stood and stared at the chaos we had created. We paid them handsomely for the extra work that was required to get things back in shape.)

There is another hidden personal reference during the Hog's reading of all the stars that will appear in an upcoming show. Note when he says, "You can also get your tickets at Duffy's Drug and Hardware Store." I'll tell you about Duffy and how that name got into the script about five albums from now. I don't want to get ahead of myself, but, trust me, it will all make sense as to why I'm waiting to share that with you.

A musical highlight here is Harold's version of the Hog singing "Sixteen Tons." This was a gigantic hit by Tennessee Ernie Ford twenty years before and was written by the fabulous guitarist Merle Travis. (I told you how we had met him in Johnny Cash's kitchen years before.) Instead of singing it in the minor key in which it was written, we countrified it in a major key and Harold botched the melody in his Roadhog voice that still just slays everyone even today. Jerry Kennedy, our producer, made the call directly to Merle himself and told him he was calling for the Statlers and explained what this album was all about and then turned the tape machine on and played "Sixteen Tons" for him over the phone. Jerry said when he put the phone back to his ear to ask Merle if he could hear it clearly enough, Merle was belly-laughing so hard he could barely get his breath. Jerry said, "Could you hear it alright?" and Merle said, "Oh hell, yes! Play it again!" Jerry played it for him three more times and he was still laughing when they hung up.

"Saturday Morning Radio Show #2"

My favorite and the most memorable part of this one is the song the Hog sings. It is a firm mixture of "Hello Darlin'," "Hello Walls," and "Funny How Time Slips Away." Even after all these years, I just had to pause the CD and laugh here in my office all by myself. (Ever notice how silly you feel when you laugh in a room all by yourself? I feel like men in white suits may be coming through the door for me any minute now.)

An interesting story on this portion of the album is about a song that didn't get included. Note that Wichita does not sing a song here but instead plays an instrumental on the guitar. Originally, we had written a parody of the Don Gibson hit "Woman, Sensuous Woman" and called it "Woman, Sensitive Woman." Anyone can record anyone's song anytime they want to unless you jiggle too much with the music or the lyrics. Then you have to have the permission of either the publisher or writer of that song in order to release it. When the publisher was called, they refused to give their legal permission because they didn't want their song butchered and quartered for the sake of comedy. At the last minute we inserted the guitar version of "Freight Train" for Wichita's feature number. Of all the songs the Roadhog gang mangled in the name of humor on this album, this is the only turndown we got. Bill Hall, our publisher, said at the time, "Don't worry about it. When this thing hits, they're going to be sorry."

"Rainbow Valley Confidential Audition Tape"

This was to be a tape that the Hog and the Boys put together of what they thought was exceptional local talent in their hometown. They wanted to send this tape to Nashville to Mercury Records in hopes of playing star makers to these fellow Rainbow Vallians. (Not a word.) We discussed the homemade sound we wanted it to have with Jerry, and he suggested instead of trying to come up with that empty, hollow sound in the studio, why not actually do it on a cheap recorder in one of our houses and we'd have the sound with no effort. Done! We all gathered at my house and we used a small Wollensak reel-to-reel tape recorder. We recorded ourselves and the new characters we created for this particular bit in my home office in Staunton. The last character was Cletus Duncan, tap dancer. This was funny to us to think they were trying to get a tap dancer a recording contract. I remember so well holding the microphone down to floor level while Harold tapped on and on and on atop our beautiful hardwood floor. When he finished, there was a four-foot square of scarred, unvarnished, raw wood by my desk. He had dug into the flooring so deeply it could never be fixed. Within months, we had the whole office carpeted wall-to-wall and the hardwood finish was nothing but a memory. Just goes to show you the lengths we would go to for a good laugh.

Lester and the Boys live on today. There have been rereleases of this album from Mercury through the years, and it has been a best seller every time. We never thought we were creating a living legend when we came up with these four oddities on that flight to Amsterdam so many, many years ago. There are YouTubes of the gang from TV shows. Tune in and catch them. Sometimes I still get to thinking they were real.

13

The Best of The Statler Brothers

1975

This was our tenth Mercury album and it was special in a number of different ways. It was the first of our albums without our images on the front cover. Instead, we put a picture of our wives as they best befitted the title. They dressed in classic early American dresses, emulating the solemn look of those old sepia-toned pictures you see in history books. I was really surprised that the label didn't raise an eyebrow at the omission of a Statler picture, but that is just more evidence of how much artistic freedom we were granted and trusted with. This was an album we had been waiting on for years. Any artist who does a "best of" collection is guaranteed monster sales because it includes past single hits. We had eleven songs on here, and only one of them was new. That would be "I'll Go to My Grave Loving You." All the rest were hits from the past five years, such as "Bed of Rose's," "The Class of '57," "Susan When She Tried," "Do You Remember These?" and more. The release timing was all based on a hit song that we didn't even have for the Mercury label, and that was "Flowers on the Wall."

There is a near-standard clause in all record contracts that states you cannot record a song on another label that you recorded on a previous label until five years after the first contract has expired. Our Columbia contract ended in mid-1970, so we had to wait for five full years to rerecord "Flowers." We did so on April 9, 1975, just three months before this album was released to the public. Everything else was ready and in place, we were just waiting for the legal timing to work out. As a matter of fact, the one new song, "Grave," had been recorded on May 15, 1974, and had just been sitting there in the can for nearly a year waiting for "Flowers" to come of age. We knew this was to be the single, and we had high anticipation that this was going to be a huge seller. It was. *The Best of The Statler Brothers* was our first gold album! It then became our first platinum album, our first double platinum, and our first triple platinum. It still sells today.

Ten of the eleven songs here were already recorded and I have already written about them, so I'll only list them for your information: "Bed of Rose's," "Whatever Happened to Randolph Scott?" "Do You Remember These?" "Carry Me Back," "Flowers on the Wall," "The Class of '57," "Pictures," "Thank You, World," "New York City," and "Susan When She Tried."

"I'll Go to My Grave Loving You"

I wrote this as a slow, heartfelt ballad. I realized the title sounded like it should be on a Hallmark Valentine card, but that was what I wanted. It captured the mood and the meaning of what I was feeling and wanted to convey. I sang it to my partners, as I did just about every song I wrote that I thought had any merit. (There were always those that wound up in the trash can and no one ever heard them.) They liked it enough that we talked about using it on a future album. But that pedestrian attitude changed in all of us quickly because of a chance happening on the bus one morning.

You may find it strange, but Harold would often go up front and relieve our driver, as he liked driving the bus from time to time. One early A.M. when I couldn't sleep, I took my guitar and went to sit in the buddy seat across the aisle from the driver's seat, and Harold and I talked while I picked around on my gut-string. He told me, at one point, to sing that new song. I did, and then he said, "Do it again and put a little tempo to it." I did a little three-finger roll with a bouncy rhythm, and as I sang it, he started singing an aftertime to it. It caught fire immediately, and in no time, with no change of lyric, we had a brand-new-sounding song. I firmly believe without his suggestion, it would have been a nice little tune buried in an album that no one would have ever heard.

Ralph Emery told us years later that of all the many years he had the late-night radio show on WSM, this song was probably the most requested he ever had.

The original way I wrote this song was recorded once as a demonstration tape for publishers. They're called "demos" in the music business, and publishing companies hire singers to sing unrecorded songs their writers have written in order to pitch them to record companies and recording artists. Robbie Harden, of the Harden Trio, sang "Grave" the way I first composed it, and it is beautiful. I get it out and listen to it sometimes just for my own enjoyment.

For years I kept a framed copy of the "Me And Bobby McGee" sheet music on my office wall to remind me daily of the perfect goal for a country song. I vowed not to take it down until I had something of my own I could be equally proud of as a songwriter. I took it down right after "I'll Go to My Grave Loving You."

Don't get to feeling sorry for Harold and his contribution with no remuneration; in the end, he got his off of this song, but I'll tell you that story about five albums down the list. Stay tuned.

14

Holy Bible

1975

The Old and New Testament

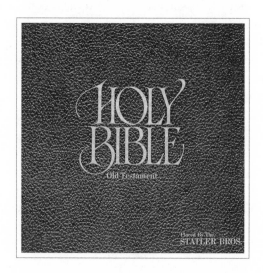

This was a double album and a body of work and love that took us nearly a decade to produce. I will write about it as I have all the others, but I think to reprint the inside liner notes from the four of us in 1975 explains it as good as it could ever be stated.

"Once upon a time we had an idea for a gospel album. That was eight years ago. Eight years ago, the first song was written for it and we thought the wheels

were in motion. But evidently the time wasn't right because circumstances didn't allow us to finish it until now. Looking back, we wonder how we ever could have thought we could put this album together in the time we had originally allowed ourselves.

"While working on other projects, albums, stage shows and recording sessions, we spent our spare time over the last eight years reading, studying, talking about and learning the Bible. We asked questions, to other people and ourselves. We listened to other people and each other. We all grew up in Christian homes thinking we knew the Bible, but as we began getting into it a little deeper, we found out there was more to the Book than we had learned in Sunday school.

"We began to see the characters in the stories as human beings. We began to realize they had the same problems, temptations, fears and doubts that you and I have. They were concerned with taxes, diseases, politics, wars, slavery, finances, family problems, social problems, crime...the same things that concern you and me today.

"We're asking you to join in meeting theses people. Make friends with them and get to know them. Look at them with a little less awe and a little more human understanding. Take them off the pedestal and put them on the street. Regard them with less adulation and more appreciation. Don't look at them with your mouth open but with your mind open.

"The one point we want to make with this album is that these people were human. What they did, you can do. God used them as He saw fit, as He may very well be using you if you let Him.

"Now Jesus is a different story. He was man and He is God so He knows the worst of this world and the best of the other. Our whole way of life is to work for something we want. To save our money and then buy it. To do something for someone so they'll do something for us. And anytime someone gives us something we have to wonder if they want something in return. But God gave us something we can't work for and earn, we can't save for and buy and we don't have to worry about returning the favor. Jesus was a gift. The greatest Christmas gift of all time. One you can't buy or earn. Just accept it and you're home free.

"This project has taken more time and been closer to our hearts than any we have ever undertaken. And there are a lot of people who have been a great help. We'd like to thank our moms and dads who instilled in us a need to believe; all our Sunday school teachers from the Toddlers' class on up who told us the Bible stories; our ministers who gave those stories more meaning; and a very special friend, Jack

Young, whose wisdom, knowledge, and interest in what we were trying to do made this album a reality for us.

"And while we're at it, we'd like to thank each other for the patience, criticism, tolerance, understanding and help that was expressed through the long and enjoyable period of putting this work together."

—THE STATLER BROTHERS

Whenever there were forty-five minutes left over on a session, we would pull out one of the gospel songs, record it, and put it in the can for later. If we had an extra day in Nashville for some reason, we'd book a session and get a few more gospel songs in the can. And in between time, on the road and at home, we would write. We began by deciding what old songs we wanted to include that would lend themselves to telling the story chronologically throughout the Bible. Then we outlined what was left and we assigned one another those songs. Lew, you write about Samson. Don, you write about the disciples. Harold, you write about the miracles. And on and on, and in time we had some of the most original gospel songs ever gathered for such an epic endeavor. With those finished, we wrote dialogue that weaved the songs together, and we each took turns narrating between the tracks. I can't wait to relisten and relive each song from each of these musical Testaments.

THE OLD TESTAMENT

"In the Beginning"

Frankie Laine was a big pop singer in the 1950s. He had an interesting habit of sprinkling in modern-day gospel songs among his major hit releases. He had "I Believe" and "Rain, Rain, Rain." And he had this beautiful piece that we all remembered as kids that we jumped on as the opening song for our adventure. We agreed we wouldn't even try to write anything to compete with it. It was a stunning description of the creation.

In the beginning the Lord made the earth
The heavens, the hills and the seas
Then he created the sun and the stars
The land, the fruit, the trees

132

The poetry and imagery here set the mood of what we hoped to capture. The chorus was powerfully sung, and it, like so many on this collection, was never again performed by us. Listening to it all today, I'm very sad for that. We should have done a gospel music tour when this double album came out. It would have been fun and, I think, an inspiration.

He made all creatures that live in the earth
And taught them to live by his plan
Then as he rested, the Lord sanctified
The seventh day for man

I understand our version of this song is also on the soundtrack of a 1994 Brad Pitt movie, *Seven*.

"Eve"

I guess the chorus contains the essence of Eve's story and the third line says it all. Debbie and I have two great friends in Bill and Judy Smith. Bill's a pastor and Judy is the perfect minister's wife and after hearing this song she walked up to me one day and quoted this third line in mock disgust:

Don't eat the fruit in the garden, Eve
It wasn't in God's natural plan
You were only a rib but look at what you did
To Adam the father of man

Musically we went from the classical melody of "In the Beginning" to our own comfortable country sound with "Eve," and we kept that pattern throughout intentionally so as not to fall into a sanctimonious presentation.

"Noah Found Grace in the Eyes of the Lord"

I was a preteen growing up in Virginia, and come Thursday nights on NBC at 9:30 Eastern, I never missed *The Tennessee Ernie Ford Show*. Only a half hour, but it was chock-full of comedy, with one guest and a closing gospel song every week.

It's funny looking back on it, because in about twelve years from me stretched out on the floor watching him on a black-and-white Motorola TV with the family, we were working concert dates with him.

Ernie had a group of twenty singers, men and women, who backed him every week called the Top Twenty. They always did his closing spiritual with him, and one of my favorites was this song. When we were looking for songs that told a Bible story, this one about Noah popped up in an instant. Although loving Ernie's version, we decided to rewrite the arrangement in a play form. I was the narrator, Lew was Noah, and Harold was God. This we *did* take to the stage, and it was a showstopper each night for the next twenty-seven years. We were still singing it when we retired in 2002. It was fast and fun, it had humor, it told a wonderful story, and we made it our own.

"Have a Little Faith"

It was so much fun and so enlightening to do the research on these songs. Yes, I knew all about Abraham, as I was born into and raised in the church, but to dig in and really study his life and all the things he did gave me a new insight into the man. Then, of course, you had to reduce all you read down to a three-minute story and make it rhyme. It was a challenge I loved, as we all did on this project.

We had a minister at our Presbyterian church at the time, Rev. Eugene Jordan. He was a brilliant scholar of the Bible and we used him sometimes as a sounding board for questions that came up. I remember, the night I wrote this song, calling him and asking his advice on the structure of a line. I had written in the fourth verse, "Abraham loved God and God loved Abraham."

There was something about the line that bothered me and I wasn't sure what. It seemed maybe I should turn it around and mention God before Abraham, but I didn't really want to because I had a good rhyme for Abraham I was going for in the next line. But Mr. Jordan said without reservation, "That's no good. You must mention God first because of 1 John 4:19. *We love because he first loved us.* Knowing he was right, I changed the line to:

God loved Abraham and Abraham loved him
It's a story to remember when your faith is growing dim
And you get tired and say, "Aw, it was different back then"

But remember that they were only just men
It's a lesson for the learning for the likes of you and me
Just have a little faith and you'll see

"The Dreamer"

This one was an assignment Lew took on. Like me, he loved writing story songs, and Joseph caught his ear. Lew always said he liked writing on assignment. Most writers like the freedom of writing what hits them or inspires them at the moment, but he liked knowing where he was going before he started. The musicians set the tone and the energy for this one before we even began singing. Good song.

"Led Out of Bondage"

See the *Oh Happy Day* album in the chapter by the same name.

"The Ten Commandments"

I will speak for Lew here in his absence. I think he would point to this song as his proudest writing moment. And I think we all would agree. It is one of the most important stories from the Old Testament, and we told it well.

Thou shall have no Gods before me is my first command
And thou shall not make any graven image by thy hand
Thou shall not take my name in vain if thou would guiltless be
Remember thou to keep the Sabbath day alone for me
Honor they father and thy mother and thou shall not kill
Thou shall not commit adultery and thou shall not steal
Love thy neighbor as thyself and show thy neighbor peace
Covet not thy neighbor's house nor anything of his

"Samson"

Is there a figure more superhero-like in the OT than ole Samson? Lew provided a good story faithful to the Scriptures, and we all four came through with a strong Statler performance.

Oh Samson, it's been said you were a mighty man
And women were your weakness, this I understand
But after all the mighty armies you went through
How could you let a woman get the best of you?

"Song of David"

Harold and I wanted desperately to write about David. Keeping his epic to a handful of verses and a chorus was the hardest part. The lyric tells more than I could ever tell in a commentary, so I'll just trust you'll listen to the song or read the Scripture. I think we hit just the right mood with King David. And I still get chills when the aftertime kicks in on verses two and four.

He was weak like you and I are
And as a sinner he certainly did his part
But God said, "This man David
Is a man after my own heart"

David was a man down in Israel
Fighter, lover, shepherd, king, outlaw
But through it all God loved him and forgave him
David, the man who done it all

"Song of Solomon"

Two of the best-known stories from the OT are Solomon asking for wisdom and then his using that wisdom to decide a conflict between two alleged mothers. Lew included them both here, and the contrast between his and Harold's voices on the solos make the stories sparkle musically.

"The Fourth Man"

See the *Oh Happy Day* album in the chapter by the same name.

"The King Is Coming"

Bill and Gloria Gaither and Charles Millhuff wrote this little master-piece. It fit so well with how we wanted to end the OT that we looked no further for any other piece of music. That was the message we wanted ringing in the air as we segued from the Old to the New. He's coming. He's coming!

The King is coming
The King is coming
Praise God,
He's coming for me

To this day, *Holy Bible* is our biggest selling album as it is still in print and still selling this very moment. It has been reissued through the years in different forms. It came out first in 1975 as a double album. A few years later it was released as two separate albums. An odd discovery came with the first sales reports from that issue. It seems the Old Testament was outselling the New Testament. Our question of curiosity was why, and after the sales department did a little research, they came back with a practical answer. It seems in the metropolitan areas, people of the Jewish faith were buying just the Old.

THE NEW TESTAMENT

"Who Do You Think?"

Harold and I set out to write a song about the first Christmas but not a song to sound like Christmas. No sleigh bells or bouncy tempo. Just straight-forward facts with some crafty turns of phrase. I think it is probably the cleverest song we ever wrote together. It follows the Scripture true to its word, all the time looking askew at the entire unusual story from a near-skeptic's viewpoint.

Who do you think could believe such a thing?
Could believe that this story is true?
Who do you think could believe such a thing?
Well, here's hopin' to heaven you do

A number of gospel groups have recorded this song, and they all did magnificent jobs. It's always fulfilling to hear how others interpret our words and music.

I have so many different files of references from all the notes and diaries I kept over the years. I thought you might enjoy a summary of the ones I found concerning the day this song was created. We were in the middle of a ten-day Texas tour. On March 16, 1975, we played two shows in Wichita Falls. We introduced "Susan When She Tried" for the first time ever on stage. During the second show, the crowd was a little quiet, so Harold, to pump things up for us and keep our spirits high, took his microphone in hand and sang both solo verses of "Whatever Happened to Randolph Scott" in the voice of Hank Snow. He knew it would bring us to our knees and it did. This was just his voice of choice that night. Other times it may be Tex Ritter or Dean Martin or whoever crossed his mind. Then with this image still in our heads, we went back to our hotel rooms and wrote this very inspired Christmas song. Such is the life on the road!

"The Kingdom of Heaven Is at Hand"

Lew took to his pen with the story of John the Baptist. Simple and to the point and just the way we liked them. There's a nice key change going into each chorus that then comes back to the original key right in the middle of the chorus. It gives a really good effect. And I mentioned earlier in this chronicle how sometimes last-minute changes were made on simple words as we were recording. There's an interesting one in this song.

He must have made an awesome sight in clothes of camel's hair
Around his waist he wore a leather band
Preachin' and baptizin' as he wandered here and there
The kingdom of heaven is at hand

On the old lyric sheets that were used on the session, and that I still have, for some reason we marked out the fourth word in the first line of the chorus. We marked through "been" and wrote in "made." Not sure why, after all these years, but we must have felt it was a better fit. Looking at it today, it looks as if either would have worked.

"Beat the Devil"

I always loved this Bible story as a kid, and I jumped at the opportunity to put it in song form. I loved Harold's reading and the character he put into his Devil role. Odd, Harold was the voice of God on the Noah song; now he's gone to the other side. The Bobby Thompson banjo and the strong, solid track demands as much attention here as the voices.

The devil left and the angels came
He beat the devil at his own game

"The Brave Apostles Twelve"

Here is my major contribution to the Holy Bible project as a writer. It took long hours of research and discernment to make the roll call and name each disciple. Why? Aren't they just listed in the Scriptures? No, not that simple at all. Four books, Matthew, Mark, Luke, and Acts, list the twelve disciples, and none of them are perfect matches. Some, not even close. Some list second names that some were known as, and you have to line them up to make sense of which ones they are talking about. (Luke and Acts are pretty good because Luke wrote both books.) We did the roll call with each of us answering in different voices and attitudes. I won't brag on the song or the performance the way I'd like to, as I don't want to appear too proud. I'll just say I am thankful and feel blessed the way this one came off.

When my grandson Davis first heard this song at the age of three or four, he found something in the lyric that very much confused him. He pointed out these lines as the source of his confusion:

Traveling 'round from town to town preachin' gets expensive
So they took along some women who took along some wealth
And the twelfth one was chosen to be their trusted treasurer
Would you believe Judas Iscariot himself?

He thought that last line was:

Would you believe Judas is scared of himself?

Maybe that wouldn't have been a bad line after all. Judas had reason to be scared of himself. Simon Peter, Andrew, James, Philip, Thomas, Matthew, Bartholomew, Simon, Judas, Judas, James, and John.

"The Teacher"

Lew had so much fun with the Ten Commandments that he wanted to tackle the Beatitudes. This was his written version and our very unique singing arrangement. On the trio parts of the verses, Harold is singing lead, and Phil and I are harmonizing around him. It's almost an Ames Brothers sound if you are familiar with that particular pop group of old. This is for sure one of those songs that would have performed well on a gospel music stage.

"The Lord's Prayer"

This is a beautiful song and I think we did a powerful presentation of it. The solos were on the mark and the harmony it built to is some of our best. The finale segment is what is referred to as a stack. This means we recorded it twice. What you are hearing are eight Statler Brothers instead of four. We were singing with ourselves, giving us a glorious choir effect. The triple "Amen" leaves me smiling at the years gone by. Pardon my gushing, but I love this very much.

This wonderful old anthem is not the easiest to play for any musician, and especially by ear without any warning. So, when we announced to the pickers present that day that we were about to record "The Lord's Prayer" in the key of C#, it sent them scrabbling for pencil and paper and making notes while conferring with one another all over the room. Except for one exceptional virtuoso, Charlie McCoy, who could play any and all the instruments on the session. He personified what the word "versatile" means. Through all the turmoil and commotion, Charlie was lying in the middle of the floor with his hands behind his head, his eyes shut, relaxed and ready.

His only reaction was, "'The Lord's Prayer' is one of my favorite tunes." When the red light went on, he was on his feet, in place with no notes, and ready to go.

140

"There's a Man in Here"

I said earlier Harold took the miracles, and he did so with a flourish. In a short time, he covers so many of Jesus's famous wonders, and in such a perfect manner. The sheet music to this song is still to this day one of our most requested. It flows like a country song but has the significance of actual Scripture.

There's a man in here who makes demons flee
Who makes cripples walk and has chosen even me
For he lives in my heart and I have no fear
I'm a better man 'cause there's a man in here

"How Great Thou Art"

I have told you so very much about this song earlier. We first recorded it on our *Oh Happy Day* album. I've told you what an important and essential part of our concerts it was. And this is not the last time we would record it or sing it. We were still singing it that last night in October of 2002 on our final album.

The one thing I may not have told you about was the evening John and June called us to see their new home on Old Hickory Lake. There was not yet a stick of furniture in it, and the electricity had not even been turned on. But John asked us to christen their home with this song. He wanted "How Great Thou Art" by the Brothers to be the first song sung in what would be their final home on earth. The six of us stood in a circle in the twilight and we sang it like we've never sung it before or since. Tears and good memories. God bless them both.

"Lord, Is It I?"

Harold and I wrote this on April 4, 1972, in a Buffalo, New York, hotel room. We were still working for Johnny Cash, and he was heavily involved in the making of his *Gospel Road* movie about the life of Christ. He wanted song material and we provided him that. This song is on the movie soundtrack sung by the Statlers. When it came time for a Last Supper song for this album, we had it ready and waiting.

Lord, is it I, Lord, is it I?
Will one of us betray, kiss and run away?
Lord, is it I, is it I?

"The King of Love"

This was on the *Oh Happy Day* album and I have already written about it. But for the continuity and flow of this album, Harold wrote a new verse more fitting to where we were in the storyline of Christ's life.

Jesus said, it has to be
The Father planned my destiny
This is my blood which I must give
I will die so you may live

"The King Is Coming"

The prophesy of the Old Testament is the same as that of the New. The king is coming is the message of the gospels and is the message of this album. We leave you with these words ringing in your ears and your hearts. THE KING IS COMING!

15

Harold, Lew, Phil, and Don

1976

The four of us are on the cover, dressed in suits and ties, sitting in Harold's living room. It's a very good picture of who we were at the time, and the music inside is a good representation of *where* we were at the time. For the first time since joining the Mercury family, we didn't record this album at the home studio. I think they had started some major renovations that sent us and all their regular customers scattering. We went just around the corner to US Recording Studio. Roy Orbison originally owned it and then Ronnie Milsap bought it. I don't remember who was in control of it at this particular time, but it was a great facility and we did our next few projects from there.

"Your Picture in the Paper"

I wrote this song on December, Friday the 13th, 1974, less than two weeks before Christmas. As these facts will tell you that even though we were off and home for Christmas and in the thick of the holidays, I never stopped working. When the creative juices stir, you have to go with them no matter where you are or what is taking place around you. I would always take notes, as I was never without a pen and pad in my pocket, and then sit up all night and turn those sketchy ideas into a song. Even on Friday the 13th.

A good topic is always whatever the most people can relate to. And everyone looks at the bridal pages in the Sunday morning papers to see who got married that weekend. Women look to see the gowns and men look to see the women. And that page is what inspired the story and the music. From the Jerry Kennedy Dobro guitar intro to the Cam Mullins string section to the final twisty punch line, it is all Statler all the way.

I saw your picture in the paper Sunday morning
Lord you sure looked pretty in your gown
The smile you were wearing was the one I remember
And your hair was never prettier except when it was down

Yeah, I saw your picture in the paper Sunday morning
By then the honeymoon was almost through
So now you've made your bed and I hope you lie well in it
And I hope you'll both be happy, you see I still lie well, too

Harold shines on the recitation. It was always a gamble for him to do a serious reading of any kind because as soon as he began to speak, fans thought he was going to say something funny. But to his credit, he was always able to set the mood and as soon as they realized he was going for the gold, they accepted his serious side without question. And it's a good thing because he was the only one of us who could do a recitation properly. Phil and Lew wouldn't even try and mine came off contrived. Harold was the man for giving it the right feeling.

However...once this song hit and we did it on stage every night, it got to be a different story. When my brother got a little bored on stage, as I have pointed out before, he was not above ad-libbing whatever popped into his head. Just to see our reaction, he would occasionally do his talking part on this as a falling-down drunk. It was hilarious and, of course, ruined the romantic nature of the piece, but who cared. It entertained and that's all that really mattered. A few years down the road, Barbara Mandrell worked with us for about three years as our opening act. Her dad, Irby, watched Harold from the wings do this one night and nearly ruptured a vessel laughing. From that time on, Irby and all of the Mandrell troupe urged him to do it once or twice every tour. Each night was funnier than the last. He was fearless and funny and never in a hole for something new to do.

"All the Times"

It looks like it was the Christmas holidays again. This time it was December 17, 1975. Harold and I got together after everyone in his house went to bed and shut ourselves in his office and wrote this song. It is just sixteen bars of simple country music set to an appealing rhythm. It tells the story of a neglectful and remorseful husband. My favorite lines are:

I remembered our anniversaries, and your birthdays and Christmas, too
But I forgot you were a woman the other three hundred and sixty-two

I mentioned Charlie McCoy, harmonica player extraordinaire, earlier and told you what a fantastic all-around musician he was. He would often overdub his featured parts after the fact on our songs, but live, he usually played the vibes. With two mallets in each hand, he would strike sustaining chords throughout the song, and it gave a full-bodied resonance to the overall sound. On January 29, 1976, when we were in the studio recording this, Charlie was late for the session because of a delayed flight coming into Nashville. We had just run this song with all the other pickers and were ready to "lay one down." Everyone was in position and waiting for the red light when Charlie came busting through the door. He threw his coat in the corner, apologized for being late, and when we asked him if he wanted us to run through it so he could hear the arrangement and the chord progressions, he said, "No. Let's cut it." Without ever hearing the song, as Harold and I had just written it six weeks before, he recorded it. The take you hear on the record is it. These are the kind of spectacular instrumentalists who made our lives so easy in the studio.

"Something I Haven't Done Yet"

As any writer will tell you, it keeps you sharp to constantly challenge yourself to see if you can describe and relay to the page anything that crosses your mind. My distinct memory of this song idea was pulling into a service station one day and seeing a pretty young woman in riding pants pumping gas into her mud-splattered Volvo. That's all it usually takes to trigger a story, and I started concocting and storing lines in my head. She was a definite "type," and I wanted to see if I could give her life with some kind of feeling and realism. Not sure how long I may have carried those notes in my mind and my pocket, but the footnotes in my song files tell me I wrote this one on 12/29/74. I had scribbled on the bottom of the page, "last song I wrote in 1974."

> *I could tell when I first saw her, her daddy was rich*
> *And her mamma played bridge in afternoons*
> *And the grace of her slim body said that she could set a horse*
> *Then dress in lace and waltz across a room*

"The Times We Had"

Old-time movie actress Marion Davies wrote her autobiography and titled it *The Times We Had.* I read her book and stole her title. So much is said in those four little yet powerful words. I transferred the high life she was writing about to the everyday life we share with those we love. Looking at the date on the bottom of my song sheet, it tells me it was another one from the Christmas holidays, as I apparently wrote it on December 16, 1975. (As I was just listening to us sing this song just now before putting these comments down, Debbie walked past the door and came in and sat down with me. We both sat here with tears in our eyes. It takes on so much more meaning now that we have become the very words of the song.)

> *When those dresses you once wore with ease are dated, frayed and tight*
> *And what little bit of hair I have left is turning white*

And the kids we took such care to raise are taking care of us
We'll smile about the times we had that no one knows but us

The house we built with so much love, the kids will sell in time
Suppertimes and Christmas Eves, birthdays and nursery rhymes
And should a tear roll down my cheek and someone wonders why
You and only you will know what makes an old man cry

"I've Been Everywhere"

When you're looking for a nice up-tempo song to flavor an album, look no further for the perfect one because this is it. We chose it for the simple reason of knowing we could bring something to it no one else could. And I think we proved that with a complicated arrangement that I challenge any other four goof-offs to attempt.

The first verse is simple and laid-back with four solos.

The second verse picks up a little speed and we alternate solos on every two words. Tricky at best.

Third verse comes on with full steam and more speed, we sing it in four-part harmony, and every word is distinct and understandable. (Something some of today's artists should strive for.)

Fourth verse at an unbelievable pulse and we rotate on *each* word. Try that!

Then we end it on a comedic note and Harold gives a little impersonation salute to Hank Snow who had a number-one record with it in 1962.

We did a twelve-day Canadian tour with Hank in May of 1975. He was opening the show and we were closing. One evening, just before leaving the hotel, Hank called the room of one of our band members to reconfirm the showtime, and our piano player laughed in the phone, made a rude remark, and hung up on him. He thought it was Harold playing a joke on him. Hank found it as funny as we did.

What you hear on this song is the first or second cut, as we had no problem getting this unusual arrangement on tape. With years of singing together, it paid off as we just fell into that comfortable groove of feeling one another and linking into one another musically. But nearly twenty years later, when we opened one of our Saturday night TV shows with it on *The Statler Brothers Show*, it became a hilarious mess. We stumbled over the words and restarted so many times we were lying on the floor laughing on camera and the audience was howling. We used all of the outtakes in the show that week for comedy. We finally got it right, but in the meantime, as we always did, we had a lot of fun getting there.

"Amanda"

No finer songwriter of country music than Bob McDill, and lots of folks tried their hands at this one. Don Williams and Waylon both had hits with it. We should have hooked up with him more often, as he wrote in a similar style as ours.

"A Friend's Radio"

Maybe the saddest song I ever wrote and to think I wrote it just three days before Christmas in 1975. I think I captured a mood even more strongly than I set out to do. If you have ever been confined anywhere for any reason and found comfort in the smallest of things, such as a radio playing down the hall or next door, you may relate with these sentiments. And the last verse is an in-depth look at true, sometimes lasting, sometimes fleeting, friendship.

In a home or a prison or a hospital ward
Each day is a promise to get lonesome and bored
And it's company listening, when you're feeling low
To the songs that they're singing on a friend's radio

A friend is just someone you use when you lie
You need when you're lonely, you miss when they die
But it's good to remember little debts you may owe
Like the songs they were singing on a friend's radio

Again, Harold and Lew just soar on the last verse. Their voices singing my words. They became friends in the fifth grade, and I can't tell you the memories, some good, some bad, that all this conjures up in me.

"Maggie"

A razor on the sidewall of the tub; a nightgown under or in the pillow-case. That's all it takes to set off a song racing through your mind. It was April of 1971 in a Holiday Inn in Nashville when I decided to put it all together, and I had, as I always had, my friendly old gut-string Giovanni guitar in the room with me. It came fast, one of those that was completed in fifteen minutes. And the only thing more fun than writing it was recording it. I just love the vocal key change in the last verse. It's a little unusual.

I just found this morning, stuffed in her pillowcase
That ole pink lacey nightgown trimmed in black
And, of course, there's that ole razor on the sidewall of the tub
That Maggie always forgets to pack

"Virginia"

Years before, I had written this specifically as a woman's song. All from the woman's viewpoint just to see if I could convincingly do it. It worked and Jean Shepard had a hit with it in the spring of 1972. Harold and I decided to turn it around and redo the verses and make it a man's song. So, three years later, in a hotel room in Lubbock, Texas, on March 21, 1975, we did just that.

'Cause I love the beauty of Virginia
I run back to her every time I can
'Cause I love being close to Virginia
Oh Virginia, I'll always be your man

Listening closely to it, Virginia can be the state or a woman. Your call.

"Would You Recognize Jesus?"

Okay, here is more information than you may need, but Harold and I were at it again out there on the road. We would travel all day, do a show, and then sit up half the night writing songs. It was August 6, 1974, and we had played an outside fair with Jack Greene and Jeannie Seely opening the show. That means nothing whatsoever to the song; I'm just setting the scene for our writing session. We were in a Holiday Inn in Elmira, New York, and we wanted to attempt a country/gospel song. Something different that had never been done. Try to posture some phrases in a way that was not trite or expected. I think we did.

Would you recognize Jesus if you met him face to face
Or would you wonder if he's just someone you couldn't place
You may not find him coming in a chariot of the Lord
Jesus could be riding in a '49 Ford

When you write a song by yourself, you have to wait till morning to sing it to someone you trust to see if it has any merit. The advantage of writing with a trusted partner is that you can correct and improve one another on the spot and you know before you go to bed whether you have a good song or not.

You can find Him in your mamma's eyes or in your daddy's face
You can find He's always there to help you win the human race
You can find Him in the mountains, downtown or by the sea
My God, here's hoping someone can find Him in you and me

Although we had been gone from Johnny Cash's employ for nearly two years, we certainly had him in mind when we wrote this one. So, when we got home, we sent it to him, and sure enough, he recorded it.

"The Statler Brothers Quiz"

Harold and I were in a mood and decided we could satisfy all of the fans' questions in one fell swoop or one swell song. The verses asked the questions and the choruses answered them, and we laughed for weeks at the honesty of it all. Yes, we did use the most-asked questions we got every day and night from the public, and it afforded us probably the most unique song we ever wrote. It was both funny and true. I won't even attempt to tease with a few lines because you have to hear it in its entirety to appreciate it. I will confess this. Of all the questions we were bombarded with every day, the most annoying to me was *Can I have my picture taken with all four of you?*

And then they would stand and wait for one of us to gather up the others. This might happen in a parking lot or a restaurant or a movie theater. We answered musically with what we finally came to answer with for real: *Sure, if you can find the other three.*

Harold, Lew, Phil, and Don. What a great title for an album. And now that I've listened to it again after about thirty years of not hearing it, what a great album!

16

The Country America Loves

1977

It was nice to kick off the new year with a new album to promote. This one was released January 7, 1977. Beautiful cover. We were standing in white boots and white suits decorated in red and blue trim. It looks like a real classy setting, but, in actuality, it was a piece of carpet and a backdrop in one of Harold's garages in his back driveway. But with the proper lighting effects, who knew? On the back cover, we again wrote our own liner notes. We liked doing this as it gave us an additional opportunity to communicate with the fans. I had to smile when I recently read the list of musicians on the bottom credits in alphabetical order that played on these selections. The first one was a violinist named Byron Bach. Hey, when you have a guy named Bach playing on your sessions, it has to be a good album!

"The Movies"

All who know The Statler Brothers likely know that our collective and collecting hobbies were movies. We had thousands of movies between us. We had 8mm, 16mm, Beta, and later VHS and DVDs. There were old westerns, musicals, mysteries, comedies, and all of the Golden Age of Hollywood that we loved to get lost in. We always carried stacks of them on the bus with us as we toured and watched one or two every night after a concert as we rolled down the highway.

Lew wrote this one by not so simply stringing together titles from every era and genre. We all had our favorites, but truth be known, we'd watch just about anything as long as it was a movie.

I love anything that moves, dancing feet to horse's hoofs
Peyton Place to Dorothy's trip to Oz
Tom Mix to David Hedison, thank you, Thomas Edison
For giving us the best years of our lives

We flew down to Austin, Texas, for the premier of the movie *The Best Little Whorehouse in Texas* starring Burt Reynolds and Dolly Parton. It was held on July 11, 1982. They wanted us to perform for the festivities and sing this song in salute to the movie industry. It was a fly-in-and-out, quick weekend. All the cast was there, and we sang and ate and mixed and mingled, and about all I remember other than that, is that we rode in a parade on a float down Congress Avenue with Jim Nabors. Hooray for Hollywood, y'all!

"Let It Show"

If I confess too many more times that I often wrote different types of songs just to see if I could, you're going to begin thinking I was an experimental lab tech instead of a hard-working songsmith. But that is the love-song truth of the matter. Earlier in this chronicle, I told about our impersonation of the Ink Spots, a black group from the forties. We did a sendup of them singing their major hit "If I Didn't Care." Then John called our attention to another one of theirs we included on an early album, "My Reward." So, sitting around the house in the early and quiet A.M. of July 30,

1976, searching for a song idea, I dared myself to write a new song that sounded old. One that I could sing to someone and they would think was written thirty years before. Why? I don't know. Just the way I like to put myself on the spot sometimes. We even used an upright bass instead of the electric and brushes on the drums instead of sticks. We got that old supper-club swing instead of a country beat, and we channeled the Ink Spots again, but this time with an original Statler Brothers song. It was like going back in a time capsule but taking your music with you. Harold did their signature bass recitation, we did the little syncopation toward the end, and it came off exactly as I heard it in my head there in my home music office all alone the night I wrote it.

"All I Can Do"

Dolly Parton sang and also wrote it. Not sure what caught our ear about it, but listen closely and you can see we gave it a similar treatment we gave "Delta Dawn." It's one of my favorite invented sounds of ours. Harold singing lead, me singing tenor down an octave, Phil singing the baritone up an octave, and Lew singing the bass part on top. Never heard any other group do it before or since.

"You Could Be Coming to Me"

Harold and I wrote this on the tour bus somewhere between Memphis and Monroe, Louisiana, on October 3, 1976. Two weeks and two days later, we were in Nashville recording it. But that was not our intention while writing it. Often, he and I would have a particular artist besides the Statlers in mind while we were writing a song. We would even put little phrasing and styles in the lines that we thought might catch the ear of that singer and might be the little hook that made them decide to record it. Ironically, though, seldom, just like in life, did it ever work out the way we planned. We wrote this one for Jeanne Pruett. Just something about it we felt was her style, so we leaned everything her way. We would get our publisher to pitch it to her as soon as we made a demo tape for it. But we never got to the demo tape because we decided to record it ourselves. Now through this period, Tammy Wynette was working the road with us. When she heard our rough copies from the session later in the month, she said she wanted it.

And sure enough, she recorded it for her *Let's Get Together* album that came out that spring, May of '77. All we had to do to in order to change it from a girl's song to a boy's song was change two nouns and one pronoun.

There's no one who knows you better than me
You need love more than lovin' and you'd think (she/he) could see
When you get tired of playing, like little (boys/girls) all do
You'll be coming home to (mamma/daddy), I'll be waiting for you

"Hat and Boots"

I was often not good with titles on songs I wrote alone. I consulted Harold many times to help me come up with a better title. While writing this one, I called it "If That Ole Hat Could Talk." Harold immediately, even though he had nothing to do with writing it, said I should change the title, and I did. Anyone could have written this little ditty because everyone has said, sometime or another, "If these old walls could talk," or "If this old car could talk." I just went with the obvious. I mean, if they could talk, I could blame them for some of the antics and get some of the guilt off me. Right?

Then I could say that it was them remembering and not me
The first time I saw her, the last time she saw me
The feeling of her fingers, the dimple in her chin
It would be so much easier to put it all on them

Jerry Kennedy and Pete Wade pickin' at their best. And yeah, that old cowboy hat I took to every session as good luck was hanging on a mic stand right beside me. Like a loyal old lap dog, it was never far from me. Full of memories and promise, it was always a comfort and a welcome sight.

If we get the chance to go back where we've been
Hat and boots we'll do it all again

November 25, 1974. Always in the early A.M., which means the middle of the night. If I were at home, I'd wait till everyone was in bed and the house was quiet, and I'd shut myself in my office and lose myself in the search of a song. If I were on the road, I'd take advantage of that "coming down" period after a show, that time you need to level out before you could go to sleep, and I'd write. I could put in a teacup all the songs I've written in the light of day.

"I Was There"

I was writing a lot and I wrote a lot for this album. This was just a little story of unrequited, young love. A thousand songs and movies have carried the theme, but I felt I had a nice view on the subject. The third line in the first verse was and still is one of my faves:

When she bought her first heels, I was there
When she combed those last pigtails from her hair
When she wore her sister's dress to the prom I must confess
When the last dance was danced, I was there

And the ultimate scene of quiet exasperation and sadness came in the third verse. You can try all night to get it right and then it just seems the Lord gives you the right words and you have a sense of not knowing where they came from:

When she walked down the aisle, I was there
When she took the vows to always love and care
With dignity and grace, I quietly took my place
With the friends of the bride, I was there

We gave it such a nice, tender treatment, and the story shined through. This was our third single from this album. It was a top-ten song and, oddly, I can't remember that we ever sang it on stage.

"Thank God I've Got You"

This was the single that led the album by about four months. Another title in question. I was calling it "I've Got You." But there was another song in the rock field at that time with that title. Sonny and Cher had had "I've Got You, Babe." Harold again suggested the title that I went with, and as usual it was the right decision. If there was an "Every song" for an "Everyman," this was it. This poor son of a gun had life coming down on him, and I think most out there in America could identify with him. Our music was good, and it always gave room for the lyrics to resonate and the story to take precedence.

"Blue Eyes Cryin' in the Rain"

Okay, it's time to back up about five albums and clear up a mystery. Remember when I told you during the *Alive at the Johnny Mack Brown High School* album I would tell you about a hidden name in the script? It read, *"...you can always get your tickets at Duffy's Drug and Hardware Store."*

May 23, 1973, at a 2 P.M. session, we were in the middle of recording this old country classic from 1945 when our publisher, Bill Hall, busted through the door and stopped all action. (He's the only person Jerry or any of us would have allowed to do that.) He said he had just gotten a call and John Wayne was waiting to meet the Statlers at a hotel out on the West End. But first a little backstory.

Everyone in Nashville knew that John Wayne was in town that week to help promote the career of the son of his ranch manager, best I recall. He was meeting with a few record execs but had put out the word he was not available for any other meet and greets of any kind. I know this sounds a little clandestine and underground, but we never did learn exactly how or why he sent word to tell the Statlers to come meet with him. But being one of our western heroes, we dropped what we were doing and headed west. Never before or since have we ever left a session with the clock running and the musicians sitting waiting on us, but this day we did.

Jerry Kennedy, Bill Hall, Harold, Lew, Phil, and I got in a vehicle with our driver, Dale Harman, at the wheel, and we headed in to heed John Wayne's summon. We knocked on his hotel door, and when it flung open, there he stood in his sock feet, smoking a cigar with a grin on his face as big as the Rio Grande. All six-foot-four of him. "Come on in, boys," he said, and he graciously greeted each of us, after which we sat and talked for a while with our hero. He regaled us with stories of old Hollywood and old cowboy stars we had grown up following, and it was an afternoon we knew we would cherish for the ages.

The Great Cowboy was sixty-six years old, had been through a number of serious health issues, and was a little hard of hearing at this time. When

Jerry Kennedy shook hands with him, he introduced himself, and John thought he had said "Duffy Kennedy," so he replied, "Certainly glad to meet you, Duffy." From that day forward, Jerry answered nobly and proudly to the name Duffy from anyone who chose to call him that. He had been knighted Duffy by maybe the biggest and longest reigning star Hollywood ever knew.

What a day! We floated back to the studio and breezed through this old Fred Rose-written gem with our heads still above the clouds. For some odd reason, this cut did not make the album we were working on at the time, which was *Carry Me Back*. It stayed in the can for four years and seven albums before we found the right place for it. But it was timeless and we knew it would fit wherever we decided to use it.

"Somebody New Will Be Coming Along"

I wrote this song with a very different and very cavalier attitude. I also obviously wrote it for a duet of two men. Not sure who or what I had in mind, but I don't think I had the Statlers in mind. As I've said, we always shared our new creations as writers with one another, and when the other three heard this song, they liked it and said let's do it. We did and it came off with a more tongue-in-cheek leaning than the bold lyrics first suggest. We often did edgy things the fans weren't expecting but they always accepted it from us. Lew and I had fun with the verses and the back-and-forth conversational lines. And the chorus, though a bit full of itself, just sounded socially confident.

Before the last one is good and gone
Somebody new will be coming along

"You Comb Her Hair Every Morning"

When you're looking for a solid country song to fit the title of this album, there is just no better place to look than here. You can't miss when two giant Nashville song makers, Harlan Howard and Hank Cochran, get together and write a hit. This didn't happen every day but when it did it was magic.

"A Couple More Years"

Yes, we've had fans ask why. Why did the Statlers cut a Dr. Hook song? We actually think of it as a Shel Silverstein song. He cowrote it with Dennis Locorriere, who was a member of the Dr. Hook group. We had known Shel for years, back to the days when he wrote "A Boy Named Sue" for John and was a better-known New York cartoonist and children's book writer than he was a country songwriter. In the early days he used to sing songs to us in hotel rooms he had just written; the ink wasn't even dry. Only problem was, Shel had a voice and a style of singing/talking a song that we could never decipher what the melody was suppose to be. Everybody who had hits with his fantastic material, John, Bobby Bare, had to sort of guess at the music and use their own imagination.

This was really a sexy song and we took interesting turns in it. Note the second verse; Lew and Phil duet, but Lew is leading and Phil is singing an alto part below him. Unusual. We seldom used electric guitar fills, but here, instead of gut string or Dobro guitar, Jerry (aka Duffy) Kennedy plugged in and fired it up. I love it. And a new string arranger was on board for the violin beds of swanky sounds. This song marked the debut of Bergen White, who would serve us well for the rest of our recording career.

So this was *The Country America Loves*, and America is the country we love, too.

17

Short Stories

1977

The two major types of country songs, or any songs, for that matter, are love songs or story songs. We had a special affinity for stories and decided to salute that particular category with an album featuring nothing but. Every entry here has a story of its own to tell; ten of them are ours and one we pulled out of the Johnny Cash file.

For the cover, it was just obvious. Where do you go to find stories? The library. We have one of those here, but the aisles were a little cramped for what we needed, so we went to the campus of Mary Baldwin College (now Mary Baldwin University) right here in our downtown area in Staunton. Their library was roomier, and a photographer was able move around for the angles needed, but we wanted something else as an eye-catcher. We contacted a lady, Gayle Aaglan, who had worked in the scenic art department of the Johnny Cash TV show with us years before. We explained what we needed, so she built and painted us a huge six-foot by ten-foot book that we carted to Staunton from Nashville on our bus.

Album titles, themes, and cover pictures were always fun to come up with. Not always easy and some times taxing, but it felt good when it all came together.

"Silver Medals and Sweet Memories"

I have told this story before because it means so very much to me. But if you haven't heard it, here it is, showing how truth becomes fiction for the sake of a song story. Our bus driver for many years, who I went to high school with, was Dale Harman. Dale was raised by his mother and stepfather, who was like a real parent to him. His stepdad was a World War II veteran, and when he passed in March of '76, I went to the funeral. I stood with the family at the graveside while "Taps" was played, a 21-gun salute was executed, and the flag was ceremoniously folded and presented to Dale's mother. I had been to other military funerals, but this particular day, standing on the hillside in that wind-blown cemetery, I was touched and moved like never before. It was as if I were overcome by the mood of that long-ago era, and as I walked to my car, my mind was working faster than my feet. By the time I got behind the wheel, I had formed verses and choruses in my head and had my opening line. I rushed home and the words and music poured out of me like the tears from the widow I had just left behind at the grave, holding that flag. I changed the facts a little to make my own story, but I used what I had witnessed and felt that day and put it all on the paper into every word and every note:

Just a picture on a table
Just some letters Mamma saved
And a costume brooch from England
On the back it has engraved
To Eileen, I love you
London 1943

We had an agent in Nashville, Dick Blake, from 1973 to 1983, who was like a father figure to us. Dick was a major in WWII and was captured by the enemy twice. By the time we knew him, his body was showing the consequences of those prison camps, but nothing ever took a toll on his spirit. He was red, white, and blue through and through. He traveled with us on every date until he just couldn't travel anymore. He always wore a small western felt, gray dress hat. He would see that we got on and off the stage properly each night, and you could always catch a glimpse of him moving about backstage while we were performing, taking care of business. Every night when we sang this song, he would walk to the edge of the stage, just out of sight to the audience, and stand with his hat in his hand. He loved this song. I got to where I watched for it. These words were something sacred to him, and I get misty-eyed just remembering the sight of him standing there at attention until this song ended every night. The Major passed in October of '83. Simply put, I miss him. We were in a hat shop out west years ago, and I saw a hat identical in shape and style to the one he wore. I bought it. I've never worn it. I just wanted to have it.

> *In Mamma's bedroom closet*
> *To this day on her top shelf*
> *There's a flag folded three-cornered*
> *Laying all by itself*
> *And the sergeant would surely be honored*
> *To know how pretty she still is*
> *And that after all these lonely years*
> *His Eileen's still his*

When Dale's mother knew her life was coming to an end, she gave me this flag. It is in my office, folded and laying on the top shelf to this very day.

"The Regular Saturday Night Setback Card Game"

Harold and I, one Sunday night on January 2 of 1977, put this one down on paper with very little fiction to add. We did change the names to protect the guilty. Take special note that FDR is mentioned twice in the verses, and we took that occasion to pronounce Roosevelt both ways. With the long "oo" and the short "oo." We grew up hearing it both ways so we straddled the fence on that one. This was a hoot to write and a type of family folk history neither one of us would have even considered writing alone. Our daddy was a character we wrote about often.

Uncle Sam left me his watch fob
Bay left me some stocks
And the Bible Uncle Clive left me was still in the box
And Daddy left a son
That remembers it so well
And a lot of other memories I don't have time to tell

"That Summer"

A Statler Brothers song with no Statler Brothers. This was the only one ever recorded like this. Harold is the only one on this, and no one, not even he, is singing. I wrote this very nostalgic lyric and sweet, far-away melody, and the spoken word was all that was needed. As I have pointed out before, Harold was great at these things. Our only risk on stage was fitting it into the show where he could get serious and the fans weren't expecting a punch line. He would take the hand mic and go sit on the piano bench with our piano player; the spotlight would follow him and leave all the rest of us in darkness. It brought a charm and relaxed energy to the moment, and I looked forward to it every time we did it. (Or I should say, every time *he* did it.)

"He Went to the Cross Loving You"

Back up a half dozen albums to 1975 to *The Best of The Statler Brothers*. I promised to tell you more about "I'll Go to My Grave Loving You" and how Harold got involved with a future song concerning it. Well, this is the future song. I had written "Grave" as a slow love ballad, and at his suggestion, we put a beat and aftertime to it to make it what it became. Sometime later, he used my original tempo and melody and wrote this pretty gospel song. We are listed as cowriters although we never actually sat down together and did any writing as we usually did. His words; my music. A powerful and concise look at the life of Christ.

THE MUSIC OF THE STATLER BROTHERS

"Quite a Long, Long Time"

This Lew DeWitt-written song was on our very first album *Flowers on the Wall*. This is one of those times we recut a song from our past. It told a nice story and we felt it was worth telling again. There were eleven years between the two recordings.

"Carried Away"

Very unusual little musical tale from Lew's stable of tunes. Nice punch at the end. Wish I knew more about where it came from and any backstory, but I just don't have much to share about it.

"The Star"

This song is the end result of being on stage night after night all of my young life. I wrote it from the stage side of the microphone. From standing in the wings, preparing to step out into the spotlight, to the personal thoughts that go through a singer's head while the routine words are coming out of his mouth. He may be singing of romance and love, but his mind is on what his kids are doing at home and what he's missing by not being there. He may look confident, cool, and even sexy to some, but in his mind, he's worried about his future and how long this stardom thing will last. It is a very deep look at a very shallow genre of a person who goes through life being a star above all else. There is little reward in tinsel and sparkle.

We did a fine job of dividing up the verses and telling respective slants on the theme. It was as if one voice was narrating it. It was probably too inside to have been a single and the production wasn't exactly country, but I loved it.

He wonders is it worth it all, the money and the lights
He'd give it all up gladly to just be home tonight
Then applause breaks his train of thought; the spot has him embraced
And the tears and the sweat melt together in his face
He's a Star!

July was always a vacation month from touring. We would take off that month because our kids were all out of school and it was mid-summer and a beautiful time in Virginia. So, as soon as our Happy Birthday USA celebration was over each year, we had lots of free time till the big fair season started in August. But my notes reveal that I never really took a vacation from writing. This one was written in July of '76, and so many others of mine were written in December, the other month we mostly took off as vacation during the Christmas holidays.

"Grandma"

Any fiction writer of novels, short stories, or songs will tell you they never discard an idea. Sometimes you carry a remnant of an idea in your head for decades. I remember as a kid of about ten years old seeing a television show one night that spooked me for days. It was one of those drama series with different stars and stories each week, many of them done live. This one was about an elderly woman who had lost her husband yet continued to live her life as if he were still with her every day. She'd talk to him; tell him dinner was about ready; discuss the news with him; discuss problems about their adult children. Just that seed of a memory was enough to create this character. I then went on and made her a little psychic. And, yes, I finally did a recitation that I had been declining to do for so long.

Wrote this one in December of '76. Did I mention that the mind never takes a vacation?

"Different Things to Different People"

The older you get the more things are revealed to you. About this time in life, I was realizing how many different people I was to all the different people I came in contact with daily. You're a father, a son, a brother, a husband, a friend, a boss, an employee, and even a memory to someone, and yet you're still you in all of these situations. Being all these things to all these people, putting on and taking off all these hats at a moment's notice, can be exhausting. But we all do it.

Different things to different people
There's so much to be and do

Different things to different people
Can I just be me with you?

December of '76 again.

"Give My Love to Rose"

Johnny Cash was a fantastic writer, especially in his Sun days and early Columbia days. This was just one of many of his compositions that we loved. Looking back on all these album selections, I can see he was a deep influence on us. We so often included a song of his as if we were paying homage to him, and I guess we were. We could easily have done an entire album in tribute to his writing talent, and I don't know why we never did. In addition to the ones we did, we could have added some of my favorites: "Come In Stranger," "Understand Your Man," "Forty Shades of Green," and a long list of others. But this one, "Rose," is at the top of the list.

"Some I Wrote"

This is a very personal song Harold and I wrote together. It also could be the national anthem for all songwriters, especially in country music. No, make that in any genre of music. I just finished reading the biography of Irving Berlin, and all songsmiths draw on their lives and private emotions in order to get their heart and feelings on paper and into a melody. I feel that we poured it all out here and performed it with as true a country sound as there has ever been.

Some day when it's all over and they come to carry me
And you're walkin' slow and wearin' black with the rest of the family
And the choir stands to sing a song make sure it's one of mine
I had a few more tunes I wanted to write but I ran out of time

I knew the night we put this one down on a scratch piece of paper that we had written my epitaph. It was what I wanted said and how I wanted to be remembered as a writer. That was more than forty years ago. Things change and now I realize it isn't as important as it was. Now I'm thinking something simpler, shorter, a little more general, a little less flamboyant. I

166

mean, forty years ago, I wore a white suit trimmed in red and blue on stage, in public. Today, I'm more of a button-down collar and V-neck sweater guy. Things change.

> *Some I wrote for money, some I wrote for fun*
> *Some I wrote and threw away and never sang to anyone*
> *One I wrote for mamma and a couple still aren't through*
> *I've lost track of all the rest but the most I wrote for you*

During the mid-seventies, we had an out-of-this-world road show. Ronnie Milsap intermission, Tammy Wynette intermission, Statler Brothers, and home. It was a killer and we had wonderful times. We were in Austin, the capital of Texas on April 17, 1977. We were on stage, I was talking between songs, and somebody in the audience threw a cowboy hat at me. I grabbed it and by instinct tossed it over to Harold. He caught it, threw it down on stage at his feet, and stomped it with his big old alligator cowboy boots. Then picked it up and sailed it back in the dark into the audience for about twenty rows. The crowd howled and roared. They loved it! Then, in the cartoon voice of one of his invented characters, Snappy Simmons, he sang "Deep in the Heart of Texas" and got the crowd to sing with him. Another notch was put into his comedy legend forever.

Later that night, while rolling across west Texas toward Tucson in the lounge of our bus, he and I wrote this heartfelt song. Just another example of how quickly you have to change moods from moment to moment in show business; and people wonder why all of us are crazy. 'Taint no wonder!

By the way, we did the ol' gender change of pronouns for Tammy, and she recorded this song, too.

18

Entertainers...On and Off the Record

1978

I came up with this little slogan that served us in lots of ways. It was on the bottom of our official Statler Brothers stationery. It was in our press kits and PR bios that went ahead of us to all our concert dates and TV appearances. Thus, it was often used by the DJs and local dignitaries who introduced us every night as we came on stage. And I promise you that 75 percent of the time, it was misspoken as, "Here they are, the entertainers on and off the road, The Statler Brothers." What? Why so many people got it wrong, I have no idea. We thought it may be good for everyone to see it in big print, so we decided to make it an album title. It was a two-faced album, and looking at it even with a close eye, you can't tell which is the front and which is the back.

On one side is a picture of us on stage at our 1977 Fourth of July show in Staunton dressed in stage suits and vests. On the other side is a picture of us in casual sweaters and jackets taken at a regional park close to home called Natural Chimneys. (Seven natural limestone rock formations that look like chimneys and reach to 120 feet plus lots of picnic and camping area.) We had an extensive photo shoot there one day and were posed on rocks and wooden tables and country lanes and tree stumps. We were tired and bored and after a few hours we told the photographers we were through and headed for our cars. They, wanting to use every drop of sunlight left, walked backward all the way across a field with cameras in hand in front of us, snapping frantically, as we strolled determinedly toward the parking lot. The picture on the album is what you see as the final, unrehearsed, and unposed moments of that long afternoon. Natural is always better than posed any day.

Our usual schedule for recording was spending days in Nashville with nothing on our minds but the album we were working on. With *Entertainers*, it was a little different situation. Looking back at my show-book calendar for January of 1978, in a week's time we guested on an NBC TV special at the Opry House on Wednesday, had meetings with our agent and publisher on Thursday, recorded three songs on Friday, played a concert date in Warren, Ohio, Saturday night, and were back in Nashville for three more days of sessions beginning on Monday.

We mixed TV, recording, business meetings, and concerts, and this was something we seldom did in order to give every aspect of our business the attention it required. But as I listen, I don't think the album suffered. And I can only hope the other factions didn't either.

"Do You Know You Are My Sunshine?"

So much has been written and told in interviews about where this song came from. What you've heard is probably true, but I'll register it here again for the record. We were playing a country music park somewhere in Indiana one Sunday afternoon. It was summertime, outdoors, and, as was our style, when we played two shows to the same audience, we would take requests from that second crowd and sing whatever they threw at us. It was fun and we always looked forward to it. A young lady motioned Harold to the side of the stage, and as he bent down to hear her request, she said, "Do you know "You Are My Sunshine?" She was, of course, wanting us to sing the old Jimmie Davis country classic "You Are My Sunshine." But Harold's creative ear heard something different. He heard the whole sentence as a lover's question. I remember distinctly on the bus after the show, while changing clothes, he said to me, "I just got a great idea for a song," and he told me what this unknown girl had said to him. We carried the idea with us, talked a little about it, but never found the right time or mood to sit down and write it. That didn't happen until months later, but the funny thing about this section of the story is that I can't count the number of people through the years who have told us, after hearing this story, that they were the person who whispered in Harold's ear that day. We still get mail from women claiming to be the mystery girl from Indiana.

Half a year later, we were in Nashville working on this album and we were one song short with one day of sessions left. We all four turned in that night and decided we would get together the next morning and come up with an old standard to fill the one empty spot. But my brother and I couldn't let sleeping dogs lie. We sat up half the night and wrote "Do You Know You Are My Sunshine." We sang it to Phil and Lew the next morning. They loved it and we took the scratch pad full of our scribblings to a secretary at Mercury just minutes before the session began and asked her to type up a lyric sheet. Then we went into the studio that morning, January 18, 1978, sang it for Jerry, and exactly two months later it hit the charts in Billboard magazine, where it stayed for seventeen weeks and reached number one.

The echo on Harold's *"Do You Know"* bass lines in each chorus was the hook. Jerry dosed it up with an almost old Sun Records echo that just reached out and made you turn up the car radio as you were driving down the road. We treated it very Statlerish, with Lew and I duetting the verses and full four-part harmony on the choruses. It's the perfect example of a true Statler Brothers song and performance.

We were on tour in Bakersfield, California, on May 16, 1978, when we got word that "Sunshine" would go to number one in all the trade charts, *Billboard*, *Cashbox*, and *Record World*, the next week. May 23rd, exactly a week later, while still on the West Coast tour, we did Dinah Shore's talk show and sang the top song in the nation. And speaking of Dinah, we did her show quite a few times. She was one genuine sweetheart.

170

We appeared in the Burt Reynolds movie *Smokey and the Bandit II* and sang this song. It is one of two of our songs I hear most often. I hear this one around my house almost every day because it is my wife Debbie's ringtone. The other one I hear a lot is "I'll Go to my Grave Loving You." That's my ringtone.

"Yours Love"

Harlan Howard was one of the best songwriters Nashville ever produced. He was prolific, commercial, and professional, and he knew his way around an unassuming melody and meaningful words. I can't say enough good things about him. This one may come as close to classic poetry as anything he ever put together. I think we gave everything musical in our version that his writing called for. We held this one in the can for two years. A standard such as this is perfect insurance to have on hand, as it can be used on practically any album any time.

May the Lord's shining grace be yours love
May the happiest face be yours love
May the last fingertips, that touch these two lips
As life from me slips, be yours love

"The Best That I Can Do"

The next three songs are listed here out of order as they appear on the album. I have grouped them together because I have something to say that applies to all three of them. They are, without question, three of the most profoundly sad and intensely desolate compositions I have ever written. I can honestly say I think they are good songs, maybe even better than that. But they are bleak and touch on miserable emotions and situations of the heart.

Tonight there must be millions of souls in misery
And Lord, if you've a second, would you check on one for me
And should you find her sleeping, let her sleep until the day
But God, if she's crying, would you wipe her tears away

I was in a Period. Call it my Blue Period. My Dismal Period. Whatever you want to call it. I was writing deeper than I needed to, and it puts me in sort of a funk listening to it today.

Please tell her I still love her
And that's the best that I can do

My misery wasn't short-lived either. I began writing this piece in September of '77 and finished it December 6, 1977 (Almost the holidays again. Merry Christmas to me!)

"I Dreamed about You"

Harold and Lew are giving it all in a duet with their contrasting voices. The chorus is good and strong but grieving in the spirit of love. I wrote this chorus in the fall of 1977. I carried it with me in my stack of notebooks that I never left home without and added the two verses in November of 1977. I never let an idea die on the vine and always went back and tried to save the good ones. I think this was a good one, but so very heavy and deeply blue.

Maybe it's silly, but Baby, it's true
I love her to sleep, then dream about you
I stood beside her and promised I do
Then took her to heaven and dreamed about you

"Before the Magic Turns to Memory"

I wrote this on the road in March of '77. Not sure where or exactly when but *after* a show was always more conducive to creating. After a show, your mind was clearer, the adrenaline was pumping, and your imagination was crystal and sharp. Your mood and time of day has a great effect on what and how you write. You will write happier songs in daylight and gloomier songs at night. The later, the gloomier. And never assume a writer, whether of songs or novels, experiences everything they write, and never presume that they don't. You don't have to kill someone in order to write a murder mystery, but then again, it might help. I don't know. Can't say. And I can't say about these three songs. I was in a mood. And I'm not sure how or why these three wound up on the same album.

We knew when we started, this could never last
We've got too little future, and way too much past
And there's only a few more hours in sight
Till morning will come like a thief in the night

"You're the First"

I can't shed much light on the creation of this song as Lew wrote it. I do like his and Phil's smooth harmony on the second verse and the background do-do-dos that Harold and Phil and I do throughout. Very nice all the way.

"Tomorrow Is Your Friend"

This is flat out a children's song. I wrote it back in 1970 to be exactly that. At the time we were regulars on the Johnny Cash TV show every Wednesday night on ABC. He often did theme shows. We did an all-western show, all-comedy, all-gospel, and even a children's circus show. So, I wrote this one and pitched it to him for the circus show. But the funny and quirky part of the story was the route it took to get there. We were sitting around on the set one day, waiting for the next rehearsal, and I sang it to John. He liked it and told me to put it on tape and give it to him. Later that day, I went to a little recording studio there behind the Ryman Auditorium and sat at the piano and sang this song. It was very good. I gave it to John that night. The next day he said, "Donnie, I like that song, but record it again with a guitar instead of a piano." So, later that day I went back to the little studio and sang it with a guitar. No further explanation, but it's just sometimes what you have to do to reach the ear of an artist and the way he wants to hear the material.

The interesting thing about the Statler cut on this song is that we recorded it on November 18, 1971, but then held it in the can until March 13, 1978, when this album was released. Nearly six and a half years from the time we recorded it until we released it. We often held songs like this in case we were in need of them, should we be busy when it came time for another album.

What a sweet little music box intro, and we sang it as if we were singing it to our kids. Come to think of it, we were.

The little boy who pushed you down and made you cry
He said when you were "it" you wouldn't hide your eyes
And like Chicken Little you think your sky is falling in
But you'll wake and find tomorrow is your friend

"The Official Historian on Shirley Jean Berrell"

This is original and innovative from the cowbell opening to the announcement of "the end" at the closing of the song. I have no record of when or where Harold and I were when we came up with this idea and committed it to paper, but I know we had a ball doing it. To think we could know someone as well as we claim in the verses is funny within itself.

I can tell you her favorite song and where she liked to park
And why to this very day she's scared of the dark
How she got her nickname and that scar behind her knee
If there's anything you need to know 'bout Shirley just ask me

And then it was the chorus that took it all to another level and made it a love song.

I'm the official historian on Shirley Jean Berrell
I've known her since God only knows and I won't tell
I caught her the first time she stumbled and fell
And Shirley, she knows me just as well

It is always risky when you use names in a song. Do you make them common names and easy to understand? Or do you make them a little unusual so they will be more memorable? We wrestled a little with those questions here. Shirley Jean rolls off the tongue nicely and is easily understood, while Berrell leans more with the latter way of thinking and it lends itself to a wider rhyming pattern. So, we had both, and after listing in three verses all the personal things we knew about ole S. J., we closed it with the perfect punch line.

I know where she's ticklish and her every little quirk
The funnies she don't read and her number at work
I know what she stands for and what she won't allow
The only thing that I don't know is where she is right now

It was the third hit single from this album and was a perfect stage song throughout our career. We often opened our shows with it or used it as the second song. When the fans heard the cowbell, they knew what was coming before we ever sang a note.

"Who Am I to Say?"

This was the second hit single from this album, and it shot immediately to the top of the charts. It was so very special to us because it was written by Harold's oldest daughter, Kim, who was only sixteen years old when she sat down and put these words in her school notebook.

She wrote it, of course, as a girl's song, and the lyric sheet from our actual session that I am looking at as I write this sentence shows me how we went through and changed each pronoun to make it a man's song.

I wish I had a dollar for every time I was unkind
I wish I'd had an answer for all the questions on her mind
I wish I'd had the time for all the times she needed me
I wish I'd realized but I was much too blind to see

This sweet, beautiful niece of mine, a junior in high school, turned seventeen just months before this song of hers hit. We thought it was an extremely good album song, but once we got it to the studio it took on a new life. I remember Jerry Kennedy saying, "Let's do something really different for Kim," as he pulled out a little electric piano that always sat in the corner with papers stacked on it. He plugged it in and got Pig Robbins to create a little intro riff on it with just a bass drum in the background. I think we all knew as soon as we heard that introduction that something magical was about to happen.

All she wanted was to love me but all I did was turn away
If I'd known how much she needed me, she might be here today
And if I'd only been more open and understood her ways
She might be in my arms tonight, but who am I to say

Kim Reid Weller wrote other songs for us through the years that I will gladly tell you all about as we come to them. By the way, Kim's middle name is Love, and she wears it with such grace.

"I Forgot More Than You'll Ever Know"

An old country standard and a blockbuster hit for the Davis Sisters twenty-five years before we ever recorded it. You may remember half of their duo, Skeeter Davis. Sadly, her singing partner, Betty Jack, was killed in an auto accident the week their record was released.

We gave it a new slant with the double-time rhythm.

"When You Are Sixty-Five"

We were in Los Angeles in the summer of 1970 to tape the Everly Brothers TV show. They were the summer replacement series for the Johnny Cash TV show. This was standard procedure back then for a hit series to have a summer show in their time slot until the next fall season. John took the summer off to tour, and we toured with him plus did all the TV we could on our own. We were staying at the Hollywood Roosevelt hotel on Hollywood Blvd., where I wrote this sitting on the bed with a guitar in my lap. It is another of those songs I have grown into.

Will you think of me as a young man or know that I've grown old
Will you think of me as a wild youth or something you controlled
Will you remember that I loved you and still would do the same
Or at sixty-five will you have forgotten that young man's name

Writing in different locations, as I had the opportunity to do, gives you fresh perspectives and angles. This may have been an entirely different song if I had written it sitting on a beach or snowed in at a Canadian motel looking out at ice and wind. You never know, and there is no way to ever tell.

But I'm glad for whatever made this one come out the way it did, because it's special to my heart and to the era in which I wrote it.

Will you wonder if I'm living or dead in pauper's grave
When you come by some old pictures or something you might have saved
Will you tell, should I be famous, your children of me
Or at sixty-five will you rather let old memories be

19

Christmas Card

1978

Most recording artists hope to have a career long enough to give them the opportunity to do two things: record a "Best of" album and record a Christmas album. This is probably truer in the pop and country fields than in the rock or hip-hop genre. It certainly was true for us. We couldn't wait to accumulate enough hits to put together that "Best of" collection, and now that we had done that, Christmas was at the top of our list.

There were old standards we wanted to include, and we had ideas for new seasonal songs we wanted to write. We wanted to have a Christmasy feeling to the songs while at the same time maintain the Statler sound and touch. I think we did that with the six original and five old standbys that we chose for this, our nineteenth official album.

The first order of business was shooting the album cover. We had decided on the very picturesque driveway that led to the front of Harold's home, and we knew we wanted a horse-drawn sleigh with the four of us riding in it. The one important thing we needed was something we couldn't rent, beg, or borrow. Snow! So, we put the man who owned the horse and sleigh on notice, and he agreed that if we called him at the first sight of gathering snowflakes, he would be there within an hour. The photographer agreed to the same deal. Everyone was spot on, and we shot the picture in no time at all. My favorite part of it all was Harold's German shepherd dog, Teabag, running along beside us. We made about three runs at it before the photographer was pleased with the lighting and the composition and what-have-you. And sweet ol' Teabag, as if on cue, ran the length of that lane every time with us in perfect frame and focus.

"I Believe in Santa's Cause"

Lew and guitarist Buddy Church cowrote this clever take on the Santa Claus yarn. The melody says Christmas, and the lyric is tricky in that many had to listen closely to understand that we were saying Santa's *cause* and not *Claus*. We did a really good and solid performance on a very deserving song.

Never heard a snowman talking, never seen a reindeer fly
Nor seen a wooden soldier walking, or met Santa eye to eye
Now there are those who don't believe in miracles or Santa Claus
But I believe what I believe and I believe in Santa's cause

"I'll Be Home for Christmas"

This was a done deal from the first day this album was mentioned. I could write all day about this jewel, which was written back during World War II. Bing Crosby had a hit with it in 1943, and every soldier in uniform, every wife or girlfriend on the home front, and every breathing soul with a blood-pumping heart shed a tear as they listened to one of the best seasonal songs ever composed. Kim Gannon and Walter Kent wrote it, and after a little lawsuit over where they may have gotten the idea, a third name was added to the copyright: Buck Ram. He was the producer and manager of the fifties group the Platters, and he had his name on a number of their hits, also. Whatever the backstory was, and I'm sure you had to be there, it has stirred the hearts and clouded the eyes of every generation since the war years. We sang our best, and Bergen White's string arrangements filled all the holes with a warm Christmas spirit. And I just love the country fiddle that shares the mid-break. If I could only listen to one secular Christmas song all season long, this would be the one. (Pardon me while I close my eyes here at my desk and listen to it one more time before I continue on.)

We did change one word:

Please have snow and mistletoe and presents on *the tree*

We changed it to *under*. It meters better and we had just never heard of putting presents on a tree. All of ours had always been under the tree.

We started putting these tracks down in January of '78. Some we did in April. This one we did June 27th. That old myth about how you have to record the songs during the season or decorate the studio with a tree and colored lights in order to capture the feeling is just that, a myth. When you have the song, the musicians, the singers, and the heart, it can be Christmas anytime you want it to be.

"Jingle Bells"

You might like to ask us why "Jingle Bells." Hasn't that been done to death? Is there anything new you can possibly bring to it? And we would have told you those two questions were the very reason we decided to do it. It *had* been done to death, and we *could* bring something new to it that would give it a fresh life and spirit. Of course, it really isn't a Christmas song at all. No mention of the word in it anywhere. Matter of fact, James Pierpont wrote it back in the mid-1800s as a Thanksgiving song. (No mention of that in it either.) It's really just a winter song. A snow song. And its original title was "One Horse Open Sleigh." Hey, that's what our album cover was all about with Teabag and the horse. Yes, we have to sing this tired old anthem to the great outdoors, and we have to give it some Statler oomph!

First, bring Bobby Thompson in to play the banjo. Then have the band play in double time and we will sing in half time. And from the opening bar, we were off and running just like that horse and sleigh. When we got to the second verse, two unusual things happened. Harold and I sang a duet. This was a rarity. As we did, we switched to double time with the music, then back to half time on the chorus, and then we all changed keys! What a fun arrangement! It still makes me smile when I hear it today.

"I Never Spend a Christmas That I Don't Think of You"

I wanted to write a teenaged romance for the season. We were home in late January, and I sat down to the piano at 1 A.M. on the 29th of that month, after my household had gone to bed, and I put this saga of young love into a song.

The year I helped your daddy trim the outdoor tree with lights
You worked part time at Penney's and I took you home at nights
The Christmas Eve you told me you loved me and I knew
I'd never spend a Christmas I wouldn't think of you

Words always came to me better late at night. There were no other sights and sounds to distract me from what I was doing. Sometimes those words surprised me and I wrote them down quickly before they left me because I knew they weren't really mine to keep. God was sending the ability to me to accept them or wait for another batch. Sometimes I waited, but sometimes I just knew it wasn't going to get any better.

The year the senior class sold Christmas trees and mistletoe
And we never thought that someday this would seem so long ago
The Christmas Eve I told you, I love you, well, I do
And I never spend a Christmas that I don't think of you

"White Christmas"

Every story that could be told about this song has been told a thousand times. Even Irving Berlin thought it was the best song ever written, and he was probably right. This is the measure every Christmas song is held to, and few survive in its radiance. Again, what could we bring to a classic piece such as this that all the artists before us hadn't already excelled in doing? Well, we just sang it in our Statler style, which I hope had a little charm and warmth of its own. And then there is that Dobro that takes a break halfway through. Nobody was expecting that, but it did remind everyone this was country music no matter who was writing the songs.

Weldon Myrick was one of the finest steel guitar and Dobro players to ever tune up in front of a mic. We knew him in our early days when he was traveling as part of Bill Anderson's band. When he settled in Nashville and did nothing but sessions, we renewed our ties and used him a lot on many of our records. That is Weldon on this song playing the Dobro and what a beautiful job he did.

Weldon was doing a session with us one night on another song, and there was a Dobro lick that he had a little trouble mastering, and he asked to do it over about three times. On the fourth try, he looked up and said, "Don't worry, guys, I'm gonna get this right if it takes every dime y'all got!"

He was a fine man and a great picker. Thank you, Weldon.

"Christmas to Me"

Harold and I arranged this song on paper before we even wrote it. In retrospect that sounds impossible, but it had to be so we would know what to write:

Christmas to me is wherever she might be
Singing carols with a choir, hanging stockings by the fire

We got together at our offices in the early A.M. of March 29, 1978, just the two of us. I played the piano while he wrote our words down on a yellow legal pad:

Christmas to me is as far as I can see
Pasture fields covered with snow, White Christmas on the radio

We would write a verse for each Statler to sing as a solo. And each verse would paint a different picture of Christmas.

Christmas to me is a tall cedar tree
Decorated and adorned with Christmas balls and strings of popcorn

182

We would record it on April 5, just a week and three days after Easter. But that didn't matter. We knew we had something different and special.

Christmas to me is the newborn baby
Lying quietly in the hay, when the angels came to say

But let's end it with all four of us singing. Just a few short lines that sum up all these different looks at the season and say exactly to the fans what we want to personally say to each one of them:

Christmas to you, may it never be blue
And may all your dreams come true
Merry Christmas to you

"Who Do You Think?"

This is the song brother Harold and I wrote for the Holy Bible album, *New Testament*. See the notes there.

"Away in a Manger"

When you're thinking a simple yet majestic carol, this one is in the race with "Silent Night." We knew we wanted to sing it, but the first time we sat down with it, we were torn as to which melody to use. There are two beautiful tunes that have come down through the ages with these words attached to them, and we had sung both in Sunday school as kids, and so have many of you. Both were written toward the end of the nineteenth century, one by William Kilpatrick and the other by James Murray. Which one did you like best? 50/50. So, we decided to use both of them. The words, attributed by many historians to Martin Luther, remained as they have been for centuries.

The first verse was melody A; the second was melody B. The third verse was Phil and Lew singing one and Harold and I singing the other against one another. For the record, there was no overdubbing involved. We sang them together, live. If you want to know the truth, it ain't all that easy to do, and we were right proud of the finished result. Never heard it done before or since. Such a tender and loving song.

"Something You Can't Buy"

This one fills me up. Harold and I had lost our dad a decade earlier and I felt we were writing about him along with every other father in the United States. Harold's talking parts over top of our singing is a technique we had never done. It was so very haunting and moving, and I've caught myself through the years at Christmastime skipping this song when I play this album in my car or at the house; it's just too emotional. The last line we used gives me pause and a challenge to the way I celebrate each year:

And to pay back all he gave me, I can't but I will try
I'll pass along to my kids, something they can't buy

And I hope I do. Our family Christmas, with the kids and grandkids, is all about doing things together much more than the giving. We gather and eat over the holidays about every thirty minutes. We have traditional breakfasts and brunches and dinners that last all week into New Year's Day. I look forward to and love every second of it more and more every year.

"The Carols Those Kids Used to Sing"

We just pointed our pens toward the paper and this one wrote itself. There is not a word of fiction in it. Our church, when we were kids, had a wonderfully active youth program, and Harold and I were simply reminiscing about all that one night. I talked about how we would pile into the back of a hay truck and ride from houses to nursing homes to the hospital and sing carols and then come back to the church and eat hot dogs and how much fun that all was.

About three nights before every Christmas
We'd load Mr. Bradley's truck with hay
Seven thirty on the dot, on the church parking lot
We'd pile in that old truck and ride away

Harold remembered out loud the year all the kids his age brought groceries and toys from home and took them to a needy family that lived down the road from the church. He remembers how bare the house was when they carried the boxes in; very little furniture, no tree. Just an elderly grandmother in a rocking chair, a single lamp, and some little kids sitting around the room.

She had told them there wouldn't be a Christmas
And the look on their faces I still see
I'm glad for what we did, 'cause we made some happy kids
Dance around where there might have been a tree

We wrote this in Nashville in a hotel room on June 26, 1978. We recorded it the very next day and still did not have a title for it. We were calling it "The Joy to the World Song" and told Jerry we'd call him later in the week and give him a title as soon as we came up with one.

"A Christmas Medley"

For the closing slot on the album, let's close big with the best there is. And to come up with the best, we each simply picked our favorite carol that we'd like to sing.

Harold: "Silent Night"
Don: "O Holy Night"
Phil: "The First Noel"
Lew: "It Came Upon the Midnight Clear"
Then we all went back and sang "Silent Night" as the finale.

We had put together our first Christmas album, and it was a fine mixture of religious and secular songs of the past and the present. It was a great success for us. It went gold, platinum, and then double platinum. But that was never our goal. It was the result but never our goal. We wanted to create something that would live on each year with some meaning and something that might bring joy to our fans and to future folks who might discover our music. Sounds corny? I guess it is but that's who we were and I'm proud of us for what we did and how we did it.

20

The Originals

1979

Four guys standing out in the middle of a field with sport coats on. You can't get a more original picture for an album cover than that. Well, yes, you can, but that wasn't the point. The border of the picture was what told the story this time. There were sketches of firsts and original things all around our photograph to tie in with the title of the album. The Liberty Bell, Babe Ruth, Gene Autry, the Flag, the first car, George Washington, and a little Methodist church in Lyndhurst, Virginia. What was so special about that little country church, you may ask. I'll tell you when we get there. And I'll tell you about all the famous musicians and the original licks they created that were reenacted on a particular song here. This one was certainly a joy to put together and to listen to again after all these years. The memories are vivid and a little startling. And away we go!

"How to Be a Country Star"

We were nominated for "Group of the Year" for the Country Music Awards in 1978. (We won nine times, but who's counting?) We were booked to sing a song for the live CMA show on October 9th. We wanted to do something besides plug our new single, as everyone always did, so less than a month before, on September 11, on our tour bus somewhere between Wheaton, Minnesota, and York, Pennsylvania, Harold and I wrote this song.

There are questions we're always hearing, everywhere we go
Like, "How do I cut a record, or get on a TV show?"
Well, it takes more than just ambition and three chords on an old guitar
There's a few more things you ought to learn to be a country star

We honored a lot of folks in the industry by mentioning their names and their gimmicks and their styles. It was written as a fun song for a TV show to be sung in front of a live audience of our peers, some of whom were in attendance that night.

You got to learn to sing like Waylon
Or pick like Jerry Reed
Yodel like Jeanne Shepard
Or write songs like Tom T.

When we hit the first note, we knew it was a winner. The crowd was with us. They were all smiles and applauding.

Put a cry in your voice like Haggard
Learn Spanish like Johnny R.
Whisper like Bill Anderson
And you'll be a country star

You can call it up on YouTube and watch it and see what I'm talking about. It was a perfect stage piece. And I only wish we could have gone on long enough to mention everyone in that star-studded Opry House. They all deserved the recognition for whatever special talent they had brought to making country music what it was at the time.

Be rich like Eddy Arnold
Say you're making more than you are
Get a gimmick like Charley Pride got
And you'll be a country star

But the final verse and punch line was the soul of the whole piece. I know as sure as there is a mountain in Tennessee that this whole thing would flop in today's social climate. We were making innocent and fun jokes, but today it would be called some sort of feminine assault and our career would have been ruined on the spot. As it was, thank the good Lord it was 1978, and the ladies, for whom we had great respect, laughed along with the men, who meant no harm from the bottom of their hearts.

But if you have no talent
And if you're not a male
If you're built somewhat like Dolly
And have a face like Crystal Gayle
Come backstage and ask for
Harold, Phil, Don or Lew
And we'll see you get auditioned
For The Statler Brothers Revue

That night, we were swarmed with questions of when was the record coming out. We felt the urgency and released a single, leading the album by weeks. As a matter of fact, by the time this album was released on March 29, 1979, "How to be a Country Star" was already number seven on the national charts.

After the singing of this song that night on the awards show, we presented the "Female of the Year" award. Instead of just reading the five nominees, we sang this special verse to the same tune:

188

First there's Janie Fricke
Then comes Crystal Gayle
Emmylou and Dolly, too
And Barbara Mandrell
Only one will win it
And to choose is quite a chore
We'll give you the winner
And we'll take the other four

Just for the record, Crystal Gayle won.

The next spring Kenny Rogers won big time at the Academy of Country Music Awards, and in his acceptance speech he said, "Now maybe I'll get mentioned in a Statler Brothers song."

"When the Yankees Came Home"

This is a terrible thing to say about a song of my own, but I still get chills and tears at the end of this song every time I hear it. I take little credit for that, as I've already said I know the words I use are only on loan to me. But this one fell in place and found a spot in my heart that only a few others of my songs permanently occupy. If I had to pick a list of my favorites of those I have had the privilege of creating, this would be one of the top four. Stay tuned to this channel and I'll tell you the other three when we get to them.

I was at home when I wrote it on our old player piano (the "player" part didn't work anymore). The New York Yankees and the LA Dodgers were in a World Series battle. And I was glued to the TV. The game that night was in Yankee Stadium, and they were interviewing Don Sutton, the future Hall of Famer and starting pitcher for the Dodgers. The interviewer asked Don, "What are you feeling tonight pitching in this historic arena?" Don said, "When I was a kid, I always dreamed of pitching in Yankee Stadium. Of course, in my dreams I was pitching for the Yankees." Wow! I was touched by that story. So heartfelt and real. But as the series went along, things didn't work out perfectly for Don that year. A few nights later, Catfish Hunter beat him and his Dodgers, and New York ended it in LA and won the whole thing in six. The news, in announcing they would cover the team landing victoriously back on New York soil, said, "Film at 11. The Yankees come home."

I had my title, and from all of this, I closed myself in my home office and wrote a baseball love song. It was October 17, and I didn't come out until I had told the fictitious story of a young pitcher who climbed to the top, losing the love of his life along the way, as so many do in pursuing their passions. She, having a family of her own, watched his big moment on TV with her two sons surrounding her and felt things no one else in the world knew were swelling up inside of her and him with every pitch.

And sure enough, there he stood like he always said he would
He was doing what he always wanted to
That New York team he loved to hate was standing at the plate
And only she knew his dream was coming true

He proudly stood his ground out there on the mound
Facing the world all alone
And the family wondered why there were tears in Mamma's eyes
'Cause she cried when the Yankees came home

Don Sutton and I got to be friends years later. We met at a Baltimore/Yankees game in Baltimore one summer and I told him this story. He loves country music, I love baseball, and we always have a lot to talk about.

"Here We Are Again"

It was the third week in March of 1975, and we were playing a rodeo in Lubbock, Texas, for four days. We did a thirty-minute show every night at 7:30, and there is just so much you can do to fill the rest of the time on the road. We went to the movies twice to kill an afternoon, *Earthquake* and *Murder on the Orient Express*. Then you pretty much had to read, which I always enjoy, or write, which I eventually did. This love song, about two lovers back together and not knowing why or where it might take them, was born somewhere on a sleepless Texas night that week. These words and this melody lay in my notebook for nearly four years before I pitched it to the other guys for this album. We put it on tape in the studio on January 15,

1979. We introduced it on *Hee-Haw* on June 6 of '79, and it was the second single from this album.

> *So here we are again*
> *Ain't we a sight again*
> *Is this a dream we're in*
> *Or is it love?*

"Where He Always Wanted to Be"

Harold and I, on any given day, would tackle the most far-fetched ideas the imagination could grasp and make a song out of it. It took almost nothing to set us off. Something someone said, just seeing an interesting character on the street, anything to make our eyes meet and we were looking for pencil and paper. We were discussing a person we both knew at the time and trying to figure out some of his motives in a business situation, and Harold said, with tongue in cheek, "But he's in country music where he always wanted to be." My immediate response was, "Hand me a pencil." We went into the Statler offices at midnight on March 31, 1978, and wrote this little magic trick of a song in the middle of the night.

The story is of any aspiring young man in the 1950s wishing to find his way into the country music industry and all the influences he experiences along the way.

> *While his friends were rockin' 'round the clock inside the high school gym*
> *He was out back in his pickup truck pickin' up WSM*
> *Carl Perkins and Roy Orbison were blastin' in the hall*
> *Outside Carl Smith and Roy Acuff and the "Wabash Cannonball"*

Throughout the song, country stars were mentioned or implied, and each time we accented the lines with familiar musical trademark sounds. Again, Jerry Kennedy worked tirelessly in putting all this together and making it make sense in a harmonious way.

> *He told everyone who'd listen, "I'm gonna be a star"*
> *They'd smile and keep on walkin' and say, "Yeah, I'm sure you are"*

He'd shake his fist and tell them, "Just you wait and see
Today you are country music but tomorrow I will be"

We called on so many friends and acquaintances to come in the studio and play just five seconds of their special licks and sounds, and every one of them so graciously did exactly what we asked of them.

Two kids he never gets to see and will never get to know
But he's had eighteen number one records in a row
But he never sees the lights of home 'cause there's no home to see
But he's in country music where he always wanted to be

These are the people who came in and did us a favor of a lifetime. God bless them, everyone!

Ray Edenton, our trusty rhythm guitar player on nearly every record we ever recorded, played the old Jimmie Rodgers guitar lick.

Scotty Moore, Elvis's original guitarist, recreated his own lick for us. (We knew Scotty from the days when he was a sound engineer for the Johnny Cash TV show back in '69 to '71.)

Mac Wiseman played the famous bluegrass guitar riff. Who better than our old Virginia buddy, Mac!

Carl Perkins. Need I say more? One of the closest and dearest friends we ever had in or out of the music business.

Brother Bashful Oswald, Roy Acuff's right-hand man, doing his famous Dobro slide.

Curly Chalker playing his Hank Thompson steel guitar lick just like he played it for Hank.

Johnny Gimble, who worked with Bob Wills way back when, giving the Bob Wills yell.

Shorty Lavender, playing what we always called the "zip-zip" fiddle intro just like he did when he played with Ray Price on all those early hits.

Ernest Tubb saying, "Aw, Billy Byrd, now."

Billy Byrd then playing his Ernest Tubb lick.

Bob Wootton, our good buddy who replaced Luther Perkins, playing those oh-so-famous six Johnny Cash notes.

Odell Martin playing the guitar break in the style of Merle Travis.

192

Don Helms, who actually was Hank Williams's steel guitar player, doing what he does best.

Grady Martin ending it with the classic final chord of his invention.

This is the kind of thing that made the country music industry what it was. It was professional and yet family at the same time. You called these folks and they came and added to your project, knowing that if they called tomorrow, you'd come for them.

"Mr. Autry"

Gene Autry was the original singing cowboy. He said in his book, "Somebody else may come along who is better, but nobody else can ever be first." He was our hero as kids, and what made him so special was that we got to know him as adults and he was still our hero. We bought his autobiography, *Back in the Saddle Again*, the day it came out, read it, and Harold and I wrote this song traveling between Norman, Oklahoma, and Nashville early in the morning, November 20, 1978. Unbeknownst to us, about ten days later, Gene signed books to each one of us and mailed them to Virginia. And, unbeknownst to him, we'd already read his book and written his song.

Dear Sir, We read your book, and you gave us a closer look
At the hero who helped us know
Right from wrong, Ah, it's been so long
Mr. Autry, We read each page, and even you improved with age
You're still the cowboy that all of us boys
Thought you were

We did a TV Christmas special in Nashville in '85. Gene said he would guest on it if we would come to LA because he just wasn't up to traveling. We did. We sat in his office and he told us Christmas stories. The next day he had us to his house, and then that night he took us to the Angels' baseball game and we sat in his private box with him. He owned the team and we owned the night.

Mr. A., We loved each line. You gave so much in your time

193

From radio to picture shows
And the songs you write, Ah your hat's still white
Mr. Gene, It's another day, and we've grown up but let us say
Just like before and even more
We want to be like you

We heard from a mutual friend, singer Johnny Western, that Gene watched our TV show every Saturday night in the nineties. I can't begin to tell you what that did to us. We grew up watching him and now he was watching us. We sang this song for him one night and gave him a personal and public dedication. We've met a lot of our heroes and some of them didn't hold up. But this one, at ninety-one years old, was still bigger than life.

And Gene, just one more thing.
If the Angels don't look good this spring
Don't worry none, You're still number one
And we still love you

"Nothing as Original as You"

The Statlers and their families were invited to Washington DC for a long Easter weekend by the Air Force Symphony Orchestra in March of 1978. For three days they gave us tours of the city, the White House, the Pentagon, the Smithsonian. They were wonderful hosts to us all, even our small kids. It all culminated with a Statler Brothers concert on Easter Sunday afternoon at Constitution Hall backed by the symphony orchestra. What an incredible sound that filled the overflowing hall and filled our senses with music and memories we will have forever.

We all had been to Washington many times as it is only a three-hour drive from our hometown, Staunton, but the sights and experiences we shared with our young ones made it so very special. Two days after getting home, I sat down at the piano and wrote a love ballad using DC as the background. It is one of the most unique love songs I ever wrote and one I still cherish every time I hear it or even think about it.

And today I saw the first airplane that flew
Saw a dinosaur and a space module, too
Saw Washington's monument and marveled at the view
But even here there's nothing as original as you

One of our favorite old Hollywood character actors, James Whitmore, was doing a one-man show at Ford's Theater (where Lincoln was shot), playing Will Rogers. We went to see him and visited with him after the show. After everyone had left the theater, he came back out and sat with us and the families and told all those old Tinseltown tales we loved to hear, just like Randolph Scott, John Wayne, Gene Autry, and so many others had done before him. We were blessed to be able to mix our business with our hobby and love of film.

Saw a play at Ford's Theater and let me tell you this
The Pentagon is something no one should ever miss
Saw Jefferson's Memorial and I saw Lincoln's, too
I don't think there was one thing I missed seeing except you

As much as I love all of this song, if I had to pick a favorite line that stands out to me, it would be the third line in this chorus:

Today I saw the first airplane that flew
Touched a moon rock and saw a Senator at the zoo
Got lost seven times on Pennsylvania Avenue
(show me anyone who has ever driven in DC who hasn't)
But even here there's nothing as original as you

"Counting My Memories"

Another good one from Kim Reid, Harold's daughter. She was writing more and we were listening closer to everything she pitched us. She has always written solid country and gospel, even as young as she was at the time. This song was the flip side of "Nothing as Original as You," which was our third single from the album and a top-ten hit.

There's an expression among songwriters, "I got a free ride." What that means is they wrote a song that was on the B-side of a hit single. (Today downloaders and digital buyers have no idea what I'm talking about.) For sales, the writer of a B-side got the same money the writer of the A-side got. So, on this one, Kim got a free ride from my song, but just the year before, I got the free ride from her when "I Dreamed About You" was on the flip side of her "Who Am I To Say?" There's also an expression called "Keeping it in the family."

I'm counting my memories, I'm biding my time
I'm so lost without you, I think I'm losing my mind
Why'd she leave me and hurt me and tell me goodbye
I'm counting my memories and biding my time

"A Little Farther Down the Road"

Lew decided to set this one in North Carolina, and I wish I had the information to tell you why and give you some insight into its creation, but I have none of that at hand. I can only tell you we recorded it on January 15, 1979, at a 2 P.M. session at Sound Stage Studios in Nashville. That same afternoon we recorded "Mr. Autry" and "Here We Are Again." It was always our goal to get three songs put down in a three-hour session. Sometimes we got lucky and got four on tape, and sometimes we ran into a snag and only got two down, but that was very seldom. We were always prepared and knew the material and, of course, had the best musicians the town or the country had to offer. This song was a good flavor for this album.

"Just a Little Talk with Jesus"

Never in the twentieth century did four males ever get together to sing gospel music below the Mason-Dixon Line that they didn't eventually sing this Cleavant Derricks classic. Derricks was a black Baptist minister who didn't stop at writing just one that would go down in history. He also wrote "When God Dipped His Love in My Heart" and "We'll Soon Be Done with Troubles and Trials." With all of that said, it is still not the reason it is on this particular album. It's here because this is the original song, the first song ever sung by the group that would become, in time, The Statler Brothers.

In high school, Joe McDorman was asked to provide some special music for a Sunday night program at his church, the Lyndhurst Methodist Church in Lyndhurst, Virginia, just a few miles outside of Staunton. Joe called Lew, Lew called Harold, Harold called Phil, and they sang that night back in June of '55 this song they had gotten together and worked up just that afternoon. The congregation liked it so much, and these teenaged boys liked it so much, they began singing around at other churches and calling themselves the Four Star Quartet. (The Statler Brothers name came later but that was all told in the book *Random Memories*.)

We knew we just had to put that first song on an album with a title of *The Originals*, so we called Joe, who was a very successful businessman, living at the time in Gallatin, Tennessee. We invited him to come sing just the second verse solo. It was a ball for all of us and a memory we were so fortunate to get on record. Because someone asked Joe for a musical favor one long-ago summer night when they were all just boys in their teens, and I was a kid of nine years old hanging around the living room listening to them practice, the Statlers were born.

"For I know the plans I have for you, declares the Lord"—Jeremiah 29:11

"Almost in Love"

We were out on tour again and Harold and I got an idea for a song we thought was really good. We wrote down the lyrics and made notes to remember the melody but never got back to finishing it. It was April of 1977 and this is the chorus we wrote:

I wish I could kiss the shine off your lips
Or mess up the curl in your hair
I'd give anything to taste the smile on your face
Or touch you where no one else would dare

Well, actually we did get back to finishing it, but it was seventeen months later before that day came. To be specific, it was September 19, 1978, in Lake Geneva, Wisconsin. We found it in one of my notebooks and looked at this very intimate and suggestive chorus and wondered what kind of verses we could complement it with. I think we did it very well.

We can only assume the others in this room
Can't tell that we're almost in love
But if anyone should see the way you look at me
They'll surely know what I am thinking of

"The Star-Spangled Banner"

We recorded this little Francis Scott Key number because we didn't know of anyone else who had ever included it on a commercial album, and what could be more original than doing that for the first time? We used it for the rest of our career to open every one of our concerts just as if it were a sporting event. A gentleman by the name of Sky Parker came in and recorded just before the music started, "Ladies and gentlemen, The Statler Brothers singing our National Anthem." This was not on the album but was put on single copies of the song that were sent out to every major league ballpark.

In 1982, when Lew retired and Jimmy Fortune joined us, Jimmy put his voice alongside Harold's, Phil's, and mine, and we had the version we would use until the end. The inclusion of this song on this album created a lot of requests for us to sing it live at so many events. We have sung it to open games for the MLB, the NBA, the NFL, and various NCAA teams and just about any other acronym you can think of. This hymn of patriotism was so associated with our live concerts that it always was the first thing you would hear at a Statler Brothers show. People looked forward to that. Our audience always stood with either hat in hand, hand on heart, or at attention with equal weight on both feet. They were respectful, thoughtful, and considerate people. We have the best fans in the world. They understood that patriotism should never be political.

21

The Best of The Statler Brothers
Rides Again Volume II

1979

Looking back, this may be the most interesting cover picture we ever did. Also, the longest title we ever had. And there was only one song on it that had never been released before. Let me explain.

With our sincere thanks to the good Lord and the loyal fans, we had accumulated enough hits to justify a second "Best of" album. Ten songs were hits from the past few years with one new one that would be the single. Then we wanted to do something different and memorable for the picture on the front, so we called up the cowboy from not-too-deep inside us and became our own western heroes. With four matching black outfits and hats in hand, we rented four white Arabian horses to round out the drugstore cowboy look. We convened at a corral on Harold's farm with the photographers and the horse trainers and proceeded to bring the Old West to life in the East. The four horses were named Serretta, Tom Collins, Kaweah, and Ph-Mondeene.

What we immediately found out when we mounted our steeds was that we had been delivered three stallions and one mare. Now this is a bad mix whether you're talking horse or human, but it is really treacherous when you're mounted atop, side by side, trying to smile for the camera as three stallions decide simultaneously they want to talk to the mare. The pose we had envisioned of the four of us on horseback sitting in a row smilingly facing the lens became a nightmare.

We finally had to dismount and just hold the horses for the quick snap you see on the album sleeve. The four individual pictures were taken in a far-off field, each of us on the same horse while handlers were loading the other three in the horse trailers.

By my count, this is our twenty-first album. If this count is off from other published sources, here are a few reasons why:

1. I am not counting compilation albums.
2. I count the "Best of" albums, where other published sources do not.
3. I count *Holy Bible* as one album. It was a double and some count it as two.

Ten of the songs here were written about in previous chapters—"Do You Know You Are My Sunshine," "Here We Are Again," "The Movies," "Your Picture in the Paper," "Some I Wrote," "How Great Thou Art," "How to Be a Country Star," "Silver Medals and Sweet Memories," "Who Am I to Say," "The Official Historian on Shirley Jean Berrell"—so I will only cover the new one.

"(I'll Even Love You) Better Than I Did Then"

Such a soft and up-close song. It was a very warm recording and performance; very romantic and sexy with some clever twist of phrase.

200

When you're lying there in bed
Late at night and all alone
With nothing on but the radio
Listening to the midnight man
Taking telephone requests
Playing songs that you and I used to know

As I listen to all these songs from so many years ago, I can often tell if they were recorded with a single in mind. I can hear it in the instruments, the voices, the little special production efforts. This one was a single in our mind from day one. We took it in the studio October 21, 1976, and it lay in the can for three years before we decided what album we wanted it on. It did everything we wanted it to do, as it was a top-ten song and helped make this second album, the best The Statler Brothers had to offer, become gold.

Do you ever think of me and all the times that we
Wasted, and can't get back again
But if we ever do, Honey, I promise you
I'll even love you better than I did then

There's an old technique they teach you in acting school about how to read a line. You approach it by putting the emphasis on different words in the line until you hit on the one that best denotes the tone and meaning you want. Example:

I *never* meant to shoot him.
I never *meant* to shoot him.
I never meant to *shoot* him.

I loved that we used this method on the ending. We sang the tag line three times, three ways, and gave it new meaning with each reading.

We were on a long thirteen-day Canadian and North West USA tour in September of '76. Bobby Bare was with us the whole trip. About halfway through, Elektra Records called and asked if we would put a new artist on our tour. They said they would pay him and it wouldn't cost us a thing. They just wanted him exposed to a lot of fans. We said sure and that was the beginnings of Eddie Rabbitt, a fine performer and a wonderful man who did so much in such a short time here on Earth.

So, it was during this tour that Harold and I started writing "Better Than I Did Then," somewhere in the cold North Country. We didn't finish it until a month later when we were in Nashville for a series of sessions. October 20, we added a verse and a little polish and recorded it the next day. To be honest, if it weren't for my voluminous note-keeping, I would never believe how often Harold and I cut it so close on readying a song for a recording session. This happened more than I realized in my memory. With touring, recording, TV, writing songs, writing our stage shows, and just generally taking care of business, we sometimes were just too tired to finish a song in one sitting. That's where my notebooks came in handy. We'd just flip back, find the unfinished page, and go to work!

The Statler Brothers

A Photo Album

Looking back I'd say I had the best childhood that money just can't buy
from "You Can't Go Home"

My mom and dad, Frances and Sidney at their 30th anniversary. We referred to them often in our songs. I loved them more than my next breath.

Carry me back and make me feel at home
Let me cling to those memories that won't let me alone
from "Carry Me Back"

A very young Bro Harold and me and his '51 Chevy in front of the house where we grew up.

And Bobby, I'd love to see him again and I would if I could
from "Carry Me Back"

Summer of 1960. Harold, Phil, my best friend, Bobby, and me. Bobby died six months later on Christmas Eve. I did a lot of growing up that year.

Do your wives ever travel with you on the road?
Did you fall out with ole Johnny? Does Harold really sing that low?
from "The Statler Brothers Quiz"

John and me sharing a dressing room and no, we did not fall out with "ole Johnny." He and June guested on our 30th anniversary television special in 1994 and after that we were at his house and sadly at his funeral.

It started March of '64, many years ago
We were hired by Johnny Cash to open up his show
Four boys, a worn-out Cadillac with a road map on the dash
For the next eight and one-half years, we got paid by Cash
from "We Got Paid by Cash"

We left John's employ in December of '72 to put our own concert tours together. This was the last check he wrote me and I never cashed it. It's worth more than money to me.

If that ole hat I wore could only talk;
and tell some of the things that it has seen
There're stories that would fill it to the brim;
if that ole hat could tell it all again"
from "Hat and Boots"

The lucky hat I was wearing our first day at Mercury when we recorded "Bed of Rose's" on September 11, 1970. I brought it to every session thereafter.

I DiDn'T come to kiss the bride
So Don'T seat me on either siDe
I Just came by to see the show
I'm close enough I'll stand right here
I can see and I can hear
I heard it all years ago

I hear the organ play a _____ melody
Is that the one they call their song
Church _____
But _____ long can you live _____

I DiDn'T come to Kiss The bride
Nor come to call the groom outside
And I don't _____ to say hello
That's not the reason I came by
I came to day to say goodbye
_____ kissed _____ years ago
to _____

Give the bride _____ my
_____ give them my best
And tell her mom and all the rest
That I was here but _____ have to go
_____ lines too long outside
And I DiDn'T come to Kiss The bride
_____ I DiD All that years ago

What God joined together, let no man put asunder
But it sure put us under right or wrong
from "Years Ago"

My original songwriting notes from the night I wrote "Years Ago," years ago. I throw nothing away! (I still have socks I wore in high school.)

THE SATURDAY MORNING RADIO SHOW

OPEN:
BILL CRAMER:
YOU'RE LISTENING TO W E A K RADIO, THE WEAK VOICE OF
RAINBOW VALLEY, WHERE THE BLUE OF THE NIGHT MEETS THE
GOLD OF THE DAY. THE CORRECT RAINBOW VALLEY TIME IS
ABOUT, AH, 9:35 AM and fm. THE LOCAL RAINBOW VALLEY
NEWS AND WEATHER REPORT IS....VERY BAD......VERY BAD.
THE UNOFFICAL TEMPERATURE OUTSIDE OUR STUDIO WINDOW IS
4 DEGREES WITH AN EXPECTED HIGHS TONIGHT OF 95.
AND NOW FOR YOUR SATURDAY MORNING LISTENING PLEASURE,
W E A K PRESENTS ANOTHER WEAK PROGRAM. LESTER MORAN,
THE OLE ROADHOG, AND HIS CADILLAC COWBOYS.

INSTRUMENTAL: *A* LIZA JANE *2 LIZA's I VER + I LIZA*

ROAD HOG:
HEY, HEY AND HOWDY TO EVERYBODY OUT THERE IN RADIO LAND.
MIGHTY NEIGHBORLY OF YOU TO LET US IN YOUR LIVING ROOMS FOR
THE NEXT 15 MINUTES OF GOOD OLE COUNTRY MUSIC. WE'RE COMING
AT YOU THIS MORNING THROUGH THE COURTESY OF BURFORDS BARBER
SHOP. YOU CAN ALWAYS GET CLIPPED AT BURFORDS. THAT'S
B-U-R-F-O-R-D. EVERYBODY GET TRIMMED AT BURFORD'S.
RIGHT NOW, TO START THINGS OFF, LET'S GET OLE WICHITA UP
TO THE MIKE PLAYING TAKE-OFF GUITAR. GOT THAT THING IN
TUNE BOY? WHAT ARE YOU GONNA DO FOR US THIS MORNING?

WICHITA:
GONNA GET HER DOWN INTO THE GEAR OF A AND WE'LL SING A
Hank Thompson RECORD. ONE CALLED HONKY-TONK GIRL. *E*

SONG
CLAP CLAP   MIGHTY FINE, MIGHTY FINE

ROADHOG:
DIDN'T KNOW IF HE WAS GONNA GET THROUGH THAT ONE OR NOT,
CAUSE WE WERE UP LATE LAST NIGHT PICKING AND GRINNING FOR
SOME OF OUR GOOD FRIENDS OVER IN HOGAN COUNTY AT MOOSE LODGE

"Mighty fine. Mighty fine."
—Lester "Roadhog" Moran

The first page of the "Roadhog" script for
the *Country Music Then and Now* album.

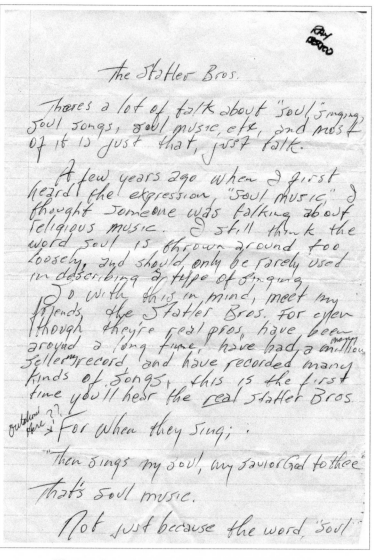

The Statler Bros.

There's a lot of talk about "soul" singing, soul songs, soul music, etc, and most of it is just that, just talk.

A few years ago when I first heard the expression, "soul music," I thought someone was talking about religious music. I still think the word soul is thrown around too loosely, and should only be rarely used in describing a type of singing

So with this in mind, meet my friends, the Statler Bros. For even though they're real pros, have been around a long time, have had a million seller record, and have recorded many kinds of songs, this is the first time you'll hear the real Statler Bros.

outblurb? here For when they sing; .

"Then sings my soul, my savior God to thee" that's soul music.

Not just because the word "soul"

We were there when June became Johnny's loving bride
And we sang the hymn that morning, our buddy Luther died
And we were there when the son was born that filled them both with pride
And we were there when John remembered God was on his side
from "We Got Paid by Cash"

The handwritten liner notes Johnny Cash gave us for our *O Happy Day* album in 1969. I love the scratch-outs and little notes all over it.

is in the lyrics, but because their souls
are singing. ~~Instead I try that~~
~~with the Statler Bros. ~~always~~ you~~
~~have true soul music.~~

And as an artist, I can say that
it's a great experience to sing from
the soul. To sing a religious song
with feeling puts the soul not!
only in communication with it's
Creator, but provides an expansion
and manifestation of the powers
of the Creator.

Here we have four friends of
mine, ~~~~~~~~~~~~~~~~~~ in harmony
with the powers of their Creator!

Here sing the souls of the
Statler Bros.

Be sure to
get —

Johnny Cash

AUTHENTIC

So, Dad, if you can hear us; if there're radios up there.
Turn it up and listen. Your boys are on the air
from "Dad"

―――――――――――

Don, Harold, Sidney (our dad) with Phil and Lew,
ca. 1966 in a theater lobby.

Making memories in everything we do.
Making memories with you, for me, for you
from "Making Memories"

Phil and Wilma, me and Debbie, Harold and Brenda, and Jimmy and Nina at Dollywood in Dolly's dressing room on September 28, 2011. We received a founders' award from the Southern Gospel Music Association.

1. BOOMARANG XXXX   12
2. One size Fits ALL XXX½ 14
3. My only Love XXXX   13½
4. You KNOW I Love you XX   9½
5. One TAKes THe BlAme XXXX 16
6. Give iT youR BesT XX½   13
7. I'm soRRy you HAD to Be the One XX½ 10½
8. One Night AT A Time XX½   13½
9. Memory LANe XXX 11
10. IF IT MAKes ANy Difference XXXX   13
11. Hollywood XXX½ 13
12. He DRops By XX½ 9

13. ATLANTA Blue XXXX
14. No Love LosT XXX
15. AngeL iN HeR face XXX½
16. MARy Lou Xxx 16

AtLANtA Blue -s
One TAKes the BlAme -s
AMAZIN New face - uP
one siZe FiTs ALL -s
my only Love -s
One Night At ATIme -uP
Give iT youR BesT - uP
IF iT MAKes ANy DiFF -s
Hollywood -
No Love LosT -
MARy Lou
BoomarAng
He Drops By
You KNow I Love

Don't ever bother to give it at all
if you can't always give it your best
from "Give It Your Best"

Our Four-Star system at work in choosing songs for the *Atlanta Blue* album. Note that we considered sixteen but chopped it down to the ten songs we thought were best.

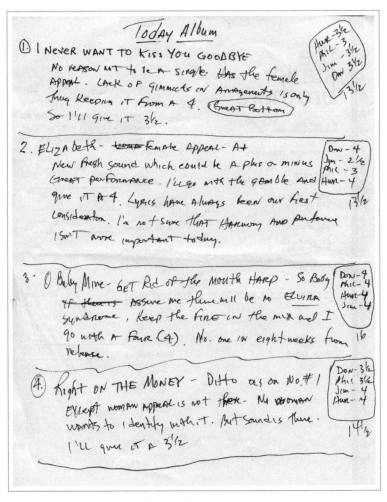

It takes more than just ambition
and three chords on an old guitar
from "How to be a Country Star"

Our Four-Star system at work after the sessions; a page of my notes analyzing what should be the next single and then our individual votes.

```
                    (MOSE)
  "The Kingsmen,"    Arbor Hill Dec. 31, 1960
  First Half.
  1.  Hide Thou Me-- D-Eb.
  2.  Search Me Lord--Eb
  3.  Amazing Grace--E-G-C.
  4.  This Little Light Of Mine.   Eb
  5.  Heavenly Love---G.
  6.  Do You Know My Jesus--Bb--Eb
  7.  Climbing Up The Mountain,--G.
  8.  He's Everywhere.-- Db
  9.  To Me It's So Wonderful.--D-G-C-
  10.  I'm Redeemed.  Bb -F
  11 Something Within.
```

I grew up a child of the fifties…
television was my friend,
I Love Lucy, Rin Tin Tin
from "A Child of the Fifties"

I was only fifteen years old and we were singing gospel songs and calling ourselves The Kingsmen. But even then, we were singing "Hide Thou Me" and "Mose" was a nickname for our piano player Sunny Samples.

He's done everything he wanted to
and more than he planned
from "Where He Always Wanted to Be"

At our Country Music Hall of Fame induction on June 29, 2008. One of the most emotional nights of my life. From the far left on the front row: Emmylou Harris, Tom T. and Dixie Hall, Phil, Wilma, Debbie, me, Brenda, Harold, Nina, Jimmy, and all of our kids seated behind us.

And the words sound so homey; so warm and so right
Bringing back memories like a friend in the night
Counting the sunsets and the days left to go
And listening to your life on a friend's radio
from "A Friend's Radio"

Standing: Harold, me, Phil, and Lew. Sitting at the desk is our producer and friend, Jerry Kennedy. He kept us on the radio for a quarter of a century. We still see each other and talk on the phone all the time. This book is dedicated to him.

22

10th Anniversary

1980

The reason behind this title was our tenth year with Mercury Records. No matter what field of music they are in, artists love to trash their record labels. It gives them someone to blame if the last couple of releases didn't hit. If their last album tanked, they can call out the producer or the promotions department or the marketing department. If they didn't fare well during the last awards show, it's because the label didn't support them with block voting. And, of course, it's always easier to blame the company than themselves. I could make you a list of the many singers we have sat with and listened to their complaints about these very issues over the years. Matter of fact, when two artists get together and the conversation heads toward the music industry (as it always will), the record label is always at the top of the list. We experienced some sour feelings in our first five years in the business with Columbia, but once we moved over to Mercury, we always had a great relationship with executives in Chicago, New York, and Nashville and all their departments. I believe this was mainly due to our producer and friend, Jerry Kennedy, who was also a vice president with the company. This album was in celebration of a decade of happiness with all these folks. On the back cover we dedicated the album to Jerry and a number of other good people at the label and closed it with this paragraph: "And to the current company President, Bob Sherwood, whom we have not known long enough to dedicate a whole album to, we dedicate any one song of his choice."

We never let a chance go by without making even the president of the whole company the butt of a joke. Bob had a great sense of humor and he took it well. He must have, as the album went gold.

You may notice that beginning with this album, we went from using eleven songs to using ten songs on each, a policy that would hold forth for the rest of our career. This was a good business move for us for many reasons. Fewer good songs were needed for each album, royalties provided for publishers and writers were now split ten ways instead of eleven, and one song would not make a difference as to whether someone would buy the item or not. This was the way the industry was headed. However, I do find it interesting that we went to ten songs on an album called *10th Anniversary*. Coincidence.

The cover was shot in Staunton at the Woodrow Wilson Birthplace. The twenty-eighth president of the United States was born in our hometown, and that is his personal 1920 Pierce-Arrow our tuxedoed selves are leaning against. It is a very classy picture of us and the car, but as I look at it today, all I seem to be able to see is the size of those 1980 bowties.

"Don't Forget Yourself"

This was a really different song for me to write, structurally. The opening line is so very important to any song, and I really like the unusual opener here. It is as if it starts in the middle of the story instead of at the beginning, and you have to do a little catch up to learn what is going on.

You're right we both could use a small vacation
It may not work but then again it might

You can go to California to see your mother
And maybe when you get back things might be right

It is rather a standard in songwriting that the verse is musically lower in range than the chorus. Going into most choruses, the song gets a lift and it registers higher on the scale. However, this, too, is backward in that sense. I actually took the opening lines of the chorus down instead of up.

Don't forget your raincoat, it gets stormy in the west
Don't forget your swimsuit, you'll have sunshine at its best
And don't forget to take some pictures everyone will want to see
And don't forget yourself when you're that far away from me

I wrote it at home on my piano on April 5, 1977. We recorded it the next month on May 25, right in the middle of recording our *Short Stories* album. We liked it so much and kept it in the can for three years, waiting for the right time to release it.

"The Kid's Last Fight"

We've been asked what led us to this old song many times. My best answer is just a childhood memory. Frankie Laine had a medium-sized hit with this in 1954, and I remember playing it over and over so much from his *Command Performance* album. (The cover was a picture of him and Queen Elizabeth in black and white.) It had that driving beat and a great narrative that lent itself so well to our style of storytelling. Note the tuba we used playing the bass line to give it that antiquated sound the tale suggests. And even though there did happen to be a middleweight boxer back in the late 1800s named Kid McCoy, this was not a true story. It all came from the brain of songwriter Bob Merrill, who was a Broadway writer at the time. He also wrote lots of hits for Patti Page, Jimmie Rodgers, Rosemary Clooney, and Perry Como.

The sustaining chord we hit before the final note gives a reverence and sadness to Kid McCoy's demise, and I have often wished we had sung this one on stage a few times. It was a jewel!

"How Are Things in Clay, Kentucky?"

Now we're getting personal, but this might be my favorite song that Harold and I wrote together. We were riding on the bus through the hot summer night of August 25, 1979. We were sitting up in the lounge with a guitar while all the others were asleep in their beds in the back. It was 2 A.M. when we finished, and we were somewhere between Milwaukee and Staunton. I say finished, but actually I should have said, "When we stopped" because we had everything written except the first line and title.

How are things in _____, Kentucky
Bet you thought I'd never care
There was a time when I felt lucky
Just to be away from there

We could not come up with a one-syllable town in the state of Kentucky. (Don't even try.) We picked our brains and scanned the road Atlas so long that we finally decided to just make up a town. We considered Bell or Lee. I have, in one of my trusty old notebooks that I keep all of my hand-written song lyrics in, with dates and footnotes, the opening line and title we decided on that morning as:

How are things in Gray, Kentucky

Sometime before the session, we scrutinized the Rand McNally one more time, and there it was! Providence again saved the day. God looks after fools and hillbilly songwriters, even when they are one and the same.

Today if you look up Clay, Kentucky, on the Internet it will say:

Western Kentucky
Webster County
Population 1179 people
Named after Henry Clay

At the bottom of the page it will close with:

This city was featured in The Statler Brothers' song "How Are Things in Clay, Kentucky?" (1980)

What it doesn't say is that we came nowhere close to doing it as good as Wilson Fairchild would do it thirty-seven years later.

We sang it on stage often. Harold would play the Dobro, Lew the mandolin (later Jimmy, the mandolin), and I played guitar. The third verse is an all-time favorite of anything my brother and I ever wrote:

I'm getting blue for the bluegrass
And how the old folks are at home
Just let me do the talkin'
'Cause I know you're not alone
I hear kids back there playin'
I hope he don't know it's me
Jesus knows I still love you
And I just had to call and see
How things are in Clay, Kentucky

"One Less Day"

We were looking for a new encore song for our concerts when Harold and I sat down to write this one. On October 29 of '79 we wrote the opening verse, which addressed our need for a closing song just perfectly:

I've enjoyed being here with you
We sure had a high ole time
But there's something better coming
That I can't get off my mind

Then when we got back to finishing it with another verse and chorus over two months later on November 5th, it took on a life of its own and turned into a flat-out gospel song:

I've got one more day behind me
How many are left I don't know

But I'm getting closer to Jesus
I've got one less day to go

It was a rouser with all of the key changes getting higher and higher as we went. It was good on the album, and it rocked a lot of coliseums and auditoriums as our stage show climaxed to a fever pitch. I can remember walking off stage to this one still ringing in the air, so many nights, so exhausted and spent we had to drag ourselves up the steps of the bus. Such wonderful memories.

"Nobody Wants to Be Country"

In the decade of the seventies, we were seeing the traditional sounds that had been the backbone of the country music industry slowly, yet surely, being forsaken. Country artists were aiming for the pop charts with each new release. It gave them a broader base if they could crossover to the Hot 100 and join the ranks of another field. It also often lost them some of their country base. They were going with beats and guitar breaks and lyrics that Nashville just did not recognize. It was a dangerous and risky move to overtly make. We spilled over into the pop charts many times with our singles and albums but never, never once tried to. If it happened, it happened, but we stayed true to our country roots and felt it our tongue-in-cheek duty to make a statement about it. So, again, with a late-night visit to our offices, on May 29, 1979, Harold and I decided to tackle the topic. And we did it with aplomb and a smile:

Nobody wants to be country, everybody wants to go pop
They've traded in their saddle, and they all try to straddle
The road that will take them to the top
They put their steel in hock and add a little rock
And wind up something they're not
Nobody wants to be country they want to go pop

We recorded it in April of '80. We introduced it to the TV public two months later when we hosted the *Music City News Awards* show. The next day, June 10th, we sang it on *Hee-Haw*. Two weeks later we sang it on the *Mike Douglas Show*, the biggest national talk/variety show at the time. We were on a roll and what appeared to be a mission.

It's a downright riddle what happened to the fiddle

And where did the banjo go
I'll tell you, friend, a mandolin
Won't get you on a TV show

Marty Stuart played the mandolin on the record, but on stage it was back to Lew, with Harold and me on the Dobro and guitar. The only thing we didn't do was release it as a single. Looking back today, I'm not sure why. I feel certain we discussed it but I can't say for sure. It was a great stage song, a great topic in interviews, and another image builder for the Statlers in relation to our being loyal and true to ourselves and those who loved us, the fans.

Nobody wants to be country, everybody wants to go pop
They got rid of their boots and Nudie suits
And now we've got a brand-new crop
That's waitin', O Lordy, for the Top 40
To make them something they're not
Nobody wants to be country, they want to go pop

To make the exaggerated contrast between old pop and country on the record we had the pickers do the famous Lawrence Welk riff at the end. I realize you have to be 100 years old, as I am, to remember LW, but those guys jumped on it and made it fit and it is still hilarious to this day.

We'll be the only ones left in country who didn't go pop!

"We Got Paid by Cash"

We had told our beginnings with Johnny Cash so many times for newspapers, magazines, radio, and TV interviews that Harold and I resolved it was time to set it all to music. Back on the bus and leaving Lakeland, Florida, for Augusta, Georgia, we wrote all night until 7 o'clock the next morning, January 25, 1980. We told the Johnny Cash/Statler Brothers story as succinctly and honestly in five verses and a chorus as it could be told.

It started March of '64 many years ago
We were hired by Johnny Cash to open up his show
Four boys, a worn-out Cadillac with a roadmap on the dash
For the next eight and one-half years we got paid by Cash

209

It was a very busy time in our career. We had been gone from John's employ for eight years and our paths seldom crossed anymore. We would see one another backstage at awards shows, where all country artists would converge and socialize, but there was never a lot of visiting time. We heard he liked the song and was honored by it, but it wasn't John's nature to go out of his way to let us know that. The chorus is the most touching and sensitive part of the song, then and now.

We were there when June became Johnny's loving bride
And we sang the hymn that morning our buddy Luther died
And we were there when the son was born that filled them both with pride
And we were there when John remembered God was on his side

I can so clearly recall the morning after we wrote it, singing it to Phil and Lew. They listened intently and their approval told us we had covered the facts and feelings we had set out to do.

We summed it up with a mention of all those lovely folks who made our early lives in this business a pleasure and a success. And on the end, we *sang* the famous Cash/Luther guitar lick with the haunting "Ring of Fire" trumpets in the background. We loved all those people.

Now John will tell you there were years when times were good and bad
But we can tell you they were some of the best we ever had
Carl Perkins and the Carters and the Tennessee Three
We were one big happy family and would have done it all for free

"Old Cheerleaders Cry"

A new songwriting team is born. Kim, Harold's daughter, who had written a fabulous hit song for us two years before, "Who Am I To Say," joined her dad for a solid country tearjerker. It's all about the sadness of looking back on youth where all the days were roses compared to today's clouds.

There must be someplace for her to go
Where are all those friends that she used to know
They might be the reason for the tears in her eyes
When the team is gone, old cheerleaders cry

210

Kim has told me how her dad would drill her about iambic pentameter or, in simpler terms, rhythm of words per line. They have to meter out, and the stress has to be on the right syllable to make it musical and flowing. It's something that comes natural after a time but is always in the back of your mind. He taught her well and she continued to write more for us as time went on.

"'Til the End"

I'm going out on a limb and tell you I love this song. As was usual, though I didn't realize it at the time, I didn't write it in one sitting. I started it in January of '79 and finished it off March 3rd, on a Sunday afternoon. The seventies was as wild a decade as the sixties got credit for being. There were leftover hippies, but it was an even more "Me" age than the previous ten years. My inspiration for this song is in the song itself. I was at a gas station one day and saw a young girl in a tank top and bell-bottom jeans that covered her feet getting her rusty old van gassed up. As she pulled away and whizzed past me, I had to smile at the sign she had taped to the back window. That's all it took for me to head home and put it on paper.

Goodbye, so long, I love you
Were the last words she spoke
Then she left for California
In a van and a cloud of smoke
With a suitcase full of blue jeans
And a strong desire for change
And a sign in her window
That said Home on the Range

Jerry Kennedy often came out of the control room and joined us and the pickers in the studio. That's him in all his glory on the Dobro guitar. And the Statlers on the chorus with the aftertime is the best example of an ex-gospel quartet singing country music one could ever possibly want.

As for the writer, well, it didn't take me long to put myself in the story of her adventure. By the second verse I had made a love song out of a gas station near-encounter.

211

I know she's never been happy
And I'm afraid she'll never be
Though she's so much younger than I am
She'll wind up older than me
So Lord, if you will keep an eye out
For things her eyes can't see
And if she gets into trouble
Send her home to me

"Nobody's Darlin' but Mine"

We wanted a country standard to round out the album, and what better one could you find than this old Gene Autry hit written by Louisiana Governor Jimmie Davis? Davis held the office two different times and kept up his show business career throughout his political profession. He even had a number-one hit record, "There's a New Moon Over My Shoulder," in 1945, while he was in office. He wrote standards such as "You Are My Sunshine" and this one that Harold and Lew shined on. It flows, easy and laid-back. Country music as it should be.

Jerry Kennedy grew up as a member of the Louisiana Hayride in his hometown of Shreveport. He knew the governor and played lead guitar for him a number of times. He also taught the gov's son to play the guitar. Are you ready for this? Jerry gave the boy weekly guitar lessons when the boy was eight and Jerry was...eleven! I wouldn't tell it if it weren't true. Two dollars and fifty cents a lesson. I just got off the phone with JK and I'm still laughing about it.

We met Jimmie Davis one night at the annual BMI Awards in Nashville. It is always an honor for me to shake the hands of the legends who paved the way for all of us who followed. He was certainly one of those heroes.

"Charlotte's Web"

The movie *Smokey and the Bandit II* was the follow up to the original blockbuster. It was an era when Clint Eastwood and Burt Reynolds were loading up their movies with hot country music acts. Jerry Reed was one of the actors, so the trend just happened to go to our field of the industry. The movie opens with a scene of the Statlers singing "Do You Know You Are My Sunshine" at an outdoor show as a plane flies over and dumps bright orange paint on us. That's all you see or hear of us until down near the middle of the story where we sing "Charlotte's Web" over a segment of Burt playing with a traveling elephant. As pretty a song as this is, the whole punch to it is that the Charlotte of the title is this elephant. We did a great job with it and released it as a single and it was a top-five hit. The movie was a hit and we got a lot of juice out of it on stage. Three West Coast writers, Cliff Crofford, John Durrill, and Snuff Garrett, wrote it for us.

Back to that bright orange paint that got dropped on us. We had trouble enough getting it out of our hair and off our skin, but the handmade red and white suits we had on looked to be a hopeless mess. Universal Studios promised to replace them as they had ruined them. And even though they were shocked to learn how much they cost, when we got home, a large five-figure check from them was waiting for us at our offices. But before cashing it, we took the four heavily stained suits to our local dry cleaners, and they were able to bring them back to life and looking brand new for $50 apiece. We sent the money back to Universal and thanked them for their concern. They called when they got the uncashed check and said they had never had anyone return that kind of money to them. They were in shock. I guess they weren't used to dealing with honest people.

23

Years Ago

1981

I think the liner notes on the back of this album tell the story of where we were in time and spirit when we recorded these songs. I share those liners with you now:

> *On the front cover of this album we are standing on the stage of the old Beverley Manor Elementary School in our hometown, Staunton, VA. Harold, Lew and Don spent their grade school years in these buildings. Harold, Phil and Lew won their first talent contest on this very stage. Tom Thumb weddings, basketball games, recess fights, marble tournaments, softball games, lunch lines and a thousand other memories are still alive in its vacant halls and empty rooms and in our minds.*

We recently purchased these old school buildings to turn these memories into our office complex. And to all those teachers who told us, 'Walk, don't run in the halls,' we're walking those halls now. And to all those teachers who tried to get us to work in those classrooms, well, we're finally working in those classrooms.

And sometimes late at night when you walk through there by yourself, you can still hear the laughter from the playground, the clatter from the lunchroom, the bouncing of a ball in the gym and smell the books in the library and the oil on the hardwood floors and feel the chalk on your fingers and a spring breeze through an open window and you're touched by it all but you can't see anything because there are tears in your eyes. And then you realize those school days weren't so bad after all.

—Harold, Lew, Phil and Don

It was the site of our offices and the Statler headquarters for the next twenty-one years until we retired in 2002. We saw to it that it became a school again. Today it is Grace Christian School, and a lot of our grandkids have gone there or are going there now. It's a nice circle of life in which we take great comfort.

"Don't Wait on Me"

Comedian and centenarian (100 years and seven weeks old) George Burns decided when he was an octogenarian (eighty-four years old) that he was going to cut a country music album. You can't say the old gentleman wasn't game! Mercury signed him and Jerry Kennedy became his record producer. JK asked us for material that might suit this show business icon whom we had always admired, so Harold and I set out to write him some original material. This is how this song was born. It's a comedy twist of things that are never likely to happen, but if they do, then I'll come back to you:

When the sun wakes up in the west and lays its head down in the east
When they ordain Madalyn O'Hair and she becomes a priest
When a San Diego sailor comes home with no tattoo
When the lights go on at Wrigley Field, I'll be coming home to you

Well, the one thing that wasn't likely to happen here was George Burns recording this song. He decided against it but decided to record two other songs we had written. "Just Send Me One" was something I wrote especially for him, and "Whatever Happened to Randolph Scott?" was one Harold and I had cowritten, and it had been a hit years earlier for the Statlers. To quote the venerable Chuck Berry, "It goes to show you never can tell." But we were honored and pleased this show business legend put two of our songs on his album.

But now what to do with this rather clever song Harold and I had put so much work into. We began working on it in July of 1980 while we were on vacation and finally finished it back on tour on August 2, just hours before we went on stage in Milwaukee at the Wisconsin State Fair.

Looking at it closer and with a new eye, we realized this was classic Statler Brothers and if it were a hit on record, it could be a killer stage song. And it was. Both.

> *When you load up on a long shot and he wins by half a nose*
> *When the Fourth of July parade is called because it snows*
> *When the waiting room is empty and the doc says, "Come on in"*
> *When Christmas comes before New Year's, I'll be coming home again*

Just a note here to show that a writer never disregards anything from his mind. When I was about ten years of age, my aunt shared with me a quiz she had brought home from a church Christmas party. One of the fun questions was, "Which comes first—Christmas or New Year's?" I immediately said Christmas because Christmas was always a week before New Year's. She explained I was wrong if you went by the calendar. I learned that night what a trick question was and I've been on the lookout for them all of my life. When we needed a last line for that last verse, it was right there ready to be inked.

But the story with this song just keeps on going. Because of the last line in the *first* verse and the popularity of the song, the Chicago Cubs called and wanted us to sing the National Anthem at the ceremony on August 8, 1988, when they did finally put lights on Wrigley Field. (They were the last MLB holdout on night games.) We were unable to be there and do that, and even when it rained and the festivities were moved to the 9th, we were not available. I always hated we couldn't because it would have been nice to have been an official part of that pop history. This also left us with a little bit of a dilemma for our stage shows. We could no longer sing *When the lights go on at Wrigley Field...*, so we changed it and sang *When they put a dome on Wrigley Field, I'll be coming home to you.* And we sang it that way for the rest of our career.

A perfect performance by all four Brothers, making this such an enjoyable record to listen to and cherish all the memoires that surround it.

"Today I Went Back"

I wrote it in 1978 and it lay around for a few years before we decided it was right for this album. I listen to it today and wonder why it was not a single. It has every element. What a fantastic track by the session pickers: a JK break on the Dobro guitar that kills, and the Statlers singing as good as I've ever heard them. I love the delayed harmony Lew is doing with me on the second verse, Harold's bass lines, the a cappella opening and closing. Wow! A missed opportunity. But it doesn't mean I can't listen to it again before I write about the next song.

The things that we vowed to that nobody else knew
The secrets we made then I still keep today
But memories ain't what I miss when I shut
My eyes at night when I lay down to pray
And today I went back to some memories I had
Some felt so good and others weren't so bad
And they all were of you and how it had been
And with a little help from you I'm going back again

"In the Garden"

What a beautiful hymn, written in 1912 by C. Austin Miles. We had all sung this in church all our lives and it took only a suggestion and a mention of the title for all four of us to jump at the chance to record it. We all did a fabulous job with it, the musicians, each Statler. But there is something about it that makes me cringe when I even think about it. You see, it was my idea to sing it at the accelerated tempo. I thought it would give something new to it. It did, but by the time I realized it didn't really need

217

anything new added to it, it was too late. I have felt all these years that my idea of using this tempo in some way desecrated this classic Biblical story and sweet melody that needed no improving. If anyone has ever listened to it and feels as I do, please forgive me and don't blame anyone besides me. On the other side of that coin, I have heard from so many, many fans who have said it is one of their favorite Statler renditions of an old hymn that we ever did. That helps salve my guilt a little, but I wish we had done it again later in a more conventional way. And I certainly hope that when I get to heaven neither Jesus nor C. Austin Miles asks me about it.

"Chet Atkins' Hand"

Chet was a musical hero to us all, but especially to Lew, who played the guitar so well himself. He had just read Chet's book and added that to all the things we already knew about him and wrote this tribute from his heart, and it was so much fun to sing. Each solo attests to our admiration of this man and what he was as an artist.

Thank you, Les Paul, thank you, Django, thank you, Merle
Are you aware of one great gift you gave the world?
Beyond the craft your hands created on your frets
You had a hand in molding those of Chet's
You set that bashful boy from Knoxville all aglow
Each time he heard you pickin' on the radio
And even though it's God alone who made the man
It took guys like you to mold Chet Atkins' hands

My son Langdon told me just recently that one of the early occasions in his discovery of The Statler Brothers and their harmony was the fourth line of this song. He said when as a kid he heard us sing *You had a hand in molding those of...*in unison and then settling in with full harmony on *Chet*, it opened his eyes to what we were doing. It has become a favorite chord, a favorite musical moment for him. This touches me. It always fulfills me on behalf of the four of us when someone tells me some little thing that we did, maybe without thinking, that impressed them forever. That's why each song and each note is important. You never know when someone is listening who

218

may remember and retain what you did. I certainly have those memories of singers and writers I was influenced by years ago.

Thank you, Maybelle, thank you Knoxville, thank you, Lord
And thanks to who it was that showed Chet his first chord
He's come a million miles since Knoxville and the Strand
I'd go a million miles to shake Chet Atkins' hand

That's Chip Young, a staple on all our sessions, playing the Chet-style finger-picking throughout the song and Pete Wade on the ending playing the famous Chet chords on the electric.

"You'll Be Back (Every Night in My Dreams)"

This was the third single from this album and it did great on the charts. Went to number three and we weren't even planning on it being a single. Lew was sick and not always available in this period of time to do anything more than tour, and we were unsure as to when he might be well enough to get back in the studio to start a new album, so we went with an extra single release to give us a little more time to prepare for the next project.

Wayland Holyfield and Johnny Russell wrote this song and Johnny had a pretty fair hit with it in 1978. Three years before that, he had come to Staunton to be our guest on the Fourth of July. We always made a deal with each of our guests to repay them in any way they wanted us to. We usually appeared at their charity event, but Johnny said he'd let us know. After asking him a number of times, he finally said what he'd really like was for us to record any song he had written of our choice. We agreed and this was our pick.

The ending was pure Statler Brothers at our best. We went out with the title line from the old Gus Kahn standard from the 1920s, "I'll See You in My Dreams."

We never missed the opportunity to have fun even if we were just entertaining ourselves.

"Years Ago"

I had already written and we had recorded and been blessed with a hit of "Your Picture in the Paper." This was about an old love marrying and leaving the past behind, and it was a serious love song. Now, for some strange reason, I began to write about the same topic but in a more humorous vein. Again, I was home during the Christmas season and wrote it December 15, 1979.

I didn't come to kiss the bride, so don't seat me on either side
I just came by to see the show
I'm close enough, I'll stand right here
I can see and I can hear
'Course I heard it all years ago

I remember so well when I first sang it to the guys. We were in a hotel and I had called them over to hear the new song I had written over the holidays. I was sitting on the bed and I sang it through once. As soon as I finished, Harold said, "Sing it again." And when I started to sing it, this time they all three gathered around me on the bed and read my notebook lyrics over my shoulder and sang it with me. I knew we had a hit before we got to the second line.

Give the bride and groom my best, and tell her mom and all the rest
That I was here but really had to go
Reception line's too long outside, and I didn't come to kiss the bride
I did all that years ago

Dailey and Vincent did a tribute album to The Statler Brothers and recorded this song. They did a wonderful job with it, as they did with all of them. Darren Vincent gets a kick out of asking me, "Now why exactly wouldn't that groom shake your hand?" And then he just cackles. He's referring to the last tag line.

There's no reason I should stay, the groom won't shake hands anyway
And I kissed the bride years ago

"Love Was All We Had"

She always brought me presents, whenever she would fly
And always thought it silly, I didn't like the sky
And tease me when I said things, like "shucks" and "bless my soul"
I liked country music, she liked rock and roll

Show me any couple, young, old, married for ten years, married for fifty, who can't identify with contrasting likes and dislikes in their relationship. You only have to come up with one, such as one likes to fly and the other is scared to get both feet off the ground at the same time, and then you can't stop naming them all. That's what I did with this seed of an idea, and I had no problem creating in my mind the little man/woman differences.

We both took communion, in different parts of town
I'd put up the window, she would put it down
I'd wake up with the sunshine, and she never heard the clock
I grew up on country, she was deep in rock

Thanks to JK, the sound of this song is a perfect marriage of the steel guitar and a bed of strings. Making those two musical sounds work was a lot like trying to make these two lovers work out and succeed. The point of the whole lyric was if you had love, that was all that was needed.

Brazenly giving you my favorites again, this final verse is one of the best, in my estimation, that I ever wrote by myself. I was able, thank you, Lord, to use some unordinary examples in expressing the idea:

We both wanted children, but she said it wasn't time
She voted Independent, I held the party line
I liked Conway Twitty, she liked Billy Joel
I'm a lifelong Yankee, she's an Oriole

"We Ain't Even Started Yet"

Always looking for something new and something that would generate excitement and applause, I came up with this line for Harold to use on stage every night after our encore number. We'd come back out to bow during the peak of the applause and he'd grab the mic and yell, "We ain't even started yet," and the audience would go wilder. It was a great crowd rouser. We closed every show in our TV series for seven years in the nineties with Harold saying, "And be here next week 'cause we ain't even started yet." It was so good a slogan, he and I thought why not write a song around it. So we did. On the bus one night, January 22, 1981, on our dad's birthday, somewhere in North Carolina heading for Daytona Beach.

I just want to say I still love you
And don't you ever forget
Some things may change but remember
Honey, you and me, we ain't even started yet

We never sang this on stage but the stage was for sure the inspiration for the song. Harold did a super job with the verses, and then on the ending we took pitches. First from the top to the bottom and then from the bottom to the top. (You may have to hear the song to understand what I'm talking about.) Nothing fancy, really, but it was always effective to do these pitches. Every singing group has done them in an arrangement sometime or another. But here is something I don't think I've ever told anyone. I hated them! They sounded okay but I never liked doing them. Whenever we did, I was always relieved to get that song behind me and on to the next one.

And now, on to the next one.

"Dad"

I just mentioned our dad's birthday. That was a coincidence when we wrote a song that day, but when we wrote this one, it was all intentional. We had written one for him, "Daddy," on an earlier album, *Innerview*, about ten years before. But this one was very personal and to the point. There was nothing general in these lyrics. They were all him, and it was so true and to the heart that the words were always hard to sing. And even harder to listen to. Looking at my old notebook notes on the handwritten lyric sheet, it says I started it in March of '81 and Harold and I finished it on April 2, 1981. Let me tell you how that happened.

My dad and I had gone to a sale together a few years before he passed and we bought a sixteen-gauge shotgun. I wound up with it, and for fifteen years it had sat in my home office, leaning against a fireplace. As I often did, I was up late writing and came up with this song idea, and as I was working on the line *He taught me how to drive a car and fire a sixteen-gauge*, that shotgun fell out in the middle of the floor at about 2 o'clock in the middle of the night. I came off the piano stool much too shaken to finish writing a song. But when I got my wits about me, I felt Dad's approval to write it. That's when I took the idea to Harold and together we wrote this memorial to him.

The original title was "Sid." That was his first name, and I honestly don't remember why or when we changed it, but we did before we got to the studio twenty days later. Harold and I loved writing this song and cherish each verse to this day.

They say he held me just the way new daddies always do
Kinda like he was afraid I would break in two
And everything he did would make me laugh so I've been told
He bought a war bond in my name when I was two weeks old

You may have to Google "war bond," but trust me, it makes sense. And, again, going back to that *Innerview* album in 1972, there was a Kristofferson song on it, "I'd Rather Be Sorry." In writing about it, I quoted a saying of our dad's that was in line with the philosophy of that song. We fitted it in this verse:

He taught me how to tie a tie and read an almanac
He taught me how to catch a horse and how to ride him back
He told me, "Son, a woman will get madder at you
For something you don't do to her than for something that you do"

We lost him way too early; he was only fifty-nine. And today, all of these verses and the ones I'm not writing down still make me smile. The tears don't come until the last one. We each had sung a solo and told the story well, but Harold and I knew it needed a finale in harmony that had to sum it all up in four lines. I think we found the perfect four lines:

So, Dad if you can hear us, if there're radios up there
Turn it up and listen, your boys are on the air

We never could repay you, no matter what we do
But we wrote this song and sang it, and we did it just for you

Growing up, our house was the hangout house. It was always full of our friends, and they all knew and loved our mom and dad. The morning after Harold and I wrote these words, we sang them on the bus to Phil and Lew. Lew cried. And so did I just now.

"Memories Are Made of This"

Number-one hit for Dean Martin in 1955. His breakthrough single. We were kids, and, boy, were we Martin and Lewis fans. We worked with Dean a number of times, including on his TV show and TV specials. We worked Vegas at the same hotel and would run into him there. He was an early hero of ours. This catchy little tune of his was written by the trio that backs him up on the record, Gilkyson, Dehr, and Miller, known as the Easy Riders. The group had as big a part in Martin's version as he does, and the only instruments were a bass, drums, and guitar. We did it the same way and sang our own background.

For stage, we had our band sing the background, and it is on our final album, recorded in 2002 at our final concert. I mentioned in an earlier chapter I would tell you the song I loved most to sing each night. This is it. We would do it about midway through the show, and I looked forward to it at every concert. The words and the melody just roll off the tongue like marbles on a hardwood floor. What a fun time we had with it each night.

I really love this album. I listen to how we were singing, so clear and strong and with such good material. I am so thankful for the ability and opportunity we were given to do what we loved and to have so many who enjoyed our efforts. God was so good to us in so many ways and still is.

24

The Legend Goes On

1982

By my system of counting, as I explained it earlier on, this is our twenty-fourth album. It is also the last album Lew would record with us. He became ill and temporarily quit touring for six months. All of this would happen after we began production on this project in the spring of 1981, but I will tell you how all of that unfolded as we go.

This cover was shot in Nashville at the photography studio of Ken Kim. Ken was a wonderful man to work with, and we used him a lot on future albums. This portrait was a portent of things to come, with us sitting on a park bench, because eight years down the road, the park bench plus a lamppost would become a trademark for our TV series. Then flip the cover over and you'll find liner notes on the back written by our good and beautiful friend, Barbara Mandrell. We toured thousands and thousands of miles together, and she will always be our little sister. Here's what she wrote:

> *"'THE LEGEND GOES ON' is quite an incredible statement, but when you are talking about The Statler Brothers, it becomes an understatement. Let me tell you about something that I call 'Statlerized.' When a song, old or new, is sung by The Statler Brothers, it becomes 'Statlerized.' This simply means that it never has or never will sound the same again if done by anyone except them. Their treatment of a song is totally unique and distinguishable. They emulate and follow no one. Instead, they are creators and trendsetters that make every recording something extremely special for all of us to enjoy and treasure.*

> *"I think you will find that listening to this collection of 'Statlerized' songs is, as usual, a big surprise. That is another wonderful thing about the Statlers. They can make us feel our memories as vividly as when they happened, like with the song, 'That's When It Comes Home to You.' I am particularly crazy about two really fun cuts on this album: 'I Don't Dance No More' and 'Whatever.' Every song is so different and they have treated each of them with the care, creativity and style that only true artists can give.*

> *"Harold, Phil, Don and Lew are legendary because they have earned it. From the very beginning, they had a desire to be givers and not takers. They have given all of us so much pleasure through their talent. They have contributed so much to American music as an Art form that they have become a National Treasure. I am so glad to know that without a doubt, 'THE LEGEND GOES ON...'*

> *"A Statler Brothers Fan,*

> *"Barbara Mandrell"*

"Whatever"

What an unusual history this little ditty had for The Statler Brothers. It began its life late in the P.M. at our offices in Staunton one night. The actual date now lost to history, Harold and I had met there to do some writing and this silly saga was the product of our efforts. It was clever and catchy and completely without inspiration or merit, just a perfect formula for a fun kind of single. And it worked! It was a top-ten hit.

Whatever bangs your shutters, Whatever melts your butter
Whatever, Whatever pops your corn, or blows your horn
Whatever peels your banana, Whatever plays your piano
Whatever, Whatever mows your lawn, let's go on
Whatever it takes to make it better for you
Whatever it takes to make you happy, I'll do

This was such a transitional time for us, and so many things took place in connection with this song, that it's hard to keep it all straight. We recorded it April 28, 1981. Lew took sick in November of that year, and Jimmy Fortune came in as a temporary replacement in January of '82 so that we could continue the show dates we were already committed to. Lew came back in June for two days. We thought all was well. In those two days, this album and single were released and we hosted the *Music City News Awards* show on June 7 and introduced "Whatever." The next day, we taped a *Hee-Haw* show with Lew singing and Jimmy playing the guitar as part of our band. That's the only time you'll see them on the same screen. From there, we went home for a couple of weeks, and the day before our summer tour began on June 25, Lew came to us and said he just couldn't do it. We sadly understood and knew his retirement was the best thing for his health. Jimmy left on the bus with us the next morning, and three days later we were back in Nashville to do the very first country music video anyone had ever done. It had already been set and history was in the making. Scene Three Productions had the sets and locations in place, the script was written, the actors had been hired, and there was no turning back. So, in that very first music video, for not only the Statlers but for Nashville as well, Jimmy lipped Lew's voice and performed on screen as the new, permanent Statler Brother. The future was sealed in this most public and unusual way. Jimmy was and is an absolute trouper and the fastest learner we had ever encountered. He became our brother in music, heart, and spirit and remains so today. I have so much more to write about him in these future chapters.

"I Had Too Much to Dream"

Harold's daughter Kim was back writing for us and stronger than ever. This is one of her most powerful songs, and we performed it with as much heart and gusto as anything we ever did. It was such a great wordplay song and has a melody that just doesn't quit. It should have been a single, and if it had come along just a little sooner or a bit later, I think it would have been. But because of the transition we were in, we were being pressured to get a new album with Jimmy on it on the market and we couldn't extend the life of this one any longer than the two singles already planned. But I loved this song and still do.

Lord, keep me awake tonight
Please keep her memory away from my life
And when I feel restless, I know what it means
I had too much to dream

"I Don't Know Why"

I remember so well when Harold and I began writing this one. We were in the studio, after a session, waiting for Jerry to rough-mix some songs so we could take copies home with us and study them. Killing time, I went over to the piano and started doodling around, and he put his foot up on the bench beside me and we started talking and writing.

I don't know why when someone is with me
I don't know why when I'm all alone
I don't know why, I never need a reason
It's just sometimes I miss you and don't know why

There is not much more to say about it except I always felt it should have been a single, also. It had the intro, the intimate verse, the hard-hitting chorus, the strings, the hearty ending. Yes, I think we missed a few in this period because of the reason I've already expressed. I go back to this one often when I just want to hear it all come together.

"How Do You Like Your Dream So Far?"

Harold and I covered a lot of musical territory when we wrote. Hardcore country, comedy songs, love ballads, gospel, and this one had that almost kiddie melody to it. But it asked a very philosophical question that would benefit every adult to ask themselves periodically.

How do you like your dream so far
Is it all you thought it would be
How do you like ridin' a star
How do you like it so far

We started it one night, May 22, 1980, in Halifax, Nova Scotia. This will show you just how our minds work in order to maintain our sanity. Brenda Lee was with us on tour, and as we all were leaving the show that night, our band bus broke down about fifty miles outside of town, and we had to leave it and one of our drivers alongside the road in wait of a mechanic. We got it delivered to us two days later over in Fredericton, New Brunswick. But this is just one of the many things that happens to traveling troubadours the public never knows about and has no reason to. But Harold and I would always find the irony in the public life and the life behind the scenes. And there was nothing more boring or discomfiting than bus trouble. So, what did we do? We wrote about it in our own sarcastic way.

You always said you had a dream
To do what you wanted to do
You proved it to the world and you proved it to me
But I wonder did you prove it to you

In time we made a love song out of it and finished it nearly a year later, just in time to include on this album.

Don't let the stars get in your eyes
I'm still your biggest fan
I'll always see your face in the moon
And write your name in the sand
Or anywhere that I can

229

A really nice sound here was Harold leading all the choruses with Phil and me singing harmony above him. Lew did the solos on the verses with an occasional lilting aftertime on the bridges. A sweet song and performance.

"A Child of the Fifties"

If ever I wrote a mini-autobiography, this was it. It was our second single from the album, and I lived and felt every syllable and note.

I grew up a child of the fifties
Learned to dance to the beat of Rock n' Roll
Television was my friend, I Love Lucy, Rin Tin-Tin
Kissed my first girl when I was ten years old

We were playing Roanoke, Virginia, April 27, 1980, on a Sunday evening. I sat in my hotel room at the Holiday Inn that afternoon and wrote this song in its entirety.

Barbara Mandrell had been opening our concert shows for the past two years. This was her last night with us. The next month, Brenda Lee joined us for about the same length of time. They both proved to be the best at what they do and have remained lifelong friends of ours. They really have nothing to do with the song, but seeing these notes in my journal, I just had to mention these two delightful and lovely ladies.

The seventies were ten years of reruns
The news of Watergate was nothing new
The Democrats got in, we fell in love again
When Elvis died we all knew that we could, too

That last line meant so much to my generation. I heard from so many who related to the hard fact that Elvis's death not only addressed their own mortality, but it was the death of an era where we only saw ourselves as young and invincible. And the final verse wrote itself, especially the second line, because this was the year I turned thirty-five.

Now I'm facing the most of the eighties
Old enough to run for President

It's hard to think it's me, the father of three
O America, I don't know where it went

"That's When It Comes Home to You"

Such a nice and pretty melody from Lew's pen. Phil does duet harmony that is just unmatchable. I so wish I had more to share with you on this, but in the absence of a backstory, I can offer some heartfelt lyrics.

When you've stumbled in vain
Gotten wet in the rain
And finally paid all your dues
When you've thrown it away
And it comes back to stay
That's when it comes home to you

"I'll Love You All Over Again"

I guess this reflects that muddled work ethic of mine, because I began writing this while we were home on vacation in December of '79 and finished it when we were on vacation in July of '80. (I never really caught the drift of that word "vacation." I honestly never did learn what it meant until I was retired and took my grandkids "on vacation." That's when I learned to let it all go and enjoy it.)

I admit the words to this song are a little suggestive. And I'll print out a sample here so you will have information that will give you insight into a related story I'm going to share with you.

I never said I hung the stars in heaven
Never claimed to paint the sky blue
And if you think I set the sun
Well, Honey, I ain't the one
And I can't lasso the moon for you

But I'll try to make you happy
I'll do all I can

And when you think we're through lovin'
I'll love you all over again

I have shared with you that my adult sons, Debo and Langdon, have been instrumental in encouraging me to write this chronicle of our music. Well, over lunch just the other day, Langdon told me a story I had never heard before. In high school, his sophomore year, I think, he had an English teacher assign the class to write love poems. He grabbed this album off the shelf, wrote the lyrics to this song, and turned them in as his own composition just to see what his teacher would do or say. She said nothing, but what she did was mark up "his" poem with all the lead left in her red pencil. He couldn't tell her or me what he had done at the time, but he wasn't the only loser. I'm wondering what all the red marks were about and what I might have done to make it more literature-worthy. And I have to laugh a little at what she thought of this tainted approach to a love poem. Langdon said she never liked him, and if she ever hears this story, she probably won't like me either.

Lew's physical condition was getting worse. There were dates we had to cancel, some we only postponed and went back later and made up. He took sick as we finished our final concert in Los Angeles at the Anaheim Civic Center, November 14, 1981. We flew him home and he went immediately into the hospital for observation and surgery. The prognosis was he would need months of rest and recovery. That's when we hired Jimmy for an indeterminable time period until Lew was ready to come back to work. This album, *The Legend Goes On*, was mostly recorded in April and March of 1981. We had seven songs in the can and ready to go, needing only three more cuts. The label and the market were clamoring for a new album, and by March 15, 1982, Lew was feeling strong enough to go to Nashville and record three songs. I don't think anyone who didn't know can find anything in our performances to denote what we all were going through. I can assure you there were eight footprints that didn't register in the sand during this period in our lives and career because God was carrying us all, all the way. These were the last three songs Harold, Lew, Phil, and Don recorded together.

"What You Are to Me"

A love song. Most songs are love songs. And just about every approach has been used a couple a million times. Finding something new and fresh to say is usually more difficult than actually writing it. It is such a good feeling when you discover that hook or that vein you can tap and maybe say something that has never been said before. It must be pretty and it's better when it's positive. I was lucky to find the right combination on this one.

Dreams come true
Love always wins
And only God knows
How it all will end
But down in my heart
I know it will be
Cause no one has ever been
What you are to me

Debbie just walked into my office as I was listening to this song. We both had a moment.

"I Don't Dance No More"

I wasn't old when I wrote this but I was old enough. It is simply the philosophy of not playing the games of youth anymore. As we get older, and hopefully a little wiser, we can forego all the games people play and waive all those foolish, boyish antics.

There was a time when I thought I could never be
Wiser than I was when I was twenty-three
I led the ladies 'round the town and 'round the floor
I'd dine 'em and dance 'em, but I don't dance no more

"Life's Railway to Heaven"

It was never planned for the final song the four of us recorded to be a gospel song. At least it was never in *our* plan. This song was decided on a year earlier. But then we always knew there was a hand larger than ours in our lives. Was it coincidence that four kids who grew up together happened to like to sing? Coincidence that they had four different voices ranging from bass to tenor? Or that one was an accomplished guitarist and one was a natural comedian? Or that three of the four of them were songwriters? When you believe in God, you don't believe in chance. We had a wonderful career together, and Lew would soon get well enough to have the single career he always wanted for a little while. Harold and Phil and I would find a new chapter with Jimmy and do more things we always wanted to do, such as a TV series. It wasn't always easy, but it was always God's plan and we never doubted Him for a moment.

> *Life is like a mountain railroad, with an engineer that's brave*
> *We must make the run successful, from the cradle to the grave*
> *Watch the curves, the fills, the tunnels, never falter, never quail*
> *Keep your hand upon the throttle and your eyes upon the rail*
> *Blessed Savior, Thou wilt guide us, till we reach that blissful shore*
> *Where the angels wait to join us, in Thy praise for evermore.*

25

Today

1983

The Statler Brothers were in the biggest transition of their lives, but the Lord had his mighty hand in it and we were headed for sunshine. After six months of leave, from December '81 to June of '82, Lew came back for two television appearances but retired for good before the touring season started in late June. Jimmy, who had been a temporary replacement for those six months and who was going to stay on as part of our band, was immediately a full-fledged Statler Brother. We were sad that Lew was ill and had to leave, but we realized a new chapter was being written for us so we faced it with a renewed energy and spirit. The last half of the year was full of touring and another medical setback with Harold having surgery, so it wasn't until

December of 1982 that we were able to get to the studio and begin a new album with our new brother, Jimmy Fortune.

The cover was maybe the best one yet in my estimation. It is simply the four of us, Phil, Don, Harold, Jimmy, standing in suits and ties, looking into the camera as if we were looking at or for our future. We were smiling and written above our heads was one word: Today. This collection was aptly titled because of all that we had been through in the past year; we realized that today was all we were promised on this earthly walk. We had decided to take that gift and give it our best shot and see what was in store for us from this moment on.

"Oh Baby Mine"

I knew all the words to this song when I was nine years old. A group by the name of the Four Knights had a smash hit with it in 1954 on the pop charts. That same year, Johnnie and Jack had a hit with it on the country charts. It was everywhere. So about twenty-eight years later, we got to hamming around on the bus, singing old songs, and this one popped up. What about it? We all agreed it was worth a chance and we loved singing it, so why not! It not only was a terrific hit for us, but it was a stage song that just wouldn't quit. Every night the crowd just seemed to wait for that intro to play and then stop abruptly as Harold hit "Oh Baby Mine." I smile just thinking about it.

Looking back over all our releases and charted hits, there is something that has revealed itself to me with the writing of these musical memoirs. Every single we ever released that featured Harold singing a bass aftertime or repeat was a hit. Sometimes just a note, sometimes a complete line. He gave us a sound with a built-in gimmick that always worked, on and off the record. Just off the top of my head I can think of: "Flowers on the Wall," "I'll Go To My Grave Loving You," "Do You Know You Are My Sunshine?," "Don't Wait On Me," "You'll Be Back," "Hello, Mary Lou," "Count On Me," "I'll Be the One," and, of course, "Oh Baby Mine."

Jimmy's blend was just perfect on this first single with us, and with most ears listening to and remembering Harold's bass lines, we felt we had done a good job of introducing the change in a subtle and musical way. We were still singing this one on stage the last night we ever performed, twenty years later.

236

"Some Memories Last Forever"

If ever there was a proven case of having too many singles on one album, this was the perfect example. From my notes of long ago, it seems that all four of us felt the same way. I have explained to you how the four-star system worked that we invented to determine which songs were singles and which weren't. Well, I found our old voting sheets and this was a sixteen-star song that just never made it to the final spot. Somewhere and somehow along the way, other songs appeared stronger and we changed our minds. But that takes nothing away from the song and the performance. If I should ever make a list of my better writing efforts, I probably wouldn't think to list this one, but maybe I should. It ain't all that bad.

Won't you look, standing here, just an old souvenir
Of something that you left behind
But don't be afraid, 'cause soon I'll just fade
Like a mem'ry that's outlived its time

It was another one of those late-night writing sessions I often did at home after the kids were in bed. It was July 31, 1982, early A.M. and I wrote this on the piano. I distinctly remember going into our offices the next day and Harold, Phil, and Jimmy were all there. I called them over to my office and sang it for them while it was still fresh in my mind. They joined in while I sang it and before we left that morning, we already had the key and the arrangement worked out and ready. All it needed was JK's touch in the studio and we were ready to go.

Some mem'ries last forever
Some are just fleeting and gone
Some last for seconds, some last for years
But some last all night long
Some mem'ries last all night long

"Elizabeth"

Jimmy tells a great story on stage today in his concert shows about his first writing experience. He explains he had never even tried to write a song until he joined up with us. He watched and listened and said to Harold one day, "If I write a song, you think the Statlers will record it?" He then impersonates the answer from Harold in a caricature bass voice saying, "I don't know, little buddy. Depends on if it's any good or not." Well, it was good.

We had a great tradition and habit of watching a movie on the bus just about every night rolling down the highway after a concert. Just the four of us in the lounge, eating popcorn, with the lights dimmed to a theater effect. Maybe our favorite collective movie is *Giant*, the 1956 Rock Hudson/Elizabeth Taylor/James Dean classic. Early on, when we found out Jimmy had never seen this film, we put it in one night and after about forty-five minutes of Elizabeth Taylor's face filling the screen, he jumped up and headed to the back of the bus and closed the door. We thought he was just bored with it all until the next day when he sang us this song. That it became the third single from this album and was a number-one record is a pretty good ending to this story.

But there comes an even better one. A number of years later, we and our troupe were visiting Old Tucson in Arizona, and by coincidence Elizabeth Taylor was also there shooting a movie. When her producer heard that we were on the grounds, he sent his assistant out to find us, and they asked if we would surprise her on the set by singing the song to her. We said sure and did just that. We had a nice visit together and a crowd, after hearing what was going on inside, gathered and waited for us all to come out. She said to us, "I'll go out and sign autographs if you'll go out with me." Again, we said sure and there are some photographs floating around of the five of us signing and talking with those folks who make our fairytale lives possible.

Oh, Elizabeth, I long to see your pretty face
I long to kiss your lips, I long to feel your warm embrace
Don't know if I can ever live my life without you
Oh, Elizabeth, I'm sure missing you

"Promise"

Jimmy came with another one and we liked it immediately. He was writing and we were happy. You can never have too much good material, and he was doing his share not just by singing but by using his head and his pen. This helped us continue to keep the album songs strong. So many art-

238

ists will spend time finding a good, appealing single and then fill their albums with second-rate tunes and lyrics that any guy on the corner can turn out. We were album sellers from day one at Mercury, and I think a lot of that was owed to not filling the spaces with mediocre merchandise. Even today, half the people we hear from will tell us their favorite Statler Brothers song, and it will be an album cut and not a single. I love that.

Jimmy had the moves and he learned fast. Harold soloed here and gave it full Statler treatment. And don't miss the ending and HR's perfect low A.

You're holdin' on to something, I don't know if it's right
But I'm a lover and a dreamer and I love to hold you tight
Sometimes I think I'm goin' up a hill that's way too steep
And you're holdin' on to a promise I don't know if I can keep

"I'm Dyin' a Little Each Day"

Harold tells me he had heard someone say, "I'd die for another piece of cake" or "I'd die for a car like that." One of those frivolous, unthinking things people often say without meaning. But his mind, as does the mind of all writers who are worth their salt and pepper, took those mindless sayings and turned them around in his head until he came up with something that meant something else entirely. That's called creativity gleaned from everyday occurrences. It's the daily fuel of those with the writing habit.

Living ain't easy when you're all alone
There's got to be a better way
I'd lay down my life for you anytime
So I'm dying a little each day

He gave us a stark story about misery and heartache. Every country album needs this kind of flavor and feeling. And just hearing the last note in four-part harmony on the ending, assured us and the world that the Statler sound had been preserved.

"There Is You"

So many emotions are associated with this song in my heart. We were right in the middle of the first tour with Jimmy on stage by our side, and we were just getting to know him, having rehearsed practically nonstop for the past three weeks. We genuinely liked him and were feeling a closeness with him even though we thought it was for only a short period of time that we would be together. That first tour took us through Georgia and Alabama and North Carolina, and Harold and I kept up the pace of writing on the bus before and after concerts each night. Some time along this route, we wrote the verses to this song. Three months later, after getting even closer with Jimmy, we were heading into Miami on March 24, 1982, when we finally got around to adding a chorus and melody. We were so excited about the finished product that we went up front and sang it to Phil and Jimmy in the lounge. As things took a natural course, we started talking arrangement and harmony and dynamics and ending, and before we knew it, we had worked up a brand-new song on the spot.

But to what avail? At the time, Jimmy was a temporary six-month replacement. We were unsure if what we had just done was even ethical. But we knew it sure was fun. So, we curbed our excitement and put the whole thing on the shelf for the time being. But later in the year, when we knew how things were going to pan out and we were looking for material for that new album, we pulled this jewel out and put it to tape. It was not meant to be a single because of all the other good stuff in front of it, but it will always stand out in my mind as the very first new, original song we worked up with Jimmy and also the very first song he recorded with us. The date was December 7, 1982. It means a lot to me.

There is you in the early morning sunrise
(there is you in the morning)
There is you when the day is just half through
(there is you) (day is just half through)
And when the sun goes down on the mountains
(when the sun) (kisses the mountains)
I know then it won't be long till there is you

It has that same feel with the aftertime as "Grave."

"Guilty"

This turned out to be one of the most difficult songs we ever recorded. I'll start at the very beginning. Harold and I started writing it in Nashville in the summer of '82 while there shooting the video for "Whatever." It lay in our stack of things to do for nearly three months, unfinished. In September we headed to LA to tape *The Glen Campbell Music Show* on the 15th and *The Mike Douglas Show* on the 16th. During that trip, we wrapped up "Guilty" and we all felt it was for sure a single. Come time for the arranging, we dropped one of the verses, as it just didn't fit into the way we saw the song. That deleted verse lay dormant and unheard for thirty-five years until our sons, Wilson Fairchild, recorded an album called *Songs Our Dads Wrote*. They included that long lost, well-intended verse in their fantastic version:

If she comes and talks to you, and asks you what she should do
Give her hope and give her help, and ask her not to blame herself
She was right more than wrong, we weren't weak, we just weren't strong
So just hold her hand and let her cry, and if she's guilty, so am I

The first day, December 7, 1982, that we started this album, we put this song down. We loved it, but in listening to it, Jerry and all four of us found it missing something. After studying it for dozens of playbacks, we felt it needed a different drum track. Try as the drummer did, it still wasn't right. In February of '83, we went back in and tried using the drummer from our tour band. Still didn't click. In March, we attempted it again with a different Nashville drummer and finally got what we were looking for and what you hear on the finished product creation. I know of no other time we faced so many obstacles in putting a song together.

If she's guilty, so am I
If she's forgotten how to cry
If she gets lonely and don't know why
If she's guilty, so am I

But there is even more to the story. That first night back in December when we first tackled it, we were having second thoughts about the way we wanted to end it. Fade it? Big ending? Stop short and let the instruments take it out? Just couldn't feel the right thing at the time when the door to the studio opened and Conway Twitty walked in. He was recording down the hall and just came by to say hello. Conway was a good friend whom we loved dearly. He stood there and listened to our dilemma for a few minutes and then said, "Would you mind a suggestion from someone who really cares?" We told him to jump in there any time as we were taking all comers.

So, it was Conway who came up with that repeating ending just as you hear it, and it was the perfect solution. Aw, we have lots of Conway stories, as he was one good man. We sang at his funeral.

"Right on the Money"

When Jimmy came to us, he brought some writing talent along with him in the person of John Rimel. John wrote some really nice things for us for a while and cowrote with Jimmy on some things you'll recognize as I tell you about them in albums to come. I haven't been in contact with John for many years, so I know nothing of any backstory on his writing and inspirations.

"I Never Want to Kiss You Goodbye"

Niece Kim Reid Weller, or to be fair to Harold, his daughter, Kim Reid Weller. I'd claim her if I could. She wrote this cute and catchy gem that barely missed being pulled out as a single. She told me how she came to write it just recently. She was lying in bed one night watching *Rio Grande*, the classic John Wayne/Maureen O'Hara western. At one point, Maureen says to Wayne, "Don't you want to kiss me goodbye, Kirby?" To which the Duke replies, "I never want to kiss you goodbye, Kathleen." Kim leaped out of bed, grabbed a pencil, and started writing as fast as she could. It wasn't until the next day she was settled down enough to put the music to it.

What a wonderful story. What a wonderful song.

No, I never want to kiss you goodbye
Don't ask me to, don't ask me why
I'll stand up today and walk out of your life
But I never want to kiss you goodbye

"Sweet By and By"

I can safely say that most of our albums had at least one gospel song on them. But I can say for sure that from this time on, a gospel song, an old hymn, or some new spiritual from one of our writers or us, was included on every album. Also, on stage we did a gospel segment in each concert. It was our beginnings and it was the core of our musical heart and soul. Never did we feel truer to ourselves than when we were singing an old Southern gospel song. Every night before we left the bus to walk on stage, we had a couple of standard rituals. One was a prayer. We took turns in having that prayer each night. And the other was we would warm up just before showtime with any old hymn any of us would throw out. "Amazing Grace." "Revive Us Again." "Rock of Ages." "When the Roll Is Called Up Yonder."

So, it was no surprise that this old revival hymn showed up to close out this first album of the new blend. And when I heard that second verse and the way Harold and Jimmy folded into one another as a duet, I knew we were home.

To our bountiful Father above
We will offer our tribute of praise
For the glorious gift of his love
And the blessings that hollow our days

Isn't it strange the little things we remember? I recall so vividly on the day we sang this song, February 16, 1983, at 2 o'clock in the afternoon, I was fighting a cold. I was so in fear that I wouldn't make the high notes on the bridge, and for years afterward I thought I could hear myself straining for them. But now, it all sounds as if a hand has taken a brush and wiped all that fretting away. Now I just hear four guys singing their hearts out and loving every note.

26

Atlanta Blue

1984

The four of us, Harold, Phil, Jimmy, and I, are dressed in different yet coordinated outfits of multi shades of blue. We're sitting on a floor of blue with a blue wall behind us and to top it all off, we're each unsmilingly carrying a blue look about our faces and body language. Get the message? We're blue. Actually, Jimmy looks a little frightened, Harold a little puzzled, and Phil and I look downright angry. Yet oddly enough, it isn't a bad album cover. We were back to using photog and art designer Ken Kim, and he was such a joy to work with.

    Some new musicians were used on the previous album (Jimmy's first) and are noted to still be on board with us here and into the future. Mike Leech on bass, Jerry Carrigan, drums, and David Briggs on keyboard. A new energy can be heard and felt from a number of different sources. We had just hired a new PR firm in Nashville and they came up with an innovative version of our name. THE STATLERS. We liked it. We never dropped the BROTHERS completely, but it was a nice casual way of referring to the group, and in reality it was what we were often called anyway. You can see it used for the first time in print on this cover. Also, just a few months before starting the recording of this album, we made another major change in our wardrobe. We dropped the custom of dressing alike on stage and went with an individual sport coat/slacks look. The maiden voyage for this outing happened in Murray, Kentucky, on March 25, 1983, at Murray State U.

We were singing strong and crystal clear. Call this our Blue Period if you like. I call it our New Period. We were getting our second wind and we were ready to run.

"Atlanta Blue"

Wow! This one had all the gimmicks. The first thing you hear is Jerry Kennedy picking the intro in pure JK and Statler Brothers tradition. Then Phil, Jimmy, and I hit the vocal intro with that falsetto harmony. I think the attention-getters are already in place when Harold begins the best bass solo ever on the two upcoming verses. He's solid and demanding, and, if I do have to say so myself, the lyric is simple and straight to the point. I loved writing this almost as much as singing it.

Just a name I remember
Just someone I used to know
Someone I never quite got over
A long, long time ago

Switching in and out of the falsetto was almost like a yodel, and to do it in harmony was a perfect little trick for the record and the stage. I remember sweating it in concert many times when my voice was less than perfect, worrying it would crack on the wrong notes. To be honest, some nights were smoother than others, but I always had Phil and Jimmy above me to make up for whatever needed smoothing over.

I'm Atlanta Blue ooo ooo
Wishing I could be with you ooo ooo
Summertime in Georgia
I'm thinking of you ooo ooo
And that makes me Atlanta Blue. Blue, Blue

Music videos were just coming on and they were hot stuff. There were video shows all over television, and it was important to shoot one for every single release and promote it for TV just like you promoted the audio for radio. We tried to, but our schedule didn't always allow for us to work one in. This one we shot on location in, where else, Atlanta. It's an odd little piece of film/tape to look at today. Mercury hired someone to write it and it time-jumped all over the place, with each one of us playing different characters in a past era. We were all over the city, riding a horse-drawn carriage through modern-day traffic and then walking through crowds in costume with cameras and lights following, stopping and doing lines with folks lined up watching every strange take. It was times like this that I knew I could never make a living being an actor. It is most uncomfortable for me to act on a location; didn't mind it in a studio, but it's a world of difference from singing to a crowd and acting to a crowd.

At one point toward the end, a baseball rolls under the carriage and I get out and bat with some kids. The ball I hit is then caught by me in Fulton County Stadium with the Braves playing in the background. The final scene is the four of us taking a bow after singing the "National Anthem" at the game that night. We sang the anthem at a lot of MLB games over the years and got to watch a lot of baseball and meet all the teams. One of my fondest baseball memories was in Minneapolis for a Twins game. In the locker room after the game, Rod Carew gave me two of his special-made bats, one for each of my sons, Debo and Langdon. They still have them. What a nice man he was.

"Atlanta Blue" was every bit the big hit we thought it would be. In those days of 45-rpm singles, Mercury released to radio a blue vinyl record for promotion. It was pretty cute and we still have a few of them laying around somewhere. So, with all those gimmicks and the MLB behind us, how could it miss? Baseball, apple pie, and country music!

"If It Makes Any Difference"

This whole album is full of heartache and heartbreak songs. Few match what Harold and I put into this one and also got out of it. We didn't often settle in and settle down to write as serious a piece as this together, and I wish I had a file on this one as to where we wrote it and when. You can be assured, though, it was late at night and we weren't in a very funny mood.

If it makes any difference and I'm sure that it won't
If you think I laugh and take it light, you're wrong, this time I don't
Look at me if you're still looking for the place the blame should fall
I'm sick and simply sorry if it makes any difference at all

The previous album, *Today*, was our first with Jimmy. I think of it as our getting-to-know-Jimmy-musically album. I'm sure JK would say the same thing from a recording standpoint. But here, I can hear the evidence that we all had found what we were looking for. You only have to listen to his harmony on the first verse to know that when we said the word "Lugan" to him, he knew exactly what we were talking about. The haunting blend and the way he glues himself to my notes just send chills across my back like an Omaha wind. The mood of the record and the sound of our voices meld together with the sincere lyric to make it one of the most perfect songs we ever cut.

If it makes any difference, I was wrong from the start
These aren't more sweet-talking words, these are from the heart
I've walked around the truth before, but this time I'm willing to crawl
What else can I say but I'm sorry, if it makes any difference at all

"(Let's Just) Take One Night at a Time"

I asked Kim Reid Weller to write me a little something to share with you about the creation of this song. I could paraphrase in my own words, but I think it's more poignant to hear it in hers: "I was living in Charlotte, North Carolina, newly married, and I asked Dad what he would like for his birthday. He replied, 'Write me a song.' He never wanted us to spend any money on him buying gifts, even though we did. So, this was the first gift he asked for that he actually got."

Just listening to the expanded intro and the sparkly hard-rocking track is evidence there is new blood in the studio. The pickers are alive and there is music in the air!

Let's just take one night at a time
Let's just hold on to those feelings it takes so long to find
Let's just keep on getting closer until we lose our minds
Let's just take one night at a time

"Angel in Her Face"

I won't try to fool you into thinking that I remember very much about the writing of this song. I don't. Not the day, not the place. However, I do remember the era, the time, the period. We were writing feelings and stories then, and we weren't ashamed to put a little hunk of our personal soul on the paper for all the world to see and hear and feel. There's a hunk of mine laid out here.

I miss the way she always knew when things were on my mind
I miss the way she'd always cling to every word of mine
I miss the way that only she could put me in my place
But most of all, I miss that look of angel in her face

Going from so very personal to so very public, I miss this kind of country music, this kind of presentation, with producers and musicians who knew how to complement a simple melody and an honest lyric without drowning it out and turning it into some kind of complicit wall of noise. I miss everything about a gentle singer who doesn't have to scream above a thunderous track in order to be heard and never understood. Yeah, there I've said it. I miss country music.

I miss the gleam she always had, in eyes that worshipped me
I miss the smile that I could feel, the warmth that I could see
And as she lies beside me now, I know I can't erase
The fact that I'm the one who took the angel from her face

"*Holly*Wood*"

It was Christmas 1983. For fifteen-year-old son Debo, we had gotten a portable recording console with multi tracks. He was playing the guitar, bass, and piano, and took immediately to putting down his own melodies. Eight-year-old son Langdon sometimes came in the music room and played the drums with us, but only under threat or boredom. On this particular occasion, four days after Christmas, I played them a melody I was working on, and the three of us put this down on Debo's new "toy" as an instrumental. It sounded pretty darn good, and as we played it back time and time again, I added words to make it a complete song. So, in all reality, the three of us recorded it before I actually wrote it. Sounds strange, but it's true.

*Holly*Wood*
You got me out here like I knew you would
And you have hooked me with your magic lure
*And there's no cure—for Holly*Wood —that's for sure*
*Holly*wood*
You have a way of making dreams come true
Anyone can see there's a different me
*Since I've seen Holly*Wood*

Leave it to trustworthy ol' JK to come through with a Dixieland jubilee by bringing in a trombone, clarinet, and a trumpet for the mid-break. And then, what just puts country smack dab in the center of Bourbon Street, Weldon Myrick finishes it off with a Dobro lick that leaves everybody dancing in the night. And if you're wondering who is doing that 1930s platinum-blonde harmony as the vocal aftertime on the verses, that's Phil and Jimmy.

*Holly*Wood*
You make me think of things that no one should
Your beauty has become a legend now
Take a bow—Hollywood—and show me how
Hollywood
I feel I'm on the verge of something grand
Who can make me feel good? I know Holly could
If only Holly would

"One Takes the Blame"

This one was painful to write. But I had written about every aspect of a man/woman relationship imaginable, and I felt a need to write this one in depth. You can never know if a song is going to be a hit, but you can know if it's good from a perspective of how well written it is. I knew it was good; it had feeling, it had the emotion, and we all four felt very strongly about it. That's how it got on the album.

When it's over
And God knows as well as we it is
When we pack up
And stack up what's hers and what's his
When we make up
The stories to cover up the shame
They never will believe, we simply fell out of love
One takes the bow, one takes the blame

After the album was out with a hit single leading it, we still felt this message and performance was original and passionate enough on its own that it needed to be heard. It became the second single from the album and a top-ten hit and in a strange sort of way, a serious anthem for breaking up. It's very sad, as it examines the relationship without offering guilt or condemnation to either party.

When we get lonely
And lonely we'll get now and then
Just remember
That somewhere we both still have a friend
Love's not forever
And ours went as gently as it came
So, for all the years I loved you, and you know I really loved you
You take the bow, I'll take the blame

"Give It Your Best"

We were on a long Canadian tour in October of '83. Reba was opening the show for us that year, and we were hitting all the good towns across the western plains of our neighbors to the north plus those of our own in Washington and Oregon. We were just leaving Calgary, Alberta, after a sellout concert on Thursday night, October 20th, when Harold and I crawled on the bus and decided to write instead of sleep. This was the result of our efforts and it certainly was fun to record.

Jerry Kennedy does some fantastic picking of the Dobro guitar as an intro and a mid-break. But then he just outdoes himself with a long segment at the end. The pickers jumped in and supported him with as robust a track as you'll ever hear. What Harold and I had written was just a nice little rhythm ditty, but what it became was an instrumental performance we didn't showcase often enough. The lyrics here are mundane but the music is worth a listen anytime you get a chance.

"No Love Lost"

Jimmy was writing here with John Rimel, a writer from Charlottesville, Virginia, we were using more and more often. They were bringing good stuff to the table as a team (which would get even better, as you will see) and as individuals. The melody had a good range to it, allowing Jimmy and me to switch leads a number of times throughout, and the words carried a nice twist by the time it got to the chorus.

There's been no love lost between us
We've kept it all to our selves
I'm praying every day, there will always be
No love lost between you and me

"One Size Fits All"

John Rimel came through for us with the customary gospel song we always liked to include. There was never a shortage of old gospel songs and hymns we could use, as we proved in the upcoming nineties by closing every episode of our TV series with one, but we were always on the lookout for a new one.

When he hands out the halos, one size fits all
When you get your crown of glory, it won't be big or small
Your stature on earth won't measure your worth
In his eyes one size fits all

Musically speaking, there is a really good key change toward the end. We go from the key of E to the key of C, and it's pretty slick. And the falsetto note I include on the last line was always fun to do. Phil and Jimmy were really good at that, but it fell to my part to do it this time. Funny, on my old lyric sheet I'm looking at from the recording session that day, January 16, 1984, I had penciled in at the bottom of the page, "swing 80s gospel ending." I don't even know what that means now, but it must have been a reminder for me and meant something to me then.

"My Only Love"

This one was from the new and trusty pen of Jimmy, and just like "Elizabeth" on the *Today* album, it was the third single from this album and it was a smash. It went to number one on December 8, 1984, exactly a year after "Elizabeth" did the same thing. There is not a lot I can tell you about this beautiful song and how it was written, but I can tell you why it was written. Jimmy's brother was getting married, and he asked Jimmy to sing in his wedding. Jimmy did him one better. He not only sang, he wrote his brother and his bride a special love song, and this was it. Once we heard it, we knew it was made for us. We also shot a video for it at a number of different locations in the Nashville area around the wedding theme.

Jim Owens Productions produced the video. Jim was a great friend, and we worked together on many projects. On this one, he hired four beautiful girls to be our mates. Harold's wedding is the focal point of the piece, and it was all shot with his "bride" in a church. Phil and his girl shot theirs on a front porch swing, while Jimmy and his partner shot theirs in a grassy field. And where did my pretty mate and I film our scenes? The guy who hates to act on public location shoots? We were standing on busy West End Blvd. in Nashville during five o'clock traffic with lights, cameras, and crew. I have to laugh looking at it today. And you can, too, on YouTube. But we always had fun doing whatever we decided to do, and this one was a blast.

This album was a first in that every song on it was written by a Statler or someone from our stable of writers. We had a number of publishing companies and we published every song here. Our writing staff would grow, as you will see, and it will include talent that will help keep the songs coming until the end. I love this album and the music Jimmy was making with us. He was feeling more comfortable with each trip to the studio and taking a healthy bite out of everything we asked him to do, from recording to stage to comedy to TV to videos to songwriting.

The Statler Brothers, or, I should say, the Statlers, were only blue in that cover picture. At heart, we were raring to go and already working on the next album.

27

Pardners in Rhyme

1985

A pretty clever title, even if I have to say so myself. And the cover was a natural, casual, and relaxed view of all the Brothers. Harold in sweater and slacks with a Dobro on his lap, Phil at an old Remington typewriter (a little bit of a stretch), me at the piano with a hat on that I often wore but seldom in pictures or in public, and Jimmy with a classic guitar on his knee that I'll tell you all about.

I had just gotten my son Debo this collectible 1968 Gretsch Chet Atkins Tennessean electric guitar with a whammy bar for Christmas. He was seventeen, and this instrument was made and marketed the year he was born. I took it to Nashville for this cover picture and everyone who saw it fell in love with it. We wound up using it on one of the songs on this album, but I'll tell you about that when we get to it. Later, I got my other son, Langdon, a Chet Atkins 7670 Country Gentleman guitar that was a 1975 model, his birth year. It's tobacco brown and has a muffler on it that gives you that Chet sound on the bottom strings. Years later, on an album further down the road, Debo and Langdon and I wrote a song called "Chet, You're the Reason," and Chet played on the session. He also autographed both guitars that day, which added a great amount of sentiment to already priceless treasures.

The back of the album is as good a picture as the front. It's of the instruments minus the Statlers, but seen in the midst of all of this is that beautiful brass music stand June Carter Cash gave me years before. It was also on the cover of the *The Statler Brothers Sing Country Symphonies in E Major* album (1972). So that makes two covers where we used June's antique music stand. It sits today in our living room by the piano.

The liner notes on the back are short and to the point. They simply read:

This album is dedicated to our producer Jerry Kennedy. It's been 15 great years. We're looking for 15 more, and we don't want to try it without JK. Thanks Jerry—you're the best.

And it was signed by Harold, Don, Jimmy, and Phil. We were a great team, Jerry and us. And there's nothing else to be said after that, so let's sing.

"Hello Mary Lou"

We had left after a concert heading to the next town, and our two buses were flying through the night somewhere in the continental United States, and that is as close as I can nail it down. The four of us were in the lounge with a couple of guitars singing whatever popped in our heads and just basically winding down from the show. Out of the fog of our weary minds and tired bodies, we started singing this old Ricky Nelson song. We were really rockin' on that chorus, with Harold adding "before" lines that were never on the original record. We were loving what we were doing, but we couldn't go any further with it because none of us could remember the words to the verses. I opened the door that connected us to our driver, Dale, and asked him to call the band bus behind us on his CB radio to see if any of them knew the words to "Hello Mary Lou." By the time we stopped at the next truck stop for gas, they had them written out for us, and we took their scratch paper and kept on singing as we rolled down the highway. As soon as we went in for the next set of sessions for this album, we recorded this Gene Pitney/Cayet Mangiaracina-written jewel and released it as soon as possible. It led the album and was a big hit single in no time. But here is the funny part.

Many years later, fans began to point out the lyric changes and ask us why we made those changes. We were baffled by their observations and really didn't know what they were talking about. Well, here is what they were talking about. Pitney and Mangiaracina wrote the first line:

Pass me by one sunny day, and the Statlers sang, *Pass me by one summer day.*

They wrote the last line of the first verse, *And though I never did meet you before* but the Statlers sang, *And though I never did need you before.*

There were a couple of other places, but we never knew about any of them until decades later. We were singing what our band had written out for us and we never bothered to check out the words for accuracy. But you know what? It didn't hurt a thing. I have to laugh every time I hear it on the radio today.

"Sweeter and Sweeter"

The video of this song overpowers the song itself to where that is what I think of when I'm trying to recall anything about the writing or singing of it. We shot it on a spring day in Centennial Park in Nashville, out on West End Avenue. We played old-men versions of ourselves as we went in and out of memories of our youth. Four gorgeous young ladies were hired to play our partners, and as this first verse played, I was singing and picking in a small club. I remember the label executives were bothered that the track was not synced up with my lips as I sang. That was a director's call and it was already done by the time they made their complaint. You can check it out for yourself on YouTube.

Gone are the days, when I was your hero
And you were my princess, so perfect it seemed

I took to pickin' and you took to playin'
And we both took to dancin' in another one's dream

Harold and I got a little philosophically clever on the word twisting, and I think wrote a pretty good song. It was the third single from the album and was a top-ten hit.

I was a loner and you were a dreamer
And we both took ourselves too much to heart
And everyone knows if you don't grow together
Sooner or later, you'll grow apart

"Memory Lane"

Jimmy was not only writing for our publishing company, Statler Brothers Music, but he was writing for us. He caught on real quick to the nostalgia slant of our style, and this song is full proof of that fact.

Maybe we can catch us a movie
Or a ballgame at the park
'Cause we don't have to worry about Daddy
Or gettin' you home much after dark
There's always someone down at the diner
And lord, you never looked finer
And it's driving me insane
Let's take a ride down memory lane

Here is a perfect example of how the writing of a song is never finished until the final seconds. Jimmy was still tweaking this one during the recording session. When he first pitched it to us, the title was "Let's Take a Ride Down Memory Lane." I have his and my lyric sheets from the session that day, January 14, 1985. Mine still has that full title on it, but on his, sometime that afternoon, he had scratched through the first five words and shortened the title to what is printed on the record and jacket cover. Good move. I like it better.

Let's take a ride down memory lane
And do some things that we used to do
Let's take a ride down memory lane
And make love the way that we used to

"Remembering You"

What a conundrum Harold and I wrote here for anyone listening to this song today. The first verse was a nice setup for a sad, lonely-guy scene in 1985.

The TV went off hours ago
Nothing but static on the radio
The house is quiet and nothing to do
And I'm just sitting here remembering you

There was just too much cultural technology in those lines, because you'd have to be forty years old today to remember when TV stations went off the air at midnight. Today, everything stays on all night.

When we started touring, there were only three cities in the US with all-night TV: LA, New York, and Detroit. And we loved it.

And then that next line about "static on the radio"—again, people today do not even know what static is. Satellite and FM radio have practically taken that word out of America's vocabulary. And check out this next verse:

The last words I heard were "home of the brave"
And I think of the home that I couldn't save
I say I'm happy but that just ain't true
The best part of my night is I remembering you

The "home of the brave" reference is the signing off of each TV station each night with the National Anthem. But there are folks today who don't remember that and have no idea it ever happened. And that's okay. But it is a lesson to all songwriters and novelists to stay away from even the most minor technology in your storylines. You can never know what changes in the world will affect and date your message. But the message in the chorus is eternal. When you keep it on a man/woman level, it will never go out of style.

I like to remember your pretty face
I like to remember your hair out of place
And whenever I have a minute or two
I just like remembering you

"Too Much on My Heart"

This one is really Jimmy's story to tell, and I won't attempt to invade on his territory. The title says it all, as he certainly did have a lot on him at the time. He was carrying loads on his shoulders and on his heart, and he took the grand opportunity to set that stress and pain to music for all the world to see. Speaking from experience, I can tell you that takes guts. And he never let up once he started.

I've got too much on my heart and I don't like to feel the pain
And I don't know where to start to make you love me once again
I don't have time to make you understand, lord, this thing is getting out of
*   hand*
Pain shoots through me like a dart, and I've got too much on my heart

It's a very dramatic song, and we performed it that way both on record and stage. It was so effective that it shot to the top of the charts, as I think the fans could hear the sincerity in every note and word. Every night on stage, as the music stopped and we all four said in perfect harmony, "Don't be so cold to me," I could feel the shivers of reality in what we were doing. This song had heart and deserved every accolade it received.

Don't be so cold to me, I know you've changed but it's still hard for me
It's too late I realize, I can see it in your distant eyes
You needed all of me, and I can't be there like I used to be
And, lord, it's tearing me apart, and I've got too much on my heart

"I'm Sorry You Had to Be the One"

Cohasset, Massachusetts, is one of the prettiest and most picturesque little towns I have ever seen. And right on the skirts of this sweet little village, a bedroom community to Boston, is a summer music theater. Every weekend there is a major show with star power like you can't imagine in such a small place. But folks come from everywhere and pack that venue all the time, and we loved playing there. That is where we were on September 9, 1983. We had two sold-out houses and were resting on the bus between shows when one of us picked up a guitar and started fiddling with a melody. The result of that fiddling was Harold, Jimmy, and me writing a song together. This particular combination had never happened before, nor would it happen again. But it was fun and produced a very pretty melody and nice lyrics. And listen to those strings that come in halfway through and just lift you off your feet.

I'm sorry you had to be the one
To say I'm sorry to me
I'm sorry is never easy to say
And alone's never easy to be

Creating words and music is not an easy thing to do with a partner. And there are many good writers who just can't work together. Style gets in the way. Egos get in the way. Feelings get hurt. People get insulted if their idea is not met with enthusiasm. You have to check all baggage at the door and try to be of one mind. Harold and I had learned to do this many years before with all the material we had written together. Jimmy fell into the pattern of give-and-take like the old pro he had already become. This song proved we could write together as comfortably as we could sing together.

I have so many fun memories of Cohasset. One morning, just after dawn, I was up and running through the town while there was hardly any traffic in sight. A car pulled beside me, and the window on the driver's side slid down, and a man said to me, "Hey. I love your music but I hate your cap." I pulled it off my head and looked at it. I was wearing a New York Yankees ball cap. We both laughed and he pulled off. But a lesson learned. Never wear a Yankees cap that close to Boston!

"Her Heart or Mine"

For the last seven years, we had been recording at Sound Stage studios in Nashville. This particular album began there, but after a couple of songs, we moved to the Young'Un Sound studio owned by Chip Young, who had been a guitarist on all of our records for the past fifteen years. (And, no, I don't remember why we switched.) I mentioned earlier about my son's Chet Atkins guitar on the album jacket. Well, that same week we did the photo shoot, we started these sessions, and I took the instrument to the studio with me to show some of the guys who I knew would be interested in it. Chip fell in love with it immediately. He wanted to play it on at least one of the songs. This was fine with us, and without a doubt this one was the perfect choice. That's him on this glorious intro and break.

She wants so much more than I can give her
And she's given about all that I can take
I think it's plain to see, it's down to her and me
Somebody's heart has to break

Harold and I wrote it, and he does a great job with such a loose and tongue-in-cheek delivery. And don't miss the mastery of JK on mixing in the Dobro of Weldon Myrick throughout Chip's picking to where it sounds like one exciting instrument. This thing has kick!

"You Don't Wear Blue So Well"

We were always on the lookout for a good song. We didn't care if it was from a stranger or family as long as we felt it had merit and felt that we could do it justice. This is how our writing staff grew within family members. Harold's daughter Kim had already written numerous songs for us, and this time out she brought her two younger sisters into the act. Kim was married and living in North Carolina when Karmen and Kodi went to visit one weekend. She sang them a song she was working on, and, as things will happen, they joined her in finishing it. It was the only time the three of them ever entered into a creative venture such as this together, but it paid off for everyone involved, and we got a good song out of it. Thank you, girls.

You don't wear blue so well
It's easy to read you, it's easy to tell
But you don't wear blue so well

Just had to share this intertwining little story. When Harold's three older daughters were teenagers, they did some singing and had some really nice harmony. After listening to them rehearse one night and watching Brenda (their mother) smile throughout, I wrote them a little fun song they did on some of their shows. It was called "Mamma's So Proud of Me." They each did a verse:

My mamma's so proud of me
She says I'm so pretty
And I'd even go so far
To say that just may-be
She thinks these two are cute
But she's proud of me

My mamma's so proud of me
She tells me constantly
I've always been the one
Who caused her less mis-ery
I guess she likes you both
But she's proud of me

My mamma's so proud of me
You see I'm her baby
And all that stuff you've heard
Is so much ba-lo-ney
She tolerates these two
But she's proud of me

My mamma's so proud of us
She frets and makes a fuss
But she gives us all A-plus
And we tell you sin-cere-ly

We're all proud that Mamma's
Proud of us all three

So, on a whim, I wrote these pretty little nieces of mine, with Harold's permission, a song. And then, less than a decade later, the three of them wrote us one. Ain't life a circle of fun!

"Autumn Leaves"

Major word play is taking place here. This is about a girl named Autumn and not about the fall of the year. Jimmy and John Rimel teamed up again and gave us a sexy little love song that has a lot of sparkle.

Autumn leaves me falling, falling, falling
In and out of love, time after time
And I believe that love is somewhere calling
And that someday Autumn will be mine

This cut is the perfect example of the strong track JK always gave us. Listen to what we used to call the "bottom." You cannot only hear the hard bass and bass drum giving you that solid, driving rhythm, but you can feel it. Two full bars of that is really all any country song needs to get my attention.

"Amazing Grace"

This song gives me chills no matter who is singing it or playing it. The blend of these words and this music makes it the perfect hymn and gospel song of all time. No, make that just the perfect song of all time, no matter the genre. This would not be the only time we would record this masterpiece. We would do it again seventeen years in the future as the last song we would ever sing together before our retirement. But this arrangement holds a special place in our hearts. Our performance, Jerry's total production values, Bergen White's string and horn arrangements—they all come together to make it a model of faith set to music.

My son Debo reminded me recently of the first time I heard the finished arrangement, all the voices mixed with the powerhouse of violins. Jerry had sent a tape to each of us at our homes in Virginia. I took it out of the wrapper and put it in the console in my home office. Debo, seventeen at the time, sat on the floor and I sat at my desk, and we were taken and overcome by what we heard. He remembers tears were rolling down my cheeks as I walked over and pushed the repeat button and we listened again with the identical reaction as the first time. I then picked up the phone and called Jerry and thanked him and told him it might be the best thing we ever did.

I listen to it today and it is as powerful to me as it was that day in my office. Our final notes and big ending is not the last word here, as it usually is with our songs. After we stop singing, it continues on and on, a full minute of just music and grace. Much like God's love does, even as we drop out of life one by one. I feel as if I'm floating by the time the fade ends. We placed it as the last song on the album so that no other sound would follow it.

28

Christmas Present

1985

I don't know who first said, "Let's do another Christmas album." It may have been one of us or JK or it may have come down from the label execs. After all, the first one, *Christmas Card*, just seven years earlier in 1978, had first gone gold and then platinum. These are the kinds of sales record companies don't forget and want more of. So, whoever brought up the idea had good reason, and we were cocked and ready to go. We wanted to explore the Christmas music scene with Jimmy involved, and we even had a brand-new writer who would shine on two compositions that would be featured on this collection. Debo, my older son, was writing melodies we just could not ignore. He didn't sing, never has, but he played guitar and piano and was beginning to bring me pieces that I shared with the guys, and we encouraged him to keep writing as he was only a teen at the time but fully had our attention and support. John Rimel continued to write for this album, as did Harold and Jimmy and myself. As a matter of fact, we, through Statler Brothers Music Inc., published all the songs on this Christmas album except "Old Toy Trains."

The cover is very understated Christmas. The four of us are dressed in winter overcoats and scarves, holding prettily wrapped packages. The photography was done in Staunton by a great friend of ours, Charles Clemmer, who had done lots of layouts and shoots and publicity pictures for us in the past. He has such a clear and perfect touch and caught that rare natural smile on each of our faces simultaneously. Ken Kim was back as our art director, and the Christmas project was officially in motion. All we needed was the music, and that began in Nashville at Young'Un Studios on April 23, 1985, and wrapped up on May 8.

We brought two of our creative worlds together with this album in a most convenient way. We had two TV specials under our belts: *An Evening with The Statler Brothers*, produced by good friend Jim Owens, in 1981. Also, *Another Evening with The Statler Brothers*, in 1983, with Jim again at the helm. Both were award-winning, as we won "Best Country TV Special of the Year" in 1981 and 1983. I don't remember who recommended we do a Christmas special to tie in with the album, but we were all of one mind to do it. With all of the already-booked concert dates, I can assure it was a busy, busy year but well worth it. Most of the songs on the album were on the special. They sold one another. The album hit the market in September and the TV show hit the air in November. The album would be a great long-time seller, and the television special would win another "Best Country TV Special of the Year" award for 1985.

As I remember, Jerry and Chip Young had someone come in and hang colored lights in the studio and put a little tree in the corner, and during one song we got visited by Santa, courtesy of Mercury's PR head, Frank Leffel. But all of the new Christmas sounds and lyrics we wrote were so fresh and creative that we felt the season's spirit in the air. We had great fun working on this, and it made 1985 a memorable year for us in so many wonderful ways.

"Christmas Eve"
(Kodia's Theme)

The first subject to tackle here is that title that just jumps up and smacks you in the face. So let's take first things first. My son, D (Harold nicknamed him Debo before he could ever walk and it stuck), wrote this beautiful melody on the guitar. Harold's third daughter, Kodi (whose real name is Kodia), was and is very close with Debo. They have been more like brother and sister their whole lives than like first cousins. She loved this tune and always got him to play it whenever they got together. Kodi sings like an angel, and they often did musical things together. When he titled this song, he subtitled it "Kodia's Theme" for her. When Harold and I heard it, we immediately heard Christmas in it and wrote the lyric. Debo's music, our words.

If dreams came true
On Christmas Eve
I'd dream you there
And never leave
I'd turn back time
And make believe
The way we were
On Christmas Eve

Did I fail to mention that Debo was seventeen years old and Kodi was nineteen years old at the time? And may I point out the piano of David Briggs and the string arrangements of Bergen White? And listen to the little vocal "ooo ooo" answers to my lines on the last verses. That's Phil and Jimmy, with no outside help needed from any female backup singers. And Harold's and my favorite lines show up in the chorus:

Like trees I've trimmed
You've never seen
Memories of you
Are evergreen

We also shot a video of it that was included in the TV special, and it was released as a single.

Turn down the lights
And make believe
You're here with me
On Christmas Eve

"Christmas Country Style"

With this song following "Christmas Eve," you can see we were wide open for any style of Christmas. Jimmy penned this, and true to the title, we countrified it with Dobro and banjo.

We'll have a Christmas country style
You can hear us singin' for a country mile
So take your coat off and stay a little while
We'll have a Christmas country style

"Brahms' Bethlehem Lullaby"

There are so many, many versions of this magnificent tune written by Johannes Brahms. The original German lyrics, the traditional English, and this Christmas version. We sang these words as kids in church, and we remembered them when it came time to record even though it had been a lifetime since we had raised our voices in Sunday school while sitting on those little wooden chairs. The words flow into this melody with such grace that even the most hardened of hearts would have to melt in hearing them.

Long ago there was born
In the city of David
A sweet, holy babe
Who was Jesus our King
Angels sang at his birth, lullaby peace on earth
Angels sang at his birth, lullaby peace on earth

From Harold's flawless solo to our a cappella verse to the full orchestra that joins us till the end, I am moved and affected by the power and the warmth of this performance. That anyone could hear this story and feel the strength of these notes of music and not believe mystifies me. And yet Brahms himself was a nonbeliever. But then we know God so often uses imperfect people to do his work, because there is no one who is perfect. But in my heart, I won't let a cloud of irreverence fall over such a piece of inspiring music that I know was God-given, even if Brahms didn't.

"Somewhere in the Night"

Debo was coming on strong with his second song on the album. He wrote this melody, and with hardly any effort at all, I sat down and added the lyric. The words just flowed over top of his melodious chords, and I felt such a thrill that I had made this creation with my son. So blessed.

A night cold and clear where angels appear
And shepherds behold such a beautiful sight
And hear as they sing the praise of a king
Who's born somewhere in the night

It is always the goal of any writer to find a new way of telling an old story. Sometimes you can do this with a fresh angle, sometimes with an unusual approach that has a little shock to it, and sometimes with just a word that has never been used before. I won't go as far to say it had never been used, but I got more mail and word-of-mouth comments about a word I used in this last chorus than any one word I ever included in a song:

Wise men will read the story and heed
Rejoice, celebrate, the heavenly neonate

A newborn child. I smile when I hear it, but I beam when I listen closely to Debo's melody.

"An Old-Fashioned Christmas"

And right back to hard, solid country. John Rimel put it all together with a sadness of cold city streets during Christmastime but a chorus that paints the perfect homey scene.

An old-fashioned Christmas with presents round the tree
A fire softly burning and you up close to me
With friends and family stopping by to help us share the cheer
For an old-fashioned Christmas, I'll be coming home this year

"No Reservation at the Inn"

This is another result of one of those many late-night writing sessions where Harold and I would sneak off to the office near midnight after our kids went to bed. We'd write all night because we had to with the schedule we were keeping. We did not have the luxury of writing Christmas songs during our December break in 1984, when it would have been so easy to get into the mood, because we had sessions booked in January of 1985 to finish up the album that preceded this one, *Pardners in Rhyme*. We had to get it ready for an April '85 release. As soon as it was mixed and shined up by JK and presented to the public, we had sessions booked in late April to begin this Christmas album. So our concentration on these seasonal songs did not begin until at least February, and that is when this bluegrass Bible story was born.

I use the word Bible loosely, as there is no mention whatsoever of an innkeeper anywhere in the Scriptures. Even though we put words in his mouth, there really was no mouth in which to put them. All that is ever said in the Christmas story over in Luke 2:7 is, "There was no room for them in the inn." In our TV special, we even cast our bus driver in the role of the innkeeper who never was. So this makes this whole song a total work of fiction, but it says so much, and I think says it very effectively. And wow! The music track. I want to point out and give special credit to Bela Fleck on the banjo, Weldon Myrick on the Dobro, and Henry Strzelecki, who is just beatin' the mistletoe out of that bass.

270

No reservation at the inn
Didn't know that you were comin' in
We're all filled up you see
We got no vacancy
No reservation at the inn

Writing about the birth of our Lord in such a rhythmic way and still maintaining a modicum of proper respect can be tricky. I think we did it with facts that fit the story even though we were creating the character and his tone and conversation as we went. We loved the challenge.

Excuse me sir, what did you say?
She's in a family way?
And you think any day now that it's due
Of course, out back we have a stable
We'd do more if we were able
Sorry sir, but that's about all that we can do

This song always sets my emotions on edge and actually makes me want to dance before it's over with. We were more than pleased with how it came off, but many years later we heard it with a new ear. Harold's and my sons, Wilson Fairchild (Wil and Langdon), were doing a Christmas concert nearby and we all went. With the stage adorned in blue and green and a big tree in full decoration, they were introduced and came on stage, took their bows, and went immediately into "No Reservation at the Inn" as a surprise for their old daddies. Harold and I were sitting in the audience, he directly in front of me. When the boys finished to rousing applause, he reached over his shoulder and I gripped his hand and just held it for a second. We both were remembering that all-night writing session and just how glad we were we had endured it and just how rewarding it was to hear our sons sing it back to us in such an overwhelming fashion. There are no words.

"Mary's Sweet Smile"

We and our writers wrote eight of the ten songs you hear here. It was our intention to present new Christmas songs on this collection in contrast to how we had structured our first Christmas album years before. In the conference room of our offices, we had an enormous glass-topped table we sat around where we worked up our vocal arrangements. On this particular early spring day, we were appraising and reviewing the material that would become our second Christmas album and realized we were one song short. Phil was not really a songwriter, but we knew that Harold or Jimmy or I could go down the hall to our individual offices and write that song and come back, maybe before the day was over, with a good and interesting entry to complete the album. But then a bell went off in our collective heads. Why not write one together while all four of us were sitting here. And we did. This is the only song Harold, Phil, Jimmy, and I ever wrote together. Jimmy played the guitar, I played a little electric piano we always kept in the corner, and Harold and Phil wrote down the words as we came up with them and agreed on them.

> *Kings from the east gave gifts when they came*
> *An angel of God gave Jesus his name*
> *That night cast a spell that the ages will tell*
> *And the world glowed with Mary's sweet smile*

This was the B-side to "Christmas Eve." We had a bond, the four of us, whether writing around the conference table, lounging on a moving bus, gathered around a microphone, staring into a TV camera, or standing in front of 50,000 people. We did good things together and loved every minute of it.

"Whose Birthday Is Christmas"

Harold owns this one all by himself. He wrote it from the standpoint of a four- or five-year-old. It was used in our Christmas television special and featured Harold and a little boy from our area. We filmed the video all over Staunton and used a lot of local folks. Even shot some of the major scenes at our home church, Olivet Presbyterian.

> *Daddy, just whose birthday is Christmas*
> *The Bible says that Jesus was born*
> *Oh, Daddy, please explain, I had to ask because*
> *You hear so much about Santa Claus*

272

There is such a sweet touch toward the end where you hear Harold singing the last chorus and in the background Phil and Jimmy are singing "Happy Birthday" to Jesus. It was just Phil and Jimmy because it was just too darn high for me. But I still just love to listen to my partners selling it! Such an all-around unique song. I can think of no other like it.

"Old Toy Trains"

This Roger Miller-written song was on both our album and our TV special. Only, on the album we sang it and on the television show, Roger did. There is hardly anyone in the music business whom I respect more as an entertainer and a writer than this man. He had it all and we loved him dearly. When he guest-hosted Dick Cavett's late-night show for a week, he called us to come to New York to do it with him. We called him for our Christmas special, and a few years later as one of the very first guest on our TV series. There was only one problem: when we all five got together, we would laugh the whole day. He and Harold would start and never stop, and we all would be on the floor before thirty minutes went by. And there is nothing that will take away the timbre and quality of your voice than laughing. We would be shot for hours and have to drink hot tea to get our throats back in shape to sing. And then, just when we thought we were ready, well, it was kind of like getting tickled in church. When you can't laugh is when you want to laugh the most. There is a picture by my chair in my den as I speak of the five of us huddled together on the set of that show, giggling like school girls on the back of a bus. I don't know how we ever got through it.

A strong link in this chain was Jerry Kennedy. He was both Roger's and our producer. Jerry cut the original hit with Roger in 1967 of this song that Roger had written at Christmastime for his little son, Dean. The last time we saw Roger was in Nashville, at the Opry House, May 6, 1992, at the taping of the TV special "Hats Off to Minnie," a salute to the life and career of Minnie Pearl. We were both guests on the show. He performed and we performed, and we talked and laughed backstage as usual. But then, during a set change, he dropped the news on us that he was sick. His spirits were high and he had every hope to beat it, but sadly he didn't. He left a hole in our hearts and in the world of entertainment. All who knew him loved him, and everybody you met in the industry had a Roger Miller story. And they were all jewels, as was he. Too soon, Roger. Just too soon.

"For Momma"

Harold and I wrote this not just for *our* mother, but for all three of our mothers. There are four verses, each separated by an old, familiar carol. Each of us honored our mothers with a verse and a story of what she meant to us at Christmastime. Jimmy's Bird, Phil's Marjorie, Harold and Don's Frances.

There's a Christmas memory I recall so well
Takes me back to when I was a child
Just her and me by the lights of the tree
We'd sit and she would softly sing awhile

The fondest memory of this song was from the TV special. We shot what was basically a video of the song with our individual mothers involved in a scene with each of us. We shot most of the special in Staunton mainly for this purpose. We wanted to get them on tape so we would always have them. They each did a wonderful job in the scenes they videotaped with us, and as the final scene of the song, our director, Steve Womack, who directed all our specials and our entire television series for seven years, had us standing on stair steps with our mothers in front of us. We were all in place, and Steve was deep into concentration setting up the scene when he looked up and said, "Okay, I'm ready. I see four Statlers but only three mothers. Where's the other mother?" The entire crew broke into laughter and Steve was startled for moment until he realized his faux pas. He ran up the steps and grabbed our mother, hugged her, and said, "I forgot for a moment that you have a double investment in this concern."

Merry Christmas to a lot of good folks who made it happen, made it worthwhile, and made it good.

29

Four for the Show

1986

Four guys sitting in a theater in tuxedoes waiting for the show to start. I love this cover. This was shot in our hometown, also, and by Charles Clemmer. The Visulite was one of three movie houses in Staunton that we grew up attending. The Strand was torn down, the Dixie is out of business, but the Visulite is still open every night showing first-run films. I went there on Saturday mornings as a preteen to see the Bowery Boys and Martin and Lewis. I went there on Saturday nights on dates as a teen and held hands. Then, years later, I took my kids and sat in the same seats and slept as they watched *Howard the Duck*. So we have history and beautiful memories with this wonderful old show place. The big difference today is that those hard, wooden seats are gone, and the ones they have now rock back and forth, recline, and have cup holders on the arms. What hasn't changed is the popcorn. Popcorn and good memories never change.

"Count on Me"

I wrote this on the road with all of that old-time gospel aftertime to it. I could hear it in my head but I had to sing it to the guys practically before I finished it in order for them to sing the answering parts to see if it was going to work. It did and turned out to be the first single from this album and a top-five hit.

Count on me (when others leave you)
Count on me (when they don't believe you)
Count on me (I'll always be true) (Count on me)

It's hard to determine how many songs I have written, but I have had north of 250 of them recorded, and some of those by multiple artists. And the more you are out there on the scene, the more of a target you become for someone who wants to take a legal shot at you. This only happened to me one time, and it was in association with this composition. Someone who had written a song that I or no one else had ever heard made the claim that I had plagiarized his work by stealing some of his melody. I never have and never would do such a thing. I love and respect the gift of songwriting that I was given at an early age too much to abuse it in any way.

As soon as I was made aware of this claim, I called an entertainment lawyer and we hired a musicologist from Vanderbilt, best I recall. He compared the song in question with "Count on Me" note by note and bar by bar. The hands-down decision was that there was nothing that could possibly be considered illegal in my song and the case was dropped as soon as we presented the results of our efforts. It still makes me a little hot under the collar just thinking about how easily someone can make an accusation without cause just to get a little attention. I honestly don't remember this guy's name and wouldn't print it here if I did. He'll have to get that kind of attention someplace else.

"You Oughta Be Here with Me"

Roger Miller wrote the words and music for a Broadway play that had a major run in the mid-eighties on the Great White Way. It was called *Big River*, based on *The Adventures of Huckleberry Finn*, and he won a Tony award for some of the best collections of original songs ever offered to the New York theater. We went up and caught it at the Eugene O'Neill Theater and were just astounded at the work he had put into it. Harold and I were captivated with a very country-sounding song from the second act and vowed to one another that night to put it on our next album. It was the kind of melody and content you just didn't hear very often in a Broadway musical.

If you think it's lonesome where you are tonight
Then you oughta be here with me
If you think there's heartaches where you are tonight
Then you oughta be here with me

We recorded it January 15, 1986, at a 2 P.M. session at Young'Un Studio, and as luck would have it, Roger was in town that week. He and his wife, Mary, came to the session and sat in the control room with Jerry while we put it to tape. It's not totally unusual for a writer to be invited to the studio when their song is being cut. I've been on the other end of that myself. I remember when John Davidson recorded "Monday Morning Secretary," I went by and listened. As I had told you much earlier, Elvis invited me when he recorded "Susan When She Tried." There were many other invitations that I just couldn't make work. We had had lots of writers and publishers come by to listen and say thank you, but we were honored to have Roger there that day and get his immediate stamp of approval.

"We Got the Mem'ries"

As a songwriter, I have always been taken by how many different ways you can make the word *memories* fit into the rhythm and rhyme of a song.

1. Memories
2. Mem-o-ries
3. Mem'ries

Every writer takes artistic liberties with this word to suit his or her immediate purpose, and Harold and I were no exception. Number three was our choice here.

Take away the house, the car, the money
And we'll still have more than we can count, 'cause, Honey
We got the mem'ries, we got the mem'ries
We got the mem'ries in our heart

We didn't use instrumental breaks in our music as much as other artists did, and I'm not sure why. But note that on the previous song and on this one, we have some really outstanding picking. Makes me wish we had done more of this. And note the vocal repeat choruses at the end. We were winging it and having fun.

"I Don't Dream Anymore"

This was a melody my son Debo had written and pitched to me. I would take his tapes, get the tune in my head, and then sit down with the guitar or piano and put what I hoped were fitting and appropriate words to his notes. Many songwriting teams through the years worked exactly this way. I told you earlier that Lew and I did this on a number of occasions, but then I was putting music to his lyrics. With Debo, I was putting lyrics to his music. Two totally different challenges. When I wrote with Harold, we sat and did the words and music at the same time.

I don't dream anymore
Not like I did before
'Cause since I met you, all my dreams have come true
I don't dream anymore

"Forever"

I'm going to tell you something right here I have never told Jimmy. Of all the wonderful songs he wrote for the Statlers through the years, this is my favorite. It's intimate and yet power-filled with a melody that just won't stop. I loved recording it, but most of all I loved singing it on stage every night. That chorus will sing itself, and you could just feel it filling up a coliseum when we got to:

Forever I will love you
I'll never get over loving you
Forever I will love you
I'll never get over loving you

This was the third single from the album and was a top-ten hit.

"Only You"

This was an old Platters hit from 1955, written by Buck Ram and Ande Rand, who were actually the same person. I think everyone in the rock field and the country field put it on an album sometime or another. It was covered more times than a lawyer's behind, and sometimes it worked and sometimes it didn't. We had a really fine record of it, but it probably should never have been a single. Listening to it today I can see that it had no real country appeal. However, we got a rather interesting video out of it.

The four Statlers, along with four actresses, spent two days, June 17 and 18, 1986, at Opryland shooting in the theme park. We rode rides and played carnival games and basically had a good time, with "Only You" blasting loudly in the background. I don't pretend to be able to remember all the actors/actresses we used in the thirteen videos we shot in the eighties and nineties, but I do recall these four ladies and you will probably know each one of them, too.

I was paired with Rebecca Holden, who guested on every major TV show in the eighties decade. You may remember her mainly from *Knight Rider*. Phil was paired with Robin Lee, a rising country singer who also toured with us as an opening act. Jimmy was with Lane Brody, who had had the number-one hit "Yellow Rose of Texas." And Harold partnered with Lorrie Morgan, who was only about three years from the string of hits that would make her a second-generation country star.

The girls were beautiful, and the video was heavy on the playlist on all the TV stations that featured those shows in the eighties. Don't think we ever sang it on stage.

Lorrie also toured with us as our opening act later. She was a part of our show when her husband, Keith Whitley, died May 9, 1989. We had told her to forego the weekend tour that started only a week after Keith's death, but when we arrived at the theater in Topeka, Kansas, on the 18th, there sat Lorrie in her dressing room all by herself, smoking, looking as pretty as ever. We asked, "What are you doing here?" And her sincere answer was, "What else would I be doing? I'd rather be working." And so she did, and the crowd was very happy to see her.

"For Crying Out Loud"

Jimmy and John Rimel doing their duet-writing again, and what a really good entry. Country music has always favored trick plays on words like this.

> *For crying out loud, you can use my shoulder*
> *For crying out loud, don't make it any harder*
> *Let the tears flow down your cheeks*
> *You'll feel a whole lot better now*
> *For crying out loud*

"Will You Be There"

Debo was really getting the hang of the melodies I liked to write to. This was a perfect one that could have gone in any direction. He gave me an open book on tempo and tune, and I chose, maybe because of the mood I was in, to take it in a very heavy direction.

> *Will you be there when all the glory is gone*
> *And only mem'ries remain*
> *Will you be there to tell my children the truth*
> *When no one remembers my name*

I was writing about a couple the age that I am much more familiar with today than I was at forty-one when I wrote these words. I thank Debo for the musical ride and can only thank the good Lord for the insight into an age to come.

When the gray in my hair doesn't matter
And the voice you hear now becomes weak
When my stories are told much too often
And my hand shakes when I touch your cheek

There's a beautiful acoustic-guitar solo midway through that I am going to credit to Pete Wade. He had such a touch, and it is never better demonstrated than on this song. This is a love song. There's no romance. No physical passion. But a deep and lifelong love that every man and woman hope to attain with the perfect mate.

Will you be there to help me pass the days
And let me know you still care
I will face whatever the years may bring
If only I know you'll be there

"I Believe I'll Live for Him"

Southern gospel music has always had so much of our hearts, and we never strayed far from it. I have often said we sang country music with Southern gospel harmony. But in our very early beginnings back home, we flat out were a young aspiring gospel quartet. We loved singing it, hearing it, and writing it. Most of our albums had one on it. All of our stage shows had two or three. So, Harold and I wrote one every chance that presented itself.

I believe he died for me so I believe I'll live for him
I may not do it right but I'm gonna try
Wherever he will take me is better than where I've been
I believe he died for me so I believe I'll live for him

The Cathedral Quartet were great friends of ours. We liked this song so much, we sent a tape to George Younce and they cut it immediately and, of course, did a fantastic job with it. But the really unique thing about this song was that we included it on this album and the very next album as well. We had never done that before. But it was just tailor-made for the upcoming *Radio Gospel Favorites*. So, consider this a preview of coming attractions.

281

"More Like My Daddy Than Me"

Both of my sons were baseball pitchers in high school, so I have attended my share of sports banquets in cafeterias, gymnasiums, and auditoriums. I loved going but didn't always love staying. All of the spring sports, girls and boys, were lumped together, and it made for a long evening for every parent there, as each person in attendance was only interested in seeing their son or daughter take the stage. And that is precisely what this song is about. Sitting through the ceremony inspired each word and note and only made me more eager to get home and commit my thoughts to paper.

I just spent an unusual evening
At a banquet that still won't digest
Watching this year's high school heroes
Get awarded for what they do best
There's a letter for the one who jumped highest
And one ran faster by far
One broke the 200-meter
And one broke her arm on the bar

I am a very sentimental guy and watching my kids do what they did in those teen years just made my feelings more tender when I wrote about them. It was as if all of this was happening to me all over again. It was as if I could see their future as I was watching their present, and it made me very introspective.

The baseball team took the honors
The MVP stole the show
The coach looked scared with a tie on
Swore next year they'd be 15 and 0
And in tomorrow morning's newspaper
There'll be pictures that surely reveal
Young men looking strange with no caps on
And tomboys in dresses and heels

That was the scene of what was going on up front. The chorus was what was going on in the audience.

282

And I've stood up there where there're standing
And never once thought I would be
Sittin' out here where I'm sittin'
Looking more like my daddy than me

Those beautiful, innocent kids had no way of knowing both sides of the coin. Only I and all those other parents sitting around me could see the full picture. It's like looking at an aerial view of your house where you can simultaneously see what's going on in both the front yard and the backyard.

Twenty some years from tomorrow
These same boys and girls will find
An old faded newspaper clipping
Yellow and torn up with time
Their daughters and sons will be standing
Up there where they used to be
And only then will they know what I'm feeling
When they're sittin' out here with me

I've stood up there where they're standing
Behind the MVP
But it's late, I'm tired and still hungry
Acting more like my daddy than me
I'm getting more like my daddy than me

When we were still young and green back in the Shenandoah Valley of Virginia, we got our first exposure on television on a local Saturday night show hosted by Don Reno and Red Smiley. They were good bluegrass musicians, and Don Reno was a banjo virtuoso of the first order. There was a story floating around the business for years that about midpoint in his career, he was on stage one night and stepped to the mic to play a break. He didn't just do the usual that night. He let his heart and mind and fingers go to places they had never been, and he hit such a pinnacle that what he played and heard affected his senses so severely that he walked off stage, laid his instrument in its case, and never touched it again for years. He had blown his own mind, so to speak, and he couldn't contend with it. Fortunately, he did come back and had many more years for us all to enjoy his talent.

My revelation was not this extreme, but I did feel a little of what Reno must have felt after I wrote this song. You may not think it is anything all that special, just another country song in three-quarter time that rhymes, but I knew it was on a level I had never written before. It was personal, and I may have come as close to poetry as I ever came. I wrote two stories at the same time: one told what was happening on stage, and the other told what was going on in the audience. I'm not bragging on it or taking any undue credit. I just wrote what I was feeling and what I was being given, but I was tuned in like never before, and I felt a pinnacle of my own with this. I didn't take a Reno-type vacation or even tell anyone about it. I kept it to myself until right now, but it still affects me after all these years when I listen to it. It's my magnum opus.

I came home from the banquet that night, and in thirty minutes put it all down on paper with the melody intact. It disturbed and excited me so much I didn't sleep all night long. I got up early the next morning and went into the Statler offices across town. Harold was already there, so I stopped in his doorway and said, "Come over to my office with me. I have something I want you to hear." I had an old upright piano in the corner, and I put my scratch paper of notes in the little grove that holds the songbooks. Harold sat on the corner of the piano stool with me and I sang it to him. I got half way through it, just finishing the first chorus, when he looked over at me and said, "You know you're killing me." It was one of the greatest writing compliments I ever got. Part of my Reno moment.

30

Radio Gospel Favorites

1986

Our daddy used to get up early in the mornings and tune the radio to WLW, Cincinnati, Ohio, and through the static listen to an early morning show of the Browns Ferry Four. This group consisted of Grandpa Jones; Merle Travis; and the Delmore Brothers, Alton and Rabon. These three acts put together this country/gospel quartet to fill a half hour that came open in the early A.M. and pick up a little extra coin. You can find them on YouTube and maybe find some of their King Record recordings somewhere on the Internet. They sang a brand of gospel with a country flavor totally different from what the Blackwood Brothers were singing on a radio station a few states west at the very same time. The Blackwoods were singing what would become Southern gospel, and all of it was a little different from the hymns you might be singing in church. It's hard to explain exactly what the differences were. You almost had to be there and grow up in that musical environment to pick up the nuances and understand what the difference between a hymn and a gospel song and a radio gospel song truly is. All of them excited us, and we loved singing them, as I think you'll be able to tell on this album.

On the cover is a simple picture of the four of us, the Statlers, singing around a modern-day microphone (at least it was then) in a radio station studio. Why we all have black hair is a complete mystery to me. Something about the lighting, I suppose, as I can assure you there was no artificial coloring going on. Or maybe it was a negative that stayed in the pan of acetic acid too long while it was being developed. Then flip it over and you'll see our conception of what we might have looked like as a 1940s radio quartet. Slick-backed hair, loud ties and bow ties, double-breasted suits and suspenders. This was our salute to those times, that era, and those men. Here is what we wrote at the time on the back of the album:

> *"As we have often said, 'We grew up and cut our musical teeth on gospel music.' It was then, and still is, our first love. We would try, at every opportunity, to find one of the great gospel groups on the radio. This picture reminds us of how we may have looked a few decades ago if we could have sung on the radio. This album is dedicated to those groups, those songs, and those times. These, then, are some of our 'Radio Gospel' favorites." HAROLD, PHIL, JIMMY, DON*

There is an added note from the four of us in the corner of the picture that reads, *"This album is dedicated to the memory of Reverend Eugene Jordan."*

This gentleman and scholar was Harold's, Phil's, and my minister for twenty-five years. I gave him some serious credit back during the *Holy Bible* production. We learned so much from him about Scripture, theology, and just faith in general. He always reminded me of the picture I have of the Apostle Paul. He was knowledgeable, stern, unwavering, and no-nonsense. Rev. Jordan was not warm and fuzzy and sometimes not even real friendly, but he was solid and intense in his beliefs, and we all just loved the man dearly. He told us one time that we were good preachers. We gave him a sideways glance and asked him exactly what he was talking about. He said, "You guys preach every time you walk on stage even if you're not singing a religious song." What a compliment that was, and what a deep observation that I didn't even try to understand at the time.

Here's some old gospel and some new gospel we sure enjoyed putting together: "Amazing Grace, "Sweet By and By," "One Size Fits All," and "I Believe I'll Live for Him." These four titles show up on other past albums, so I won't rewrite about them here.

"A Different Song"

This was another song that was on a previous album back in 1972—*Innerview*. But what makes this different from the ones I listed is that we recut this one, so it is really a new rendition. Being the sole writer, I have tried hard to make a decision over the years as to which cut I like best, this one or the one from fourteen years before. The early one was more country, in the key of F, and slower. This one is more gospel-flavored, in the keys of D and E, and faster. If I had to make that decision, and thank God I don't, I think I would just throw a dart over my shoulder and take whichever one it landed on.

"There Is Power in the Blood"

Usually considered a hymn, but you will be hard-pressed to find it in a standard Presbyterian, Methodist, or even Baptist hymnal. Not a Southern gospel standard. You won't often hear it at many quartet concerts. But a good example of a radio gospel staple. You are more apt to find the words and music in a thin paperback songbook given out at a tent meeting along the highway in the first half of the twentieth century. As a matter of fact, it was written by Lewis F. Jones in 1899 at a camp meeting in rural Maryland. It has the charm and the feel and the spirit of the era in which it was written.

There is power, power, wonder-working power
In the blood of the lamb
There is power, power, wonder-working power
In the precious blood of the lamb

Our arrangement is less than two minutes long but it is powerful. We never ran over and usually leaned toward running a little short. We never wanted to wear anyone out listening to our music. We figured if you liked it, you could just play it again!

"We Won't Be Home Until Then"

I was in a philosophical and retrospective mood when I wrote this one. I remember distinctly sitting at the piano the night I was so moved and giving it that particular rhythm to fit the words I was hearing in my head. JK set the perfect laid-back, bluesy mood with the electric guitar from the first note. The piano of Larry Butler picked it up, and from there we gave what I felt was a perfect reading of a hard gospel song with lyrics that meant something.

Leave the world a better place
And pay the debts you owe
The price to get through heaven's doors
Was paid up years ago

And we won't be home until then, praise God
We won't be home until then
Till that final release, when my soul is at peace
We won't be home until then

Larry Butler was on the road with us during the Johnny Cash years in the sixties and seventies. He grew up in gospel music just as we did and was a fantastic piano player at a very early age. You get to know people really well when you travel together day after day. We liked Larry a lot. When our Lester "Roadhog" and His Cadillac Cowboys characters hit, we would joke with Larry about doing another album of gospel quartet satire and call ourselves "Woody Burns and the Gospel Flames." We joked about it so much it almost happened. Oh boy, I am so glad it never did.

After we left the Cash troupe in '72, Larry produced John's records, along with so many other artists such as Kenny Rogers, Mac Davis, John Denver, and more than I can list. He came and did these sessions with us, and I'm so glad he did. I tell you all that to tell you this. Larry and Jerry

Kennedy, both being such successful producers, had no qualms about working for and with one another. Jerry was just as likely to go play on a session Butler was producing the next day. You would think there would be high competition, but these guys were so good at what they did and so confident in what they knew, they didn't mind sharing their talents with one another.

We used to ham around backstage on the road with Larry at the keyboard and sing all of those old gospel songs we all knew as kids. Here we got a chance to do it together for real.

"Blessed Be"

Kim Reid Weller was directing our church's youth choir for a Bible School closing service. She needed a song for the children to sing. Something special that had not been done year after year. Something the kids would look forward to. Something new and fresh. So, she wrote one, and this was it, and we knew this was it as soon as we heard it sitting in the pews.

Blessed be
The children who are free
It blesses me
That they come to see
And come to know
His love he has to show
And it will glow
And it will grow

"A Beautiful Life"

There could not be a better example of a radio gospel song. We used to sing this when we were wee-tiny kids and sing the aftertime just like we heard it on the kitchen radio.

Each day I'll do a golden deed
By helping those who are in need
My life on earth is but a span

When we got to that last line, we had a friend we grew up with who misheard it, the way we all do with some songs, and always sang it, "My life on earth is buttered Spam." I can't hear it without remembering that and smiling.

But back to this very serious and very good old song. It was written by William M. Golden in 1918 and it still holds up today.

Life's evening sun is sinking low
A few more days and I must go
To meet the deeds that I have done
Where there will be no setting sun

This isn't the only standard classic of this genre that William M. wrote. He also penned "Canaan's Land," sometimes titled "Where the Soul of Man Never Dies." Why we didn't put that one on here, also, I have no idea. It would have been a perfect addition.

While going down life's weary road
I'll try to lift some traveler's load
I'll try to turn the night to day
Make flowers bloom along the way

This is The Statler Brothers as I like to remember them. We were bright and energetic and the harmony was robust, close, and had authority. Listen to the duets. Listen to Harold's low notes on the last chorus and to Jimmy's high note at the end. I love this sound and this style and this kind of music. I loved these guys and making music with them.

William M. Golden wrote most all of his gospel songs while in prison for an eight-year stretch. Not sure why he was there, but he certainly made good use of his time. He was killed in a car accident in 1934 near Eupora, Mississippi.

"Over the Sunset Mountains"

Jimmy brought us this song. We three had never heard it or heard of it before, and that is a rarity. It was written by John Peterson, who had written other gospel field standards such as "Heaven Came Down" and "It Took a Miracle." We were not only taken by the beauty and simplicity of it, but when Jimmy told us it was his mother's all-time favorite song, that put the capper on it. We not only recorded it here, we also used it in the closing of our TV show in the nineties more than once. Such a sweet and picturesque gospel/hymn.

Over the sunset mountains, someday I'll softly go
Into the arms of Jesus, He who has loved me so
Over the sunset mountains, Heaven awaits for me
Over the sunset mountains, Jesus my savior I'll see

31

Maple Street Memories

1987

As soon as we had the concept for this album, we knew we needed an all-American house with a summertime front porch for the cover. Just down the street from me was the picture-perfect setting we were looking for. At 359 Sherwood Avenue (you can easily see the house number in the picture), these neighbors gave their consent for us to invade their privacy one morning long enough to get shots for both the front and back of the jacket. Again, Charles Clemmer was the photog, and Ken Kim handled the art direction for us. My favorite part of the picture is the bicycle flopped in the yard the way a kid (and haven't we all) will just jump off it and leave it.

Recorded at Young'Un Sound Studio in Nashville in its entirety, it was started thirteen months before it was released. The first track was laid down on June 16, 1986, and the album dropped (a word meaning "released" today but was not in use back then) July 20, 1987. You read all the time where artists say, "It took us five years to make that album," or "We spent a year in the studio getting it right." Don't believe it. It just means it took a year fitting it in the schedule. But saying "a year in the making" really makes it sound like a great effort. It's an old interview trick everybody uses.

"Our Street/Tell Me Why"

This might be the most unusual and original piece of material we recorded in our whole career. Harold and I had the idea to try to recreate a lazy summer evening in a typical small town without the benefit of video. It had to all come from the audio side of the coin, with the music, the spoken word, and the sound effects. Jerry Kennedy, bless his old Southern heart, knew exactly what we wanted and came through with those sound effects, such as crickets chirping, kids playing in the background, and a porch swing creaking that just blew our minds. The scene was set and the story was told before we even got to the written word.

Phil kicks off the recitations with a story we wrote for him about a girl from his past who broke his arm and his heart. It's as if he is looking down this street and reminiscing as he talks. We each follow suit with stories that overlap and tell them as if these scenes from our childhood and teen years were coming to us as sweet but distant memories. The one we wrote for me was a true story about our dog, King. He saved my life, and to this day he makes me cry by just the mention of his name. I can't listen to this story. Sometimes the years give you things your heart just can't handle. Oh, how I loved that old dog.

Jimmy's story is about trying to kiss his girlfriend goodnight on her front porch under a glaring overhead lightbulb. And Harold's is a wrap-up and overview of the street on any given summer evening, anywhere in America, with family and dusk close by and a peace we all try to recapture with each passing year. Note that in his story, Harold mentions two girls who used to sit in a front-porch swing and sing. Shirley Jean Berrell and Charlotte Thompson—two names we borrowed from other songs of ours. Shirley Jean from "The Official Historian..." and Charlotte Thompson from "Susan When She Tried." Just a little sidebar of how we let even our fictitious characters live on in other settings.

When these two neighborhood girls (in reality, session singers Jean McCracken and Diana Rae) begin to sing, they're singing an old pop song from 1945, "Tell Me Why." Harold and I remember the high school girls who would sit on the very back seat of the school bus and sing all the way home every evening when we were kids. Invariably they would get around to singing "Tell Me Why," and without fail there was always one of them who knew that walk-down harmony part. We knew we couldn't capture the era or the mood without two girls singing this beautiful old love tune just one more time. Then we, Harold, Phil, Jimmy and I, sing it a capella. And it is as good as four-part harmony gets, even if I have to say so myself. There, I said it and now on with business.

If you count this piece as one song, as it really is, that only makes nine cuts on this album. As you may have noticed, the Statlers never recorded long arrangements of any one song. Two and a half to three minutes was about our average whereas most artists would think nothing of adding half that again to any recording. I'd say Roger Miller and the Statlers cut the shortest songs in the business at the time. Roger, due to his writing style, and us, due to our arranging. But here with "Our Street/Tell Me Why," we were dealing with 8:09, eight minutes and nine seconds. Our dilemma was how many total songs should be on the album? This led us to take a relook at our record contract, and we saw that it called for "nine to ten sides or 28 minutes of music." Problem solved. We went with nine cuts and easily had thirty-one minutes of music.

"Maple Street Memories"

We were playing Seattle. Saturday April 26, 1986. I distinctly remember it was a high-rise hotel, and I spent the day watching TV and reading until my mind and my eyes glazed over from boredom. On the road, all day long, you doze and eat and then doze some more. Finally, I rode down to the lobby, walked out to the bus, and got my guitar and took it back to the room with me. I sat there on the bed, and on a yellow legal pad I wrote these words:

We were both nine years old when you came to town
I remember the big Allied Van
My mom went over and took you all lunch

294

And my dad gave your dad a hand
The first time I saw you was through the screen door
When the paper I threw missed the porch
Lord, it's been years since I carried the News
But I still carry the torch

I remember sitting there and staring out the window, trying to decide exactly where I wanted to go next with this. I knew I had a great opening verse. (Originally that second line was "I remember the big moving van." After a while of staring, I thought Allied gave it more realism.) I also knew if I was to have a love song, I had to get into the personal relationship pretty quick in the next verse. As I began writing that verse, I had no way of knowing that before I finished it I would be given maybe the best line I would ever write in a song:

We played Hide and Seek in the buildings out back
I was easy to find, I admit
As the years flew away it got harder to hide
The fact I thought you were It
Then we stood by the lilac bush in your yard
Your pink prom gown late in May
Your mom took our picture, I took your hand
And you took my breath away

By the driveway where I grew up on Route 3 in Staunton, Virginia, there was a huge lilac bush. Mom always had us stand by it for family pictures because of the colorful background it offered, even though a lot of them were in black and white. There's a picture of me in a tuxedo when I was in the Tom Thumb Wedding in the first grade, a picture of Harold in his ball uniform, and one of my sister Faye in her prom gown. There are Easter morning pictures of all of the family, and every one of them is posed by that lilac bush at the edge of the driveway. Mom's lilac bush. In one sentimental afternoon, in a lonesome hotel room in a far northwest city, I was able to pay homage to Mom's lilacs and then write the line that would keep me writing for years to come, trying to top it. Don't think I ever did.

Your mom took our picture, I took your hand
And you took my breath away

295

I spent the rest of the day finishing what I had started, and on the way to the show that night, on the bus, I sang it to my Brothers. The ink was still wet, so to speak, and the emotion of these new words were still so fresh my voice shook a little as I sang it. They loved it as much as I did.

I never go back I don't stand in the yard
And look at your window upstairs
In my mind I see you combing your hair
And blowing kisses at me in the air
Then one time at Christmas I saw you come home
Your arms full of children that day
And it was later that night when I put mine to bed
I put my Maple Street memories away

The Statlers were famous for their strong, definite, and harmonious endings. I think this is the only song we ever sang where one voice did the last line as a solo. It just seemed to call for that kind of intimacy.

We shot a video of it in our hometown in the summer of '87. We used a lot of our sons and daughters and their friends in it. There was one girl we hired to play the main character in the last verse because she was so pretty. I didn't know her but we all thought she was perfect for the part. Turns out now, thanks to Debo, she's my daughter-in-law and the mother of two of my grandchildren!

"Déjà Vu"

Speaking of my son Debo, he again brought a new melody he had written to Harold and me. We knew it was not a country song, but it had so much old-school, 1950s charm that we could not resist trying something with it. It would be a great album flavorer, but with his titling it "Déjà Vu," the challenge was on for appropriate lyrics. We could have asked him to change the title but that would have been too simple. We liked the dare and the contest of seeing how far we could run with it.

Déjà vu
Is the only way I have you
And my heart can never reveal
All the things that I feel, for you
And it's true
That a memory will have to do

And I know in my mind
It's just a matter of time
Déjà vu

There was a great strength in Debo's melody that lent itself to a comparison with some of those powerful instrumentals of the fifties such as Nelson Riddle's "Lisbon Antigua" or Les Baxter's "The Poor People of Paris" or any Roger Williams record. And JK gave us a glimpse of that by bringing in the full orchestra and recording them first; after they left, we sang to the track—something we seldom did. But I think the true nature of the melody is heard in the instrumental break with the piano work of David Briggs along with Bergen White's string arrangements. That section alone could have been a hit within itself.

Debo has recently told me he wrote this song on his orange Chet Atkins Gretsch guitar. As a teenager, he had a little studio there at the house with a four-track recorder and mixing board. He added the bass and drums and fills and played the finished product for me. That's what Harold and I worked from as we added the lyrics.

"Am I Crazy?"

Jimmy Fortune writing at the top of his game. Love this song. On my old lyric sheet from the session that day back on November 18 of 1986, I made a note in pencil above the first verse. It said "Ames." Remember the "Lugan" notes we would write on our sheets to remind ourselves to emulate the Louvin Brothers? Well, this is a similar note to remind us to follow that same course concerning an old pop group from the 1950s, the Ames Brothers. We sang that verse in the vein of the Ames Brothers—heavy and broad with a full, solid, yet quiet body of harmony. You almost have to feel it as you sing it. And then we opened up on the chorus with a more country feel to it.

Am I crazy or losing my heart
I don't believe how fast, I've fallen so far
You made love easy right from the start
So am I crazy or losing my heart

"The Best I Know How"

Kim Reid Weller learned from her daddy all about songwriting—what to do and what not to do. She also learned to store up facts and feelings for use at a later date. When I contacted her and asked her for any story she might have about the writing of this song, she said an old boyfriend actually said these words to her during a breakup. She carried the thought and the rhythm of the line with her until she found a use for it. And here it is in the title of this song.

I've given all that I have to give
And I can't take anymore
What I'm trying to show you in the way that I hold you
Is I've loved you the best I know how

The musical charm of all this is in the presentation we made in the bridge. It is so vocally animated, with each of us singing a different version and different pattern of the song. Listen closely and you'll hear us intentionally not singing together but giving it a special energy with individual interpretation. For the lack of a better term I'll call it "contrived improvising." We happened on it as we were sitting around the table arranging it, and somebody said, "Remember what we each just did and let's do it just like that." This was the third single, and it did its job keeping the album viable as it reached into the top fifteen on the country charts. Good song and fun to sing.

"I'll Be the One"

Debo brought me another tune I just couldn't ignore. This one was up-tempo with a clever built-in chord change in the melody that then flowed back into the original key. Putting words to his music was always a pleasure, as he didn't write like the typical instrumentalist. You never had to cheat a syllable here and there to make it fit. The lines were in time and in accord with one another. All I had to do was make 'em rhyme and we were in business. On this one, we even worked in that ever-pleasing before-time bass line for Harold, added Bela Fleck plunking on the banjo, and we were off and running. This was the single that led the album. Two minutes and three seconds long—the perfect radio song, and it went into the top ten in no time. We had so many good writers creating on our behalf that it was hard not to put good songs on each album.

I'll be the one, standing in the shadows
When you think the world has been unfair
I'll be the one walking beside you
When no one else is there

I'll be the pillow you lie on
I'll be your midnight lullaby
I'll be the shade on the window
To keep the stars from your eyes

Debo gave me an insight into this one that I really don't recall. He said he played the verse for me, and the next day, just before dinner, I sang him the four lines I had written to his melody. Only problem was I told him it needed a chorus. So he rushed through dinner and wrote a bridge that he played for me that evening. He said he never heard anything about it again until we came home from our next trip to Nashville and I played him the finished record. His first single. He said he bought his first car, a Nissan Maxima, with the royalties.

"Beyond Romance"

I wish I had more to tell you about this one. But maybe it doesn't need much else said about it. It speaks for itself in the mature and understanding way the feelings are laid out. And the performance is so solid and pure. I'm very proud of this Jimmy Fortune/John Rimel song and the heart that all of us put into it. It's love and good writing and good singing all wrapped up in one package.

If you're lucky you may
Fall in love one day
So hold on to what you can save
Old memories pass
Life goes by too fast
So be there when love comes your way

"I Lost My Heart to You"

And here is that Fortune/Rimel team again. It's strange, but I don't remember meeting John Rimel but about twice in our whole relationship. Jimmy would bring these songs in and play them for us, and John just stayed across the mountain in Charlottesville and wrote. They complemented one another nicely and fed the Statler style like they had been with us from day one. Just look at and listen to those nostalgic lyrics:

Summer nights and ponytails
Eyes sparkling blue
Take me back to yesterday
When I lost my heart to you

I have had so many fans through time tell me how they liked the way we would often tease a couple of lines with all four of us singing in unison and then hit harmony with a vengeance that would bring them out of their seats. The chorus here is a perfect example of that. I wish you could hear it as you read it. And maybe you can find some of these more obscure songs on the Internet.

I lost my heart to you
Time after time, it's true
I fall to pieces
And lose my heart to you

And don't miss the Jerry Kennedy Dobro guitar intro and turnaround. Sometimes he would come out of the control room and pick while we were singing, but most of the time he would add his in after everybody left the studio. Either way, it was always magical. Some of the most enjoyable and creative get-togethers we ever had were when just the five of us would go eat supper after every session. We had our favorite restaurant in Nashville, The Peddler Steakhouse, and we would talk about what we had recorded that day and what we would record the next day. It was always relaxing to have those private moments with just us—Harold, Phil, Jimmy, Jerry, and myself. And the years have not changed that one jot or tittle. There has been no better friend and sounding board for me than JK throughout the writing of this chronicle. Now we talk over the phone instead of over a steak, but it's still just as much fun.

"Jesus Showed Me So"

An economy of words and music. Harold and I didn't waste much. We liked to make each word count. These lines were short and brisk and to the point with no room for flowery adjectives. I love the boldness and matter-of-factness of this song.

Some men do
Some men don't
Some men can't
Some men won't
Others say they may,
but still
Jesus always will

Each Statler showed out with a solo here, as we often did, giving our own interpretations to a verse. I like listening to how different each one of us read these lines. And there is a lesson here on never throwing away anything. I have told you about the notebooks I carried with me daily in which I entered ideas and lines and outlines and scribblings for songs, many of which were never used. But as we were writing a verse for each man for this song, I went to one of those old yellow notebooks in my briefcase and found four lines I had written more than ten years before. We used them as the fourth verse intact, word-for-word, and it fit the meter and philosophy of the song perfectly. Don't tell me God doesn't look out for fools and songwriters alike.

Somebody laughed
Somebody cried
A babe was born
An old man died
Nothing lasts too long down here
But Jesus is always near

This *Maple Street Memories* album was all original material written by our staff of writers: Kim, Debo, John, Jimmy, Harold, and myself. And we had more writers coming for future albums we weren't even aware of yet. But I get ahead of myself. We were always so thankful for the talent we were surrounded by and the good things that were happening to us.

301

32

The Statlers—Greatest Hits Volume III

1988

Well, let's start this one off with a little prayer of thanksgiving. I can so easily remember how excited and unbelieving we were thirteen years before,
back in 1975, when we put together our first "Best of" album. And here we
were with volume three! The cover picture shows us sitting around the pool
at Harold's house drinking lemonade, looking cool and laid-back. But pictures can lie, even if they are worth a thousand words. We were still, after all
those years, in that I-can't-believe-this-is-happening-to-us mode. We were
singing and doing with our lives what we always dreamed of doing, and we
never for one moment at any time in all our career took any of that for
granted. I have pinched myself on stage in front of thousands, in recording
studios, at the White House, while meeting one of our childhood heroes,

accepting awards—and I silently thanked the good Lord for a blessed life every time. Still do. Released on October 3, 1988, this collection of recent hits and three new ones that would chart with success was a milestone along a golden, grateful, and appreciated path.

Seven of the songs here were written about in previous chapters, so I will only cover the three new ones. "Elizabeth," "Count on Me," "The Best I Know How," "Guilty," "My Only Love," "I'll Be the One," and "Atlanta Blue."

"Let's Get Started If We're Gonna Break My Heart"

This single led the album and was already number twelve on the country charts when this volume of the "Greatest Hits" was released. Again, Debo, who never attempted to write lyrics to his really catchy and exceptional melodies, brought this one to Harold and me to put our brand of country music libretto to it. I find the subject matter we broached here a little laughable, to be honest. We wrote about the dating scene, something that neither one of us knew anything about except in our distant memories. But being writers, we were always observing and remembering, and I think we captured what we were going after in a very expressive way.

> *I knew where the night was going*
> *When I first saw you smile*
> *But this tired old get-to-know-you routine*
> *Takes a little while*
> *We'll talk about fads and fashion*
> *That's a good place to start*
> *And I know we'll wind up talkin' about*
> *Our astrological charts*
> *So come on let's get started*
> *If we're gonna break my heart*

That's Jerry Kennedy on the intro and the mid-break playing the electric guitar. Jerry would sometimes sit in the control room and plug his guitar directly into the board and play. This set the tone at just how easy and relaxed our sessions were. As for us out in the studio, sometimes we'd stand and sing, sometimes we'd sit on tall stools. Sometimes we'd stay in the room and encourage a picker who was having trouble getting a particular lick. We served as cheerleaders to one another. Recording sessions were serious fun to us.

> *Just a little more conversation*
> *Cause we're playing by the rules*
> *We'll tell each other how some other*
> *Made us feel like fools*
> *Now here's where we gotta go easy*
> *So we won't upset the cart*
> *We'll talk about books and movies*
> *And Norman Rockwell art*
> *By then you should be ready*
> *To start to break my heart*

As I look back over my notebooks of schedules and the days that were surrounding this May 23, 1988, recording session, I'm overwhelmed by what we packed into short periods of time to achieve everything that had to be done. In that one week, we, the Statlers, were in Washington, DC, to do *The Larry King Show*. The next evening, we shot across town and performed at the White House Photographer's Dinner at the request of President Reagan. (We were with him a number of times during his administration, but this would be the last time we saw him, and the picture taken that night is a very special memory.) From there we headed to Nashville to record this song plus five others and then over to Opryland the following evening to guest on *Nashville Now*, Ralph Emery's nightly TV show that was a must every time we were in town. It was a constant whirlwind that leaves me out of breath even today thinking about it.

Looking at my old tattered 1988 datebook, I also see that in that short period of time, I missed four of my sons' baseball games by being away from home. That's what breaks my heart the most.

This was in that period of time where we were shooting a video of almost every single to get play on the many video shows being aired all over the country. VJs, or video jockeys, were sprouting up all over the TV screens with early morning and afternoon shows. We, like all the other artists of the day, tried to keep them happy. This one was shot in the Nashville airport in the middle of the night. This cut down on the crowds we would have to work around. Lorianne and Charlie of *Crook and Chase* made cameo appearances. The story was about the four of us rushing to catch a flight and then waiting to board it. We each played a dual role that got worked facetiously into the script as we posed as characters sitting in the waiting area with all the other passengers. It was a fun shoot. Phil appeared as Indiana Jones, Jimmy as an Asian tourist, Harold as an early aviator celeb, and me as an Arab sheikh. We started around 11 P.M., shot all night, finishing about 5 A.M. the next morning. I can honestly say I never had an inkling as to how much a video added to the sales of a record. It was hard to figure. They've gone out of style, so I have to think it was proven it was money not too well spent. But we had a good time spending it for them.

Note: If you can find it on the Internet, this was a period where Harold was wearing a full beard. Not sure why, and I don't remember his wearing it for long, but I do remember we all told him it made him look mean. I'm not sure if that's why he grew it or why he shaved it off.

Let's begin with "I don't know you that well"
And move on to "I'd really rather not"
By midnight we should be close enough so that we
Could get started if we're gonna break my heart

"Moon, Pretty Moon"

Kim Reid Weller at the piano and typewriter again. Such a bright and jaunty little tune that just makes me smile every time I hear it. Kim told me she was on a business trip with her husband, Scott, when they pulled into a hotel parking lot one night down in North Carolina. While he went inside to check them in, she sat in the car, mesmerized by this enormous full moon in the sky, and wrote the whole thing in her head before he got back. And I know from experience that ain't easy! I've only written one song without a piano or guitar close at hand, and I know she had neither in the car, so my hat is off to her for carrying that sweet melody in the caverns of her mind until she could get to an instrument and work out the chords.

Moon, pretty moon
Bring my baby back to me
Shine your light in her eyes

And make her remember
Moon, pretty moon
Keep her real close company
And when you see her looking up, shine her home

When Kim submitted a song, we would always have to change the gender of her pronouns. Where she had he, him, or his, we marked through and made it she, her, and hers. Small price to pay for a good song.

"More Than a Name on a Wall"

Jimmy and John Rimel presented us with another major career hit for The Statler Brothers. This one exploded on the charts and has kept pace through the years, long-lasting and meaningful. It is all about the Vietnam Veterans Memorial Wall in Washington. The song tells a story that engulfs a nation even though it's told from a very personal point of view.

I saw her from a distance as she walked up to the Wall
In her hand she held some flowers as her tears began to fall
She took out pen and paper as to trace the memories
She looked up to heaven, and the words she said were these

I had gone to Washington years before to see this wall. It was very poignant and silently affecting to my generation. I had come within an airplane's ride of serving in that war when I was turned away at the induction station and sent back home for physical reasons. (Uncle Sam said I had too many heartbeats per minute.) I had gone to funerals of my contemporaries and classmates who weren't sent home but sent straight into the battle to a land we hadn't even studied about in high school geography. I had helped put their flag-draped coffins in the ground, so I had a personal reverence for this somber memorial.

I walked the length of that wall and read the names and studied the faces of those walking slowly beside me. They were all searching for a name or maybe just for a reason. I saw mothers and dads, wives and children, walking in silence as if they were in a cathedral instead of outside in that Washington, DC, sun. I was moved beyond words. So much so that I got out of bed that night in a nearby hotel and walked down to see it after dark.

306

It was then that I stopped and touched names and allowed myself a few conversations and some private tears. They were vibrant people who now were only names carved in a granite wall. This is not much comfort for a mother overcome with a grief that will outlive her and cause her to catch her breath between painful sobs.

Lord, my boy was special and he meant so much to me
And oh, I'd love to see him, just one more time you see
All I have are the memories, and the moments to recall
So Lord, could you tell him, he's more than a name on a wall

We sang it every night on stage right down to our final concert in 2002. I said basically the same thing each time as an introduction over the music as it played softly underneath:

"And then we sang a song about one of the most sensitive eras in American history that most of us have lived through. And if you have ever, or should you ever, visit Washington, DC, you should see the wall. And you should see it at night and you should touch it. And it, in return, will touch you. This song is for all of those whose names are there and for all of those who risked having their names there, on the wall."

Not a night went by that people didn't stand at the end, and never once did we misinterpret it as praise for us. No, it was a tribute to those names and those memories and those soldiers and those guys I went to school with who never had the chance to hear this song.

33

Live and Sold Out

1989

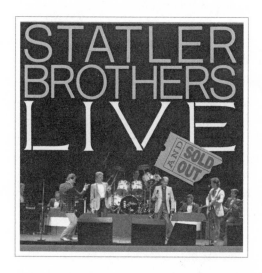

We had done every kind of album imaginable. Straight country. Numerous gospel albums. Two Christmas albums. A comedy album featuring the Roadhog and his gang of misfits. The only type we had not tackled was the "live" album. Some other artists did these, and they were always exciting to listen to. (There were some artists who actually recorded an album in the studio, put canned applause after the songs, and sold it as "live." We weren't about to stoop to this level of trickery.) The four of us and Jerry knocked the "live" idea around over lots of dinners and ultimately decided on a town that we felt totally comfortable with, so Jerry arranged for all of the mobile equipment to be there on such and such a place and time.

That such and such place and time turned out to be the Capitol Music Hall in Wheeling, West Virginia, on June 23, 1989. This was the home of the Wheeling Jamboree. Second only to the Grand Ole Opry, this was the oldest and biggest live country music radio show in America. The theater, perfect for concerts, was also set up with great sound equipment, even though Mercury did bring in a sound truck for the recording. We loved the audiences there and through the years we played it more than twenty times, always with multiple shows each night and usually multiple nights. Our agent, Marshall Grant, booked us two shows that night, and Jerry and his staff recorded both of them. We did identical shows for both audiences. Our thinking on this was we could cut and splice and interjoin any song that might be better on one show than it was on another. Our band could fix and tweak the track if anything was needed, and this gave us a backup for any tech problems that might occur. We basically just had a good time and let things fall as they may, as we always did on our concert shows. We talked to the crowd, Harold ad-libbed with them, we did comedy routines, we encored and did everything as naturally as we did each night. This was the first live recording of our stage show ever, and we wouldn't do it again until our final concert, thirteen years later, on October 26, 2002.

The sound you hear behind us is our road band, the Cowboy Symphony Orchestra. That name was a little tongue-in-cheek as there were only five of them.

Billy "Boopie" James: Bass
Carroll "Bull" Durham: Piano
Don "Mousey" Morton: Drums
Jerry Hensley: Lead Guitar
Charlie Hamm: Rhythm Guitar

"The Offical Historian on Shirley Jean Berrell"

Yes, this song was on an earlier album, *Entertainers...On and Off the Record*, 1978. I have not been writing about songs that have been previously recorded, but I wanted to point out what a different song this was by this time and how differently we used it. Originally, it was a nostalgic story song that fit perfectly into the Statler vein of singles. But now you will notice some changes. The tempo is faster and we use it for an opening concert song. It's a familiar hit to the fans in the audience plus we are emphasizing the energy of the song more than the story inside it. We did the same thing with "Do You Remember These?" through the years. These songs tended to serve other purposes for us on stage than they had on record. An evolution that you will notice that takes place with most recording artists. That is the mystery and the magic of music and how it serves us as we age and grow, giving us the chance to find new ways for it to fulfill various objectives.

As Harold and I play with the audience after this song, you'll hear me mention the cowbells and you may hear some ringing from the crowd throughout the show. This is a custom of that theater that was born of the Wheeling Jamboree through the years. I have never known how it started or what it means, but many concertgoers would be seen with their personal cowbells in hand as they came through the doors. They loved ringing them, and we always found it funny and loved hearing them.

"A Hurt I Can't Handle"

Jimmy wrote this toe-tapper, and it was the single from the album. Oddly, it was backed with the stage version of "Don't Wait on Me," and both sides wound up on the charts. I'll talk more about that later in this chapter, but here are a few good lines I wanted to share with you:

This is a hurt I can't handle, and it cuts right through my skin
I've gone and burned my last candle, till it's meeting at both ends
I swam across love's muddy river and I've sailed life's stormy seas
But this is a hurt I can't handle, and lord, it's killin' me

"Bed of Rose's"

This, of course, was the same song we had a major hit with in 1970, and yet, at the same time, a very different song. After years of singing it on stage every night, we again morphed slowly into a much faster tempo. We used the speed and energy of the song in a new way from how we used it originally. Stage versions of our songs took on a life of their own after hundreds and hundreds of performances. And then there was the comedy that we always allowed to enter into it during a concert. Harold and I were always looking for ways of including the audience in any way possible.

On this particular night, as you can hear, someone brings a rose to each of us while we're singing. In all honesty, this happened most nights during this song because of its title, and Harold would usually play with whomever had the nerve to put themselves in the spotlight each night.

"Foggy Mountain Breakdown"

We always featured our band, the Cowboy Symphony Orchestra, in concert. We would leave the stage while they played. Although it appears as the fourth song on the album, it was actually performed toward the end of the show each night. It not only gave them an opportunity to be featured, it gave us a break to wipe the sweat from our faces backstage and get a drink of water. We also took our coats off and came back on stage in our shirtsleeves.

"When the Roll Is Called Up Yonder"

The applause you hear just before this song is for the band as they lay their instruments down and walk off stage in imitation of our walk-off just before their song. The setup was that they had performed without us and now we would have to perform without them. After some banter, Harold gives us a note on the piano and we sing this wonderful old hymn a capella.

One night in the late nineties, the Cathedral Quartet was booked to perform at the Salem Civic Center just up the road from Staunton. These five men were great friends of ours, and as much as we loved their music, we loved them even more. We got word a day before that both George Younce and Glen Payne were ill and would not make the show, but the other three, Ernie Haase, Scott Fowler, and pianist Roger Bennett, would be there and do the show. We called Roger and told him we were at home off tour and if he needed us, we'd come and do a few numbers to help out. He said, "Please."

We showed up, they introduced us, we came up from the audience, and the first song we sang was this one. After some back-and-forth joking, Roger asked if we needed him to play for us, and I said, "No. Just roll us an F. We do this one a capella." Without missing a beat, he threw his hands in the air like the fabulous instrumentalist he was and said in disgust, "A capella! The devil's music!"

"I'll Fly Away"

We always included a gospel song in every concert. Usually two or three, because we just loved singing them and it became expected of us. Albert E. Brumley wrote this old classic in 1932, and it is reputed to be the most recorded gospel song of all time. I can easily believe that is true. We started singing it back in 1961 when we scored a summer job at a local outdoor country music venue, Oak Leaf Park, in Luray, Virginia. We opened the shows every Sunday as the staff quartet for performances at 2 P.M. and 5 P.M. for whichever star was headlining that week. Buck Owens. Loretta Lynn. Cowboy Copas. The Stanley Brothers and so many more. I was only sixteen, but I learned so much that summer just watching and listening to all these starfolks. (That's not a word but it should be.)

Back then it was just the four of us, Harold, Phil, Lew, and me, with Lew playing the guitar. No band of any kind. But this was the vocal arrangement we did then, just as you hear it here. Even then we stopped the show with this old standby every week. I don't know why we waited so long before we put it on record, because as far as I know this is the first and only time we ever recorded it.

If you listen to our rather unique version, you'll notice how we do the little step ups on the chorus in a jerking kind of pattern. When this album came out, I gave my mother a copy, and after a day or so she called and said something was wrong with it. She said it skipped. I gave her another one and she said it was doing the same thing. Turned out it was our arrangement that she was mistaking for glitches in the tape. She didn't care much for the way we sang it, and she was never shy in telling us so. The most lovable and honest human being I have ever known.

I'll fly away O glory
I'll, I'll, I'll fly away
When I die Hallelujah bye and bye
I'll fly away

"Walking Heartache in Disguise"

Debo was back at work with his four-track recording deck. The inspiration for this song started with some chord progressions he heard in his head. From that he created the melody, and a new song was in the making. He remembers that he and I rode around in the car and listened to his tape over and over. I tried, at this point, to encourage him to write his own lyrics to it, but I was never successful at talking him into that half of the writing process. So again, Harold and I wrote the lyrics, and the three of us had a new Statler cut.

> *She's got the look of an angel in love*
> *She's got the face dreams are made of*
> *You may get lost in the magic of her eyes*
> *She's a walking heartache in disguise*

In the sixties, when Waylon Jennings and the Statlers were young and full of spit and vinegar and just starting out, we worked a lot of dates together. We liked each other's music and each other's writing, and we'd sit up all night and sing each other songs. Somewhere along the way, I wound up with Waylon's Fender guitar from his Buddy Holly days. This was the guitar Debo wrote this song with. Waylon came to our TV show in the nineties in Nashville, and I had him autograph it to Debo and Langdon. I also had him sign a box set to Langdon. He wrote: "Langdon, you got a good dad, Waylon."

"Tomorrow Never Comes"

This was an old country song from the forties written by Ernest Tubb and Johnny Bond. I cannot remember when we first started singing it on stage, although we did put it on our first Mercury album, *Bed of Rose's*, in 1970. But the stage arrangement goes back to the Oak Leaf Park and "I'll Fly Away" days. We did it big with a building crescendo, and it became identified with us in the same way "How Great Thou Art" and "This Ole House" did, even though they were never single hits for us.

"Don't Wait on Me"

As I related earlier, we recorded this song for the album *Years Ago* in 1981, and it was a hit single for us at the time. Of course, in 1988, as I explained then, the lights really did go on at Wrigley Field in Chicago, and even though we were invited to sing this song there the night it all happened, we were not available to do so. Harold tells this story in a comedic way on the album as an introduction to the song, as he often did each night in concert. And another difference you may notice in the arrangement from the original back in '81 is that in the spot where Lew and I originally did the back-and-forth duet, now Phil and I did it. The reason Phil did it with me instead of Jimmy was more of a logistic nature than a musical one. When Jimmy hit the road running with us in early '82, we only had a couple of weeks of rehearsal time. He had a lot of material to learn, musically and lyrically, and we took the load off him wherever we could. This was just one way of giving him a little relief at the time, and Phil and I did it like this until the end of our career.

I smile to myself listening to the ending of this song. Note that we each come in at different times on the last note and we hold it an unusually long time. I'm the first to hit my note, so I am holding it longer than the others. This did not go unnoticed by my three stage brothers, and each night they would hold it just a little longer until they saw me getting blue in the face. It was a fun challenge and one of those little inside things that so often happened. That's the kind of stuff I miss about my three buds.

"I'll Go to My Grave Loving You"

Just as I have explained about other hits of ours, this signature song took on a new cadence and tempo in concert. Much faster than the hit record, it served as our near- closing song. Jerry Hensley, lead guitarist in our band, served as our emcee, bringing us on and taking us off stage each night. When we sang this one, we and all of our regular fans knew the show was about over. Encores would follow, sometimes one, two, or three, depending on the fever of the crowd, but "Grave" would always signify the beginning of the end of the night.

"This Ole House"

So many memories are associated with this grand old piece of music. We have used it as a gospel song, as it was originally written. We have used it as a comedy routine, which Harold and I wrote on stage as a series of ad-libs very early on and then used extensively anytime we needed it through the years. We have used it as a rousing show-closer. But one of the sweetest uses of it takes me back to the Johnny Cash days when we were with him for nine years. His mom and dad would often come to the concerts whenever we were close to where they were living, and we got to know Carrie and Ray very well. Mr. Cash was a much shorter man than you would expect, having the image of John in mind, and he was always very quiet and gentle-spoken. The first time they caught our show we had included "This Ole House," and Ray requested/demanded that we sing it every time thereafter when they would come. Either he would hunt us down backstage and say, "Now, boys, you're gonna sing my song for me tonight, aren't you?" Or John would knock on our dressing-room door and say, "Hey, guys. Daddy's here tonight. You know what that means." And we would sing it one more time for Mr. Cash.

34

Music, Memories, and You

1990

This was the first album of ours that would not be released as vinyl. The era of the 33 1/3-rpm was over. (Well, almost, until it was brought back in retro fashion some decades later.) From here on out, everything was cassette and compact disc until it went to digital downloading. I suppose the next step will be mental telepathy, but I don't have one of those machines yet.

Eight of the ten songs here were recorded before the last album, *Live and Sold Out*, was even thought of. Somewhere along the way, just before finishing this one off, the idea and opportunity for the live concert album came up, and we put everything here on hold. *Live* was released October 3, 1989, and while it was on the charts, we went back in the studio March 26,

1990, and recorded the lead single and a gospel song for this one. Released in June of '90, two songs came from it that were also done as videos.

"Small, Small World"

This song was not written by any of the Statlers or any of our gang of writers. It came from Nashville, in the mail, from two songsmiths for whom we had great respect. Gary Scruggs, son of Earl, and Thom Schuyler. Thom wrote "16th Avenue," the anthem of all country songwriters, and "Old Yellow Car," the anthem of all of us who ever saved up a few precious bucks as teenagers to buy that first, sacred car.

We tragically lost Gary not long ago, but I've been in contact with Thom in recent years. I never knew him personally, but one day I just emailed him to tell him how much I like his talent and his style of writing. "Old Yellow Car" ranks among my top-ten favorite all-time country songs. We had a great conversation, and I was glad to tell him how much I admired his work. I do this quite often with people I know and with many I don't. It makes me feel good to express to them what I feel about their craft and/or their life. Thom was working with youth at a Nashville church when we last communicated.

Two guys meet and converse about the girlfriend they don't know they have in common. One coincidence after another keeps cropping up in their conversation until they finally realize they have more to talk about than they first thought. We liked the song from the beginning and knew we could do the comedy delivery it needed and also make it a good stage song. Ninety percent of the song is conversation between two men, and it was only a natural assumption that Harold and I would do it, as this was just like the back-and-forth banter we had done on stage all our lives. But our speaking voices are so similar that we knew it could be confusing when you only had audio to rely on. Simple solution—Harold and Jimmy would do it, and there could be no mistaking which character was talking and when.

They did a fabulous job on not only the record but on the video we shot. We also did it as an opening number on the *TNN-Music City News Awards* TV show we hosted live June 4, 1990. The punch of the song required beautiful twin girls, and we used two who had been popular as the Doublemint Twins in those chewing gum commercials from that era.

317

This would be the last Statler single that charted. Our career was about to take a new and different turn. The very next day after that awards show, on June 5, 1990 (my birthday), the four of us and Marshall Grant, our agent, met with Dave Hall, president of the Nashville Network. It was in this meeting that we were offered the opportunity to produce and host a Saturday night variety show on TNN that would last for seven years and never leave the number-one position on the network.

We would continue to record and release albums, as our album sales were always strong till the end and way past retirement. But our focus was now on TV and not on the single charts and keeping up with the changing music scene. Our image and style had been set, and our fans were loyal and growing, and the albums of music that would come were what they most wanted. And then there was the time issue. Writing, producing, and starring in a weekly TV show, keeping up a standing-room-only concert touring schedule, and then writing songs and recording often left us little time to eat and sleep. We never worked harder than we did in the nineties. I wound up more than once in the doctor's office and ERs around the country with a racing heartbeat and even had to have a heart ablation to fix the problem by 1999. But I loved every minute of it and would do it the same way all over again!

"Nobody Else"

This is one of the most hard-core country songs I have ever written and the Statlers ever recorded. It rings in that open E key and the lyric is simple and straight to the matter.

When I lie down beside you
And your attention's all on me
There's nobody else that I would rather be
When I look across the table
And you're looking back at me
There's nobody else that I would rather be

We made a video of this song in Nashville on October 11, 1990. Buck Ford produced it. Buck was Tennessee Ernie's son, and we had worked concerts with his dad many times twenty years earlier. (Did someone say it's a small, small world?)

No picture in the paper
The movies or TV
Nobody in the news or history
When our babies call me daddy
And throw their arms 'round me
There's nobody else that I would rather be

On the same day we recorded this song, January 13, 1988, at Chip Young's Young'Un Sound Studio at 2 P.M. on a Wednesday afternoon, we recorded a song I had written titled "Old Habits of Heart." For reasons now lost to the ages, it was never released, still hasn't been released, and I suppose never will be released. It and "No Letter Today," an old country standard written by Ted Daffan, are the only two songs of ours still in the "can" at Mercury. It has been a lifetime since I've heard either, although my sons assure me they have copies of them. But don't look for them on the Internet because they are just not there.

"Jealous Eyes"

Debo brought me this killer melody, and, again, all I had to do was drop a few words into it and make 'em rhyme. But before you get to either the music or the words, you are regaled with one of the best intros I have ever been associated with. What and who you are hearing are two acoustic guitars being played by Jerry Kennedy and Chip Young as only they could do. Chip was finger picking while JK was pulling the strings. Pete Wade does the electric fills throughout the song. It was some of the best and most fantastic instrumental work from everyone on this cut.

Jealous eyes you're not crying
I realize something's dying
Somewhere we both gave up trying
But I still miss the memory of those jealous eyes

"Holding On"

In your arms is where I long to be
Holding on to memories
Holding on to things that used to be
Holding on to you and me

Another beautiful love ballad from Jimmy and John Rimel. I remember so clearly when we recorded this on a cold January day in 1988. We had decided on a fade ending with just the instruments and no voices. After a playback, Jimmy said, "Here is what I hear picking as the music goes out," and he played it for Jerry on the guitar. Jerry said, "Why don't you just do it?"

And he did. That's Jimmy playing the guitar on the very end.

"Think of Me"

There is an art to writing short stories that I think gives songwriters a leg up on most novelists. Songwriters learn early on to make each word count, to be able to say it all with an economy of words, and to cram a lot of story into a small space. I think Harold and I did just that with these short, jabbing lines. Before the first verse is half over, the scene is set and the story is afoot, as Arthur Conan Doyle (master of the short story) might have said.

I can feel it coming, it's started up again
You hung the phone up quick when I walked in
You go out with your new friends, but never have them in
And then get mad if I ask where you've been

We wrote this in the old camp-meeting/convention-singing style of the early Southern gospel songs, only it's a country song through and through. In the vein of "I'll Go to My Grave Loving You," it has that sing-a-long after-time chorus that we loved. Then add Brent Rowan's electric guitar fills and it ain't half bad.

Think of me before you go
There's one more thing you should know

You'll have regrets, just wait and see
But when you do, don't think of me

"You Gave Yourself Away"

As I listen to these songs so many years after their initial recording, I hear things I was not even listening for back in the day when they were released. The entire musical track on this cut and on this whole album is so strong and energetic. JK sprinkled a few new faces among the old and established pickers, and it seemed to spark everyone. We seldom got involved in choosing the musicians we used. We depended totally on Jerry for that. He had worked with every instrumentalist in Nashville. He knew their strengths and personalities, so we trusted him without fail or regret to bring the right ones together for the good of each album. Again, I love the intro and fills on this Jimmy Fortune/John Rimel-written jewel. From opening bar to closing line, it is in a rhythmic groove that can't be ignored. And that's Phil and Jimmy doing the duet on the verses. I love their sound together.

I was blind and never saw the writing on the wall
Though the end was closing in, I'd no idea at all
In a million years I never thought our love would end this way
Suddenly it's clear to me, you gave yourself away

"I Never Once Got Tired of You"

This is a good genuine country song that Harold, Debo, and I collaborated on. It was in that era when we were first seeing the country flavor that we had known all our lives slowly drift away from the industry. The musical tracks on the new blood that was flowing into the Nashville sound, to my ear, was more Guns N' Roses than it was George Jones. That three- and four-chord song that historically built the town was traded in for melodies that sounded like warm-up vocal scales. So, in putting together the lyrics for Debo's country melody, my brother and I made it a love song, but we didn't shy away from also getting in a shot and saying what was on everyone's mind at the time.

Sometimes I get tired of evening sunsets
Sometimes I complain if the sky's too blue
I get tired of what some call country music
But I've never once got tired of you

"What's on My Mind"

This very special love song is buried in the depths of all of this good material but rises from the ashes with a certain flicker after all these years.

I could buy you Valentines
Pretty cards with rhyming lines
Candy decorated like a heart
Or I could send you roses
Red and yellow by the dozens
But even then, I don't know where to start

Without the magic touch of "Pig" Robbins's piano and the lavish strings of Bergen White, these words and this melody would not have been as romantically effective as they are. This kind of talent was just an example of the support and complement given the Statlers throughout our career.

I could hire a plane to spell
Love notes on the clouds and tell
The world how much you've always meant to me
Or I could rent a billboard space
With just a picture of your face
So everyone who passes by could see

Everything I wrote then I still mean today.

But that won't say what's on my mind
I need words I just can't find
And even though I've loved you all these years I love you more
Right this very minute than I ever have before

"He Is There"

When I asked Kim Reid Weller for the inspiration that led to the writing of this song, here is what she told me. "I was inspired by the beautiful mountains we get to enjoy everyday living in the Shenandoah Valley. My favorite part of the day is the evening when the sun starts to filter through the trees onto the ground as it starts to descend. I can see Him everywhere. And you always hope people can see Him in you."

I would be a crass fool to try to add anything to that.

He is there, everywhere you look
Because he loved us all, our sins he took
He will always be beside you, whomever you may be
He is everywhere you look, just look at me

"My Music, My Memories and You"

On the bus again. January 1988. Going from a concert in Bloomington, Indiana, to LA for the *American Music Awards*. We often flew when we went to the West Coast, but this time we didn't, so we had lots of time to watch movies, read, sleep, and write songs. Harold and I went to the back of our bus, closed the doors, and gave life to this rather unique composition. After about thirty minutes, we went back up to the front lounge and sang it to Phil and Jimmy. We arranged it immediately and everyone picked the solos they wanted. The only harmony we sang was on the very last line. It was a simple arrangement in which the instruments we each sang about were featured after our solos.

Don: *Like two violins that get sweeter with time*
You've got your memories and I've got mine...
And then Buddy Spicher plays the classic violin transforming into the country fiddle.
Phil: *The guitar seems to play a song just for you*
It's soft and it's pretty, all the way through...
JK's acoustic guitar splits this break with Weldon Myrick's Dobro guitar.
Jimmy: *Like a fine old piano, you've always been grand*
You give me such comfort when we're hand in hand...

323

Keyboard virtuoso and Elvis's piano player David Briggs gives it a
    beautiful touch.
Harold: *As the band keeps on playing, it's always our song*
And it seems to get better as time goes along
The guitars, violins, and piano all play together and bring us to:
When it all comes together, it all rings so true
My music, my memories and you

The picture on the cover of this CD, which is of the four of us standing
in front of a large piece of sheet music, is as casual and relaxed as I have ever
seen us. In our faces and our body language I can see a restful attitude and a
peaceful countenance in our smiles. This was in March of 1990 when we
had no idea of the pace, the stress, and the explosive goodness and extreme
work this decade was about to rain upon us.

35

All American Country

1991

The cover is the perfect pose and message of who The Statler Brothers were at the time and in the decade to come. We are standing in front of a large American flag, dressed in suits and ties. This was our mood and the mood of the country, and this was the television look that we carried throughout this decade and into the new century and to our retirement. This album is very transitional in more ways than just our appearance. We recorded these songs the latter part of '90 and the first few months of '91. During this very same period of time, we also were writing and taping our new television series for TNN. Our doors were never closed to outside writers, but if they were ajar all those years, they were now swung wide and welcomed a larger scope of songwriters. You will see that evidenced in this collection of material.

Jerry Kennedy also filled the studio with new blood, blended in with the old, in the persons of Brent Mason and Brent Rowan, two of the hottest new electric guitarists in town. Mark Casstevens and Kenny Bell joined the acoustic-guitar section, Larry Paxton was playing the bass, and Steve Turner and Jerry Kroon rotated on the drums. JK mixed fire and power into the tracks, and we were floating atop a new bed of music, and it felt good and fresh. We filled the album with songs that justified the title. It was pure, new country, and it was bookended with patriotic numbers that could raise the hackles up and down your spine. In my mind, we had about four different stages to our career, and I liked this stage a lot. I liked who we were and what we were doing.

"Remember Me"

This John Northrup/Gordon Payne-written song came to us during a highly sensitive and nervous era in our country. The Gulf War, Desert Storm, Desert Shield, and a half dozen other names described the conflict we were embattled in over in the Middle East. The lyrics were very subtle and indirect, but it was a war/love song by no mistake.

> *How could I have known this would take me away*
> *Could be into fall, maybe longer they say*
> *Our lives have been torn apart, our dreams are on hold*
> *But my heart I'll leave with you, till I get back home*

The melody was big, and we made it even bigger and more dramatic. Sentiments and emotions were high as lots of soldiers were deployed. We sang it each night in concert, and there was an electricity in the air with each performance. Also, during this period, whenever we played a concert anywhere close to a military base, we gave free tickets to all the families who had a soldier in battle. For the love and safety of us all, it was the least we could do.

> *Remember me, for the love we share*
> *Remember me, like I'm standing there*

326

And in time I will be
Till I return, Remember me

"Dynamite"

A new writer who would become part of our stable of music contributors joined us with this album. Wil Reid, Harold's son, now part of the country duo, Wilson Fairchild, wrote his first song and submitted it to us. It was in the novelty vein with a great rhythm, and it was fun arranging it.

Honey, I think you're dynamite
But I hope you don't explode
The roses that I sent you
Are just a piece of what I owe

I talked to Wil recently, and he shared what was going through his mind back when he wrote this at the age of seventeen. This multi-versed song about all the things his girlfriend got upset with him about was the first song he ever completed. When it was finished, he was leery of singing it for his dad or any of us because lines two and four were not "true" rhymes (explode/owe). He knew what a stickler his dad and our style was for exact rhymes. But he gave it a shot, and it gave us a good, cute, and energetic song for our repertoire.

I have told you about how the Statlers leaned toward short songs. I have had verses deleted from songs I've written because we didn't want to run too long on any one cut. This happened on Wil's first. He wrote four verses and we cut one and turned it into a Brent Mason guitar break. So, for the benefit of a little folk history, here's the verse we left out, now put back in!

I kinda gave your diamond earrings
To my sister to wear to the ball
She danced all night and had a great time
But she can't find your earrings at all

"Everything You See in Your Dreams"

Such a sad love story. I'm not sure what determined the type of song Harold and I would write together when we sat down with pens in hand. Sometimes it was comedy, sometimes tragedy. After not hearing this one for about twenty-five years, I have to think we must have been in very melancholy moods or maybe severely depressed states of mind.

Leafing through the time-worn pages of an old book from my shelf
Found an envelope I hadn't seen in years
In a hand that I'd forgotten, words written long ago
I read through a cloud of memories and tears

It started with "I love you and you know I always will
But there's something that I feel I have to say"
Then the hurt I felt the first time, washed over me again,
Old feelings that had never gone away

Jimmy leads this one and Phil joins him singing tenor on the verses. The two of them singing together with this arrangement of harmony just makes me smile all over. I love the sound they have, and I'm really falling in love with this song all over again.

I folded up the letter, put the book back in its place
And I'm sure I'll read them both again someday
The book I never finished, so I still don't know the end
And we know some things are better left that way

But I guess I know the answers, before the question's hardly asked
Cause life is full of best-laid plans and schemes
And what I've learned from living is that you can't believe
Everything you see in your dreams

"Who Do You Think You Are?"

Frank Dycus and Dean Dillon, two of Nashville's most prolific hit writers, sent this to us. It was so very different from anything we had ever done before or since that it caught our ear immediately. We weren't even sure why they had bothered to send it to The Statler Brothers. It wasn't our style, our meter, our phrasing. Nothing. But this is what we were hearing with our new open-door policy. So, we decided to record it. And here it is.

Oh, who do you think you are?
Some kind of angel from some distant star
That could walk right in, put an end to my pain
And who told you I was blue?
In desperate need of somebody like you
Oh, who do, who do you think you are?

"There's Still Times"

I remember distinctly wanting to write a very country song but include things that would make it modern in text. In the first verse I wrote about a "two-line telephone." Well, that's outdated today as so many people have a "no" line telephone—just their cells. By trying to update the lyrics, I just made it easier for them to go out of date. But I still like this song so very much.

Got a home in the country, with a two-acre lawn
A garage where I know where everything belongs
Got a dog we call Tilly, who won't stay at home
Three kids we love dearly, and a two-line telephone

I mentioned a TV dish in the second verse and also a computer on the shelf where I used to keep my record albums. I think many folks could relate with those changes that were taking place in most households at the time. But my favorite line is the reference back to ol' Tilly. It feels so good when you can tie it all together like that.

Got a dish in the backyard, but nothing's on TV
Computer in the den where my records used to be
Got a hedge that needs trimmin', a rose vine gone dead
And just like ol' Tilly, I got prayers that need said

329

And there's still times when I get crazy, and think that I'll survive
Times I think I'm happy, and glad to be alive
And there's still times when I get lonely, times when I get blue
And times I go for minutes and never think of you

Something about this song that has always bothered me. All songwriters have to hedge and twist from time to time to make things fit. We sometimes have to use contractions to make the rhythm fit the words. Sometimes "ain't" just fits the bill and says it better than "isn't" or "aren't" ever could. Sometimes just bad English has to be used to get the point across. This song is a perfect example of what I'm trying to say. "There's still times" rolls off the tongue better in a song than "there're still times" which, of course, should have been the proper title. You take artistic license and hope it's better. I think it is but it still bothers me a little.

"Put It on the Card"

Again, two songwriters we didn't even know, Tony Haselden and Stan Munsey Jr., got their song to us. I remember this day so clearly. We had accumulated a stack of cassettes that Jerry had gathered for us at Mercury in Nashville and sent to Staunton. One morning the four of us went into our offices to have a listening session, and somebody suggested breakfast, so we rode around town and listened to the whole stack while we ate donuts and drank coffee. This one stopped us cold. It had comedy and a built-in arrangement. Phil, Jimmy, and I would sing the setup and Harold would do the punch lines. Add that jaunty little tempo and Weldon Myrick's Dobro licks and it was a natural. It was good on record, stage, and TV.

Sometimes I think my honey thinks money grows on trees
She blows through our bank account like a whirlwind goes through leaves
When there's nothing left but branches and the green's all gone oh, lord
That's when she pulls that plastic out and says, "Put it on the card"

"If I'd Paid More Attention to You"

Jimmy came through with flying colors in writing this one. It was fun to sing and flowed so easily over that clicking track. Drummer Jerry Kroon and, again, Weldon's Dobro chops are standouts to me as I listen to it all come together here. On the verses, Jimmy and I are duetting, as we so often did, but this time he's leading and I'm harmonizing below him. A whole different sound that worked.

I might not be lonesome or all by myself
I might not be feelin' this blue
You might not be somewhere with somebody else
If I'd paid more attention to you

"Jesus Is the Answer Everytime"

It was January of '91, and Harold and I were deep in the writing of the twenty-six episodes we needed for the first season of our TNN television show. The two of us wrote every show for all seven years. We wrote on a long table in our conference room five days a week until we had to leave on tour or, in this case, finish an album. One morning, during a coffee break from the script writing, we got to looking at our schedule and realized the album we were going to Nashville to finish in February still had no gospel song. We liked having one on every album if at all possible, so we stopped writing TV, changed hats, went down to my office where the piano was, and wrote this song.

When there's no good in your good mornings, too much hell in your helloes
And your kind heart is something less than kind
When you're thinking more about the thorns than you are the rose
Jesus is the answer everytime

Roger Bennett of the Cathedrals told me years later that they always wanted to record this song. They loved what it said and the point it made but that opening line kept them from it. They felt "hell" was too harsh a word for a gospel group to sing in that context. I've always regretted they didn't say something so we could have written them a new opening line. We would have done anything for those guys.

When you're thinking more about the glory than you are the deed
And there's less than good intentions on your mind

331

When your prayers are filled with things you want instead of things you need
Jesus is the answer everytime
Use the Bible for a rule book and I think you're gonna find
Jesus is the answer everytime

"Fallin' in Love"

Debo brought the melody, I brought the words, and we had us one heck of a song. It should have been a hit for someone. Maybe not us, but it has Texas written all over it in melody and lyric, and it would have been a killer for the right artist. And that's Phil and Jimmy with the oo-oo background that sounds like two girls.

It was a late hot summer evening, first time I felt her breeze
She danced by me pretty as you please
There's someone here, a friend said, I'd like for you to meet
And we two-stepped the night away in the August heat

Fallin' in love—Fallin' in love
She was dancin' to the music while I was fallin' in love
Fallin' in love—Fallin' in love
She was only dancin' while I was fallin' in love

About a year after this came out, Walmart got in touch with us with a jingle idea of using this song. We rewrote the chorus and recorded it one night after TV rehearsals. I still have a copy of it and it's interesting to hear. But as often happens, the project fell through on their end and it never happened.

Prices fallin'—Walmart callin'
Callin' and fallin' again
Fallin' again—Fallin' again—Fallin' again
Prices are fallin' again

"You've Been Like a Mother to Me"

This is the same song I wrote about back in the chapter concerning the album *Sons of the Motherland*. The same song that President Reagan jumped to his feet to salute and honor. The same song we used to close so many of our Fourth of July celebrations in Staunton. Yet this time we gave it even a little more. We rerecorded it for this album and then Mercury wanted to shoot a video of it. We traveled down to Richmond, Virginia, and shot for a day in an old warehouse. It was June 5, 1991, my birthday again. (Seems like we were always doing something on my birthday.) The director interspersed beauty shots of America and American families and activities with film of us singing. It was and is an impressive piece, and you can easily find it on YouTube, as you can most of our videos. This one will make you feel good, and I hope the words will make you feel good, too. That's why I'm going to share them with you just as I originally wrote them.

She's seen me through lots of trouble, she's stayed up nights so I could sleep
She's given me more than comfort, she's given me something I can keep

I love her and I need her and I want to be with her all the time
I'd fight just to keep her and I'd die if I thought she wasn't mine

I love her every morning, thank God for her every night
I worship the ground she stands on and I stand on the ground she'll
*   be alright*

When you need me, you know I'll be there 'cause you've always been there
*   for me*
America, God knows I love you, 'cause you've been like a mother to me

America, we've been through troubles and we'll make it again just wait
*   and see*
America, God knows I love you, 'cause you've been like a mother to me

America, stand up and show it, that you're proud of the red, white and blue
You love her and you know it, 'cause she's been like a mother to you

36

Words and Music

1992

One of the best titles we ever had for an album. Simple, to the point, and meaningful. And this is what we were all about. Words and music. Truth be told, probably more words than music. The melodic side to our songs was simple. We took more care and more pride in the lyrical side. I have cowritten with a number of writers, sometimes I would add the music, sometimes the words, sometimes we did both at the same time. But I always felt I was getting a free ride when I added the music because it took less time and thought. When I added the words, then I felt I had done my share.

The cover picture was taken high above Staunton, Virginia, on a little mount called Betsy Bell. There are two historic hills side by side, and the other one is called Mary Gray. Back in the 1700s, Virginia settlers named these hills after two girls from Scotland. There is a long, winding, rutted, dirt road leading to the top of Betsy Bell Hill. Teenagers for many decades have driven up there and used it for a parking place. Families have driven up there and used it for picnicking. The Staunton City Council is bound by contract to make an annual walking trek up there due to a stipulation in the deed when it was given to the city from God only knows who. We drove up there in a couple of trucks with photographer and friend Charles Clemmer and took this photo one spring morning. You can see behind us the fantastic vista of the eastern side of our city. And now to the songs, because all of this has nothing whatsoever to do with the album. I just wanted to tell you a little about the picture and our little town.

"A Long Story Short"

Open that proverbial door and let those writers in! And here they come! Ron Irving, Wayland Holyfield, Susan Holden, and Larry Wayne Clark. All four of them wrote this one song.

And what a sweet song it is. It couldn't be anymore a Statler song if the four of *us* had written it. The melody, the chord progressions, the bounce. And hats off to Mark Casstevens on the acoustic and our oldest friend in Nashville, Jimmy Capps, on the electric guitar.

> *Some folks are famous for turning a phrase*
> *You have your Shakespeare and your Hemingway*
> *I can't weave words the way they do*
> *But here beside you at the break of day*
> *My heart is almost bursting with things to say*
> *I hope these simple words will do*
> *To make a long story short, I love you*

Jimmy Capps has been an A-lister in the music circles in Music City practically all his life. We first crossed paths back in 1961 at Oak Leaf Park, the Sunday afternoon gig I told you about a few chapters back. We all, Jimmy and the four of us, were mere kids looking for a future in this business we call entertainment. He was playing guitar for Charlie and Ira, the Louvin Brothers, and we hit off a friendship with him immediately. We ate lunch that day together backstage and found that we were all about the same age

335

with the same burning desire. When we got to Nashville a few years later, Jimmy was there already, playing sessions, doing early-morning TV shows, and becoming a regular member of the staff band on the Grand Ole Opry. We continued to bump into each other all the time. We all were regulars from 1969 to 1972 on the Johnny Cash ABC TV show, as he was a part of the Bill Walker Orchestra, and I can't begin to tell you how many award shows we did together over a period of nearly forty years. When we hired the Bill Walker Orchestra for our TV series from 1991 to 1997, Jimmy was right there with us for every rehearsal and show. Now our sons, Wilson Fairchild, think the world of him, as they have worked with him so much on their television dates. And oh, yeah, he's the sheriff on *Larry's Country Diner*. Oldest friend in Nashville? Uncontested. We still see him and his wife, Michele, often when we're in town.

"It Only Hurts for a Little While"

This was an old Ames Brothers hit from 1956. The answer as to why it is on this album is irrelevant. The real question is why hadn't we recorded it years ago? This was a part of our musical heritage. Those pop groups of that era when we were kids were the 45-rpms we were buying every Saturday afternoon on our way home from the cowboy movies. The Four Aces. The Four Lads. These were words and music from our past. And this one was written by Fred Spielman and Mack David. David was a Broadway and movie songwriter with eight Oscars for songs such as "The Hanging Tree," "Hush, Hush Sweet Charlotte," and "Bibbidi-Bobbidi-Boo" from *Cinderella*. We gave it the full Ames treatment for old memories' sake.

> *It only hurts for a little while*
> *That's what they tell me*
> *Just wait and see*
> *But I will hurt till you come back to me*

Our TV series debuted October 12, 1991. TNN sent us on an interview tour of all the talk shows on radio and television across the country at the time. Two weeks and two days before the first show went on the air, September 26, we were in New York doing the *Today* show on NBC. Just the four of us and our piano player, Scott Cash. We did the interview with

Bryant Gumbel, and then he asked us to sing a song. This is what we sang. Bryant beamed all the way through it because this was his era as a kid, also. He remembered all the old songs that we did, and we had a good time that morning. I liked Bryant and was sorry to see him go.

"A Lifetime of Loving You in Vain"

Now I had both sons interested in music. We would go into our music room with all the instruments propped against the wall near the piano and drums, and we would pick and sing and record. This was the fruit of our labors for one night over the Christmas holidays in 1991. Two months later, the Statlers were in the studio being treated to one fantastic track underneath Debo's, Langdon's, and my song. Wow! This thing pops!

It'll be days before it finally hits me
It'll be months before I feel the pain
It'll take years before I get over
This lifetime of loving you in vain

Harold's solos are dead on, and the echo fullness that JK gives Phil, Jimmy, and me on the chorus is robust and sturdy. (Makes even me want to boogie!) And let's not overlook Brent Rowan's guitar and Larry Paxton's bass. And on the piano is Gary Smith. We toured many thousands of miles with Gary when he was Barbara Mandrell's pianist.

"The Rest of My Life"

And then you have to come down sometimes and just write a quiet, homespun country song. Put a fiddle intro on it (Glen Duncan) and leave all the frill and fancy behind. I was never more relaxed in the studio than when these moments came along. Smooth and pretty. I like Jimmy's wailing cry on the choruses, and I like the message that it leaves with us. I have no particular recollection of when or where I wrote this one, but it haunts me a little whenever I hear it.

If I could just be a part of your memory
You would carry the rest of your life

337

If I could just be a ship that was passing
You'd remember sometime late at night
Then I'd be gone like a wild wind in winter
Knowing I had done one thing right
If I could just make you happy for a moment
I'd be happy the rest of my life

"Some I Wrote"

In the chapter *Short Stories*, I told about this song. The feelings I had for it, the writing history, and I shared the lyrics with you. It was in 1977 when Harold and I wrote it and the Statlers recorded it—fifteen years before we decided to redo it, this time with Jimmy singing tenor. The Jimmy Capps guitar break at the end is worth the trip to the den or wherever you keep your CDs. The thinking behind recutting this was in keeping with the title of the album. These are words we wanted preserved and thought they bore repeating.

"Nobody Loves Here Anymore"

A nice play on words. It was written by LaDonna Brewer-Capps, Jimmy Capps's daughter-in-law. Odd thing about it, Jimmy was on much of this album but not on this particular song. We did a very unusual vocal ending here, and to tell you the truth, I didn't like the ending very much.

Nobody loves here anymore
This old house ain't the home it was before
We both still live here, but one thing's for sure
Nobody loves here anymore

"Same Way Everytime"

I'm not real sure, even today, if I wrote this tongue-in-cheek or in a flat-out rage of anger. I said exactly what I wanted to say, but each word was probably not dripping with love and comedy. The country music industry was about to fall on its face and change its look to where it might never be recognizable again. The cowboy hats were coming in or, I should say, coming back. The music was getting louder and closer to the rock world. The lyrics were being buried and treated like they weren't needed. We opened up this song with a spoken intro:

*THIS IS THE STATE OF THE UNION MESSAGE ON
COUNTRY MUSIC*
A lot of them sound like George, a lot of them sound like Merle
Most of them sound alike, 'cept the one that sounds like a girl
I'll grow old just waitin' around
To hear an original sound
'Cause half of them sound like George and the other half sound like Merle

I was missing the originality of those wonderful old voices that didn't have to be announced on the radio. When the record started playing, you knew in three seconds it was Hank Snow or Willie Nelson or Kitty Wells. They had style. They had distinction. You didn't mix up Marty Robbins and Ernest Tubb. You never had to wonder if that was Tammy or Loretta. You didn't have to wait till the end of the song to see if the DJ was going to say it was Conway Twitty or Sonny James. The new crew was coming in and the labels were cutting them all from the same cloth.

Black hat, white hat, dress hat, any hat is fine
Old song, new song, country song, sing it with a whine
Count your lucky stars and thank the likes of Lefty and Hank
'Cause the new way and old way's the same way everytime
Big girl, little girl, pretty girl, any girl is fine
If she sings country music she wants to sing like Patsy Cline
Well, honey dream on, don't stop
But don't sing "Rocky Top"
'Cause the new way and old way's the same way everytime

I had nothing against the song "Rocky Top." I think it's even one of Tennessee's state songs. But every girl singer that came along used it on stage like some kind of anthem just because it had a fast tempo. I got tired of hearing it and, again, just wanted some inventiveness shot into the new acts instead of sameness.

Duo, trio, quartet, any group is fine
But no-hat harmony is a little out of line
What radio thinks is new, Ernest Tubb did in '42
The new way and old way's the same way everytime

So much for my soapbox and message songs. We had fun with it—in the studio, on TV, and on stage. Probably made some folks angry, but that's okay. I really don't care.

We always gave the new acts in town a spot on our TNN TV show. There was one we sat and talked with during rehearsals one day who confided, almost tearfully to us, that he really liked the way we dressed. He went on to explain that his record label took him shopping, picked out and bought his clothes, took him to the salon and told them how to cut his hair, and handed him songs and told him what he was going to record. They told him how to look and how to sing and how to handle himself on stage. It was the beginning of a cookie-cutter era that sometimes gave the appearance of freedom, but in honesty was controlled completely from the top. The boy never made it. He was gone from Nashville in a matter of months. I still think about him and feel sorry for him and what he got caught up in. I wish some of those know-it-all record execs had been around and tried to tell Faron Young or Johnny Cash or Jerry Lee how to sing and conduct themselves on stage. Yeah, I'd like to have been there for that.

"Is It Your Place or Mine?"

Harold's daughter Kim Reid Weller is back and stronger than ever. This started as a play on words for her. She took the old come-on line and made it mean something thoughtful. Two people who care for one another trying to decide who's move it is in making it right. Jimmy leads the verses and I harmonize with him, and then we do sort of a jigsaw thing with lines three and four. We sing overtop of one another, and I love the effect it has. It accents the story of confusion and indecisiveness that Kim set with the whole song.

Kept hoping you'd call, or maybe drop by
Hadn't seen you at all, since we said goodbye
The phone rang today, didn't get there in time
Should I try to call you, is it your place or mine

340

Listen for Phil, the best harmony singer to ever jog in a pair of cowboy boots, on this chorus and on the ending. He bends the notes almost to the breaking point. What he knows and what he can do still fascinates and amazes me. My favorite line is the third one coming up. Some lines just hit you and you can't let 'em go.

Is it your place or mine, to say, "I'm lonely"
Is it your place or mine, to say, "I was wrong"
I don't think I'm healing, the way that I'm feeling
I wish I knew just what we'd do
Is it your place or mine

"He's Always There for You"

And here is the last addition to our close-knit staff of writers. My son Langdon was just coming of age, and after a lot of pushing from his brother and me, and a lot of rejecting from him, he decided he liked playing and singing and writing music after all. This was his first entry into the world of songwriting, and we would never have chosen to record it if it hadn't been worth it. Look and listen to the power of these words and this melody, and it's hard to imagine how young he was in years when he created them.

Was your day sorely spent with frowns and discontent?
Were you never introduced to a single compliment?
Were there times you felt you were treated unfair?
Remember life is fragile, so handle it with prayer
Do you sometimes wonder why you feel the need to cry?
And nothing else will help, no matter how hard you try
Whenever your heart seems to be untrue
Remember, He's always there for you

Langdon is busy with his career now with cousin Wil in Wilson Fairchild, and they have scores of original songs under their belts today. But I went to him for a little insight on his remembrances of this first composition. I loved hearing it from his vantage point and in his words and thought you might, too.

"The fastest way to a Statler Brother's heart is with a southern gospel quartet song. I didn't know much for a fresh 16-year-old, but I was paying attention enough to the old man's music that I did know this for sure. I knew through writing poems in school that I enjoyed words and especially rhyming words that were unique and unexpected. I loved hearing an unusual word at the end of a rhyming line and trying to guess what its match was going to be. As a challenge to myself, I went the unusual and unique way with the verses in this song. Discontent/compliment, unfair/prayer, said/instead. The overall theme of the song is the constant daily struggle of always coming up short or basically, *when something goes wrong with every-thing you do...* I knew that was definitely a relatable idea. And again, if I had learned anything from the classic writing style of the Statlers, keep the chorus simple and get a little deep and get your 'wordplay' in the verses. (*Remember life is fragile so handle it with prayer.*) I knew the first time out of the chute had to be good enough for them to like it and prove myself as a legitimate writer.

"I wrote it on the piano and played it first for Mom. I knew that if it wasn't any good at least she'd say she liked it! Her immediate review was, 'I can definitely hear them singing it. Make sure your dad hears this and at least give him the chance to say no.'

"I did and guess what? He nor his brothers said no. And getting this song cut was a lot more inspiring to me than those stupid poems I was writing for English class!

"I wrote it on March 18, 1991. Statlers recorded it February 27, 1992. I went down to Nashville for the recording session, which was a pretty big deal...not because I was missing school but because I was missing the first week of Varsity baseball practice.

"Then, the Statlers recorded it for their show-ending gospel segment on the TV show. And for my 18th birthday in 1993, Dad gave me the lyric page of the TV script and all four Statlers signed it and wrote me a note on it. It hangs on my wall above my desk in my office to this day."

I'm hearing some of this story for the first time as I read this. I am touched to tears by Langdon's sentiments. And I'm moved by his commanding words and music.

He's always there for you
In every walk of life you walk through
When something goes wrong, with everything you do
Jesus will still be there for you

"Thank You for Breaking My Heart"

This was sent over to us from Mel Tillis's publishing company. It had Mel's name on the stationery even though one of his writers, Jim Martin, had penned it. That's probably why we opened it and discovered this cute little ditty of a song. It's very "inside," and all about the music business, but it added a nice flavor to our album, and the pickers had a great time with it. It's a one-joke song, but as they used to say on *American Bandstand*, "It has a good beat and you can dance to it."

The postman delivered my royalty statement today
Telling me how many records I sold and how many times they'd been played
'Cause when you did me wrong, I wrote me a song
About the misery and how far I sank
And it's made so much money, it ain't even funny
So I'll cry all the way to the bank

Thank you for breaking my heart
Thank you for tearing my world all apart
I'm rollin' in dough at the top of the charts
Thank you for breaking my heart

37

Gospel Favorites

1992

Even I can't keep up with all the compilation releases. *30th Anniversary: Statler Brothers—Legendary Country Singers* for Time-Life, *The Gospel Music of The Statler Brothers Volume I & II*, a Bill Gaither production of the closing hymns from our TV series, *The World of The Statler Brothers, Statler Brothers—The Definitive Collection, The Statler Brothers—An American Legend, Statler Brothers Gold, The Statler Brothers—The Gospel Spirit, The Statler Brothers—A Reader's Digest Collection*, a Canadian TV offer—*The Statler Brothers—Now And Forever, Today's Gospel Favorites*, and I could go on. It always amazed me how all of these albums plus the TV offers could sell so extremely well and still never hurt our regular releases.

Back in the seventies, we had an agent who started us on the track of promoting and producing our own concert tours. His name was Major Dick Blake. He was a World War II vet and a very shrewd and fascinating man whom we all just loved. He would set a concert for January in, say, Columbus, Ohio, and then book us into the Ohio State Fair in Columbus in August. We would tell him that it was too soon to go back into a town, that the folks there had just seen us seven months before. And his invariable answer was, "Not the same people. The same people who go to a concert aren't necessarily the same people who will go to a fair." This tested out to be true and that was just another reason why we loved him. We lost him in October of '83 and I still miss his humor, his wisdom, and his friendship.

Thus, the same philosophy held true for records. Regular releases verses TV releases. To quote the Major, "Not the same people." Those who would order from the television screen were not the same folks who would go to the record store. Of course, nearly everyone today orders their music from the computer screen or through their cell phones. It's a different time but we, in our era, had the best of both worlds.

I explained earlier in these pages that I would not try to acknowledge all compilation albums. To do that would be a researcher's nightmare, and I'm not sure I even have all of them in my files or on my shelves. But all Statler-recorded songs represented by those compilation albums are just reissues of songs already released under other original covers. With that said, this album is a little of both, but there is enough original material here to warrant treating it as a first release. This was a television-offer-only album that you couldn't walk into a record store and buy. (Today's buyers are saying, "What's a record store?") Heartland Music in New York, in cooperation with Mercury, released a double album of twenty-two gospel songs of our choice. We went with thirteen songs we had on previous albums and recorded only nine new ones for this collection. (Four of these nine were actually rerecordings, but I'll explain that as we go and tell you why we did what we did.) At the time, this was the biggest selling TV offer Heartland ever did, and they did many. It was a gold album, and the sales record was never broken for their company until we broke it with another double album three years down the road.

These thirteen were on previous albums I have written about:

"When the Roll Is Called Up Yonder": *Live and Sold Out* (1989)
"Blessed Be": *Radio Gospel Favorites* (1986)
"One Size Fits All": *Atlanta Blue* (1984)
"Sweet By And By": *Today* (1983)
"Amazing Grace": *Radio Gospel Favorites* (1986)
"There Is Power in the Blood": *Radio Gospel Favorites* (1986)
"This Ole House": *Live and Sold Out* (1989)
"Jesus Is the Answer Everytime": *All American Country* (1991)
"Over the Sunset Mountains": *Radio Gospel Favorites* (1986)
"I Believe I'll Live For Him": *Four for the Show* (1986); *Radio Gospel Favorites* (1986)
"A Different Song": *Radio Gospel Favorites* (1986)
"A Beautiful Life": *Radio Gospel Favorites* (1986)
"I'll Fly Away": *Live and Sold Out* (1989)

"The Old Rugged Cross"

This is one of the few examples of feedback Heartland Music offered us. I think some survey they had seen showed this old hymn to be among the most popular through the years, and I'm sure that's true. No one had to twist our arms to include it. An album involving hymns in any way is not complete without this old Rev. George Bennard classic. The reverend wrote it in the fall of 1912, and there is a plaque in his hometown of Youngstown, Ohio, in the Lake Park Cemetery commemorating him and the writing of this beautiful old classic standard. Never take familiar old songs such as these for granted. Don't sing them by rote. Sing them as if they're fresh and new and listen to what the words are really saying.

On a hill far away stood an old rugged cross
The emblem of suffering and shame
And I love that old cross, where the dearest and best
For a world of lost sinners was slain

"Precious Memories"

When you're singing timeless and elegant pieces of music such as this and others included here, the best thing you can do is not get in the way of the beauty and structure that has been passed down through the years. This song has endured generations, and it needs no great production and certainly no changes to make it effective. It's built in. Written in. The glory is in that flowing poetry and simple melody. You only have to present it in the manner in which it was created and then just sit back and enjoy it.

Precious memories, unseen angels
Sent from somewhere to my soul
How they linger ever near me
And the sacred past unfold

"Rock of Ages, Cleft for Me"

When I was a kid growing up in our old brownstone church on the highway, we would always have Sunday night song services in the summertime. The doors were flung open, the stained-glass windows were raised to their ultimate height, the organ would blast into the night air, and we would sing all our old favorites out of the blue Presbyterian Hymnal, copyrighted 1927. It had all the old good ones, and this, of course, was one of them. Written by Thomas Hastings and Augustus M. Toplady. I mean, what kid is not going to remember a name like that. Oh, how I loved those times.

And then we just recorded it as simple and as pure as we could. Jimmy glides into his verse with such grace and charm, but Harold's solo on the second verse is the most perfect and sweetest of his entire career. I listen to it and tear up to where I can't even write about it.

Could my tears forever flow, could my zeal no languor know
These for sin could not atone, Thou must save and Thou alone
In my hand, no price I bring, simply to Thy cross I cling

We were in Cumming, Georgia, for two shows on Saturday night June 5, 1993. (My forty-eighth birthday, but that has nothing to do with this story.) From there we were headed to Nashville to perform on the *Music City News Awards* TV show. We got the news before ever leaving Cumming that Conway Twitty had died of an aneurysm in a Springfield, Missouri, hospital. We were crushed. Conway was a good man and a good friend and we loved him. The tone backstage all through the awards show rehearsals for

347

the next two days was glum. The show itself went on as scheduled, but neither the fans nor the industry had much joy. We had a scheduled session on Tuesday with plans of heading home immediately afterward. But when Conway's funeral was planned for that Wednesday in Hendersonville, Tennessee, we stayed to attend. (Seems like we were always going to funerals in Hendersonville, and this wouldn't be the last one.)

Conway's family asked us to sing. Others were there, also. Vince Gill sang. The Oaks sang. We went with the intention of singing "How Great Thou Art," but when Connie Smith expressed her desire to sing that, we switched at the last minute to this old heartfelt hymn of the ages. It was a very moving day, and I clearly recall Reba coming up from the congregation to the pulpit to offer a word of remembrance. She said she never got a chance to tell Conway what he meant to her, and she was not going to ever let that happen again. So, standing there she thanked Dolly for what she had meant to her career and thanked the Statlers for giving her the break she needed early on in this business by taking her on tour with us. It was a beautiful, sad, and emotionally filled afternoon for us all. And I never hear this glorious old song that I don't think of Conway and what a generous and unassuming friend he always was.

"Love Lifted Me"

This old revival hymn, written by James Rowe and Howard E. Smith in 1912, can be found in just about any book of hymns and spirituals you pick up. It has a sing-a-long chorus that can't be matched. Just one of many that we didn't need sheet music or lyric sheets for when we went to record because all four of us were born knowing the words to these wonderful old tunes. Again, a no-brainer including this gem on an album of old gospel hymns. Harold and Jimmy duet a verse. You might find it interesting they sang the first half of the second verse and the last half of the third verse simply because the words spoke to us better this way.

Souls in danger, look above, Jesus completely saves
He will lift you by his love out of the angry waves
Love so mighty and so true merits my soul's best songs
Faithful, loving, service, too, to him belongs
Love lifted me, Love lifted me

When nothing else would help
Love lifted me

When the rock group the First Edition broke up in the mid-seventies, this song was Kenny Rogers's first solo single. An odd but good choice for him in making his transition. We had worked television with the group in the sixties and, of course, knew Kenny as he entered into the country music industry. He had grown up in Texas with the same musical influences as we had grown up with in Virginia.

One of Harold's daughters, Kasey, at six years old, came home from her first day in the first grade. When Harold asked her, "Did you learn a lot to-day?" her answer was, "Yes, I did. I learned there are two things I don't know. I don't know how to read and I still don't know who Kenny Rogers is." Weeks later, Harold and I were eating breakfast in a hotel dining room in Nashville, and Kenny was sitting at a table by himself. As we left, we stopped to say hi, and he invited us to join him. Harold told him this story, and he loved it and laughed himself silly. He said he was doing *The Tonight Show* the next week and was just sitting there trying to think of a good story to tell. He asked if he could tell this one about Kasey. Harold assured him it was all his, and we said good day and went our separate ways. We were working and didn't see the show, and I never thought to ask Kenny through the years if he used it.

"Turn Your Radio On"

Albert E. Brumley, that wonderful old songwriter who wrote more hit gospel songs than most people have ever sung, penned this one also. This just might be his best one. I love, love, love it. From the opening of Jimmy Capps's popping guitar and Phil's in-command solos to that ending that was so much fun to do, it rings! I had a creative-writing teacher in school who used to tell us all the original subjects had been written about so what we must do as writers was find a new way of telling an old story. Boy, did Albert ever know how to do it.

Turn your radio on and listen to the music in the air
Turn your radio on, heaven's glory share

Turn the lights down low and listen to the Master's radio
Get in touch with God, turn your radio on

My friend Ace Collins is the novelist, historian, and author of so many music-related books. Whenever either one of us has a new publication, we always send the other a copy with a note inside. We're kind of big fans of each other's work. We've got a mutual admiration thing going. One of his books about the backstory of some of those amazing old gospel songs is actually titled *Turn Your Radio On*. Ace tells a story about the writing of this masterpiece that just gives me chills. Mr. Brumley said that whenever his friends and neighbors heard someone singing one of his songs on the air, they would call him on the phone and say, "Albert, turn your radio on." This is all the nudging a master songwriter such as he needed to sit down and write a classic such as this.

"Noah Found Grace in the Eyes of the Lord"

This is the same composition we included on our *Holy Bible—The Old Testament* album in 1975. I wrote about it earlier. It had become such a great stage song for us that when we transitioned from Lew to Jimmy in 1982, we rearranged it and kept on singing it each night in concert. As I explained back in the chapter featuring *Live and Sold Out*, when I wrote about "Don't Wait On Me," Phil took on some of Lew's solos to relieve Jimmy from having to learn such a myriad of words in such a short time. The same principles held with "Noah." We did it nightly on stage with Harold and Phil and me doing the characters in the play form and Jimmy shining on the last two choruses and last note, so this was a perfect opportunity for a do-over and a fresh new recording. What a song and what a fantastic arrangement!

"Just a Little Talk with Jesus"

Turn back to the chapter on *The Originals* and you'll see this song was the absolute beginning of The Statler Brothers. Joe McDorman, the high school boy who made that first phone call to his friends to put together a singing group so his church would have some special music for their Sunday night service, started it all. Joe, Harold, Lew, and Phil sang this song that night back in 1955, and we had Joe come in and sing it with us on that album back in 1979. It was always the perfect standby song we would go to whenever we needed another one for the stage or just whenever we felt like we wanted to sing it. And this album just cried out for it, so we recorded it again, with Phil back to singing the solo like you have never heard him, Harold rocking that final swing chorus, and Jimmy ringing out that last note. Wow, I love these guys!

"In the Garden"

In the chapter discussing *Years Ago*, I told you all about my feelings of guilt in the way we recorded this beautiful old classic in 1981. We double-timed the tempo, and it was all my doing. I also said, "I wish we had done it again later in a more conventional way." That was just a little suspense tease and a writer's liberty, because we did do it later in a more conventional way. Sweet atonement. This cut is proper, pretty, and everything it should be. Thank you, Lord, JK, Harold, Phil, and Jimmy for giving me this second chance. I feel so much better now.

And he walks with me and he talks with me
And he tells me I am his own
And the joy we share as we tarry there
None other has ever known

"How Great Thou Art"

I have told you just about everything about this song there is to tell. I've told you we sang it for Luther's funeral and for the christening of John and June's house. We sang it during every concert and recorded it more times than any other song in our career, at least four that I can recall. But at this point, in 1992, we had not recorded it with Jimmy. It was a must for this album. Without this song and this powerful arrangement, anything titled *The Statler Brothers' Gospel Favorites* would have been incomplete and a total lie. I am struck anew by the simplicity of these words and yet the authority and beauty they carry.

Then sings my soul, my Savior God to Thee
How great Thou art, How great Thou art

The third album of our career, *Oh Happy Day*, in 1969, included this song. The liner notes on the back of the album were written by Johnny Cash, who had listened to us sing it night after night for five years and would hear it many more times in the coming years. Here, in its entirety, are those liner notes:

"There is a lot of talk about soul singing, soul songs, soul music, etc., and most of it is just that, just talk.

"A few years ago, when I first heard the expression "soul music," I thought someone was talking about religious music. I still think the word "soul" is thrown around too loosely and should only be rarely used in describing a type of scene.

"So, with this in mind, meet my friends, The Statler Brothers. For even though they're real pros, have been around for a long time, have had a million-selling record and have recorded many kinds of songs, this is the first time you'll hear the real Statler Brothers.

"For when they sing, 'Then sings my soul, my Saviour God to Thee,' that's soul music. Not just 'cause the word 'soul' is in the lyrics, but because their souls are singing.

"And as an artist, I can say that it's a great experience to sing from the soul. To sing a religious song with feeling puts the soul not only in communication with its Creator, but provides an expression and manifestation of the powers of the Creator.

"Here we have four friends of mine. In harmony with the powers of their Creator.

"Here sing the souls of The Statler Brothers."

—Johnny Cash

38

Home

1993

I don't remember which came first, the songs or the album title, but I do recall that when the title came, the picture came easily with it. The old house the four of us are standing in front of is the farmhouse Harold's and my dad grew up in. The family lost the entire farm in the middle of the Great Depression. Just a few years before this picture, it came on the market and Harold bought it and used it as sort of a summer camp just to have it back in the family. We've had a lot of fun reunions on that front lawn. It's located out in Augusta County, about fifteen miles from Staunton, and this photo, taken again by the talented Charles Clemmer, holds a lot of dear and heartfelt sentiments for us. Our grandmother Maggie, who we never knew, passed away sitting on those front steps one night in May in 1931.

"Dream On"

Debbie and I live in a beautiful old stone house in Staunton that I bought in 1988. Originally built in 1922, it carries the name "The Whitestone" from the previous owners. When we purchased it and moved in, there was only one piece of furniture that conveyed with the house. It was an old grand piano sitting in the north corner of the living room. We never moved it. Debbie just arranged the rest of the house around it, and it is still pretty much the centerpiece of our living. It's what the extended family would gather around at Christmas while singing carols. It's where all the family histories are displayed in the form of dozens of pictures in all sizes of frames. And it's where I wrote practically all my songs from this period on. I have been extremely happy in this home, but you would not know that from this song. It is sarcasm personified and I just love it. The track is full of energy and verve from the pickers and the harmony is dead on.

If you have a crazy thought sometime
Miss me and think maybe I'm
Somewhere all alone and missing you
Dream on, Dream on, Dream on, Dream on

"The All-Girl-All-Gospel Quartet"

We grew up under the influence of Southern gospel quartet singing, but I cannot, for the life of me, remember ever hearing an all-girl, four-part singing gospel group. Country, yes, but not gospel. This all came from somewhere deep in my imagination, as did their whole story and background. I distinctly remember the day and night I wrote these words and this music on that very piano I just told you about.

Both my sons, Debo and Langdon, were outstanding baseball pitchers for their high school here in town, and I was so proud of them both. One night in April of '93, Langdon was pitching in a home game. He was hot and attracting a lot of attention from colleges and MLB scouts who would come and sit inconspicuously in the bleachers. I never missed any of their games when I was home, and I reveled in every pitch thrown. This particular afternoon, I had sat down at the piano and this song began coming to me. A story that was falling together like little pieces of sunshine from heaven. I was deep into my creative mode, which usually takes me to a plane where I don't even hear phones ring or voices that are talking directly to me. (Just ask Debbie if you don't believe me.) What finally brought me out of this writing trance was Debbie actually laying her hand on my shoulder and saying, "The game starts in fifteen minutes."

I sat in the seats behind home plate and cheered every strike, but I could not shake the storyline of this song. Between innings I was testing rhymes and counting out meter on my leg. It was as if my two worlds had collided and I couldn't escape either. When the game was over and we won, I headed back home to the piano bench and finished this one off. I have often said it is one of my three favorite songs I ever wrote. Can I say that last verse, even to this day, gives me chills and brings tears? Yes, I can, because I know these words aren't mine. I was given these words simply because God wanted me to have them.

If any of the four of you hear me, there's a song I never could find
It's the one where Alma played guitar and Bonnie Mae sang aftertime
And it's sad how no one remembers, though I find them hard to forget
And you would if you'd ever heard them, the all-girl-all-gospel quartet

And their harmony sounded like angels
And I can still hear them yet
Alma and Flora, Bonnie Mae and Little Louise
The All-Girl-All-Gospel Quartet

The studio engineer on the albums from this period was a young man name Brent King. His wife was a member of the country singing group the Girls Next Door. The Girls—Doris, Cindy, Diane, and Tammy—worked a lot of show dates with us on the road. The perfect ending to this song was to actually hear the All-Girl-All-Gospel Quartet. So, thanks to these ladies, they came in and gave us the perfect ending.

"Chattanoogie Shoe Shine Boy"

As a little kid in the 1950s, I would lie on the floor in a darkened living room on Saturday nights and watch Red Foley on *The Ozark Jubilee*. That's where I first saw Brenda Lee. She and I are the same age, only difference she was on TV at ten years old and I was on the floor in the living room. Brenda toured with us for years, and we consider her and her husband, Ronnie, great friends. She was the one, by our choice, who hung the medallions on our necks the night we were inducted into the Country Music Hall of Fame. But I digress. Red Foley sang this often on the Jubilee as he had a major number-one hit with it in 1950 on both the country and pop charts.

And then everybody recorded it. Crosby. Sinatra. Phil Harris. But nobody did it with quite the snap and polish as my brother. He outdid himself and all those others on this performance. (Try saying, "Hoppity, hippity, hippity, hoppity, hoppity, hippity hop" fast and in time.) Just listen to it crackle and pop with some out-of-this-world guitar work from Jerry Kennedy and Mark Casstevens.

"He'll Always Have You Again"

Okay, this is just a darn good piece of songwriting from my niece and Harold's oldest daughter, Kim. She was at the top of her game. The chords are beautiful and the lyric is heart-wrenching and there was just so much emotion already in this song by the time she sent it to us. I talked to her about this recently and she confided it all came from a heartbreak but, thankfully, not hers. As a true professional, Kim had found that you don't have to experience everything you write—just observe it. She saw this happening in someone else's life who was probably close to her and she captured their desperation. The Statlers, every one of us, are singing with strength and heart here. The whole package is very powerful and very well done.

And you know it's wrong to leave him
And you know you shouldn't want me
But what is a man supposed to do
When all I have is you

Kim sent me a note that said, "It was this last line that brought the song full circle. It made me feel I was channeling my dad and my uncle with their story songs. A successful feeling. Thanks Pop and Unk."

How can I not love this girl?

"Feeling Mighty Fine"

Mosie Lister was a Baptist minister, a gentleman, and one of the most prolific writers of Southern gospel music the world has ever known. He wrote such classics as "Where No One Stands Alone," "Then I Met the Master," "Till the Storm Passes By," "How Long Has It Been?" and so many more. We knew them all growing up in the South, being glued to the radio, as we were, and enthralled by the all-night singings of the gospel groups. One of our greatest thrills was playing a town in Florida one night and being told Mosie was at the stage door. What a joy it was to have a hero of ours at the concert, and you can be assured we sang this song that night with him in the audience. For years after that, Mosie sent us each a crate of oranges for Christmas. What a sweet and gentle man and what a song crafter.

Whenever we sang this on stage, the crowd would start rising when we did that unexpected chord change in the middle of the last chorus, and by the time we hit the ending, they were standing and we were floating.

Well, I'm feeling mighty fine, I've got heaven on my mind
Don't you know I want to go where the milk and honey flow
There's a light that always shines down inside this heart of mine
I've got heaven, heaven on my mind and I'm feeling mighty fine

"My Past Is Looking Brighter"

From three Nashville writers, Huffman, Dobbins, and Morrison. A good job by Jimmy on the solos and leads. Singing is Statler-solid.

"That Haunted Old House"

We have a new writing team on our staff of writers. Harold and his son, Wil, tackled this nostalgic theme together for the first time. It is so typically Statler material and so well done that it stood no chance whatsoever of getting overlooked. They used a fictitious old, empty house that apparently an ex-girlfriend lived in as the setting and catalyst for the story. The teller is considering walking about the shambles of the house and his memories, with scenes from the past flashing before him. Though they're all good, the third verse is my absolute favorite:

Although it was quiet, I swear I could hear
The record I bought you by the Platters that year
I walked up the front steps but stopped at the door
There's nothing for me in there anymore

The chorus tells the whole story in perfect country fashion:

I can't remember if it was your fault or mine
And you can't trust a memory when its had too much time
I'm haunted by things like your smile and my pride
Like that haunted old house, I'm empty inside

"Chet, You're the Reason"

I guess June 8, 1993, was father and son day for us in Nashville. That afternoon, at a 2 P.M. session, we cut "That Haunted Old House" and this little gem. Debo, Langdon, and I wrote this Chet Atkins salute, made a tape of it with the boys playing all the instruments, and pitched it to the Brothers. We asked Chet if he would guest on the record and used that same tape to show him where we wanted him to play. A couple of months later when he guested on our TV show and did this very song with us, he leaned over to me during rehearsal and said, in that slow Knoxville drawl, "Don't know which one of your boys is doing that picking, but he does a pretty good imitation of me." Langdon still holds that comment and compliment in the highest of honors.

There was a group of little guys grew up together
In the fifties when rock n roll was hot
And every time they turned on a radio station
Chuck Berry and Little Richard was all they got
And then one night they heard the Country Gentleman
Playin' something new in a brand-new way
Chet would you play...

At this point Chet picked as, of course, no one else can do. And then the session guys just jumped in with a gang cluster of country licks like you've never heard. JK, Pete Wade, Casstevens, Sonny Garrish. The floor of the studio raised up just a little. It was fabulous.

We only met but never got to know him
Till our first TV special years ago
So then we called and asked him if he'd come by
And do a little pickin' on our show
And there we sat in front of all America
Like we used to sit in front of our radios
And Chet would play...

Chet was always so very complimentary and gracious. Years before this, in 1981, he guested on our very first ninety-minute TV special. We introduced him, and he stepped into the spotlight to perform a medley of fifties songs he had arranged in honor of our nostalgia theme. But before he began, he totally surprised us with a little salute he had written to us to the tune of "Do You Remember These?"

It all started in high school, harmonizing in the hall
Now you're even singing for presidents and you're acclaimed by one and all
So many hits, so many awards and let me tell you, please
You, you deserve all these
Growing hair, losing hair, fighting off the fans
It must be fun while you're young fulfilling all your plans
Harold, Don, Phil, Lew, my message don't you miss
'Cause you, you deserve all this.

The most difficult thing to handle is when your heroes become your fans. This happened to us on many occasions, and I never quite got used to it. It left me feeling so blessed and honored but also so awkward and unsettled. It kind of leaves you scratching your head and staring at your boots.

"I've Never Lived This Long Before"

One of my main duties when we were home between tours and TV and record sessions was doing interviews on behalf of the Statlers. Some we would all do, but the bulk I did alone. I did all the pre-tour interviews with radio stations, newspapers, magazines, and call-ins to local TV shows in the towns we were heading to, whatever was needed. Some days I'd go into the office, close my door, and do easily fifteen interviews before coming up for air. I've answered every question you can imagine and dodged all that I didn't want to answer. And, every once in a while, someone would ask a really nice, original question I'd never been asked before, and I lived for those rare moments. One day some faceless voice out there somewhere in America on the other end of the line asked, "Besides the awards and the hit records, what has been the most rewarding part of your career?" Taking just a beat, I surprised myself with my answer. I said, "It has afforded us the opportunity of meeting all our heroes." It was a quick yet deeply accurate response that took me to the piano in the corner of the living room before the week was over, and I wrote that first line:

I've met all my heroes and shook all the hands
  of all I wanted to meet
I've kissed all the women that once were the girls
  I dreamed about fallin' to sleep
I've looked up the bullies from grade and high school
  and gave them a piece of my mind
I've even looked up some old teachers I had
  and 'pologized for being unkind

That verse was part fact and part fiction, as all verses tend to be, but then I got very personal on the second verse, as songwriters are wont to do.

I talked to my mamma and told her I knew
  I hadn't done all that I could
She just smiled and kissed me and said, "After all,
  you know prayers answered late are still good"
and Daddy, there's things I'd love to tell you,
  but you died 25 years ago

360

'Cause just now I'm learnin' a few of the things,
I thought for years you didn't know

I have absolutely loved writing story songs such as these. Having two on the same album ("The-All-Girl-All-Gospel Quartet") was very unusual for us, but that was the mode I was in. "All-Girl" was 5:58 and this one was 5:57. That was pretty unusual for us, also. I won't give you all five of the verses, but I will share the third one as it is an interesting mixture of amusement and philosophy. Or as close as I can get anyway.

I find myself reading the Bible more now
than I did, say, ten years ago
And I find myself lookin' at young girls and thinkin'
that's somebody's daughter, you know
And what does it mean when they call me Mister
and say things I don't comprehend
And to tell you the truth, more often to me
their mammas look better than them

And there's nothing I've done that I wish I'd done less
but there's a few I wish I'd done more
And the thing I find hardest to believe is I'm here
'cause I've never lived this long before

This is one of the oddest writing stories I may have ever shared. I wrote this song and titled it "1994." To understand that, you have to know that the original last line was *and it's almost 1994* instead of *'cause I've never lived this long before.* We were at the session and getting ready to record it when Harold pulled me aside and said, "There's something that's bothering me. That title and that line dates this song. I think you should get rid of the whole 1994 thing." I thought about it and agreed but I couldn't come up with a new line or a new title. He and I sat and discussed it, mulled it over, and he was the one that finally said, "How about 'I've never lived this long before?'" Perfect!

At that point he got part of the song credits and became cowriter because he saved it from having an expiration date on it. That's not the first time big brother saved my bacon, but then that would be enough material to write another book.

"What We Love to Do"

Another new writing team: Harold's son, Wil, and my son Langdon. They have written so many great songs together since, but this was the first. They also had been touring a lot already at this time, and January 15, 1993, found them in a white Jeep Cherokee, with two guitars thrown in the backseat, heading for a date somewhere in West Virginia. I'll give you the rest of the story in Langdon's words as he gave it to me.

"The best advice we ever got from the best songwriters was to 'write what you know.' So we did. The journey, struggles, balances, ups, downs and the ultimate chasing of the neon rainbow. The life of an entertainer is a beautiful thing! When we set out to write this song, we were just capturing all the elements of the road and lifestyle. It was never our intention to write it for the Statlers, but after we completed it, it seemed like a natural."

We like to pick and sing and it's not a nine-to-five
It may not be a real job but it keeps our dream alive
We've sung for more than many and sometimes quite a few
Either way, it doesn't matter, it's what we love to do

The song was so good and so Statler, we not only recorded it immediately, we also shot a video on it. And we tailored the video to the perfect lyrics they had written. Most all of it was shot on our bus, backstage at our sound checks, and on stage in concert. It's not only our life on the road, but the life of any entertainer in any field of music. It's a wonderful breath of freshness showing how the sausage is made. And then they capped it with a dash of a love story. Nice touch.

Backstage we say a small prayer, then do what we do best
The band begins our music and we'll do all the rest
The ride home will be the long one, as soon as the show is through
I know she'll be up waiting, it's what we love to do

39

The Statler Brothers Sing the Classics

1995

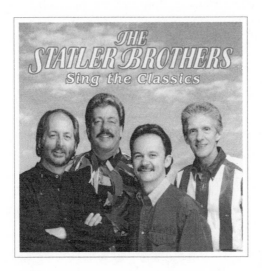

The Nashville Network TV series was eating up so much of our time that we were just not getting in the recording studio as much as we used to and as much as we wanted to. There was something about making records that appealed to all four of us in a special way. Performing on stage or TV was more show and less creativity. Making records required no particular dress, no flash, because no one was watching, and not trying to recreate a sound or arrangement, because here is where it all began. All you had to concentrate on was the audio. JK always had such a relaxed atmosphere for us that was so conducive to trying some new twist without the fear of embarrassment or failure. We might get a complete vocal and instrumental track down, and while listening to the playback, the five of us would look at one another and say, "This isn't working." No problem. We'd just change a tempo or a lead or an instrument. That is what the creative process is all about, and it was a sweet victory when it all came together.

This double album was another Heartland production for TV. The enormous-selling *Gospel Favorites* album was three years before this one. Since then, Mercury had released a twelve-song compilation version of it called *Today's Gospel Favorites* in '93, our regular *Home* album in '93, and the big three-CD package, *30th Anniversary Celebration* in '94. This was in commemoration of our thirty years in the music business, measured from the time we were discovered by Johnny Cash in 1964. All sixty-two songs on it were rereleases, but a pretty darn good history of our professional career. I guess if you had only one Statler album, that would be the one to have. Unfortunately, it's out of print today. Inside was a great little booklet and some pictures that had never been seen before or since. So, enter again Heartland, who had been wanting us to do another TV offer, and this time they asked for an album of the old classic country and early rock songs that most influenced our growing up. We went for it and picked some of the greatest old songs we ever heard on the radio. Harold, Phil, and I have said publicly that this is a favorite of ours and that we all four are singing better here than ever in any period of our lives. This album, reissued in 2018, is one full of fun and joy.

"Memories Are Made of This"

This is *the* pop song from my youth. I had the 45-rpm and wore the grooves flat on it. Dean Martin was a pop idol of ours, and we saw every Martin and Lewis film on Saturday mornings at the theater that they made. I own copies of all sixteen of them. So, it was a special thrill to finally get to sing this Dean Martin classic. We did TV with him a number of times and told some stories about that in a previous book (*Random Memories*), but I have to say he was the perfect example of our being afforded the opportunity to meet and mingle with our heroes.

Note also on this song two good friends who were backup singers on our TV show, who came across town and did the background vocals for us. And what a beautiful job Wendy Suits and Jeanine Walker did.

Then add the wedding bells, one house where lovers dwell

Three little kids for the flavor
Stir carefully through the day, see how the flavor stays
These are the dreams you will savor

I was only ten years old when this went to number one, but I guess I was already developing a writer's ear. Terry Gilkyson, Richard Dehr, and Frank Miller penned it and taught me a new word. Savor. I remember looking it up as a kid, but I very much remember, as an adult, admiring their finesse in using it as a rhyme. Can you think of any other song in which this word was ever used? I don't think there *was* ever another one. I so love this kind of innovative thinking in a writer.

We played the big showroom at the MGM Grand in Las Vegas often in the eighties and nineties. Martin played there a lot for a week at a time and sometimes we would follow him when we came in for our week. We would get into town to get everything set, usually on his last day each time, so we would go down and catch his show. He always had us stand up in the audience, and he would introduce us as "four beautiful boys from the Shenandoah Valley of Virginia." Then we'd go backstage and visit with him. One night we were in his dressing room, and Harold asked him, "How come you never sing 'Memories Are Made of This?' Martin shook his head and said, 'Lord, that's been twenty years ago.'" Harold said, "Well, more like thirty, but we'd still like to hear it." He laughed, but he never sang it. He never sang any of his hits from the Martin and Lewis era. I think he had some sort of mental or emotional block about that. We were with Jerry Lewis on a number of occasions, also. Even visited backstage with him when he played Broadway in the nineties. And he, in return, never mentioned Dean either.

"The Great Pretender"

The Platters. 1955. Number one. Tony Williams singing lead. This was their follow-up hit to "Only You," which, of course, we also did. The story is that Buck Ram, who wrote both hits for them, wrote this one in twenty minutes in the washroom of the Flamingo Hotel in Las Vegas. I don't know if he was standing up or sitting down, but it worked.

We put the Statler touch to it by arranging it in a Southern gospel style. It starts with a pretty piano roll (Pig Robbins) with me leading. I'm the setup man. I always set up the jokes for Harold's punch lines, and I always set up the songs for the exciting chord change near the end, when Jimmy would take it and slay. And that's exactly what happens here. We stop and Pig gives the 1950s eighth notes with the Bergen White strings swelling in around us. We did use the Platters' ending. However, as we performed it subsequently for years on stage, it became more and more Statlerized. But I'll tell you about that when we get to the very last album.

"Gone"

Ferlin Husky. 1957. Number one. Ferlin went to the top of both the country and pop charts with this one, and then a few years later did the same with "Wings of a Dove." Such a talented man on stage and on record. We always loved his rendition of this song and never realized what great Statler material it was until we stepped to the microphones in the studio. I think this is just an exemplary performance by all four of us. I could listen to it all day.

Ferlin was one of the best stage entertainers in country music. He sang his hits, did comedy and impressions, and always left the audience wanting more. We loved working shows with him. But there was one non-show of a very serious nature that still makes me laugh. When our dear buddy Luther Perkins, Johnny Cash's guitarist, died in '68, we sang Luther's favorite song, "How Great Thou Art," at his funeral at the First Baptist Church in Hendersonville, Tennessee. Ferlin was a pallbearer but was late arriving at the front door as we all walked in. All the pallbearers followed Luther's widow, Margie, down the aisle, and we followed them for a short distance. At a certain point, Harold, Phil, Lew, and I veered off and went into the choir loft, where we would sing later in the service. Ferlin, rushing in at the last minute, saw us and fell in behind us and went right up in the choir loft with us.

Now there we stood, the five of us in front of the church and the four of us not knowing exactly how to correct this situation with proper decorum. Phil was closest to him, so he leaned over and whispered, "We're going to sing. You're supposed to be down there." Ferlin nodded big, winked, and gave us the okay sign behind his back as he headed out the loft and down the aisle as the funeral party waited on him to be seated. As hard as it was to sing without crying that day, it was just as hard to watch Ferlin scooting down that church aisle without laughing. And Luther, bless his generous and loving heart, would have been laughing the hardest.

"Naughty Lady of Shady Lane"

The Ames Brothers. 1954. Their first hit with a long line of others to follow. This song was so cleverly written by the New York team of Sid Pepper and Roy C. Bennett. They wrote hit after hit for everyone from Guy Lombardo to the Beatles. Elvis recorded more than forty of their songs. They certainly had a touch, and even a country touch for NYC Jewish pop writers. This song had a twist at the end that you usually only found in Nashville. The lady you sing about all through the song turns out not to be the lady you thought it was at all. Sort of a comical-mystery hook. As songwriters, we just couldn't turn down the opportunity to do it, and as fans of the Ames Brothers, it was a must. We also sang it on our TV show and even put it in the stage show for a while. In case you've never heard it, I won't spoil it for you here, because the last line will, for sure, make you smile.

"She Thinks I Still Care"

George Jones. 1962. Number one. Written by our friend Dickey Lee. And, no, you are not having déjà vu. We recorded this one twice. The first time was on the *Innerview* album in 1972. We did it again here because it just fit the bill so perfectly and we had been doing it on some shows in recent years.

When Jimmy came in '82, there was such a workload on him learning so many new arrangements and lyrics that one day during rehearsals on the stage in our office complex, we called a halt to all work. We asked him to just sing something to us that he enjoyed singing. Something he knew all the words to and felt 100 percent comfortable doing. He rolled a D chord on the guitar and stepped to the microphone and started singing this song. We stood and listened for a couple of lines and then joined him on the third and fourth, and we had a new quick and easy stage song the fans just loved. And Jimmy shines and sparkles on every note.

Just because I asked a friend about her
Just because I spoke her name somewhere
Just because I rang her number by mistake today
She thinks I still care

"I'll Go to My Grave Loving You"

This one was lifted from our *Live and Sold Out* album. Heartland insisted we have a few Statler Brothers hits on here, and this is one of them.

"Moments to Remember"

The Four Lads. 1955. Their first hit, also, with a long line of others to follow. So, going back through the pages of time, turn to our fifth album, *Pictures of Moments to Remember.* I told you then we recorded this song again and teased by not telling you the name of the lady who sang the intro here and did the recitation midway through. As I have said, our TV series was in production all during this time frame, so one day we asked Crystal Gayle, who was a regular on our show, if she would come in and do us the honor of singing and talking on this particular cut. Her answer can be heard clearly here. There has never been a sexier and more intimate reading of these words than what she gave us. We love you, sweet Crystal.

> *January to December, we'll have moments to remember*
> *The drive-in movie is where we'd go*
> *And somehow never watch the show*

But I have to give great credit to the real stars of this piece. Again, two Jewish NYC songsmiths, Robert Allen and Al Stillman, who wrote hit after hit together. "There's No Place Like Home for the Holidays" for Perry Como. "Chances Are" for Johnny Mathis. "No, Not Much" for the Four Lads again and so many more. But here Allen wrote one of the most beautiful melodies two human hands could compose on a piano. (He was Como's pianist for years.) And Stillman just makes me weak in the knees with the pictures of youth he paints throughout.

> *The New Year's Eve we did the town*
> *The day we tore the goalpost down*
> *We'll have these moments to remember*
> *The quiet walks, the noisy fun*
> *The ballroom prize we almost won*
> *We'll have these moments to remember*

"Chattanoogie Shoeshine Boy"

From our *Home* album, 1993. And I'll still bet you can't say "hoppity, hippity, hippity, hoppity, hoppity, hippity hop" fast and in time.

"Making Believe"

Kitty Wells. 1955. Top of the charts. Flat-out country music. Mandolin and fiddle abound. Good song, good singing, and hearing Phil's little note-bending excursion on the final chord is worth the listening.

With every celebrity comes an interesting or memorable story. And most who spend any time in this business are colorful enough that there will be stories or rumors flying all over the place about them. Back in the 1960s, when we were a part of the Johnny Cash show, there were tours where he would add more acts to the show for certain areas of the country or certain cities or maybe just for weekend nights. There was a period of time when he would add the husband-and-wife team of Kitty Wells and Johnnie Wright, who had been half of the duo Johnnie and Jack. They would always have their band and their daughter, Ruby, and their son, Bobby, who was a regular on the hit TV show *McHale's Navy*.

They were all wonderful, down-to-earth folks. Ruby was cute. Bobby was funny. Daddy ran the show (word around town was that he would not let Kitty cut any song that had more than three chords in it), and Kitty was the obvious star of the family, due to her legendary history of hit songs. But what made Kitty Wells so outstanding and clearly unique, besides her one-of-a-kind voice, was the fact that there was absolutely nothing to re-tell about her whatsoever. No rumors. No scandal. Not even a funny story here and there. She was quiet, unassuming, ladylike, and would perfectly meld into the scenery when not on stage. This, in itself, makes her so peerless and memorable as a show business personality and star. Kitty "Keeping It Real" Wells.

"Tom Dooley"

The Kingston Trio. 1958. Number one. Maybe one of our best performances ever committed to tape. From Harold's booming talking intro to his booming singing on the exit line, it's a perfect execution of an execution song. I won't bother to print any sample lyrics below, because is there anyone alive who doesn't know the chorus to Tom Dooley? I loved recording this and still love listening to it. Such a simple track and simple melody with a masterful mix from JK.

"Love Letters in the Sand"

Pat Boone. 1957. Number one. (And then there was our old Virginia bluegrass pal Mac Wiseman, who had it on the Dot label even before Pat.) I so well remember going to the Dixie theater in downtown Staunton to see Pat's first movie, *Bernadine.* He sat with his feet propped up on a chair and crooned it. I was only twelve, but I knew I'd like to sing that song someday. And here it is.

Brother Harold owns these choruses by the time we're through with it. Smooth and with a hint of swing, it just flows out of him. Another exceptional performance from us all, if I do have to say so.

From a twelve-year-old fan of his music and his movies to a friendship in years to come. Pat guested a couple of times on our TV series in the nineties. The seventh and final season, he became a semiregular. Harold and I wrote a special Hollywood segment featuring popular music from the movies. Pat did half of them with us and Glen Campbell did the other half. I would often sit in rehearsals in front of the orchestra as we all ran through our scripts and our music and look over at Pat sitting in a circle with us and see that image of him with his feet propped up on that chair in his first movie, and then I'd see that twelve-year-old image of me in the balcony. In this business it's sometimes hard to separate the dreams from reality.

"Hello Mary Lou"

Ricky Nelson. 1961. Big hit. Statler Brothers. 1985. Big hit. This is the same cut that was on *Pardners in Rhyme.* And I still don't know how to pronounce Cayet Mangiaracina, but he and Gene Pitney wrote a good song.

"Unchained Melody"

Al Hibbler. 1955. You don't know him but he had a great hit with this one. Roy Hamilton did, also. They raced one another up the charts. Most everyone remembers the Righteous Brothers' version in '65, even though it was only *one* "brother" singing, Bobby Hatfield. It all came from a B prison movie, *Unchained*, in '55 and has become a pop standard to this day.

The rare beauty of the song dictated we had to include it, and I loved singing it, but the standout memory for me is in the last chorus. We began the song in the key of G, did a dominant key change midway, and finished the last chorus in C. Thus, at one point in this bridge, I sang a G note. That is probably the highest I ever sang on record or on stage or on a bus or in a car or just anywhere. I sweated that note for weeks. I'm very fulfilled by the sound of it today, but I wouldn't want to do it again. I leave all my high lifting to Phil and Jimmy.

"The Battle of New Orleans"

Johnny Horton. 1959. Number one. It was written by an Arkansas schoolteacher, Jimmie Driftwood, who also wrote "Johnny Reb" and "Tennessee Stud" and lots more. Our producer, Jerry Kennedy, grew up playing guitar for Horton and touring with him. Johnny Cash and Horton were best friends, so we have heard many great stories about him, even though we never met him, as he had passed by the time we got to Nashville in the midsixties.

The structure of this song always fascinated me. It has two choruses. One starts with:

We fired our guns and the British kept a-coming

And the other one starts with:

They ran through the briars and they ran through the brambles

You just don't find that often, and I was always drawn to it by this simple little writing quirk. Also, Johnny Horton and others who sang it always sang that last line in verse four as:

371

Then we opened up our squirrel guns and really gave 'em...well...

By the time we got to it, we figured it was 1995, and it might be a little prudish to skip over that word the way they had in the fifties, so Harold sang it:

Then we opened up our squirrel guns and really gave 'em hell

This whole arrangement really worked, and it proved to be a really rousing stage song for us for a long time.

"I Can't Stop Loving You"

Don Gibson. 1958. His first hit and he had a gang of others that followed, too. Someone will correct me and say I should have said Ray Charles. 1962, number one. And you'd be right, also. But Gibson not only wrote it, he beat Ray to it by four years. However, the Ray Charles hit had quite an emotional and nostalgic effect on me.

I graduated from high school on June 4, 1962, when I was sixteen years old. The very next day I turned seventeen. Where I was when the midnight tolled on that long-ago hot spring night is not a story I'm inclined to relate at this juncture, but this song, for sure was with me. It was the hit that radio could not get enough of that summer, and I still reach down and turn it up when an oldies station plays it just for old times' sake.

I know I told this story in the *Random Memories* book, but it is just to good not to repeat it here, also just for old times' sake. On the Johnny Cash television show that was taped each week in the Ryman Auditorium in Nashville, we were regulars and featured on every broadcast for the three years it was on ABC. The Statlers went out each night before the taping and warmed up the live audience for John. Then I hung around and introduced each guest to the studio audience before John intro-ed them to the television audience.

I was standing backstage with Ray Charles, and I explained to him that I would intro him, his man would lead him to the piano, and then John would introduce him on camera. From that point then he would kick into his song. Perfect. Ready to go. I walked center stage with a mic in my hand and simply said with all my heart, "Ladies and gentlemen, the incomparable

Ray Charles." The Ryman went wild, Ray went to the piano, got seated, and waited for the applause to die down and then said, in his best tongue-in-cheek voice, "What dat dat man call me?"

He was a master at what he did. I've often wished, as I watched him perform, that he could have seen the smiles he put on the faces of the people.

Phil and I would often switch leads and harmony for a line or two with one another for different and various reasons, but on this one, he leads it all the way. And what an extraordinary job he does. The choruses are full and solid and it was always fun for me to get to sing harmony all the way through an arrangement. Don't miss the verse where Jimmy echoes Phil on certain lines. It has a wonderful, almost "Sparkling Brown Eyes" effect. (This is in reference to a 1954 Webb Pierce/Wilburn Brothers partnering that resulted in a very well-performed hit record. Look it up and give it a listen.)

"Bye, Bye Love"

Everly Brothers. 1957. Their very first hit and, wow, so many, many more to come. Our version was rockin' from the opening bar. That's Jimmy Capps leading us in and out of the verses with a cracklin' electric guitar as only he can. Every Everly song we ever sang was fun every time we ever sang an Everly song. Now, say that last sentence as fast as you can and take two aspirin and go to bed.

The Everlys had a summer TV replacement show on ABC in LA in 1970. We had met them on the set of *The Johnny Cash Show* that spring, and they invited us out to do a couple of the shows with them. There is a YouTube of the six of us singing "Columbus Stockade Blues" from one of those appearances, and to be brazenly honest with you, it's pretty darn good.

"Only You"

This one can be found on the *Four for the Show* album from 1986.

"Have I Told You Lately That I Love You?"

Gene Autry. 1946. In a long, long list of many, many hits. This is one of those songs that was before my time yet I still grew up knowing all the words. Songs would become a part of the radio world that we lived in, and by osmosis it would seep into our brains and live there forever. I have hundreds of examples of songs from twenty and thirty years before I was even born that I just know the words and music to and have no idea how.

My lyric sheets from the session on May 1, 1995, tell me we changed this arrangement at the very last minute. Originally, in the key of D, we all four sang the first verse and Harold sang the second. Then, for some reason, we scratched that and Harold sang the first verse, we changed to the key of E, and Phil did the second. I don't any more know why we did this than I know how I knew all the lyrics when I was a kid. But I do know this melody is very laid-back and unassuming, and it's the words that hold all the power. You can just close your eyes and hear the truth.

This was written by Scotty Wiseman, one half of the married singing duo of Lulu Belle and Scotty. Years ago I heard this very touching story about him writing this song. His wife, Lulu Belle, was in the hospital for some surgery. He visited with her the night before, and as he was leaving her room, he stopped at the door and turned around and said to her, "Have I told you lately that I love you?" Then he went home and wrote it.

Have I told you lately that I love you
Could I tell you once again somehow
Have I told you with all my heart and soul how I adore you
Well, darling, I'm telling you now

"Oh Baby Mine"

From the *Today* album, 1983.

"It Only Hurts for a Little While"

From *Words and Music*, 1992.

"He's Got the Whole World in His Hands"

Laurie London. 1958. Number one. You could hear this song on the radio without even turning the radio *on*. It was everywhere. And this gets real personal real quick, because I would get up extra early that late winter and take my clothes to the relative warmth of the kitchen and dress there so I could hear this song before going to school. The DJ played it at the same time each morning, 6:30 A.M., and I then he'd play "Sugartime" by the McGuire Sisters and "Twilight Time" by the Platters while I ate breakfast. Same times every morning. But it was the Laurie London hit that initially got me out of bed that early. Who was it? Was it a boy or girl? The voice and the name just added to the mystery. Turns out it was an old spiritual from the 1920s someone had dug out of the archives and a thirteen-year-old English boy recorded it and set the world on fire. Sadly, and oddly, he never had another chart record. This was it. A one-time biggie.

But then all the Southern gospel groups started singing it. Children's church choirs, school talent shows, and kids at camp around the campfire. It became a folk/gospel classic in a short time. Everybody who can carry a tune can sing a verse or two for you. Just ask! We decided to divide it up with solos for each of us and made it the ultimate sing-along. It's still fun to listen to our arrangement and to remember Laurie London's.

"Bed of Rose's"

From the *Live and Sold Out* album, 1989.

"Love Me Tender"

Elvis. 1956. Number one with a bullet! Such a rich history behind this lovely old song. It was an old Civil War folk piece called "Aura Lee." Ken Darby, an Academy Award-winning composer and songwriter in Hollywood, took that beautiful old melody and wrote new romantic lyrics to it and pitched it to Elvis.

Allow me to divert for a moment and tell you that when Elvis recorded "Susan When She Tried," which I wrote back in the seventies, I was invited to the session the night he cut it. My publisher warned me that his people would approach me and demand 50 percent of the song. I was not able to go that night and the negotiation was never brought up to me. However, Elvis did cut it, and it is on his *Today* album, and it is still 100 percent mine. Now, back to Ken Darby's story.

The powers that be in Elvis's organization did approach Darby and tell him Elvis would need 50 percent of the song and his name on it as cowriter if he wanted a Presley cut on his ballad. Darby agreed, but when he turned in the contract he used a pseudonym—Vera Matson—his wife's name. When someone asked Darby why he put his wife's name on the song as cowriter with Elvis, he said, "Because she didn't write it either."

Our history with this song is not nearly as funny as Ken Darby's, but it may be a little more sentimental. I went to the Visulite Theater in downtown Staunton (it's still there) in 1956 and watched E. P. on the big screen in the black-and-white film by the same name. Eleven-year-old boy that I was, I fell in love with his costar, Debra Paget, and listened to the girls in the theater scream each time he sang a song and heard them cry when he met a fatal end in the dust at the finale. Even then I knew the song was better than the movie, and it ranks with me as one of the best all-around performances of The Statler Brothers on or off the record. With Pig Robbins at the piano, Bergen White at the orchestra, and Jerry Kennedy at the controls, mix in Harold Reid, Phil Balsley, Jimmy Fortune, and Don Reid doing what they do best and this one can't be beat. Not a solo in sight, just full, solid Statler Brothers harmony singing a beautifully written song the way Vera Matson meant it to be.

"Goodnight, Sweetheart, Goodnight"

The McGuire Sisters. 1954. Top ten and their first hit in a long line of fifties winners. This one swings, and that guitar-string-pulling theme throughout is Jerry Kennedy playing the Dobro guitar. (Jerry still laughs today that Harold always called it the "upright Dobro.") These old songs from the fifties decade just suited our style and fit our voices to where it sounds as if a lot of them were written with us in mind. We liked singing this one so much we added it to our stage show. It was standard that we used "Thank You, World" as a first encore song each night. "This Ole House" became our standard second encore, and then we'd just walk off to the applause as we were always spent and exhausted by that time. It was such a sweet tribute we felt each night as we could still hear the audience and feel the love as we exited the backdoor.

But we decided instead of leaving after "This Ole House," this would make a nice goodnight song to the crowd. It worked and I looked forward to it every show.

I have never told this story, and I hope I don't get in more trouble than I can handle by telling it. The McGuire Sisters guested one week on our TV show in 1993. It was our Christmas program that year, and we even sat on the set and sang carols together during rehearsals that weren't even included in the show. It was great fun rubbing musical shoulders with these ladies. Our production staff offered them three dressing rooms, but they said they only required two. Chris and Dot were in one and Phyllis was in the other. The world knows, as there was even a movie made about it, that Phyllis had a long-standing relationship with Sam Giancana of Chicago/Kennedy/Sinatra/Exner fame. And even though Sam bought the farm one night in 1975 with seven deadly shots to the head while frying sausage in his kitchen, his influence lived on.

Nearly twenty years later, there was still an immaculately dressed gentleman with a dark aura who sat outside Phyllis's dressing room door, allowing no one to enter or even knock but he himself. He was very friendly but nary a script girl, makeup, hair dresser, producer, director, or star could approach without his permission.

Goodnight, Phyllis, Goodnight.

A Footnote

Langdon and Debo have reviewed each chapter as I have written it, and they have pointed out something to me that I just never realized. The influences of the songs and the artists that are represented on this one album speak in depth as to who The Statler Brothers were musically. We have always been very vocal about our Southern gospel and country influences, but this collection of songs goes a bit deeper into the songs and the singers who had our attention growing up. And as I was digging into old files, I found handwritten notes and scribbled-up sheets of notebook paper that offered song titles we had to cut from our list of possibilities. Here are just a few that didn't make the final cut for this album: "Wings of a Dove," "Ain't That a Shame," "Sentimental Me," "Irene, Goodnight," "April Love," "You,

You, You," "Blueberry Hill," "Chantilly Lace," "The Three Bells," and "Secret Love."

The list goes on, but the point is there is no true stopping place when you begin analyzing what soaks through your senses in a lifetime of listening to music. Growing up, we had radios by our beds, in the bath, in the kitchen, in the car. We had record players in our rooms and in our living rooms. There were jukeboxes in all the teenager hangouts we frequented. There was music in the movies we went to and variety shows full of songs and singers on TV every night. Even old hymns and gospel songs at church every Sunday morning and Sunday night. At our high school, we had a large gathering room called the Social Center. Every morning for about forty-five minutes, you could go there before classes started and just hang out and socialize, and there were current records playing constantly and people dancing, even at that time of the morning, Monday through Friday. So, there was just no way we could or ever wanted to get away from music. It was everywhere, and I thank the good Lord that it was.

40

Showtime

2001

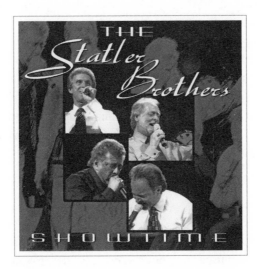

Our career was ever changing and, thankfully, ever growing. In the decades of the sixties, seventies, and eighties, we were driven by the record industry. In the nineties, we were driven by the TV industry with our series that ran for seven years in the number-one spot on the network. All of this had a great influence on our concert touring. The only change we ever saw in our audiences was the tone and flavor of the individual members of the crowds. Never the numbers. We still had full houses, sellouts, and SROs. They only changed from record buyers to TV watchers, but they were still our fans. Until the very day we retired, we were still blessed by and enjoyed packed theaters and coliseums and concert halls. However, we were so accustomed to bouncing back and forth between the road, the recording studio, and the

TV studio that we missed any aspect of the business we were not involved with at the moment. We had been with Columbia records for the first five years of our professional career and then with Mercury for twenty-six. Few artists and record labels have a relationship such as that, and we have nothing but good to say about them and the role they played in our success. But things change.

Jerry Kennedy was no longer VP in charge of the Nashville office. He had left and formed his own company, JK Productions. He still produced our albums but as an outside contractor. The pickers we were so comfortable with for so many years were backing off or retiring completely. Some had health problems that didn't allow them to continue working. We were having less and less time for all the facets of the business, but we knew we wanted to get back in front of the microphones, put the headphones on, and create some new music.

And that is how we came to this particular album. We formed our own label and called it Music Box Records. The four of us were there with JK at the controls but with mostly all new faces on the musicians. We had our staff of writers and a stack of good, all-new songs, ready to face the twenty-first century.

"She Never Altogether Leaves"

I'm looking at the lyric sheets from the session that February day in 2000. There is one with a note printed on it written to one of our secretaries that says, "Shirley, re-type this and change all the hes to shes. Thanks, HR."

This can only mean one thing—a new song by Kim Reid Weller that needed just a little pronoun adjustment. She handed us the melody and lyrics, and JK and Mark Casstevens handed us some guitar pickin' that constituted a kickin' track. Every songwriter keeps his/her mind open to any thread of a conversation that might lead to an idea or even a title. When I asked Kim for any remembrance of the writing of this one, what she gave me was something every writer can identify with. Here are her words sent back to me in an email:

> "It was an episode of MASH. Hawkeye's love had left the unit and he was sad. I think B. J. said it would be easier when she leaves, to which Hawkeye replies, "She never altogether leaves.""

380

Being by myself is not so bad right now
An empty closet and just one mouth to feed
It's only late at night that I remember
That she never altogether leaves"

"Too Late for Roses"

Wil and Langdon, two young men in their mid-twenties, offering up wisdom and a philosophy that we all can benefit from at any age. We gave their words a good country treatment, but still the message steals the show in this piece. Come all ye men, weary and tired and beaten by life, and take notice of what this chorus is saying to you.

Don't wait till it's too late, too late for roses
You can't say you're sorry, once the flower shop closes
It's too late to miss her, once another proposes
When you're pushin' up daises, it's too late for roses

Langdon has pointed out the rhyme pattern and choices that they put to such good use. And I commend them for that—roses/closes/proposes. So many writers will rhyme the word but give no thought to the *s* on the end of the word. It is so nice when it all matches perfectly, and that is the difference in spending time rewriting yourself and just going with the first thought in your head.

In the years before they each married, Langdon and Wil spent a lot of time at the old farmhouse you see pictured on the *Home* album. They would go there, with two guitars, to write and work on new music. It was there, on July 10, 1998, that they committed this one to paper.

And before we leave this song, let me just break off a little chunk of verse two's insight and perception for all of us to chew on and learn from:

So don't take tomorrow for granted
'Cause today might be your last chance
Now's the time to start thinking with your heart
And hold her like it's your last dance

381

"You Just Haven't Done It Yet"

Pat Wertman, who is the bass player for Wilson Fairchild, joined the two philosophers, Wil and Langdon, and gave us a jaunty little melody with a lot of crux and pith wrapped up inside. The verses offer up problems we face in life that sometimes just scare us to death and leave us in fear of failing. But then a single little thought of wisdom settles our nerves and gives us the stamina and resilience to charge on through. Well put together, and it all came from a sentence uttered by Pat while they were on tour. Langdon immediately jotted those words down, and a few weeks later, in a hotel room in Nashville, he and Wil wrote the song. (In the second verse, there is a line about having "second thoughts." They tell me today, that was a salute to their dads and a song we wrote by that very title. It's one of their favorites and one they included on their album, *Songs Our Dads Wrote*.)

> *It was the longest night, before our wedding day*
> *I wasn't having second thoughts, I just had more prayers to say*
> *I sat there in the church alone, asked my Father man to man*
> *Can I live up to a promise, when I don't know if I can*

We recorded this on February 23, 2000, Langdon's birthday, and he and Wil were in the studio with us when we did. I always loved having the writer at the session, and especially if they were one of our own.

> *Then my dad told me the secret*
> *That I never will forget*
> *He said, "It's not that you can't do it,*
> *You just haven't done it yet."*

"In Love with You"

My son Debo did not have to twist my arm to put words to this melody. He told me while I was writing this chapter that this is his favorite melody of all he has written. I can believe that because it may be my favorite of all *anyone* has written. He wrote it years before we collaborated on this song, and I carried it in my head for maybe a decade, trying to find the right expressions and syllables befitting such lovely notes. It always reminded me of an old Santo and Johnny hit or maybe something Ferrante and Teicher would perform on the pianos. It still gives me chills.

With Pig Robbins's 1959 piano licks and Bergen White's drive-in-movie string arrangements and the Brothers belting out these beautifully written and aligned quarter notes, well, it's just almost more than this old heart can take. Debo was there for these sessions, also, in February of 2000. And I'm glad he was. We finally saw his melody become a song.

I've been rich and I've been poor
I've done with less but never more
'Cause I have never been in love
Like I'm in love with you

Songs can be divided up with any percentage the writers agree on. Usually, if there are two writers, each will take 50 percent, but that is not written in blood. I don't get into telling these kinds of behind-the-scenes business facts, but I felt this melody was so much the whole song that I insisted we split this one 75 to 25 percent. And I was honored to get a quarter of it.

"Too Long Ago"

It had been fifteen or maybe even twenty years since Harold and I had sat down and wrote a flat-out nostalgia song like we turned out back in the seventies. We got credit for creating that style of memory songs with "Class of '57," "Do You Remember These," and "Carry Me Back" and so many more. For this album, we just decided one night to see if we could still do it. Could we still set that mood of looking back and painting that picture of the past that might tug at a few heartstrings?

It's been too long ago, there's so much we don't know
It's been years since I've been this close to you
Standing here on the street, like strangers when we meet
O God knows it's been too long ago

Harold and I were always on the same page when we wrote together. There was never a discussion about the direction we would go in or what we should say or not say. We wrote with one mind. And we never had to salve one another's feelings when we wanted to reject a line or a rhyme. We'd just say, "No," and then sit there till one of us came up with a better one. We wrote best when I held the guitar and he held the pen. And the later the night, the better the song. Feelings and memories get more tender after 2 A.M.

I won't try to lie to you
'Cause time just won't let us
Play the games we once had the time to play
We're both a little older
But lord, you don't look it
And when you smile I feel eighteen again today

"All I'll Need from You"

A superb performance of a superb piece of writing. It begins painting a beautiful picture of a classic romance with the opening lines:

I know you're a woman, the sensitive kind
A fairytale princess with hearts on your mind
Who needs to be showered with candy and flowers
And told that you're loved all the time

The melody and the chords caress the charm of these words and float through a portrait of a relationship everyone should experience.

I know you need kisses and hugs everyday
Phone calls and letters, whenever I'm away
You need to believe in faraway weekends
Puppies and Valentine's Day

Langdon describes it today as "a Hallmark card put to music." With Jerry's intimate guitar break and Bergen's strings suspended over each line, it's a card I wouldn't mind hearing every day. Lang and Wil use a nice technique here. After two verses and a chorus, they begin what you think is going to be a repeat of the first verse, but halfway through, new words prevail for a perfect capper and closer. Just good all-around music whether you like it country or sentimental or just plain pretty.

"Darlin' I Do"

Here's an interesting songwriting team. Gordon Kennedy (JK's son) and Steve Wariner. We had known Gordon since he was a kid and Steve for years as a friend and one of our favorite artists. They wrote this song for us and we loved it. It was country with a snap that fell right into an easy style.

Gordon has produced Wilson Fairchild albums and performs with them on stage sometimes. So that family connection lives on. And Steve, one of the best singers and guitarists in the business, has another talent you may not even be aware of. He paints. Hanging on the wall of my office, and I just turned and looked at it, is a picture Steve painted. It's five cowboys in varied western dress, standing in line as if posing for a picture. It's signed by Steve and I wouldn't take a gold album for it.

"I've Had a Good Time"

I've written a lot of story songs, and, quite frankly, I don't always remember this one when I think of them. But I would have to list it as one of my favorites. I was able to sum up a lot of my career and my life in these three choruses.

I've had a good time, had a good life
Had a good home, had a good wife
Had a little rain, had a little sun
Had a little sin, had a little fun
Been up on cloud nine, been down on my luck
Made a few friends, made a few bucks
Then fell in love a couple more times
I've had a good time

My hat is off to the pickers here who all did an outstanding job. But a special tip of the hat to JK, Kevin Grant, and Jeff King. They shine.

I've had a good time, had a good run
Sometimes I lost, sometimes I won
Wrote a few songs that still get sung
I didn't give up and I didn't die young

I've been up, I've been down, I've been to the wall
But I've been blessed, Lord, through it all
Even fell in love, two or three more times
I've had a good time

The next chorus says, "Got no regrets, well, maybe a few." One regret is that we didn't include this as a concert song during our final yearlong tour of 2002. This would have been a perfect statement each night as we left the stage.

I've had a good time, had a good ride
Sometimes I laughed, sometimes I cried
Sometimes I looked, sometimes I touched
Sometimes I took just a little too much
But I never looked back, got no regrets
Well, maybe a few, but even yet
I'd love to do it again, just one more time
I've had a good time

"It Should Have Been Me"

I was writing the nostalgic-looking-back song from a very adult position. It was a reflection of things that never were. A lament of what could have been. And I'm right proud of the way it came off and how we did it. I wasn't writing near as much or as often as I had most all of my career, so I tended to savor those private moments more than I ever had before. No more writing on the run, no more leaving notes and ideas on the piano to finish the next day, no more getting up in the middle of the night to jot down a new line that had come to me from somewhere in the night, no more carrying that little black rhyming dictionary in my guitar case because there was no more carrying my guitar. I was settled and satisfied and was taking the time to appreciate a breeze of creativity any time it blew through my window. Nice song. We did it a lot on stage.

It should have been you—it should have been me
It should have been the way things turned out to be
It could have been now—it could have been how

We both dreamed that it would be
But we both know where dreams come true
In fairytales they do
But in life, having you
It should have been me

"Look at Me"

Listen to that intro and those strings throughout. And it's all about those sad and lost lyrics from Jimmy's pen. This one just cries and clutches for the heart. Jimmy's performance is a glimpse of what you were to hear from him in the ensuing years as a solo artist. He has such a rich voice with no frills or fancy footwork. Just flat out gettin' it. His singing always makes me smile, and, to be truthful, *he* always makes me smile. Even when he sings such an unhappy, lost-love song as this. I smile at the talent and the joy he puts into every note.

Look at me, you can't even look at me
I don't know what happened to what we used to be
How can you say you love me
You can't even look at me

"The Other Side of the Cross"

The immediate effect this song had on our audience was overwhelming. I wrote it as a closing gospel song for *The Statler Brothers Show* for TV in mid-1995. We sang it that season and the show aired on February 24, 1996. The response was like no other gospel song we had ever presented. We were flooded with requests as to which album it was on and where the sheet music could be bought and when we would sing it again on TV. We had no answers for any of these questions. We did repeat it again the next season (October 24, 1997), and we made sure sheet music was available for all the choirs and churches that were demanding it. But it wasn't available on any of our records until this album in 2001. We were singing it on stage nightly, and it found a voice of its own from the very first performance.

Bill Gaither called us in early '99 and told us about an album and video he wanted to do for the Cathedral Quartet, who were retiring that year. We assured him we were on board for anything he had in mind because we loved those guys and wanted to be a part of the celebration.

On May 18, 1999, in Nashville at the Ryman Auditorium, we sang this song for Glen Payne's and George Younce's retirement concert. We went free of charge and took no fees for any of the CD and DVD sales. It all went to Glen and George, and it was one of the most fulfilling and emotional nights we ever spent on stage. The pews in the old Ryman were full of their contemporaries and our heroes. James Blackwood, Jake Hess, Ben Speer, and so many more were standing with the rest of the audience when we came off stage, and they all said so many wonderful and nice things.

But the one that touched my heart the deepest was James Blackwood, my musical hero since I was nine years old. He grabbed me and hugged my neck there on the floor of the Ryman, where we had bought tickets as kids to go hear him sing, and said in my ear, "Don, I think you have another hit." Only Jesus could know how much I loved and respected that man and what I was feeling somewhere down deep in my soul of memories. Thank you, James. This song brings me great peace. Harold has said many times it's his favorite of anything I ever wrote. Thank you, bro.

On the other side of the cross
The side that no one could see
Hung the spirit of things yet to come
Hung the future of you and me
And what He gave that day on the cross
Not one bit of love has been lost
Hold my hand, stand up and say
If you were there on that day
On the other side of the cross

"I've Got Jesus on My Side"

I wrote this simple little a cappella number to use on stage with never a thought of recording it. Each night for a couple of years, we would do this in a pin spot just before singing "How Great Thou Art." It has everything any Southern gospel song could ever want or need. Camp meeting aftertime, bass lead-ins, a tenor lead on the chorus, and a big, robust ending. It never failed the crowd and never failed to excite us. Just a fun and inspiring song we looked forward to each concert. And a message that holds true for the ages. I'm glad I was given these words. Looking back on them and listening to them again, they mean more today than they even did then.

And some day soon, this weary pilgrim
Will take that final glory ride
Then all is well, and all's forgiven
'Cause I've got Jesus on my side

Thank you, Lord.

41

Amen

2002

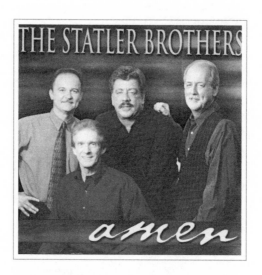

"AMEN. The word means 'truly,' 'certainly,' 'may it be so,' 'so it is,' and 'so be it.' It's used after a prayer or a song to express approval in church, such as, 'The covered-dish supper will start at 7 P.M. Amen.'

"Most of the songs are new with a few familiar ones thrown in for flavor, but they all share one main thing in common, the old-fashioned message of the old, old story. And to this we say, 'Amen.'

"We had some great second-generational help in the songwriting department from Kim, Debo, Wil and Langdon. We're, of course, proud of the songs and even prouder of the kids. To this we say, 'Amen.'

"As always, this project was produced by our friend Jerry Kennedy. We have not walked in a studio in 32 years without him. We give him our best and he always makes it better. And to this we say, 'Amen.'

"But the album is not complete. And it won't be until you listen and enjoy and approve. It will only be complete when you say, 'Amen.'"

—*Harold, Phil, Jimmy and Don*
The Statler Brothers

These were the liner notes packaged inside our purported last album. We felt pretty sure going into it that it would be the last time we darkened the doors of a sound studio for an album before we retired. We had not told anyone yet of our intentions and wouldn't until months after this album was finished, but for us and only us, there was a sentimental cloud hanging over the entire production. For it to be a gospel album in dedication to our gospel beginnings was befitting. That it would carry the name *Amen* was certainly more than irony and coincidence. We again produced it on our own Music Box label, and we filled it with twelve of the most heartfelt and sincere songs in our reach. I write about it with a certain smile and sadness that only retrospect can offer and only love and remembrance can understand.

"A Place on Calvary"

We began this album on May 30, 2001, but Langdon tells me today that he wrote this song four years before this. He tailored it to have the Southern gospel appeal to us and even wrote little gospel bass lead-ins to each line in the chorus that we were so noted for, and then we didn't use them. What's that they say about the best-laid plans? Then he added, and I'll offer it here in his own words, "But the low A note Harold hit on the end made me forget all about those lead-in lines." From the time we recorded it, it became a part of our stage show. We sang it every night in our gospel segment right up to and including our last concert. Also, Dailey and Vincent recorded it and used it as their closing song for a long time on tour. It's hard to find a better one than this to leave ringing in the air as you exit a building.

It had great charm and appeal. It reminded us of some of the old Statesmen songs from the 1950s. Even the arrangement we gave it was in the style of Hovie Lister and his men of song, who were one of the best quartets to grace any all-night sing.

Lower my body and lift my soul
And tell me to come on home
Let me leave this world of sin
'Cause heaven's where I wanna roam
I will bow my head, raise my hands
And get down on my knees
I just beg and pray that I someday
Will have a place on Calvary

"It Might Be Jesus"

One was standing on the corner with a tin cup in his hand
One was walking down the highway all alone
One was asking for my time when I had no more time to give
One was looking for a handout or a loan

Phil, Harold, and I still go to the church we were born into and grew up in: Olivet Presbyterian. We're all three ruling elders there and have been for many years. The absolute inspiration for this song came from within the walls of Olivet. Back in the nineties someplace, there was a middle-aged man who lived in a nearby halfway house. He was scruffy and, to be honest, downright dirty of body and clothes. He started coming into our church service and continued to come for about a year. He would ride his bike, park it by the front door, and then track mud up the center aisle, leave a mess of wrappers each week in the pew, and offend the olfactory senses of anyone who came remotely close to him. But no one, and I stress no one, ever mentioned any discomfort whatsoever. He was treated warmly by every member and encouraged to continue to attend even though any attempt at conversation with him was met with silence and a vacant stare.

Another elder there, Harry Hogshead, and I went shopping for him one day and bought him some clean clothes and toiletries and took them to his door. We were met with the same lack of greeting we got on Sunday mornings from him, but we knew in our hearts we had done the right thing. I found it difficult to shake his image and his possible story from my conscience, so, in time, this song was born. I don't know where Kevin is today, but I think he was used by God, as we all are, and is in his care somewhere this very minute.

One came into our church with dirty hair and filthy clothes
Tracking mud across our Christian floor
One was preaching on the sidewalk where no one stopped to hear
And two came and knocked on my front door

The chorus is a sermon unto itself and also an admonishment for us to be on the lookout for those around us. I take no credit for these words, but I'm honored they were given through me. If they have never done anyone else any good, they certainly spoke to me.

It might be Jesus
   it might be Jesus
That lonely stranger
   someone let in
It might be someone
   you turned your back on
It might be Jesus
   it might be him

"He's Gettin' Me Ready"

I remember when Jimmy brought this one in and sang it to all of us. We saw it as a throwback to the old quartet style of the south. It's a perfect rhythm song and one that would just stop the show at any gospel sing below the Mason-Dixon. The track is on fire and it was so much fun to sing.

He's gettin' me ready for what's waitin' down the road
He's gettin' me ready to carry this heavy load
Gonna see what Jesus has waitin' there for me
He's gettin' me ready for eternity

"God Saw My Need"

I used characters in the Bible to punctuate and accent the message in each verse. And I can't honestly say I knew I was going to do this when I started writing this song. I think it made for some clever turns of phrase, and I liked the final product, but those things just come in the creative process, and you write down on paper what runs through your head at the time. Often, that is all the credit you can take, and to claim more would be dishonest.

Merle Haggard once told me he wrote "Leonard" using automatic writing. This is my favorite song Merle ever wrote, and when he guested on our TV show, we talked one day about how good it was and how outstanding it was from a songwriter's point of view. That's when he said it all came from him just holding his pen on the paper and his hand moved involuntarily, forming letters and words with no input from him. You may not buy that particular belief and process, although it is an actual subconscious and spiritual free-writing technique many people have believed in for centuries. It isn't too far removed from believing that God puts the words in your mind and heart and you put them on paper.

I could name you every book in the Bible
And I knew all the pretty words it took to pray
But like Zacchaeus I was short on things that mattered
Till the Lord stopped in at my house one day
It's a thin, thin line between a good man
And one who knows he's been saved
Like Lazarus I'm now a friend of Jesus
And this body's all I'm taking to the grave

"Keep Your Eyes on Jesus"

Let me address the singing and picking first. I love the opening a capella verse. It seems we were doing a lot of that at the time, both on stage and on record. We were exercising our harmony in ways we didn't in our younger years. Not sure why—just something we grew into. The instruments join us with that rocking-chair rhythm, and it turned out to be a bluegrass sound even though we were just going for a real country treatment. But when a banjo leads out and is joined by a Dobro, you can't deny it's not a bluegrass sound. (The Dobro may be my all-time favorite instrument for a country break.)

I sat in a dressing room with Jerry Douglas for a couple of hours one day backstage at the Country Music Hall of Fame. I'd never met the guy and didn't know until we'd left who I'd been talking to all that time. I so hate I didn't tell him how much I love his playing. He does things with the Dobro no one else has thought to do. Hey, to you, Jerry.

Wil and Langdon again brought us this little gem. As Wil recently told me, he and Lang were in a writing groove at the time and were turning out all kinds of songs and topics. Langdon said the idea hit him as he sat in his Religion and Philosophy class in college. His professor was saying, "You've got to keep your eyes on Jesus." He wrote that on a yellow Post-it Note and later that day, March 16, 1998, the two cousins wrote these words and this music.

Keep your eyes on Jesus, focus on his love
When you believe, you'll receive visions from above
When your eyes are open, you can see his point of view
So keep your eyes on Jesus, 'cause he keeps his eye on you

These two writers keep every scrap of paper, just the way I always have. They still have the original lyric sheet in pencil with a list of water words they wanted to use such as: winds/waves/night/ship/sea/sail on one side of the paper. On the other side they have: Matt. 14:25/Mark 6:45–52/John 6:15–21.

You can't miss with those kinds of references!

"If It Only Took a Baby"

This Kim Reid Weller song not only needs to be heard but also felt. It's a beautiful lullaby melody with meaningful words that bring the peace and grace the season calls for and demands. A Christmas song for the whole year. And with the single fiddle/violin echoing throughout in and around our voices, it will make a way into your heart.

If it only took a baby,
Peace on earth must soon be here
If it only took a baby
Lullabies should ring with peace

"Far Side Banks of Jordan"

I'll admit my steps are growing wearier each day
Still I've got a certain journey on my mind
Cares of this old world have ceased to make me want to stay
My one regret is leaving you behind

I can't say enough about the writing of this song. Terry Smith, a schoolteacher turned songwriter, wrote the perfect gospel/love song. I have always loved this little-used genre and have contributed to it a couple of times myself. But this creative effort stands heads above all others. There's a chill in each line, and each line means more with each passing year. It was a joy to sing and the picture that chorus paints is one that is with you forever once you hear it.

I'll be waiting on the far side banks of Jordan
I'll be sitting drawing pictures in the sand
And when I see you coming, I will rise up with a shout
And come running through the shallow water reaching for your hand

We had first heard John and June do it, and I always saw John on that second line sitting drawing pictures in the heavenly sand, waiting for June. But we learn many lessons in life. Never try to time the market, never tell a joke twice to the same audience, and never try to out figure the good Lord. It was June who was waiting on John.

If it proves to be His will that I am first to cross
And somehow, I've a feeling it will be
When it comes your time to travel, likewise don't feel lost
For I will be the first one that you see

"When I Take My Vacation in Heaven"

This wonderful old gospel song was written by a gentleman by the name of Herbert Buffum. I don't know much about him besides this song, but I have heard that when he passed, back in 1939, the *Los Angeles Times* called him "the king of the gospel songwriters." Also, at the time, *Ripley's Believe It or Not* claims Herbert set a record by once writing twelve songs in one hour. A dubious record at best, and one I would never contest. But with all this said, it should take nothing away from the charm and appeal of this old popular piece. It became a part of our repertoire during the TV show years. Hardly a week went by we weren't barraged with mail requests to include this at the closing of one of our shows. Always willing to please the public, we did, and it was an instant crowd pleaser.

I'm willing to conjecture right here that this was not one of the dozen ole Herbert wrote in sixty minutes, because there are some heartfelt lines in the chorus that I want to believe took a little more time and emotion to the matter.

When I take my vacation in heaven, what a wonderful time that will be
Hearing concerts by the heavenly chorus, and the face of my Savior I'll see
Sitting down on the banks of the river, 'neath the shade of the evergreen tree
I shall rest from my burden forever, won't you take your vacation with me

"I Should Have Known You, Lord"

I have a weakness for songs of faith that come straight from the Bible. The first half of this one does, as it tells Mary Magdalene's story at the tomb. Then it transitions into a story each of us can relate to.

I should have known you, Lord
After all the sins you've forgiven me for
I've found you and I won't be lost anymore
I should have known you, Lord

Father and son, Harold and Wil, wrote this one together, and I think what Wil told me about the writing of it is so consequential that I'll just give it to you in his words: "This song is so special to me because I wrote it with

Dad. It was a great idea written and inspired from Scripture that applied to all of us. It's easier to write with a writer who is better than you. All I had to do was play the piano and stay out of his way."

Such a nice tribute to my old writing partner.

"A Living Part of You"

When Debo would bring me a new melody, unless he denoted it, I had to decide if it was a love song, a novelty song, a country song, or a gospel song. Without reference or bias, I would just let it lead me wherever it so desired to take me. This one had the beauty and structure of a gospel song, and I think I was led in the right direction as I put the words to the notes.

Something about these verses is very special to me, but it is more in the arrangement than the lyric. Phil and I sing a duet throughout both verses, and it was a rare treat. There has never been a better harmony singer in all the world or a more modest one. He fitted and complemented each note with so little effort or glory. There will never be another like him in any music industry. He shined in his ability not to shine but to support. He never swayed from that position, as that was his chosen and desired place to be. He had to be pushed to solo, often coaxed to even duet, and took bows and applause only because it was expected of him. He was never nervous in front of a microphone but never completely comfortable. He wanted to be blended more than heard. He was the brains behind the music we made, as he knew each of our parts before we did. He knew each of our vocal ranges and could tell us what key we needed to be in in order to do the ending we wanted to do and what keys we needed to not be in. When we performed anything without benefit of an instrument, we never needed a pitch pipe. We had Phil. And he could hum the starting note in the right key at any given moment. All of this is why these verses are so very special to me. I sang them with Phil.

With my time getting closer and my days getting few
Lord, make my heart a living part of you

"Hide Thou Me"

I might not be able to write about this one. It conjures up so many emotions and memories with each note that I'll be typing through tears before it's over with. Not knowing where to start, let me grab a piece of my childhood with both hands and start at the beginning.

Somewhere about the time I was ten years old, there was a Southern gospel trio formed by the name of the Sons of Song (Bob Robinson, Cal Newton, and Don Butler). Don Butler had the richest and most demanding baritone voice I had ever heard. We bought and lived with their albums and their fresh style of presenting those old classic songs. They sang this one like no one else ever had before, and Butler performed that opening verse and just mesmerized me with his tone and quality. We started singing it around in churches when I was about fifteen. I know I did it no justice, but I relished in trying every chance I got. Of all the good folks in the gospel industry we met and became friends with, I never once met Don Butler. He was a real musical hero of mine, and I would have loved to have shaken his hand and told him what his singing had meant to me.

So, come the mid-nineties, we planned to sing this song as a closing hymn on one of our TV shows. A few days before we taped this particular segment, I called his office in Nashville (he was head of the Society of European Stage Authors and Composers [SESAC] at the time, best I remember) to say hello and invite him to the taping. He wasn't in, but I left a message with his secretary, and she assured me he would be so pleased to hear from me and that he would call me and make arrangements to attend. But he never did. Didn't call or come. Maybe he never got the message. Maybe he had other plans. So, I never met the man for whatever reason, but he was still a great inspiration to me and made this song very special to me all my life. Odd that we never got around to recording it until our last album.

Sometimes I feel discouraged, I think my work in vain
I'm tempted then to murmur, to grumble and complain
But then, I think of Jesus and what he's done for me
Then I cry O Rock of Ages, hide thou me

We were sitting around with Bill Gaither one afternoon reminiscing about the history of all the old gospel singers we grew up admiring, and the name George Younce, bass singer of the Cathedrals, came up. Harold said, "George is the best bass singer there ever was." Bill said, "Why put the word bass in it? How about just the best singer there ever was." We all readily agreed.

And that may be the way I feel about "Hide Thou Me." Ask me my favorite hymn and I'll quickly say "At the Cross." Ask me my favorite old pop standard and I may say, "I'll Be Seeing You." Or my favorite country song, and it may be anything form "Today I Started Loving You Again" to "I Wonder How the Old Folks Are at Home." But take all the adjectives away and ask what's my favorite song, this might be it.

Debo, Langdon, and Wil were with us throughout the sessions on most of this album. My sons remember distinctly and have insisted that I include this little tidbit of a story that I'm rather uncomfortable telling. As we listened to the playback in the studio that night, the musicians and everyone in attendance stood and applauded as I finished this verse. I can only be thankful for their generosity while admitting there is no other song where I'd rather have had that happen. When complimented and congratulated on the performance, they remember me saying, "Well, thank you. I've been practicing on that one since I was ten years old."

After we retired, Harold, Phil, Jimmy, and I would often get together with our wives, usually around Christmas, and eat dinner, and without fail, we would all wind up around the piano before the night was over. Sometimes a carol or two was harmonized, all the time old stories were told and laughed about, but *every* time a special song was sung as we ended the evening. I would play the piano, key of D, and I could feel the three of them standing behind me as I began to sing that verse that I learned from so many, many years ago. I learned it by heart and I sang it by heart. And when we would start singing that chorus, with all the power and love of all those years together, there is no emotion I have ever experienced that could equal it. The little starts and stops in the harmony we didn't even have to look at each other anymore to accomplish, the soft to swell dynamics and volume that comes so naturally without even a nod, and the changing of parts on the last two lines when we would build into an ending that would ring in my ears throughout the season and into another year. And then we'd stand and hug one another and say our goodnights. And that's how I want it to end.

There's a note in my file by the side of my desk in my office with instructions for the music at my final memorial and funeral concerning what I want played by The Statler Brothers. It's not a long list for anyone to worry with, and it won't take up a lot of anyone's day. The note simply says, "Hide Thou Me."

"Jesus Living Next to Me"

And then there was one. One more song to record. June 15, 2001. This would be the last song we would sing in a studio full of magnificent musicians who worked so hard to simply make us sound good. The last time we would look through the huge glass-divider window and see Jerry Kennedy sitting by the soundboard giving us a smile and a thumbs-up sign. The last playback we would gather in the control room to listen to. And the last feeling of accomplishment that was such a mixture of highs and lows as we wrapped up another album of love and went off to celebrate with dinner.

Tomorrow I'll be living
Where I've always wanted to be
Yes, I'll be moving in tomorrow
With Jesus living next to me

Langdon wrote it all—words and music—both so elegantly done. And he told me this story: "I was standing in a graveyard with Mom, attending a funeral of a family friend, listening to the minister talk about changing our address for that last time. My mind took off. I asked Mom for a pen when everyone bowed their heads to pray. She shook her head and handed me one. She knew what was happening. She drove home so I could finish it. This was March 12, 1994. I thought it was kind of cool thinking of heaven as a neighborhood and Jesus as my neighbor. I look forward to it."

And then there were none. The last album was finished. The last studio album of new material, anyway. There would be the recording of our final concert, but this was it for Nashville and the sessions that had been so much a part of our lives for the past thirty-seven years. From that first session John took us to on April 3, 1964, where we sang "The Wreck of the Old '97," to this last song, it was a lifetime of joy and stress, happiness and worry, work and play. Would I want to do it all again? No way. Wouldn't have the energy for it, but it has been fun remembering it all with you.

401

42

Farewell Concert

2003

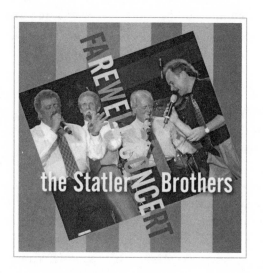

Our last, final, concluding, no-turning-back concert was in October of 2002. We had been considering it for a couple of years, talking seriously about it among ourselves for more than a year, and planning on it since our Christmas break in 2001. We had faced something similar to this before, and let me share with you how we dealt with that.

For twenty-five years, we did a free, flag-waving Fourth of July concert in our hometown of Staunton, Virginia, from 1970 to 1994. (Wilson Fairchild do it now and do a fantastic job, I might add.) After about seventeen or eighteen years, even though the concert was becoming more popular with each turn of the calendar, we were of a mind to retire from that commitment but were unsure of how to step down. We knew we might hear and feel some resistance and resentment from the town "powers that were" to the disappointed fans from around the world who swarmed Staunton every year. Should we announce before the concert this would be the last year or after the concert was over? Should we cut it off at twenty years? Or should we just stay until we were too old to climb the steps to the stage? After discussing all this for a few years, all of a sudden, we were already at the twenty-year mark and near twenty-one.

A close business associate and friend of ours, Denny Henderson, happened to be in our offices one day when we were knocking around strategy on the matter. Denny offered, "Why not announce you will do it for a total of twenty-five years, giving all who have never been here a chance to come and all who want to come back a chance to attend as many as they can. That way no one can take offense at being slighted nor hold any hard feelings whatsoever. A quarter of a century seems like a fair and round number." Buy that man a Coke! The perfect solution, and that is exactly what we did.

So, we applied the old Henderson tactic to our retirement and officially announced in January of 2002 that October 26 would be our final concert. In the meantime, we continued to tour all over America for the upcoming ten months. We played seventy-four dates ranging from the Great Northwest down through California, extensively through the Midwest, the East Coast, the Northeast, and the Deep South. Just like Denny suggested, we gave everyone who wanted to a chance to see the Statlers that final year. And it was a tour of memories and bliss. The only sadness was each night, as we walked out of an auditorium that had become so familiar through the years to where I knew every twist and turn in the hallways backstage, every step up to a dressing room, and could find the exit stage door even in the dark, I would stop and say to myself, "I will never be here again." I soon learned I had to quit saying that and get on with the next chapter of life.

Each night about midway through our stage show, we would stop and talk about our retirement plans. This gave us a chance to tell the fans our feelings, make a few jokes about it all, and be honest about our reasons and goals. Each night I told them there would likely be more albums to come depending on time, health, and scheduling of our individual plans. As it was, those future albums didn't pan out for a number of reasons—mainly because we found out you are either in the business or out of it. You can't keep one foot in and one foot out. Once we walked off the stage, we realized we were ready to hang up the boots and saddles and enjoy the peace and quiet we had missed more than we knew. (I have taken my grandchildren to school each morning more than I ever took my own kids. That's the stuff you miss and can't get back.)

This final album came about by accident. We had never allowed anyone to videotape one of our stage shows. Never. We felt it played a vital role in the huge crowds that always came right up to the last night. If they had a video of the excitement, the comedy, the hits, the spontaneity, and the ad-libs right there in their cozy dens, what would make them want to come out to see us? So, no matter how much money we were offered through the years, it was always a definite no to taping our concerts. We had security throw out pirates who tried on the sly more than once. But then a gentleman named Doug Grau, who owned Yell Records in Nashville, approached us at just the right time with just the right idea. Record the final concert and release it into the fast-growing video market. There would never be another Statler concert, so this way everyone could have their very own memento of our career. "Not a bad idea," we started saying to one another. Yell even agreed to hire Jerry Kennedy as the audio supervising producer. "Sounding better all the time," we said to one another. And after the video was out, we'd release it as an audio album into the music market. "We can't find anything wrong with any of this," we said to one another. And it was done. The album went gold. The video went gold multiple times, and it was a wise move for everyone involved.

And that is how this very last album came to be. I considered not including it in this book because there is no new Statler song material on it, making it actually a compilation album. This also means I have already written about every song in this collection, but it has become much too important to our overall career to exclude. So here we go, back to October 26, 2002, to the Salem Civic Center in Salem, Virginia, just eighty-five miles from home.

Introductions

Jerry Hensley, our lead guitarist, recognized dignitaries in the audience and read a letter of greetings from President George Bush. Then he introduced Jimmy Dean, who introduced us. Dean had joined us in prayer on the bus just before we all came to the wings of the stage. I loved the man dearly, and he had a heart bigger than his ever-present white hat. After doing an impromptu commercial for his sausage business, he brought us on stage for the last time with a Texas/Virginia flurry. We each hugged him and then embraced the audience for the next ninety minutes.

"Do You Remember These?"

This was our opening song more times than any other song we ever used. It was up-tempo, a familiar hit, and it featured each one of us on a solo. There was not one better we could have ever used. I think people were past listening to the lyrics anymore. The fans knew it was a Statler song, and they just heard that rhythm and it said to them a theme was being set for the night. Nostalgia. Memories. And Fun.

A funny story you may not know about this song. It was banned in England back in 1972. There's a line in it that refers to *knickers to your knees*. Over here, knickers were a style of short pants for men. But across the pond, they were ladies' panties, and that line took on a whole other meaning. The BBC didn't take kindly to it, and the all-American Statler Brothers, who made a point to never offend anyone, got banned in the land of the Beatles.

"Do You Know You Are My Sunshine?"

This is the tune we were singing in the first ten minutes of *Smokey and the Bandit II* when the airplane flew over and dropped bright orange paint on the entire cast. I talked about this earlier (see "Charlotte's Web") but here are a few more details. We had it in our hair, in the fabric of our stage suits, in our mouths, and in our eyes. Our bus was nearby the set where we were shooting in Las Vegas, so we made it to the bus door. We stripped off the clothes and put on others for the ride back to our hotel. But that orange glow was still on our skin, and our hair was still a deep carroty color as we exited the bus in front of our hotel and the four of us trekked in the front entrance, through the crowded lobby, and into the elevator. We couldn't have attracted more attention if we had all been naked. Jackie Gleason was on the set and saw all this happen and took great pleasure in telling all who would hear that our suits were worth $5,000 a piece and Universal Pictures had ruined them. Gleason was a solemn and serious kind of guy, as so many comedians are in real life. But what a talent!

"Susan When She Tried"

There was a Dr. Charles Yates who kept contacting us and wanted to book us for a private event in Houston. We didn't do a lot of private situations, an occasional convention maybe, but not often. Dr. Yates was relentless, and in talking to our agent, Marshall Grant, said he could and would pay us our going price if we would do a private thirty-minute show for his and his wife's twenty-fourth wedding anniversary. Come March of 1988, we were booked to do the Houston Rodeo, the biggest in the country, with 40,000 folks in attendance. Marshall told Dr. Yates we could stay over and do his anniversary, seeing as how we were already in town. The doctor booked a small theater there and paid our price, invited about a hundred of their family and friends, and they turned out to be two of the nicest and friendliest folks we ever met. Just before the performance, he told us "Susan When She Tried" was his wife's, favorite song. So we had it made up in advance and sang it as "Sally When She Tried." They loved it!

We lost contact with them and never saw them again. Well, not until the night of this final concert in Salem, Virginia, fourteen years later. When I looked down from the stage, I saw Dr. Charles sitting on the front row beside my wife, Debbie, with his wife, Sally, on the other side of him. We had no idea they were going to be there.

"Too Much on My Heart"

This was the song that made Jimmy Fortune a songwriter. We had had great success with the first he ever wrote, "Elizabeth," and then the very next year he brought us "My Only Love." But the proof of his talent didn't set in with him, I don't think, until he saw he could do it a third time. This proved he was no fluke or flash in the pan. This proved he knew his craft and how to put his heart where his words were. This is when I knew he would write more good songs, more great songs. This one showed the world he hadn't just written a song or two but that he was a songwriter. Slow, heartache ballads don't always work on stage when the audience is there to have a good and fun time. But this one did. It never failed to reach the crowd or touch the singers. I loved this one every night.

"The Class of '57"

When we were putting our TV series together in 1991, our old friend and musical genius Bill Walker became our music director. He had served in the same capacity for Johnny Cash on his series in the sixties, and we had the fullest love and trust for the man and his talent. One of the first questions he asked was about our choice for a theme song. Thankfully, we had a lot to choose from. We gave him a list that included "Flowers on the Wall," "Bed of Rose's," "I'll Go to My Grave Loving You," "Elizabeth," "Carry Me Back," "My Only Love," and quite a few more, and, of course, this one. He considered them all, and it was his choice to write the arrangement for our twenty-piece orchestra using this 1972 hit.

Every time we sang it, I would picture the real people in my head that Harold and I had written it about. So many of them are gone today but not in my head.

"Bed of Rose's"

Singing this song always made me remember two people. One who loved it and one who didn't. Jimmy's mother, bless her sweet heart, never liked this one at all. The subject matter was just too much for her, and she cringed every time we sang it. But on the other side of that coin, Charley Pride sat in the hotel lobby after the CMA awards in 1971 with a guitar in his lap. Everyone who came by to congratulate him on winning "Male Vocalist of the Year" was met with, "Yeah, but have you heard this song by The Statler Brothers?" and he'd sing them "Bed of Rose's."

"Oh Baby Mine"

I can't begin to explain what can go through your mind standing on stage while you're singing and performing a song in front of thousands of energetic fans. Sometimes it's funny and sometimes just downright silly.

I grew up in a big county in Virginia (Augusta). So big that there were two fleets of buses to and from the elementary school in the mornings and evenings. The first caravan of yellow buses would leave the school at 3 P.M. and come back empty to take the next group of kids home around 3:30. When I was in the third grade and waiting for that second shift, the teacher, Mrs. Switzer, would always let those of us remaining in the room for thirty minutes have what today would be called "open mic" time. We could go up front and recite a poem or tell about a book we were reading or a movie we had seen or, if brave enough and a little bit of an exhibitionist, sing a song. Jimmy Coffey and I would often choose the latter, giving our renditions of the current hits of the day. I distinctly remember us singing "Ricochet Romance," a hit by Teresa Brewer, who would be a guest on our TV show forty-two years later, and "Oh Baby Mine," a hit by the Four Knights that would also be a number-one hit for us thirty years later.

These are the things that keep you sane. Or is that insane? I'm not sure.

"Moments to Remember"

I have already told you how deeply I feel about this song. We sang it every night that last year of concerts, and without any staging or discussion at all, it just became natural that we all four walked toward one another to center stage as we sang:

> *Though summer turns to winter, and the present disappears*
> *The laughter we were glad to share will echo through the years*

And then the music would stop. Everything came to a long quiet pause. And as we began to sing the next lines, with no music, just our four voices, we walked away from one another as if going our new separate ways, which certainly we were, just a matter of minutes after singing these words, never to sing them together again.

> *When other nights and other days*
> *May find us gone our separate ways*
> *We will have these moments to remember*

We never missed a beat or a note, but it was not easy to keep it all together. I still find it difficult to watch.

"The Great Pretender"

I told you earlier that we used the Platters' ending here, but after singing this song on stage, the ending got Statlerized, and in time, we owned it. It was as good an ending as any song has ever been blessed with on any stage, anytime. We paused and stopped and dragged it out and held it out,

408

and that last note must have lasted for fifteen seconds. It is a stone-cold killer, and we loved playing with it and juicing it up a little more every night.

Now, I have also told you about the lovable George Younce, bass singer extraordinaire with the Cathedrals. George was a very demonstrative and outspoken friend. He would call just anytime of the day or night to tell me a joke or just say he loved me. What a friend he was. When he was reading a new book I had written, he would sometimes call after each chapter just to tell me what he was thinking and feeling at the time. One night, right after this DVD had been released, Debbie and I were pulling into our garage and the house phone was ringing. I jumped out of the car and answered on the garage extension, and it was George. He was laughing and completely out of breath. When I picked up the phone and said, "Hello," he started right in with, "All the family is over here and we're watching your Farewell Concert video. We just got to the end of 'The Great Pretender' and I hollered, 'Ernie, quick, hit that pause button. We gotta have some relief here.'"

What a compliment from a man who has sung endings that just lifted me out of my seat so many, many times. But it took George to put it in words I will never forget.

"Whatever Happened to Randolph Scott?"

This song disrupted Randolph Scott's quiet and peaceful retirement. His last movie, *Ride the High Country*, was made in 1962, and he stepped away from any involvement in the show business world at all. He became a Beverly Hills businessman and spent every day in suit and tie, sitting in his office managing investments. We wrote and released this song eleven years later, and the media went wild. He told us that in a week's time of it reaching the top ten, he got calls from all the major talk shows begging him to come do an appearance. Johnny Carson, Dick Cavett, Mike Douglas, Merv Griffin. And yet, even though we were responsible for this distraction in his life, he and his wife, Pat, treated us most graciously. At one point, as the five of us were sitting around his desk while Pat and his secretary sat in the outer office with the door open, one of us asked who his favorite leading lady was. With a sly, handsome smile, he leaned way out and looked toward the doorway and said in a low voice, "I was always fond of Irene Dunne."

"More Than a Name on a Wall"

I left business college during the second semester of the first year when we went on the road with the Johnny Cash show in March of '64. I turned nineteen three months later. I had made some pretty good friends at that little college in the short time I was there, and it was only a year and a half later, still short of twenty-one myself, that I drove to a little cemetery near the West Virginia line to help bury John, one of the guys I'd met at the school. He had been called to Roanoke for his physical about the same time I was, but they didn't send him home. They sent John right on to boot camp and then to 'Nam. All of America was seeing people die in the jungles on the evening news every night, and it hardened a generation, with all that realism so much in your face day after day. And yet nothing prepared you for carrying a coffin of a twenty-year-old past a weeping family and setting it at the feet of grief-stricken parents while "Taps" was played and the flag was folded.

The drive home by myself that fall day is still vivid and intense in my mind, and it was every night when we sang "The Wall." I tried to lose my thoughts in the blue spotlight but I never did. Never have. Never will.

"Flowers on the Wall"

One of those FAQs that we always got was, "Do you ever get tired of singing 'Flowers on the Wall'?" And I understand why they asked. We sang it on every show for nearly thirty-eight years. But, no, we never got tired of singing it because they never got tired of hearing it. A couple of little-known facts about "Flowers" that few people know:

1. Lew was stuck for a title. You might think the title was obvious, as it was the first line to each chorus, but it isn't always as easy to decide on the perfect title when the song is still new to your ear. For months after he wrote it, he called it "The Big Kick." Now, nowhere are those words in the song, but that described it best for him, so we all referred to it by that title. It wasn't until we actually recorded it and had to fill out the official sheet that we said to him, "Are you sure that's what you want to go with?" After a little thought and discussion, we decided on the title you're familiar with today.

2. "Flowers" hit about a year after the Beatles and all the other English groups had invaded America. As we were new to the industry and the record was just as big a pop hit as it was country, every place we went to plug the record, disc jockeys, promoters, and even the public thought we were British. They swore they could hear an accent in our singing. But once they heard us talk, they knew for sure that accent was just simply Shenandoah Valley of Virginia.

"Elizabeth"

We shot a video of this song back in 1983 when we first recorded it. It spanned a lot of decades, with each of us doing scenes with an actress from varied times in history. Harold was in a Civil War uniform, and he and a Southern belle beauty were saying their romantic goodbyes to one another. Then cut to Phil in the 1920s with his beautiful flapper as he puts her into a Model T and kisses her goodbye. Jimmy shows up in the 1940s in a sweater vest and bow tie and makes a little whoopee with his sweetie in a porch swing. And then it's me, in modern times, at a wedding where apparently my ex-girlfriend is getting married.

When we all showed up on set early that morning, the first shocker came when I found out that when they booked these four actress/models for the roles of our girlfriends, my girlfriend was sixteen years old. I put my foot down immediately and told the director and producer I was not going to hug or kiss a sixteen-year-old girl. I was thirty-eight at the time and prisons are full of guys like that. But I will say after hair and makeup got through with her that morning, she easily looked to be in her late twenties. Still, I made sure the script was altered to where there was no touchy-feely with me and a young girl who could have been my daughter.

"I'll Go to My Grave Loving You"

We were taping an all-star variety television show in Nashville at the Opry House one night, years ago. One of those where all the cast is lined up on stage for the closing number. There were a myriad of country stars all over the place, singing and smiling and waving goodnight. I felt a shadow come over me at one point, and suddenly a huge figure loomed above me and whispered in my ear. He had stepped out of his marked place on the

THE MUSIC OF THE STATLER BROTHERS

stage and didn't seem to care who he was blocking. He had something to say and looked like a man who was not going to be kept from saying it. It was David Allan Coe. He said to me, "'I'll Go to My Grave Loving You' is great. It's one of my favorite songs." I thanked him, and when the show ended, we talked. However, I still don't know if he's a redneck, a hippie, or a cowboy.

"Bus Fumes"

We featured the band every concert, and this is an original song they all five wrote together. It gave them a spot to shine while giving us an opportunity to leave the stage for a few minutes. We were able to step out of the spotlight, wipe the sweat from our brow, get a drink of water, and regroup with any verbal notes we might want to exchange with one another. The title of this song was also created by the boys in the band because they said when we got to this point near the end of the show, they could almost smell the bus fumes that were about to take us home.

"A Place on Calvary"

Seldom did a song get on back-to-back albums of ours. This is a rare exception. It was on *Amen* and now here it was again. By this time, it had become an intricate part of our show. Way back in the early years, we always did one gospel song per show because that was just who we were. In those days, as part of large package shows where nobody really knew who The Statler Brothers were, we might only be allowed twelve minutes per show. But even then, one of the four songs we would sing would be an old gospel favorite. As our career grew, that one song became a segment, consisting of maybe three or four, and that is where we were by Farewell Concert time. When we came back on stage from our little respite each night, we would have our coats off and be ready for some serious down-South-camp-meeting-hymn time.

Note that even though this is the same song, written by Langdon, as on our penultimate album, it is musically a new and fresh song. We are so much freer with the performance on stage than in the studio. The tempo is up a little, Jimmy and I are looser with the back-and-forth duets, and we all four are taking exciting liberties with the melody and harmonies. And the ending still leaves me with a smile on my face.

412

"How Great Thou Art"

I know exactly what I was thinking while singing this that October night in '02. "Can this really be the last time we will ever sing this song together?" And yet, in my heart, I knew it was. And at the end of the song, as we waited in the dark before the spotlight came up on us for the encore that had happened every night with every audience at the same place, I knew we were about to sing that final chorus and those final ringing notes and that I would never feel the comfort and excitement of these combinations of words and music coursing through me again. What got me through it without my voice breaking was knowing they were all there on the stage with us. Luther. John. June. And Lew.

"This Old House"

Oh my golly! This was on our *first* album, and here it is on our *last*. I'll bet we sang this song more times than Stuart Hamblin and Rosemary Clooney put together. I thought about Ray Cash, John's dad, and how he loved it. I thought about the comedy routine Harold and I wrote around the second verse and how many, many times we had pulled that out of the hat. How long does it take for your life to flash in front of you? You may think split seconds. I think it's however long it takes to sing "This Old House" because this old jewel covers me from about 1954 to the present. I love it!

"Thank You, World"

In the normal run of things, this is the song we left the arena on. It was our walking-off song. It said exactly what we wanted to say to the audience. We praised them with it. We thanked them for their loyalty and support with it. We bowed to them with it, waved, and left the building. But not tonight. We came back because there was more we needed to say tonight.

"Amazing Grace"

The night of this concert, I said all that could be and needed to be said. If you listen to the CD or watch the DVD, you hear me say this was the first song the four of us ever sang together and that we wanted it to be the last.

November of 1981, we were in LA for a week rehearsing and taping *The Barbara Mandrell Show*. We finished up the week on Saturday night, the 14th, with a concert at the Anaheim Civic Center—Lew's last one with us. He was too sick for the remaining dates booked for the rest of the year, so as soon as we got home we cancelled December: Athens, Georgia; Asheville, North Carolina; Johnson City, Tennessee; Williamsburg, Virginia. His doctor told us he would need at least four to six months complete rest. Our decision was to either take that time off or find a temporary replacement who could become a part of our band after Lew's return. We had so much on our plate at the time and so many commitments we decided on the temp route.

Sometime in December, we met Jimmy for the first time when he came over to our offices. He was living in Nelson County, Virginia, about thirty-five miles across the mountain from us. We liked him immediately, and once we walked to the piano and pulled a song out of the air that we were sure all four of us knew, we immediately liked his singing. That song happened to be "Amazing Grace." The rest and how it all fell into place is a part of our history, recorded in the book *Random Memories*. But the history and the power and meaning of that song to us as Christians and the friendship and bond it produced in us never left us. We knew how we wanted it to end and on what note we wanted to leave it. We sang it that last night with more heart and love than ever before, and when we stepped back from the microphones, with the crowd already roaring, you can see me say something to my three Brothers that no one else could hear. I simply said to them, with the last notes ringing in the night, "I love you guys."

I meant it then. I mean it now.

Thank you for listening to my story.
Don Reid

Acknowledgments

Acknowledging and thanking the people who helped me put this book together can come at the beginning or the end. I always like it at the end because then the reader has a fuller understanding of what all took place. I'm going to start with my sons, Debo and Langdon, who were the instigators of this project and who served as my agents. I told them from the beginning, when I finally succumbed to their insistence, that I would write it if they would do all the other work of developing the whole production, finding the publisher and making the deal. And they found the best.

Dr. Marc Jolley at Mercer University Press and his staff, and notably Marsha Luttrell, have been a joy to work with. (See they even occasionally let me end sentences with a preposition so I have to love 'em.) Mary Pearson was an astute and eagle-eyed copyeditor and made the whole process painless and even enjoyable. Of course, my old pal and legal advisor, attorney Russ Farrar in Nashville, was always there looking out for me. And I would like to take this opportunity to recognize Alice Holtin, who wrote a discography on the Statlers nearly twenty-five years ago. I appreciate all her work even more after writing this book of my own and digging for all the facts and memories. Brandon Hatcher helped so much with the layout and reproduction of all the photographs that have made this book come to life. Fellow writer Ronda Rich, bless her sweet Georgia heart, was the glue that put the boys and Marc Jolley together from the very start. And how about a shout-out to Joe Ruoto, webmaster extraordinaire, who keeps me in touch daily with the world at my website donreid.net. Photographer Mike Miriello did a wonderful job at making even me look presentable.

Then, to my personal sounding boards who were invaluable. After writing each chapter, I would send it to Debo, Langdon, Jerry Kennedy, my writer friend Charles Culbertson, country music historian Mark Stielper, and my brother, Harold. They read the chapters and discussed them with me, and I was able to make wonderful adjustments from things they offered. But mostly they offered their encouragement and their assurance that this was a history that needed to be told. I have come to believe in this book so much that I urge and even challenge other recording artists to do the same with their body of work. Their stories should be told and remembered and enjoyed by the public who still cares and wants to relive those memories with them.

As I wrote about each album, I listened to it while sitting in my writing office on the second floor of my home in Virginia. Often, my wife, Debbie, would pass by the door and then come back and sit down, drink her coffee, and listen with me. Sometimes we never said a word, but it was a comfort to have her there to share those moments.

It was a process that took about two years from the day my sons and I first started talking about it during our weekly lunches together at the Depot Grille, table 23, on the left in the back, in the corner. It's become a sacred place to us every Wednesday. Full of laughs, full of life, full of memories. And who knows, maybe another book idea will come before the salad does.

—Don Reid

Index

This index does not include: Phil Balsley, Lew DeWitt, Jimmy Fortune, Harold Reid, Don Reid, The Statler Brothers, The Statlers, and any names mentioned in lyrics.

Aaglan, Gayle, 161
Acuff, Roy, 70, 73, 192
Air Force Symphony Orchestra, 194
Allen, Robert, 368
Ames Brothers, 49, 140, 297, 336, 367
Anderson, Bill, 4, 5, 44, 103, 182
Arnold, Eddy, 107
Arnold, Mary, 74
Ash, Glen, 23
Atkins, Chet, 218, 255, 261, 358, 359
Autry, Gene, 70, 100, 186, 193, 194, 195, 212, 374
Bach, Byron, 152
Balsley, Marjorie, 274
Bare, Bobby, 108, 109, 159, 201
Baxter, Les, 297
Beatles, 27, 73, 367, 405, 411
Bell, Kenny, 326
Bennard, Rev George, 346
Bennett, Roger, 311, 331
Bennett, Roy C., 367
Berlin, Irving, 166, 181
Berry, Chuck, 10, 216
Bill Walker Orchestra, 336
Blackwood, James (& The Blackwood Brothers), 30, 33, 34, 55, 61, 105, 106, 285, 388
Blackwood, Ron, 106
Blake, Dick, 162, 345
Bond, Johnny, 45, 313
Boone, Claude, 87
Boone, Pat, 370
Bowery Boys, 275
Braddock, Bobby, 21, 22, 23, 25
Bradley, Harold, 40, 56
Brahms, Johannes, 268, 269
Brewer-Capps, Ladonna, 338
Brewer, Teresa, 408
Briggs, David, 244, 267, 297, 324

Brody, Lane, 279
Browns Ferry Four, 285
Brumley, Albert E., 312, 349, 350
Buffum, Herbert, 397
Burford, 123
Burgess, Wilma, 73
Burns, George, 215, 216
Bush, President George (41), 117
Bush, President George W. (43), 404
Buskirk, Paul, 87
Butler, Don, 399
Butler, Larry, 106, 288, 289
Byrd, Billy, 192
Campbell, Glen, 33, 370
Capps, Jimmy, 335, 336, 338, 349, 373
Capps, Michele, 336
Carew, Rod, 246
Carrigan, Jerry, 244
Carson, Johnny, 409
Carter Family, 16, 19, 53
Carter, A.P., 53
Carter, Anita, 16, 19, 86
Carter, Helen, 16, 19
Carter, Mother Maybelle, 16, 19, 27, 53, 73
Carter, President James, 117
Cash, Roy Jr., 7
Cash, Carrie, 315
Cash, John "Johnny", 3-11, 13, 15, 17-19, 22, 26-28, 31, 32, 39, 45, 49, 52, 59, 68, 69, 72, 73, 76, 79, 92, 124, 141, 150, 153, 159, 160, 166, 173, 176, 192, 209, 210, 288, 315, 340, 351, 352, 364, 366, 369, 371, 372, 396, 401, 407, 410, 413
Cash, June Carter, 4, 5, 16, 18, 19, 32, 45, 52, 69, 72, 73, 76, 79, 141, 255, 351, 396, 413
Cash, Ray, 315, 413

Cash, Scott, 336
Cash, Tommy, 28, 67, 102
Casstevens, Mark, 326, 335, 356, 359, 380
Cathedral Quartet, 281, 311, 331, 387, 400, 409
Cavett, Dick, 273, 409
Chalker, Curly, 192
Charles, Ray, 372, 373
Chase, Charlie, 305
Christian, M., 53
Chuck Wagon Gang, 30
Church, Buddy, 179
Clark, Larry Wayne, 335
Clayton, Paul, 26
Clement, Cowboy Jack, 15, 52, 63
Clemmer, Charles, 266, 275, 292, 335, 353
Cline, Patsy, 56
Clooney, Rosemary, 11, 205, 413
Cochran, Hank, 158
Coe, David Allan, 412
Coffey, Jimmy, 408
Collins, Ace, 350
Como, Perry, 73, 205, 368
Copas, Cowboy, 99, 312
Cormier, Mary Lott, 120, 121
Cowboy Symphony Orchestra, 309, 311
Crofford, Cliff, 213
Crook, Lorianne, 305
Crosby, Bing, 11, 12, 179, 356
Crosby, Fanny, 11, 33
Daffan, Ted, 319
Dailey & Vincent, 220, 391
Darby, Ken, 375, 376
David, Mack, 336
Davidson, John, 277
Davies, Marion, 146
Davis Sisters, 176
Davis, Jimmie, 170, 212
Davis, Mac, 83, 288
Davis, Skeeter, 176
Dean, James, 238
Dean, Jimmy, 404
Deepvoice, David, 123
Dehr, Richard, 224, 365

Delmore Brothers (Alton & Rabon), 285
Denver, John, 288
Derricks, Cleavant, 196
Dillon, Dean, 328
Doddridge, Rev Philip, 31
Doublemint Twins, 317
Douglas, Jerry, 395
Douglas, Michael, 95
Douglas, Mike, 409
Doyle, Arthur Conan, 320
Dr. Hook, 159
Drake, Pete, 41, 63, 79, 84
Driftwood, Jimmie, 371
Dudley, Dave, 75
Duke of Paducah, 4, 5
Duncan, Cletus, 125
Duncan, Glen, 337
Dunne, Irene, 409
Durham, Carroll "Bull", 114, 309
Durrill, John, 213
Dycus, Frank, 328
Dylan, Bob, 17, 26, 84
Eastwood, Clint, 212
Edenton, Ray, 40, 95, 192
Edwards, Darrell, 55
Edwin Hawkins Singers, 31
Emery, Ralph, 129, 304
Evans, Dale, 4, 5
Everly Brothers, 176, 373
Exner, Judith, 377
Favorite, Larry Lee, 59, 60
Ferrante and Teicher, 383
Fisher, Eddie, 11, 55
Fleck, Bela, 270, 298
Florida Boys, 30
Foley, Red, 355, 356
Ford, Buck, 318
Ford, Tennessee Ernie, 10, 68, 124, 134, 318
Foree, Mel, 70
Fortune, Bird, 274, 407
Four Aces, 49, 336
Four Knights, 236
Four Lads, 49-51, 336, 368
Four Nights, 408
Four Star Quartet, 197

Index

Fowler, Scott, 311
Francis, Connie, 62
Frazier, Dallas, 24, 41
Frye, Kodi Reid, 18, 261, 267
Gaither, Bill, 30, 31, 137, 344, 387, 399
Gaither, Gloria, 137
Gallico, Al, 14
Gannon, Kim, 179
Garrett, Snuff, 213
Garrish, Sonny, 359
Gayle, Crystal, 189, 368
Giancana, Sam, 377
Gibson, Don, 22, 125, 372
Gilkyson, Terry, 224, 365
Gill, Vince, 348
Gimble, Johnny, 192
Girls Next Door (Doris, Cindy, Diane, &Tammy), 355
Glaser, Tompall, 108
Gleason, Jackie, 405
Golden, William M., 290
Grant, Kevin, 385
Grant, Marshall, 15, 18, 19, 309, 318, 406
Grau, Doug, 404
Gray, Claude, 87
Greene, Jack, 24, 149
Griffin, Merv, 409
Groah, Danny, 6
Groah, Lucille, 6
Gumbel, Bryant, 337
Guns N' Roses, 321
Haase, Ernie, 311, 409
Haggard, Merle, 69, 394
Hall, Dave, 318
Hall, Tom T., 8, 109
Hall, William "Bill", 81, 106, 125, 157
Hamblen, Stuart, 11, 413
Hamilton, George IV, 4
Hamilton, Roy, 371
Hamm, Charlie, 309
Harden Trio, 129
Harden, Robbie, 129
Harman, Buddy, 40, 88, 107
Harman, Dale, 123, 157, 161, 255
Harris, Phil, 356

Harvesters, 30
Harvill, Karmen Reid, 261
Haselden, Tony, 330
Hastings, Thomas, 347
Hatfield, Bobby, 371
Hawkins, Hawkshaw, 99
Helms, Don, 193
Hemp, Faye Reid, 295
Henderson, Denny, 403
Hensley, Jerry, 309, 314, 404
Herman's Hermits, 73
Hess, Jake, 388
Hibbler, Al, 36, 371
Hoffman, Elisha, 32
Hogshead, Harry, 392
Holden, Rebecca, 279
Holden, Susan, 335
Holland, W.S., 18, 19
Holly, Buddy, 16, 313
Holyfield, Wayland, 219, 335
Horton, Johnny, 371
Houston, David, 24
Howard, Harlan, 87, 88, 108, 158, 171
Howard, Jan, 44
Hudson, Rock, 238
Huffman, Dobbins and Morrison, 357
Humperdinck, Engelbert, 22
Hunter, Catfish, 189
Husky, Ferlin, 4, 366
Hutchens, Bobby, 90
Ink Spots, 11, 153, 154
Irving, Ron, 335
Jack, Betty, 176
Jackson, Alan, 6
Jackson, Stonewall, 103
James, Billy "Boopie", 309
James, Harry, 56
James, Sonny, 4, 5, 94, 95, 339
Jean, Norma, 73
Jennings, Waylon, 148, 313
Johnnie and Jack, 236, 369
Johnston, Bob, 17, 20, 25
Jones, George, 4, 5, 15, 21, 52, 55, 62, 72, 123, 321, 367
Jones, Lewis F., 287
Jones, Louis Marshall "Grandpa", 117, 118, 285

Jones, Mark, 118
Jones, Ramona, 118
Jones, Tom, 21
Joplin, Janis, 46
Jordan, Rev Eugene, 134, 286
Jordanaires, 70
Kahn, Gus, 219
Kennedy, Gordon, 385
Kennedy, Jerry (JK), 22, 23, 39-41, 46,
    47, 51, 62, 65, 69, 70, 73, 77, 80
    84, 87, 88, 94, 96, 102, 106, 108,
    119, 124, 125, 144, 155, 157-159,
    170, 175, 185, 191, 204, 211, 212,
    215, 217, 221, 228, 237, 241, 245,
    247, 249, 251, 255, 261, 263-266,
    270, 273, 277, 288, 289, 293, 297,
    300, 303, 308, 309, 319-321, 323,
    326, 330, 337, 351, 356, 359, 363,
    370, 371, 376, 380, 384, 385, 391,
    401, 404
Kennedy, President John F., 377
Kent, Arthur, 94
Kent, Walter, 179
Key, Francis Scott, 198
Kilpatrick, William, 183
Kim, Ken, 225, 244, 266, 292
King, 293
King, Brent, 355
King, Jeff, 385
Kingston Trio, 7, 369
Kipling, Rudyard, 12
Kristofferson, Kris, 46, 60, 223
Kroon, Jerry, 326, 330
Laine, Frankie, 132, 205
Lambert, Herb, 53
Lavender, Shorty, 192
Law, Don, 8
Lawrence, Steve, 85
Lee, Brenda, 229, 230, 355, 356
Lee, Dickey, 62, 65, 367
Lee, Robin, 279
Lee, Ruby, 123
Leech, Mike, 244
Leffel, Frank, 266
Lewis, Gary (& The Playboys), 14
Lewis, Jerry, 365
Lewis, Jerry Lee, 15, 340

Liggett, Milo, 94
Lincoln, Harry, 53
Lister, Hovie (& The Statesmen), 30,
    33, 34, 55, 391, 392
Lister, Mosie, 357
Locorriere, Dennis, 159
Lombardo, Guy, 367
London, Laurie, 375
Louvin Brothers, 55, 62, 82, 99, 297,
    335
Louvin, Charlie, 55, 82, 99, 335
Louvin, Ira, 55, 82, 99, 335
Lulu Belle and Scotty, 374
Luther, Martin, 183
Lynn, Loretta, 72, 312, 339
Malden, Karl, 95
Mandrell, Barbara, 8, 145, 226, 230,
    337
Mandrell, Irby, 145
Mangiaracina, Cayet, 256, 370
Martin and Lewis, 224, 275, 364, 365
Martin, Dean, 10, 55, 138, 224, 364,
    365
Martin, Grady, 15, 193
Martin, Jim, 343
Martin, Jimmy, 73
Martin, Odell, 192
Mason, Brent, 326, 327
Mathis, Johnny, 94, 368
Matson, Vera, 376
McBain, Ed (Aka Evan Hunter), 115
McCoy, Charlie, 45, 76, 84, 140, 145
McCoy, Kid, 205
McCracken, Jean, 294
McDill, Bob, 148
McDorman, Joe, 196, 197, 350, 351
McEntire, Reba, 27, 251, 348
McGuire Sisters (Chris, Dot & Phyl-
    lis), 10, 36, 49, 375-377
McGuire, Phyllis, 377
Merrill, Bob, 205
Miles, C. Austin, 217, 218
Miller, Dean, 273
Miller, Frank, 224, 365
Miller, Jody, 73
Miller, Mary, 277

Index

Miller, Roger, 9, 21, 22, 46, 74, 273, 277, 294
Millhuff, Charles, 137
Milsap, Ronnie, 143, 167
Montgomery, Melba, 4
Moore, Bob, 40
Moore, Scotty, 192
Moran, Lester "Roadhog" (& The Cadillac Cowboys), 65, 76, 77, 122-126, 288, 308
Morgan, Lorrie, 279, 280
Morton, Don "Mousey", 309
Mullins, Cam, 51, 55, 63, 92, 118, 144
Munsey, Stan Jr., 330
Murray, Anne, 74
Murray, James, 183
Myrick, Weldon, 182, 249, 261, 270, 323, 330, 331
Nabors, Jim, 23, 153
Nelson, Ricky, 255, 370
Nelson, Willie, 15, 87, 339
Newbury, Mickey, 22, 23
Nitty Gritty Dirt Band, 73
Nixon, President Richard, 117
Northrup, John, 326
O'Hara, Maureen, 242
Oak Ridge Boys, 348
Orbison, Roy, 96, 143
Oswald, Brother Bashful, 192
Owens, Buck, 99, 312
Owens, Doodle, 41
Owens, Jim, 252, 266
Page, Patti, 205
Paget, Debra, 376
Parker, Sky, 198
Parton, Dolly, 153, 154, 348
Paxton, Larry, 326, 337
Payne, Glen, 311, 388
Payne, Gordon, 326
Pearl, Minnie, 4, 273
Pepper, Sid, 367
Perkins, Carl, 15, 18, 19, 27, 32, 75, 76, 104, 192
Perkins, Luther, 6, 18, 19, 36, 192, 210, 351, 366, 413
Perkins, Margie, 366
Peter, Paul & Mary, 7

Peterson, John, 290
Phillips, Sam, 52
Pierce, Webb, 373
Pierpont, James, 180
Pitney, Gene, 256, 370
Pitt, Brad, 133
Platters, 179, 279, 365, 366, 375, 408
Prather, Bob, 33
Presley, Elvis, 12, 27, 56, 69, 94, 115, 116, 192, 230, 277, 324, 367, 375, 376
Price, Ray, 22, 60, 192
Pride, Charley, 41, 407
Pride, Rozene, 41
Pritchett, Jimmy, 87
Pruett, Jeanne, 154
Putman, Curly, 21, 23
Queen Elizabeth, 205
Rabbitt, Eddie, 202
Rae, Diana, 294
Ram, Buck (aka Ande Rand), 179, 279, 365
Ramsey, Wichita, 76, 125
Reagan, President Ronald, 117, 304, 333
Reddy, Helen, 86, 87
Reed, Jerry, 16, 17, 21, 212
Reeves, Del, 73
Reeves, Jim, 15
Reeves, Kathleen, 54
Reid, Brenda, 73, 123, 262
Reid, Davis, 139
Reid, Debbie, 119, 133, 146, 171, 233, 354, 355, 406, 409
Reid, Debo, 120, 121, 232, 246, 249, 254, 255, 263-265, 267, 269, 278, 280, 296-299, 301, 303, 312, 313, 319, 321, 332, 337, 354, 358, 377, 382, 383, 390, 398, 400
Reid, Gloria, 342, 401
Reid, Langdon, 47, 52, 105, 120, 218, 232, 246, 249, 255, 271, 313, 337, 341, 342, 354, 358, 362, 377, 381, 382, 384, 390, 391, 395, 400, 401, 412
Reid, Maggie, 353

Reid, Sidney Boxley, 55, 57, 65, 163, 184, 222, 223, 285, 353

Reid, Wil, 52, 105, 271, 327, 341, 357, 362, 381, 382, 384, 390, 395, 397, 400

Reno, Don, 283, 284

Rexode, Wesley, 76, 123

Reynolds, Burt, 153, 171, 212, 213

Richey, George, 29

Riddle, Nelson, 297

Righteous Brothers, 371

Riley, Jeannie C., 23, 96

Rimel, John, 242, 251, 263, 266, 270, 280, 299, 300, 301, 306, 320, 321

Ritter, Tex, 4, 99, 100, 106, 138

Robb, Chuck, 119

Robb, Lynda Bird, 119

Robbins, Marty, 15, 90, 339

Robbins, Hargus "Pig", 40, 79, 175, 322, 365, 366, 376, 383

Rodgers, Jimmie, 11, 192, 205

Rogers, Kenny (& The First Edition), 23, 39, 74, 189, 288, 349

Rogers, Roy, 4, 70, 100

Rogers, Will, 195

Roosevelt, President Franklin D., 162

Rose, Fred, 70, 158

Rowan, Brent, 320, 326, 337

Rowe, James, 348

Russell, Johnny, 108, 219

Ruth, Babe, 186

Sam The Sham and The Pharaohs, 73

Santo And Johnny, 383

Schuyler, Thom, 317

Scott, Jack, 81

Scott, Pat, 96, 409

Scott, Randolph, 95, 96, 195, 409

Scruggs, Earl, 53, 73, 317

Scruggs, Gary, 317

Seely, Jeannie, 149

Shacklett, Ronnie, 356

Shepard, Jean, 149

Sherwood, Bob, 204

Shiflett, Frances Reid, 54, 55, 57, 274, 295, 312

Shook, Jerry, 65

Shore, Dinah, 170

Silverstein, Shel, 159

Sinatra, Frank, 356, 377

Smiley, Red, 283

Smith, Arthur "Guitar Boogie", 34

Smith, Bill & Judy, 133

Smith, Connie, 348

Smith, Gary, 337

Smith, Howard E., 348

Smith, Terry, 396

Snow, Hank, 138, 147, 339

Sonny & Cher, 156

Sons of Pioneers, 4, 5

Sons of Song (Bob Robinson, Cal Newton, Don Butler), 399

Sousa, John Philip, 116

Speer Family, 30

Speer, Ben, 388

Spicher, Buddy, 65, 79, 114, 323

Spielman, Fred, 336

Stanley Brothers, 312

Stillman, Al, 368

Stone, Cliffie, 69, 70

Strzelecki, Henry, 270

Stuart, Marty, 209

Suits, Wendy, 364

Sumner, J.D., 105

Supremes, 73

Sutton, Don, 189, 190

Switzer, Mrs., 407

Taylor, Elizabeth, 238

Teabag, 179, 180

Tennessee Three, 4, 5, 76

Thomas, Cal, 115

Thomas, Susan, 115

Thompson, Bobby, 42, 82, 114, 139, 180

Thompson, Hank, 192

Tillis, Mel, 23, 343

Toplady, Augustus M., 347

Travis, Merle, 45, 73, 124, 192, 285

Tubb, Ernest, 45, 192, 313, 339

Tucker, Tanya, 86

Turner, Steve, 326

Twitty, Conway, 27, 42, 43, 72, 241, 242, 339, 347, 348

Vallee, Rudy, 12

Vandersloot, F.W., 53

Index

Vassy, Kin, 74
Vincent, Darrin, 220
Vines, Red, 76, 123
Wade, Adam, 94
Wade, Pete, 155, 219, 281, 319, 359
Wagoner, Porter, 21, 43
Walker, Bill, 407
Walker, Cindy, 69
Walker, Jeanine, 364
Wariner, Steve, 385
Warren, Ed, 94
Washington, President George, 186
Watson, Doc, 73
Wayne, John, 157, 158, 195, 242
Welk, Lawrence, 209
Weller, Kim Reid, 175, 176, 195, 196, 210, 211, 228, 242, 247, 261, 289, 298, 301, 305, 306, 323, 340, 356, 380, 390, 395
Weller, Scott, 305
Wells, Kitty, 99, 339, 369
Wertman, Pat, 382
Western, Johnny, 194
Wetherington, Jim "Big Chief", 34
Whiffenpoofs, 12
White, Bergen, 159, 180, 263, 267, 297, 322, 366, 376, 383, 384
Whitley, Keith, 280
Whitmore, James, 195
Wilburn Brothers, 373
Williams, Don, 148
Williams, Hank, 24, 70, 87, 193
Williams, Mason, 106
Williams, Roger, 297
Williams, Tony, 365
Wills, Bob, 56, 192
Wilson Fairchild, 52, 55, 105, 107, 207, 241, 271, 327, 336, 341, 382, 385, 402
Wiseman, Mac, 53, 63, 114, 192, 370
Wiseman, Scotty, 374
Wolfe, Thomas, 54
Womack, Steve, 274
Wood, Kasey Reid, 349
Wootton, Bob, 192
Wright, Bobby, 369
Wright, Johnnie, 369

Wright, Ruby, 369
Wynette, Tammy, 21, 27, 72, 96, 123, 154, 167, 339
Yates, Dr. Charles, 406
Yates, Sally, 406
Younce, George, 281, 311, 388, 400, 409
Young, Chip, 40, 94, 95, 219, 261, 266, 319
Young, Faron, 340
Young, Jack, 131